'Wendy McCarthy has always been a not accept inequality or injustice. Sh powerful advocate for change in Austr what is right so we can advance our social agenda. Her legacy is vibrant, dynamic and reformist, but I am sure the best is yet to come!' **—The Hon. Julia Gillard, AC**

'An extraordinary story of a life magnificently lived with passion and purpose . . . and one that has paved the way for women everywhere.' **—Lisa Wilkinson, AM**

'A tale of daring, determination and a downright refusal to take no for an answer when it came to equal rights for women. Wendy McCarthy is and always has been a trailblazing feminist and a warrior—but I just think of her as a really great woman. This is her story.' **—Fran Kelly**

'The title of Wendy McCarthy's book, *Don't Be Too Polite, Girls*, is a call to action for women and girls everywhere. Through her stories of five decades of relentless community engagement, feminist activism and corporate work we see her steely determination and fine intellect, peppered with her quick wit and irreverent sense of humour. Wendy's book charts her eighty years of life experience in parallel with her observations and involvement with some of the most significant social movements of her time. Wendy McCarthy is a personal friend, a mentor, a confidante, a role model and in my opinion, a national treasure.' **—Dr Kerryn Phelps, AM**

'*Don't Be Too Polite, Girls* is an incredible memoir of an extraordinary life forged by a determined country girl. More than a memoir—it's a manifesto on how to live well with gusto, heart and ambition. This book is testament to the fact feminism, fun, family and fashion can co-exist. Like Wendy herself, *Don't Be Too Polite, Girls* is wise, generous, accomplished and an absolute riot.

A fuller life than Wendy McCarthy's is impossible to fathom and this rollicking read captures it all.' **—Georgie Dent**

'Here is a portrait of a very well-lived life indeed. No, politeness may not have been its hallmark but essential civility was, interpreted in a very broad, big-thinking way. A lot of us have been the beneficiaries and continue to be so. It sounds like a lot of fun too!' **—Geraldine Doogue**

'Fearless, wise, witty and intelligent: Wendy McCarthy is one of the great Australian feminist superheroines of the last 50 years. Her book is a fascinating piece of social history as well as a clarion call to the next generation of feminists, male and female.' **—Jacqueline Maley**

'Nothing beats the wisdom drawn from a woman's lived experience and Wendy McCarthy's long life experiences have been so rich and diverse, and her accomplishments so radical and necessary that it is both a pleasure and an education to read how she did it all.' **—Dr Anne Summers, AO**

'My advice? Take Wendy's advice. She is smart, strategic and effective. She's never rude, but always challenging. She gets shit done, even if it ruffles feathers. She is also warm, funny and engaging—just like her book.' **—Jane Caro, AM**

'Wendy McCarthy nails it again! This enlightening work says so much about the history of the feminist movement in Australia of which Wendy has been a trailblazing headline act. In typical style, Wendy cheekily and deftly guides the next generation of young women on how to carry the torch and continue the fight for women's rights. Her wit, wisdom and guidance deliver a must-read for all.' **—Sandra Sully**

'Beautifully written, relatable—like sitting at your dining room table, drinking rosé and talking. Brilliant!' **—Avril Henry**

ABOUT THE AUTHOR

Wendy McCarthy is an experienced manager and company director who began her career as a secondary school teacher. She moved out of the classroom into public life in 1968 and since then has worked for change across the public, private and community sectors, in education, family planning, human rights, public health, overseas aid and development, conservation, heritage, media and the Arts. She has a long track record of advocating, campaigning and fundraising for women's issues in public life.

Wendy has held many significant leadership roles in key national and international bodies. She has established several businesses, including the national consulting practice McCarthy Mentoring, which is now owned by her daughter Sophie McCarthy. Wendy McCarthy is an experienced speaker and facilitator and is regularly asked for comment on social and political issues.

ALSO BY WENDY McCARTHY

Your Body, But Whose Right to Choose?

Sex Education and the Intellectually Handicapped: A Guide for Parents and Care Givers

A Fair Go: Portraits of the Australian Dream

Don't Fence Me In

The Guide for Mentees: How to Be an Effective Mentee

The Guide for Mentors: How to Be a Valuable Mentor

Teaching About Sex: The Australian Experience, edited by Wendy McCarthy

Raising Your Child Responsibly in a Sexually Permissive Society, by Wendy McCarthy and Sol Gordon

Sexuality and People with Intellectual Disability, by Wendy McCarthy, Lydia Fegan, Anne Rauch

Don't Be Too Polite, Girls

A Memoir

WENDY McCARTHY

First published in 2022

Allen & Unwin
83 Alexander Street
Crows Nest NSW 2065
Australia
Phone:(61 2) 8425 0100
Email:info@allenandunwin.com
Web:www.allenandunwin.com

A catalogue record for this book is available from the National Library of Australia

ISBN 978 1 76087 830 6

Index by Puddingburn
Internal design by Post Pre-press Group, Brisbane
Set in 12/18.2 pt Janson Text LT Pro by Post Pre-press Group, Brisbane
Printed in Australia by SOS Print + Media

10 9 8 7 6 5 4

The paper in this book is FSC® certified. FSC® promotes environmentally responsible, socially beneficial and economically viable management of the world's forests.

This book is dedicated to my children
Sophie, Hamish, and Sam
and my grandchildren
Elias, Lara, Aidan, Luca and Freya

Special thanks to Jane Palfreyman, my publisher, who was constantly encouraging and a source of sound professional advice.

And to my niece Savannah Nichols, who worked with me during the life of the book and managed to wrangle me and the computer to get it done.

It is easy to forget that there is more to a book than an author.

Contents

Prologue

> I don't want us just to tell them how we felt. I want us to tell them what we did.
>
> Kamala Harris, *The Truths We Hold: An American Journey*

And so do I.

On Thursday, 19 September 2019, I was sitting in the NSW Parliament listening to an excruciating debate on the Abortion Bill. The debate was becoming circular and all the key players were exhausted. Any hope that this would be a benign legislative change to remove abortion from the Criminal Code had long gone. It was feral.

I was booked on a flight to London on 22 September, a reservation already twice deferred because of this debate. After 30 hours in the chamber and the prospect of another extension, I sent a text to the Minister for Health at 6 p.m., when the session ended, asking: 'When will this be done?'

His response was: 'We have to go through this but we are nearly there.' That night, the Premier closed the debate down to further extensions; the general consensus was it would finally have a safe passage. I decided I would trust the process and leave as planned. I was looking forward to the flight as an opportunity to sleep and reflect on the two years of campaigning that had led to this anticipated triumph.

I watched the rest of the debate in NSW Parliament on live stream in the United Kingdom and could now relax, secure in the new reality that no woman or her doctor will go to jail and be treated as criminals for this particular medical procedure.

It had been a long, hard slog—fifty years, in fact.

It is a story to treasure and hold close when we feel cynical or disbelieving that planned change never happens.

At a personal-political level, it was the accomplishment of my life to lead the Pro-Choice campaign to this result. I never doubted it was the right thing to do. As my friend Susan Ryan was fond of saying: *Just Keep Going*.

I had had an illegal abortion in 1964, which I had never disclosed until I did in a national newspaper in 1972. Putting this information in the public domain was a deliberate political act that challenged the police to lay charges on the women who had signed the double-page spread advertisement for their criminal behaviour. At that time, an abortion was a crime for both the woman and her doctor/abortionist.

Eighty of us had outed ourselves. The police did not lay charges. It was liberating to stare down the secrecy and fear that had surrounded our actions. It was a relief to publicly own this and refuse to accept shame and regret. Strength came from standing our ground collectively and not being bluffed and intimidated by threats.

It reminded me of when I was an adolescent and I refused to be diminished by the boy who told me my father was a drunk. My response was, 'I know.' I refused to let him destroy me with those words. He never mentioned it again.

Our culture offers us inner scripts and codes for our lives. If women of my generation had accepted those and stayed inside the proscribed boundaries, Australia would be a very different place. Changing the culture changed the script, and gave us opportunities unknown to our mothers and grandmothers. But we can't take for granted that the trajectory for change will be as we wish unless we defend and fight for it.

I have learnt there is a cause for everyone somewhere, and when it matters so much you will march for it, you are on your way. And even amid the tough parts of life are moments of humour, fun and satisfaction that come from being an engaged citizen. There is less *I* and more *us*, and we learn to keep our head and heart connected. Learn to say yes to opportunity and risk, and worry later how to manage it.

As Glen Tomasetti sang through the seventies: *Don't be too polite, girls. Show a little fight.*

Or as Gandhi advised: *Be the change you wish to see in the world.*

Memoirs remain a powerful way of sharing stories. There is a hunger to hear from those who have gone before us and in whose footsteps we follow. We ask them, 'Tell us how you did it?' Currently I'm thinking of the women in Port Kembla who challenged the BHP steelworks and won their long Jobs for Women Campaign, 1980–1994. How wonderful it was to see the 2020 movie *Women of Steel*, which tells their story.

Often it is in the writing of a memoir that you find out what encouraged you to *Just Keep Going*. It has been twenty-two years since I first wrote about my life and being sixty is very different to being eighty. For starters, I think anyone under sixty-five is young. The expectations of appropriate lives for women over sixty are being revisited, and I am really happy to be part of it.

At eighty, we have a long view and the past often seems to be repeating. It sometimes feels like shopping for clothes when there is nothing you haven't seen or worn before but then you're surprised. But secrets and lies are uncovered.

For instance, it seems no one knew my father had been court-martialled in 1943. How could that be? Had I not been questioning discrepancies in his recorded birth dates and gone to check his army records, I may never have found out. It has profoundly changed my view of my father. When I read his testimony, I could hear his voice, something I found poignant and moving.

When I wrote *Don't Fence Me In*, I was astonished to think I could write a book that sold. This will be the last memoir . . . I have run out of song titles.

CHAPTER 1
First families

> Call it a clan, call it a network, call it a tribe, call it a family. Whatever you call it, whoever you are, you need one. You need one because you are a human. You didn't come from nowhere. Before you, around you, and presumably after you, too, there are others . . . even if you live alone, even if your solitude is elected and ebullient, you still cannot do without a clan or a tribe.
>
> Jane Howard, *Families*

There is something supremely elegant about a birth certificate. It records, in one succinct page, the details that give you a place in the world for the rest of your life. I saw my birth certificate for the first time in 1964, when my husband Gordon applied to Registry of Births, Deaths & Marriages in Sydney in order to establish my identity and apply for a passport.

I was born at Kallara Private Hospital on 22 July 1941, in Orange, New South Wales. Wendy Elizabeth Ryan is recorded in the birth register as number 35703 in District 493. My parents, William 'Bill' Rex Ryan and Audrey McGillivray Taylor, were listed as 'drover' and 'no occupation'. For my mother, her maiden name and birthplace are also included. The birth certificate gives their marriage date and declares they had no previous issue.

I was lucky to live in a country where births are recorded. When examining this certificate I was reminded once again of how the accident of birth can define a person's life. Today, one in four children under five worldwide remain unregistered, which means that 166 million children around the world have no human rights. They are not named. They can be trafficked. They have no entitlement and, as Article 7 of the Convention on the Rights of the Child states, without immediate registration a child is stateless. Their lives are considered unworthy of a record in our human story.

I asked my mother about the circumstances of my birth some years later. I was born late at night, after a long labour. It was a tough first birth, and my father, over the moon to have a daughter, apparently went AWOL to visit me. I was not aware, though, that she and my father had been married for only six months prior to my birth.

My mother gave me no indication that the Ryan grandparents were part of the wedding. I do know that my father's sister, Shirley, was married with a big wedding the same month I was born and this probably took the limelight. She was marrying up. I wondered if there was much family disapproval. It turned out to not be a topic my mother wanted to discuss.

Though I'll never know, I do wonder how welcome my mother was in the Ryan family. Her mother made my father's first dinner suit, I was told, and she certainly knitted my mother's wedding outfit, but there were never any photographs on display or a sense of any joy attached to their wedding. I know it was wartime, but I had a feeling she became the camp follower of my father's regiment partly because she had nowhere else to go. When my father enlisted, they were living with Nana Ryan.

If I am right, it would explain a lot about my mother's independence, and her upward aspiration, which she expected a man to provide. She saw her role as providing a happy family home. I didn't write any of this when my mother was still alive because it upset her to think that people would judge her. But, really, I wanted her to know that I admired her. Bill was the man she wanted to marry.

As a grandmother myself, I am increasingly interested in the family histories and stories of my grandparents. The Ryans and Taylors lived across the road from each other in Orange for about ten years. The Ryans had come from Ireland; the Taylors from Scotland and England. They saw themselves as quite different people, and in country towns back then there was a clear divide between graziers and townsfolk.

The Taylors had a large block of land that included an orchard and a vegetable garden, as well as a modest but comfortable house for their six children. My grandfather worked in the post office and had served in Gallipoli. They were country townsfolk.

The Ryans were from Coonamble, 300 kilometres north-west of Orange, where they had property growing sheep and wool. Their cottage in Orange had been bought as a base for their daughters to attend the Presbyterian Ladies College. It was not until the death of my grandfather Ryan that this cottage became a permanent home to my grandmother. Grandfather Ryan died before I was born.

I loved both my grandmothers. Nana Taylor, my maternal grandmother, grew up in Andover in England, and was from a comfortable family. She met my grandfather, Jock, in England when he was on leave from fighting in Gallipoli. She came to Australia with no domestic skills, but in time she became an expert seamstress and provider for her six children.

Her dressmaking was legendary. My mother remembers her sewing well into the early hours of the morning to add to the family income.

Jock was passionate about music. He conducted the many and various bands he established over his life. He also had a reputation for being mean and a hard Scot. He played almost no role in my life. My mother always seemed slightly fearful of him and thought him a hard husband and father. There seemed little generosity in purse or spirit to his life. His passion was Police Boys Club and bands. In his later years he separated from my grandmother and lived in Broken Hill. She moved to Tamworth, breaking the links of family in Orange.

The last time I saw Jock was when I was about seventeen and attending university, which had made him very proud. He was living alone in an austere dark farmhouse in Minto, surrounded by books. My mother felt she should visit him and so we went together. He gave me a silver vase and his copy of Giovanni Boccaccio's *The Decameron* when we left. I treasure these items and wonder about the missed opportunity of knowing who he really was.

My Nana Ryan, born as Elsie Mary Phelps, married William 'Will' Ryan, who died before I was born. The story is that Elsie and Will were engaged to be married for a long time because she was Methodist and he was Catholic, and a common religion could not be agreed upon. It's a reminder that marrying across religion back then was, for some, akin to marrying across cultures now.

On 22 December 1910, at the Pilliga School of Arts, with the Reverend Bonner of Coonamble officiating, Will and Elsie were married. It had been agreed that the children would be christened Methodist but, when the time came, William Ryan would still receive the last rites and be buried as a Catholic in the family vault at Rookwood Cemetery. The local newspaper described the bride as looking charming in a trained white ivory silk gown trimmed with white silk fishnet of real lace. Elsie was attended by three bridesmaids, just like me. The article notes approvingly that the presents were numerous and, in some instances, costly.

Today Will Ryan survives only in family folklore and a few photographs. A piece written after his death, in 1934 at the age of fifty-eight, was treasured in the family. It was written by his former teacher, Mr William Hagen, in a letter to *Country Life* magazine:

> Billy and I were great mates in the grassy West in those days, in the early 90s. He was the apt and big-hearted pupil and I was the newly appointed teacher. Elsie Phelps was also a pupil at the old Milchomi and Cashel Half-Time School. Since then, I have been in many centres from Come By Chance in the West to Longreach in the North. At times like Wolseley, riding the waves of glory, but more often like Hopeful on the rocks of despair. And if I were asked to write a name in letters of gold, it would be Will Ryan of Cashel.

Will and Elsie had three children between 1914 and 1920. My father, William Rex, was the middle child and only son. He grew up on the Coonamble property Ellim-eek. A place of horses and wide-open plains, and an annual cycle of life that followed farming sheep. He was eighteen when his father died and assumed responsibility for the family property. During the Great Depression, he drove mobs of sheep for months at a time and survived by buying and selling the sheep he fed and agisted on the public stock routes. In his own terms (and to my mother's horror), he was for a time, as he wrote on my birth certificate, a drover.

Will's sister 'Bubbles', christened Myra, was described as a bit funny—she had meningitis when she was a baby, something for which Coonamble could offer little medical attention. She certainly suffered from epilepsy, and never learnt to read or write. As children, we knew we had to be nice to Bubbles. But the worst punishment was having to take her down the street, even when she was so much bigger than us, and risk meeting someone we knew and having them laugh at us or feel sorry for us. Still, I learnt to stare them down.

My grandmother's life in Orange revolved around Bubbles' needs, and she led a frugal life so that when she died Bubbles would be provided for. My grandmother's constant worry was that Bubbles would be put in Bloomfield Hospital because no one else would know how to look after her.

I learnt my love of radio from my Nana Ryan. ABC Radio played constantly, and it was the voice of authority in her household. It was in those early childhood years that I became addicted to my first radio serial, *Blue Hills*. When the music to it started, all activities were suspended as we sat down for the daily episode. My mother was never really interested in soaps and was rather dismissive of them, especially when I announced that I wanted to listen in. But that love of radio, which has stayed with me to this day, I'm sure began in that little house in Orange.

I spent quite a lot of time with my Nana Ryan in Orange before we went to live in Goulburn when I was seven. I have photographs of me standing in the snow in the backyard of that cottage. She often took in boarders from the University of Sydney, particularly from the Vet School, and so there was a constant flow of people through the house. The earnings from these lodgers were invested for Bubbles' future.

My father was witty, entertaining and fun, and liked to be the performer at the party. Some of his grandsons are the same. And it's easy to see how he could have swept my mother off her feet. She was beautiful, young and inexperienced. She had innate style and would rather go barefoot than wear the wrong shoes. She always had great taste and could make something out of nothing. She had a strong view that looking your best was next to godliness. And when we got new clothes, we kept them for best. Even now I keep new things for best weeks before I'm due to wear them, much to the amusement of my friends.

In our family, the look or smell of poverty or disadvantage was to be avoided no matter what. My mother thought that being poor defined you in a negative way. When the feminist movement spoke of discrimination, she argued that it did not apply to her. She insisted that we always look our best, had perfect table manners and never discussed personal issues outside the family, and she did not want charity—even when she needed it.

My father enlisted for war service at Orange in July 1940, joining the Australian Light Horse Regiment. Over the years, I've met people who remember him as Bill Ryan from Coonamble. As recently as 2008, I met some of his contemporaries at a Coonamble Festival with my grandchildren. We later visited the family property, which had been lost to our family during the Depression.

My father was often described as a larrikin in the army, as well as being engaging, charming and not amenable to authority. When I was working with the Australian Bicentennial Authority, I met military historian John Laffin, who wrote to me about him, recalling their time based at Orange Showground in 1944:

> Bill was a militia man, that is he had an Army Number, and was expected to fight only in direct defence of Australia. He was a Sergeant member of the instructional staff. Bill's job was to convert the men at Orange into competent infantrymen. These men were not exactly ideal soldiers, some of them were tough, rough and rebellious. Some hated the Army and all had been guilty of some Army crime or other. Bill Ryan's great strength in approaching this job was that he could talk their language. Though always firm, he had a quick easy smile and a casual manner. I thought several times, he would have made a fine Light Horse trooper of the World War I type . . . Bill was a happy go lucky man and laughed a lot. He certainly liked to be popular. He was generous and gregarious. The roots of his liking for drink lay in these traits. He just liked to yarn and he did this best with a glass in his hand. The trouble was that he did not know that he had reached the point where . . . he had had enough . . . Bill liked the open country life and though he was in the Army with three stripes, he was not cut out for responsibility. While he did a good job as a Non-Commissioned Officer, he was really at heart one of the boys. He was a man who loved children. I recall him with affection because of his genuineness and sincerity. He put on no airs and graces and there was no pretence about him. He was just Bill Ryan.

I was very grateful to John Laffin, a world authority on world wars and conflicts. I felt so lucky to meet him as he had spent so much time with my father during the war. I treasure his letter. It seems to get to the heart of the man I loved as a father, and it helped me understand why he became the alcoholic he was in later life—which was not a long life.

When I reread John Laffin's letter, I see both myself and my father in ways I hadn't before. In my early teaching career, I was also given the naughty kids to look after, just as my father had been. It gives me a quiet sense of connection to him.

In more recent years, I have been driven by a curiosity to find out more about my father. I discovered the joy of Trove, the online service from the National Library of Australia. It provides access to content from many rural newspapers that became important records of life in country towns.

My father had various mentions in local news during the Depression when he was droving mobs of sheep for months at a time. In 1936, he was fined £2 for travelling his sheep only twenty-two miles in twenty-five days along the stock routes. The headline in the *Dubbo Liberal* was: 'Sheep travels slowly'.

When a conflict in a birth date took me to the Australian War Memorial to check their records, I discovered to my astonishment that he had been court-martialled in July 1943. The charge sheet read as follows:

> The accused, NX.144790, Cpl. RYAN, William Rex, 6 Aust. Detention Barracks, is charged with having, whilst being a soldier of the Military Forces of the Commonwealth of Australia on War Service, committed the following offence: —
>
> FIRST CHARGE. A.A. 40. Conduct to the prej.—wrongfully acquired from Spr Lynch, a military greatcoat, public property, issued to Spr Lynch for military purposes.
>
> SECOND CHARGE. A.A. 40. Conduct to the prej.—wrongfully sold to one Keith Clover WARRENDER, a civilian, a military greatcoat, public property.

He was found guilty of both charges, and he was sentenced to be reduced to the ranks and fined £5. He returned to the barracks to continue in his role and was subsequently discharged from the army on 10 March 1947.

It was his testimony in that trial that I found so moving. I could hear his voice. He was sixteen when his father died and, in his words:

> At no time did I think I was doing anything wrong. I have no knowledge of Military law; my education was of 12-months' duration attending a secondary school, and a couple of months before that I was doing a correspondence course. I am a sincere soldier; I love it. I have never done anything to prejudice or that might prejudice my military career. It is correct that a man without education has got a good fighting chance to circumstances which arose out of this greatcoat was entirely ignorance on my part.
>
> My people had a grazing property the other side of Coonamble. Later I was left with the property. My father died when I was 16 and I attended to the property until the Depression years and I was forced out of it. I was about 200 miles west of Bourke, kangarooing when the Japs attacked Pearl Harbor. It was 2 or 3 days after their entry into the war when I left things very valuable to me and I came back as quickly as I could and joined the 6th Light horse.

CHAPTER 2

Country girl

> The landscape contains the spiritual essence that is part of me. I am in the landscape and the landscape is in me.
>
> John Olsen

At the age of three, I was enrolled at Trinity Grammar kindergarten, which was based in a little bluestone church hall in Orange. Its principal had a double-barrel name and was much admired by the locals. Mrs Pender-Brooks ran a tight ship, and all the young mothers were in fear and awe of her. She launched a rigorous campaign to convert my left-handedness, which included summoning my parents into a meeting. My mother said she was terrified. She assumed I must have done something really shocking for my father to be asked along.

The principal explained: 'Wendy is left-handed and refuses to use her right hand. We have done everything we can and she just refuses. She is not rude about it, but just very politely sits down and keeps using her left hand. It will be a terrible handicap to her.'

Apparently, my father, looked at her and said, 'I wouldn't try changing her mind, she is very determined.' I remain left-handed and not visibly damaged by it.

I can almost remember my mother from when I was growing up and old photographs reinforce these memories.

When I was a child, she was finding her feet socially in Orange, and flourishing in her role as a young wife and mother. Post war, my father found a job as an auctioneer with Farmers and Graziers, a stock and station agency, where at least he worked with country people. His charm and persuasiveness enhanced his auctioneering skills, but he really wanted to be back on the land.

It was a great relief to him when he found a job managing a sheep station on the Murrumbidgee River, in 1948. The property, Nanangro, was remote, and my mother was pregnant with her third child—by this time, I also had a brother, Kerry. It was agreed that we would live in Goulburn, the nearest town, and visit him occasionally. Now I see that this was my father's first serious escape from domestic responsibility. It would begin a pattern he would repeat for the rest of his life. But I don't think we recognised the signs back then.

My mother, Kerry and I had our little brick cottage in the centre of Goulburn. My sister Deborah was born in 1949, soon after we arrived. Most of my memories of Goulburn are of my mother having the life of a young, attractive matron, going to picnic races and the polo, wearing beautiful clothes. For the first time she had some domestic help. I have little memory of my father's presence during the six months we lived there.

We visited our father at Nanangro a couple of times. It was remote and scary. Visits were major expeditions, which involved driving to the Murrumbidgee River and boarding a punt to cross the river, then a horse and sulky carriage journey on narrow, hilly tracks for miles to the manager's house where my father was living. I'd never seen alpine country before. The river was cold, turbulent and pristine, and the trees were tall and ghostly. Even the horses seemed different—and in fact they were, because in that country there were wild brumbies.

My father had chosen a brumby to break in. He was called Bobtail. In order to ride Bobtail, someone had to chase him and then strap his leg to get up on him. Invariably this attracted an audience, which my father loved. My brother Kerry and I were terrified of Bobtail, so we were given quiet ponies to ride. And even though they were not well mannered, the ponies would be ridden constantly so they were too exhausted to bolt.

It was an unsettling time for our family. Nanangro was remote and the life there best suited a single man. A life not unlike the one my father had enjoyed as a younger man. There was no community life for a young family. For my mother, with three children, including the new baby, life in Goulburn must have looked a whole lot better.

In my new school in North Goulburn, I was the odd one out. The other children were blond and beautiful, and many were the sons and daughters of Baltic immigrants who had come to work on the Snowy Mountains Hydro-electric scheme. They looked very different to this small, dark-haired, freckled, skinny girl. I thought they had all come out of *The Swiss Family Robinson* books.

The playground was a rough place. I wasn't the only child victimised; the Balts had a hard time, too. This is when I first learnt the language of difference: *Balts* and *reffos*. It took me quite a while to work out who they were and why they were despised. I think in the end I came to understand it was just because they weren't like us. Whoever *us* was in Goulburn.

The only girl I really made a friendship with was from Estonia. She was clever and beautiful, but our parents made it very clear that we did not have a friendship beyond the school gate. That had a profound effect on me, in the way that all these things do before you turn ten. After school, we dispersed to our different lives. Goulburn, like most Australian country towns, was fearful of difference, and the local children reflected and articulated the prejudices of their parents. I seriously hated the place. It was not a long stay there, only six months, and I never felt I belonged. It was my only unhappy school experience.

In February 1949, my father received a letter advising him that he had won a block of land in a ballot. It was in a subdivision of the Boyd Estate in a little place called Garema, seventeen miles west of Forbes. These ballots were part of the postwar soldier settlement schemes.

We were off to Garema. It was totally unknown country. My mother was apprehensive, even scared. She had moved from Orange, the only place she had ever really known, to Goulburn, and now had to move again. But my father brooked no objections: he had won the ballot and considered it to be his natural entitlement to be on the land and have us together as a family.

We arrived at Garema in late 1949. It was yellow, brown and flat. Just one tiny hill could be seen on the horizon. Our thousand-acre block was fenced but had no buildings, no sheep and, of course, no house. Not even a postbox where the mail could be delivered. In the little village of Garema, the dominant buildings were the wheat silos on the railway siding. To me, as a child, they seemed enormous.

Our property was named Ellim-eek after the Coonamble property of my father's family, and our first dwelling was a large tent with an outside fire and copper. We kids thought this was fun for a week or so but, as it rained and rained, our new home lost its appeal and we fantasised about a real house. How my mother put up with that outside shower and the rain with a baby, heaven only knows.

As life got harder, my father organised for us to live in a long row of shearers' huts, which he transported over from a property some miles away. These would be our home until we could afford to build a house.

It turned out our thousand-acre block was best suited to mixed farming, which meant my father couldn't be the grazier he wanted to be. For a couple of years, during the wool boom, he concentrated on sheep, but it was a short period of good times. We would be high on the sheep's back until the market dropped and we were in trouble again. Our neighbours who planted wheat prospered. We didn't.

My mother set up house in this long, dark-green wooden building. Shearers' accommodation was not designed for a young family and it required a great deal of ingenuity to reach a degree of comfort. From a child's point of view, being near a creek was fun and a source of endless entertainment. That changed whenever the creek flooded and we had to be rescued, usually by the neighbours, because Daddy was 'away' (our code for a drinking bout). When not away, he would be the rescuing hero and we would be so proud of him.

When we arrived at Garema, it was suggested that Kerry and I would do school by correspondence. We thought that sounded fun and that we would mostly play; however, it was not to be. The Garema School was within the qualifying distance and so the Correspondence School was not prepared to service our schoolwork.

Garema was a one-teacher school. Imagine a weatherboard portable building, an entry porch, one classroom and one teacher, two outside lavatories, a playground and an all-weather shed. But it was a happy place. We were welcomed warmly; they needed extra pupils to remain viable.

Twenty-five seemed the base number, and that included five to seven children whose fathers were railway fettlers who came and went.

One teacher responsible for all grades meant it was always bustling. I was the good girl and the teacher's helper; when not, I retreated to my own world of books. I rode my Malvern Star bicycle three miles there and back from third grade, which I had to repeat, through to sixth grade. At special times, when the road was wet and my bike got bogged, I was allowed to ride my favourite pony, Stella, a twenty-year-old grey who didn't mind having three or four kids on her back. Sometimes I just doubled Kerry on her. Stella was happy tied up to the fence for the day, with a break for rides by kids who didn't have a pony of their own.

I was usually the only person in my grade. Sometimes, there was another girl or two, but usually it was just me. I spent my time listening to ABC Radio and reading to the little kids. I read and read and read. My enduring love of books surely comes from those years.

Garema School pupils came from the families of graziers, railway workers, wheat cockies, village shopkeepers and postal staff. Teachers in one-teacher schools were invariably male and they struggled to be part of the local community and bring a veneer of civilisation to their students. This was a typical Australian railway village, and the social and class distinctions were drawn early. It was assumed that only those who left Garema—the graziers' children—would make it.

There were black children in our school, and we were always told they were Indian. I had no reason to disbelieve this; I had never seen a black child before. I wonder now how the community kept those secrets, for of course they were Aboriginal children. What conspiracy was it that had us all thinking that Aboriginal people were Indian? Why would it be better to be Indian than to be part of our First Nations people? We loved it when the Dunns, who were a large Aboriginal fettler family, arrived because they were great at sport. And on the school picnic day they won every game.

Other people passed through Garema. There were caravans of gypsies, who were off limits to local children whose mothers had warned of unknown terrors for those that played with them, which of course added mightily to their attraction. I would sometimes go down and peek at the exotic haberdashery in the caravans and would usually see one or two of the local families there buying beautiful fabrics.

By the age of ten, I knew in my own childish and inarticulate way that my father drank too much and could not accept long-term responsibility. Country children see a lot of their parents. My father was often moody and violent. He lied about his drinking, which made me angry and sad. When he went to town, we would be frightened about how long the journey would take, because every couple of miles (and it was only a seventeen-mile trip) he would stop the truck and lift the bonnet, claiming engine problems. After each swig behind the bonnet, his driving became more erratic.

There were occasions when we had no working vehicle on our property. Like the time when my sister Deborah was kicked in the head by my horse, Starlight, who had been tied up at the fence. My father hopped onto Starlight and galloped to the neighbours' place for help. They took Deborah and my parents to the hospital, and my sister battled for her life as the doctors warned of brain damage because she had a fractured skull. We were advised we would not know the extent of the brain damage until she came out of an induced coma.

The stress was too much for my father. After the first couple of hours waiting in the hospital, he disappeared on a bender, leaving my mother to manage. Despite him knowing he needed to be there to learn whether she was brain damaged and whether she would be able to recognise him, he couldn't stick around. I knew my father was not someone to be relied upon in terms of the safety of our family. It was our mother we had to turn to.

With my father still nowhere to be found, one of the neighbours took my mother to the hospital to bring Deborah home. A day or so later, my father returned, contrite, remorseful and hungover. But sober. I simply could not understand how he abandoned his little girl whom he adored more than anyone. It seemed he just simply could not cope with stress. I was so grateful that Deborah was home; she had looked so frail lying in hospital. And since I had been the one supposedly looking after her at the time, I was extremely grateful that my parents never blamed me for what happened. It was just treated as an accident. She made a complete recovery.

All this may make my family sound completely dysfunctional. Strangely, it wasn't. Our income was unpredictable and unreliable. My father had a drinking problem. And yet this doesn't tell you the real story of our family. And it doesn't tell you how much we were loved, encouraged and nurtured by our parents.

I called my first memoir *Don't Fence Me In* partly because my father used to sing along to it with Bing Crosby and The Andrews Sisters. Some of my happiest memories of him are of me riding my pony beside him and singing, with the endless horizon of flat farming country. It epitomises the sense of space growing up as a country child—a belief that there were no boundaries.

Still, as children, Kerry, Deb and I learnt to avoid provoking our father when he was drinking. These were the dark times. When his truck would come home, weaving up the road, one side to the other, we would run to bed and pretend to be asleep. But, really, we were just lying there to protect our mother in case he flew into a rage at her. Sometimes he would stay away for days and the neighbours would come to check on us. They would have seen him somewhere on a bender.

In the early years, the drinking sessions were few and far between. During the good times, we would be laughing, singing, playing games and pretending we had won the lottery. A good season could cover up many tensions with a cushion of money. We would have new clothes and books, summer holidays were planned at the beach, our parents would go to parties and our father would sing.

We had wonderful friends and neighbours. Two of our female neighbours had had careers before they married. They fired my imagination. Val McDonald had done war service and Dulcie Doust had been a nursing sister at Manly Hospital. Such exotic occupations. I determined then, at age ten, that I would be a nurse.

Where I would go to secondary school was a pressing issue. It meant I had to leave home as there was no school bus into Forbes, and most of the boarding schools of choice were in Sydney. The last-ditch option was the local convent, but it was a desperate choice. Anglicans hated Catholics and saw them as socially inferior.

My teacher thought I should sit for a state bursary to help with the cost of secondary education. He thought I would easily be successful. I was not. It was a shock to open the mathematics paper and find it almost incomprehensible. Knowing my times tables didn't seem to be much help.

Despite our financial position, my mother pushed for me to go to boarding school in Sydney. But schools in our price range, such as Queenwood and Claremont at Randwick, were at that time closing their boarding houses. I would never wear one of the uniforms I had fantasised about. I had read so many books about girls at boarding school. I wanted to be someone like Hilary of the Upper Sixth, or Wendy of the Upper Fifth. Reality set in. Boarding school was simply not affordable.

It was decided I would instead board at St John's Anglican Hostel, adjacent to Forbes Intermediate High School, where I would attend school. I began my secondary education in 1952. Writing this book in 2021 reminds me yet again how the first ten years of our lives, and particularly the first three to five, shape who we are through life, left-handed or not.

It was a shock in my first year of secondary school to find that other children had done maths. Numeracy was not strong at Garema, as evidenced by the test for the state bursary. However, I caught up, with the only significant damage done to my pride. My unusual pre-school and primary education gives me the confidence to continue to reassure parents that good education can be found in a variety of settings. Who else had a pony tied up in the schoolyard? What matters are the teachers, and I have been blessed with some of the best.

I've spent my life being an advocate of early learning. I was fortunate to have parents who sent me to pre-school when neither my mother nor father had completed secondary school. They gave me a life advantage: I learnt to read early. I had a head start in formal learning. Education is a remarkable gift. No one can ever take it away. It is yours to do as you wish. I have always treasured my educational opportunities.

Waiting to be asked to dance

Leaving home at eleven to board at a hostel was not a particularly unusual experience for a country schoolchild. I loved living there. Established by the Anglican Church to assist rural families in educating their children through secondary school, it was a remarkable and idiosyncratic experiment. There were forty boarders: twenty girls upstairs, twenty boys downstairs. We all shared the domestic chores.

Our warden, whom we called 'Padre', was Don Shearman, a twenty-seven-year-old Anglican minister who had been a Bush Brother with a short stint in the Air Force. He and his wife Faye were newly married when they were posted to St John's. But it was later heartbreaking to find out that he had sexually abused one of my girlfriends. And extraordinary to think that I had no awareness of what was happening. I could never have imagined he would be charged with sexual abuse.

For me, St John's Anglican Hostel was a happy and safe place. Padre introduced us to classical music and religion. It was an unusual boarding experience being entirely co-ed, as well as attending the local co-ed high school. We were encouraged to have friendships with both boys and girls. And apart from the division of domestic chores, there was little perceived difference between genders. We all had special boyfriends and girlfriends—until it came to the school social.

The school social was a serious event where girls were taught their place. No dancing until the teacher said 'gentlemen, take your partners'. The twelve-year-old gentlemen would then slide across the floor, made slippery by preparation known as Pops, to grab a girl for the foxtrot, Pride of Erin or the barn dance. We knew that to be a wallflower was social death but under no circumstances were girls to be bold. We had to wait to be asked to dance. Boldness was speaking out and being pushy. It was the antithesis of being a good girl. And it was usually followed by the advice to be polite, not forward, and never make a show of yourself.

Wait until you are asked to dance has always resonated with me.

Boarding was fun, and so was school. I loved my school uniform—a black box-pleated surge tunic with a white shirt and tie, blazer, black stockings in winter, white socks in summer and shiny leather shoes. In my first year I was streamed into class 1A, which offered mathematics 1 and 2, French and Latin. Sadly, the Latin teacher quit in my first term, and to my great regret I have never studied the language.

All girls did domestic science, a subject I loathed. I thought the cooking and sewing teachers were prissy, and I couldn't see the point in making bloomers large enough to cover two people. The domestic science teachers didn't like the A-stream girls much in turn and tried to cut them down to size. My revenge was to top the class. I knew that as an A-stream girl I would not be in the class for more than one year—I would have other options. I now look back and think, I owe those teachers an apology because I now adore the domestic arts, which is a surprise. While I am no Nigella, I love to cook and be a homemaker.

The school struggled to offer the same number of subjects as the larger schools. At that time, there were just over forty intermediate high schools scattered throughout New South Wales. Their objective was to educate and retain children until the end of compulsory school age, which then was fourteen years and ten months. When Forbes Intermediate became a high school in 1953 and prepared students for the Leaving Certificate, the town celebrated.

There were many able children from Forbes Intermediate in my intake to Forbes High School. We pushed each other along with much help from our very skilful teachers. Of the fourteen students from that first-year who presented for the Leaving Certificate, more than half went on to be university graduates. There are some distinguished Australian achievers among them, including Dr Bruce McKellar AC—a theoretical particle physicist who enjoys international recognition.

School for me was all-consuming. There was no activity that escaped my curiosity and engagement. I loved team games, something you don't get in a tiny school. I turned out to be competent at hockey and softball, which meant I could play in the local competition. This provided a sense of community and belonging that I craved. And it helped ease my anxiety about my mother's position back at home.

When my father went on a bender, life was hard, money was scarce, and it was my mother who had to hold it all together. Simple and drastic inconveniences occur for a family living in a remote place with only one car. If the vehicle was elsewhere, the family was grounded. It wasn't until 1953 that we had a telephone and then I could speak to my mother during the week.

During that first year, I was swimming well enough to get into the school team. Such achievements were rewarded with many bus trips to towns that were nearby but still seemed faraway, like Parkes. This was a pre-travel era, and these trips were coveted for the competition they provided. It was a powerful incentive to succeed at sport as it offered not just an experience out of the town but also the chance to meet new people.

In the 1950s, the Education Department provided incentive for its teachers to do country service. Forbes Intermediate High School was probably not a particularly desirable post as Forbes was a small town. But we were blessed with teachers who worked so hard to broaden our horizons. We had a German mathematics teacher, an Indian geography teacher, and a Welsh French teacher. More diversity than anything offered to my children some thirty years later.

And away from school we had a highly organised Christian education, too. At the hostel, we attended church three times a week. As I prepared for my first communion, I moved easily into the language of the High Church Mass and Evensong. Some of us went to church and polished the altar brass with great love and devotion. The legacy is an ease and familiarity with the language of the High Anglican Church—the hymns, the prayers and the order of service for communion are remembered and comfortable.

Meanwhile, my father's drinking habit worsened. The time between benders was shortening and money had become a major issue. I worried about my mother being often on her own with Kerry and Deborah. I also knew my part of the deal was to be a good girl, to succeed at school and at St John's so that I could stay on, because after the first year my father wouldn't—or couldn't—pay the fees.

When Padre and the local towns solicitors discovered the Canteen Trust Fund, which had been set up with the proceeds from the staff canteens during the Second World War, was offering funds to support children of the military, they applied for a scholarship for me. In 1954, I was awarded a scholarship, but school reports had to be provided and renewed each year. This was a strong reason for me to keep succeeding at school, which I did. The fund supported me until the end of the fourth year, after which time I changed schools.

I learnt from that experience the notion of social reciprocity. It wasn't a term I would have used in those days but I came to understand how important it was for me to return in some way what had been offered to me. People had relied on me and put faith in me, and I had to deliver.

At the end of third year, then known as Intermediate, many of my girlfriends left school. People still asked the question: why waste education on girls when they are going to get married anyway? My mother, supported by Don Shearman and the teachers at the school, ensured that I would stay on to finish my education, even though things were tough at home.

The year 1956 was one of tumult in our family. Ellim-eek had to be sold as the debtors were circling. Despite my father's failure and despair, he was offered a position as manager of a large remote sheep property at Warialda in north-west New South Wales. Full of contrition, and with promises to stay sober, he persuaded my mother, Kerry and Deborah to go with him. It was a nightmare. He began drinking heavily again and it was clear to my mother that he would not survive in the job very long. He grew frustrated, humiliated and reproachful. My mother, in searing heat and ugly circumstances, was doing her best to make a home out of the very ordinary little fibro house, euphemistically described as 'the manager's residence'.

But what to do with me at the end of my fourth year? I couldn't stay at the hostel. So it was decided that I would stay with some family friends of my grandmother's, the Beckenhams, and attend Tamworth High. It was hardly a prospect to look forward to—I was happy where I was and had a sense of belonging and security. And to move for my final year was very unsettling. I'd have to start all over again. There would be no rewards for having so far survived four years of high school. But I had to accept it, and I wanted to be near my family, so I said my farewells to Forbes and headed to Warialda for the Christmas holidays.

School had been such a safe place, so it was a surprise when I got to Warialda. I had forgotten how badly my father had deteriorated. I begged my mother to leave him—I was truly frightened he would hurt her. And we did leave a couple of times during those holidays, when the pressure got too heavy and there was no money to live on, but we invariably returned because we believed he cared about us and wanted to be better. And we wanted to be a family.

This is so often what happens when families are fragmenting. Finally, my mother packed up again and left Warialda for good. It was a dramatic exit and done in secrecy. Again, my Nana Taylor took us in at her very modest house in Tamworth. Weeks later, my father sobered up and found a job managing another property at Breeza, near the village of Currabubula, which strangely is my sister Deborah's home now.

We all agreed to try again. The property had a marvellous house, which was a great attraction, and for a while things seemed to be working. Kerry was sent to Farrer Agricultural School, and I continued to board privately in Tamworth with the Beckenhams and their three boys.

Tamworth High School wasn't easy, especially as I was the new girl in fifth year. I had left a group of fourteen at Forbes High School and moved to a year level of more than seventy students. The students at Tamworth High School were light-years away from my peer group in Forbes: they drank, smoked, drove cars and listened to recordings of the Broadway musical *My Fair Lady*. I could have landed on another planet.

My subjects weren't compatible with the timetable in Tamworth either, and no one was too interested in changing that. For the first term, parts of my physics and chemistry course had to be individually supervised by a science teacher who made it clear that this was a total waste of his time. It was bad enough to have a girl doing physics and chemistry. Any boy who chose me as their partner in the experiments was called a sissy or a sex maniac. It made me determined to do well. And when the numbers went up at the end of the year, I got an A-level pass in combined physics and chemistry. It felt like a well-deserved revenge.

Tamworth High was also my first experience of a community where many of the girls were groupies and observers, rather than participants. At Forbes, there hadn't been enough boys to play in team sports, so girls were invited to join in. But in Tamworth the clever girls frequently chose not to play sport. They saw sport and drama as opposites. This was incomprehensible to me. I represented the school in hockey, swimming and ball games, but I did not make the school play that year.

My teachers encouraged me to apply for Teachers College and Commonwealth scholarships. It caused great drama. My father, who disliked authority of any kind, refused to sign the form. My mother ended up persuading one of my aunts to sign the guarantee form with her, in full knowledge they would never be able to pay back the money if I broke the five-year bond attached to my teaching scholarship.

I was disappointed with my results, an A in physics and chemistry and five Bs—I had been hoping for six As. Still, two days later I discovered I had won both Commonwealth and Teachers College scholarships to attend the University of New England. It was agreed I could go. Life was about to change.

On my own

I was sixteen in 1958 when my mother and father drove me to Armidale to begin my student life at the University of New England. My father gave me £10 spending money for first term. That did not last long—my memory says one month. Fortunately, my scholarships had a substantial living allowance.

My mother and I had been very worried about what I would wear on campus. What did university students wear? Certainly no one in my family knew. My mother made me a new dress and I had a new pair of shoes, my first Bedggood pigskin stacked heels. I thought they looked beautiful with my green wool academic gown, which all undergraduate students in New England wore each day on campus. It was a blessing as it covered all your clothes. I was now financially independent and settled. I had a job in the university dining room as a waiter. I also had my allowance, and I was working hard.

After my father's job at Breeza ended badly, he found another at Blayney, near Orange, with a stock and station agency. In fifteen years, he had gone full circle: stock and station agency, managing properties, managing his own property, going broke, managing properties again, with the grog always at the centre of it. Life for my mother was out of control.

In Blayney, they had rented half a house in the wrong end of town. My heart ached for my mother and Deborah, who both had to endure it. Kerry and I saw it merely as a place to visit when school and university were on break. But my mother and Deborah were stuck there.

My father's new job lasted only a few weeks. And, as his drinking became acute, he was admitted to Bloomfield, now Orange Mental Hospital, suffering from delirium tremens.

When I visited him, he looked pale and sad. I begged him to go to Alcoholics Anonymous to give himself a chance, but he said it was for drunks, not him. He also thought it was silly for him to stay on in hospital because he really didn't need the sort of treatment he was being provided.

That was the end of the road for our family as a unit. After Blayney, we never again lived with my father. He went and stayed with his sister and brother-in-law at Manildra. My mother went back to Garema to stay with friends. She then moved to Sydney with Deborah to find work. I went back to university, my brother Kerry to boarding school, with the Canteens Trust Fund agreeing to support that financially.

After that first year at university, I joined my mother with our Garema friends for Christmas. I knew the festivities would be temporary as I had to decide what to tell my mother about my first year at university. I expected to fail at least two out of my four subjects. How was I going to explain that I had wasted my opportunities, missed lectures and spent a lot of time socialising, especially when she was struggling yet again with the departure of my father? It was clear that we could not depend indefinitely on the generosity of our friends, the Dousts and the McDonalds.

After some discussion, it was agreed that I should go to Sydney and find work over the summer break. My Tamworth boarding family arranged for me to stay with their relatives in Manly. I went to the Manly Unemployment Bureau and found a job as a mother's help for three weeks in Dee Why. After that I moved to Palm Beach, where I worked with three different families, minding their children for £5 a week, seven days a week, which included board. I guess the bonus was that I lived on the Northern Beaches in Sydney, an area of which I'd had very little experience until then.

However, there was a brutal truth awaiting me back at the university. I was not going to be saved from humiliation. When the marks were posted, my name appeared in only two places: History and Psychology. I had failed Economics and English. I was now in grave danger of losing my scholarship. Suddenly, my university life looked amazingly wonderful and nursing no longer held the attraction it had been up until then. I loved the learning, the collegiality, the energy of campus life, and the opportunity to be a teacher.

I decided to ring the Department of Education and make an appointment to ask them for a second chance. I pleaded the instability of my family's circumstance and, that given a second chance, I would pass six subjects by the end of my second year, which meant I could still complete my degree within the three years covered by my scholarship. They agreed.

I returned to university in 1959 knowing I was there by the skin of my teeth. And that I must return to my former self and understand that there was a reciprocity in the relationship between someone funding my education and my performance.

I knuckled down to work. I replaced Economics with Geography, Psychology with Education, repeated English 1 and moved on with History. Good things were happening at university. I was selected to play in the First university hockey team, in Intervarsity down in Hobart. Unfortunately, it cost money, which my teaching allowance would not cover. I was desperate to find a job when the mid-year break began in May.

I joined my mother in the Upper North Shore Sydney suburb of Killara, where she was now staying with a friend, and while walking through the streets I saw an ad for domestic help at Dalcross Private Hospital, which was a couple of blocks from where she was living. Within a day, I got the job as hospital cleaner, and I worked out that I could earn just enough to get me to Hobart for Intervarsity. Even the task of cleaning the operating theatre after bloody operations failed to deter me.

This all came crashing down a week after I started when my father died from a haemorrhaging gastric ulcer. Intervarsity became an unrealised dream. His death was sudden. We had a phone call from Nana Ryan saying he was in hospital and wanted to see us. My mother and I flew to Orange to be with him. He was very ill, very frightened and very contrite.

As he worsened, the doctors decided he needed to be in Sydney. The ambulance took him to Royal Prince Alfred Hospital, ward C1, in Camperdown. It was dark and frightening in there. He was incredibly remorseful when my mother and I said goodnight. We were barely asleep when the phone rang at midnight to say that he had died. He was forty-three years old.

It was my second experience of sudden death. The first being the death of four of my classmates in an air crash in my third year of Forbes High School. But my reaction to my father's death surprised me. It was relief. We no longer needed to feel guilty or worried about him. His life had been unhappy. Now it was all over. And for my mother, it would be better to be a widow than a divorcee, something she had considered becoming at the time. For us children, it was better for your father to be dead than to be a violent alcoholic. No more secrets and lies. Just the simplicity of the statement: 'My father died.'

After his death, our family dynamics started to alter. In the past, I had been my mother's confidante and adviser, and she had always been my emotional support. I could not have asked for a better mother during those first seventeen years of my life. Our relationship changed after that and that was okay for me because I was happy to withdraw and focus on my adult life. I knew I had to pass my exams in all subjects so I wouldn't be a burden on my family. It would also enable me to retain my independence.

The University of New England was an interesting experiment as all students lived on campus. There was an equality and collegiality about that situation, which would be very hard to find in any other university in Australia at that time. For many country parents, these living arrangements were a wonderful option. Many students in my year, in particular girls, were the first in their families to attend university. Professor James Belshaw, Dean of the Faculty of Arts, wrote in the orientation handbook:

> The University of New England is the only university in Australia, outside the capital cities and the large urban centres. Because of that, it was once described as our bucolic university. Certainly, it is a university in a rural environment . . . There is no other Australian university that is a university community in quite the same sense.

And what a wonderful community it was for me and my friends. Teenage girls growing up in challenging but relatively safe spaces. My college principal, Audrey Rennison, was a remarkable woman. A hospital almoner and social worker, adventurous, single. In retrospect, I can see the many battles she fought for the women in her college. And, if I replay some of the incidents and conversations in my head, I can only think of what a tough world it was for her and the women of Mary White College to battle the male hierarchy in the white maleness of New England. I discovered all this subsequently from conversations when she expressed her annoyance at men ignoring her in meetings, especially less-competent, less-educated men. C'est la vie. The more things change the more they stay the same.

For me, a girl who had come out of a co-ed school and co-ed boarding accommodation with male leadership, it was remarkable to see the leadership of women at the university, and in particular Audrey Rennison. She was a Cambridge graduate and had high personal and academic standards, with a great commitment to ensure that the girls graduating from this college would make contributions to the world.

I loved my four years at the University of New England. I fell in love with the New England landscape. Snow gums, mountains, alien trees—maples and oaks—freezing mornings, amazing crisp night skies with visible stars, frost and snow, deer in the park. My first impressions in the height of summer had been misleading. I had seen only the parched landscape. Living there during autumn and winter was a seasonal rhythm I had not experienced before, and one which I now constantly seek.

Inevitably, I fell in love. I met a city boy in 1959, who became my first major relationship. City boys were pretty unusual at New England. Most of my male friends were from the country. We were just different to the city folk. The city boys and the occasional city girl, like the journalist Caroline Jones or the late writer Dymphna Cusack, who each came to Armidale from the University of Sydney—an unknown place to me—were considered rather exotic and beautiful creatures. (I still think that of Caroline, who remains a friend to this day.)

The city boys at New England were often those who had failed at city universities and had been sent out there by their parents, probably for penance and an opportunity to do some extra subjects, before a return to the natural order of things. Alas, for this boy's parents, he was a romantic and a dreamer who loved boats, women and the theatre. Law became an elusive idea for him. We became a couple within a week of meeting and remained that way for the two years he attended the university.

I kept my commitment to the Department of Education. I passed all my subjects, while remaining fully involved in college and university life. At the end of 1959, I returned to Sydney for the summer break, happy with my life and looking forward to my job as a nursing aide at Neringah Home of Peace: A Home for the Terminally Ill. It is now part of the Hammond Care Group and remains a significant part of elder care in Australia. There I would learn to pack bedsores and lift immobile people in and out of bed. I also learnt about compassion.

By now my mother had gained a modicum of independence. She was involved in a relationship with a man she would subsequently marry. He was a lawyer and offered her security and a chance for a new life. I spent that break between the nursing home, my boyfriend and my family. It was a wonderful summer.

I thought often of my father, but still with a sense of relief that the struggle was over. These days I reflect that I have only one letter from him and in the end he was a man that I really didn't know very well much beyond my tenth birthday.

In 1960, I returned to university and was a member of the Orientation Committee. That was an honour. My descriptor on the program was: 'Wendy Ryan, Arts 3 and Education. Wendy is treasurer of the women's hockey club. The Review is one of her main interests and much of the social program is Wendy's work.'

I was in love with university life, in love with learning. I had gifted teachers, a wonderful college principal. I flew through the year to graduation.

The following year, 1961, I was enrolled for a Diploma of Education, my postgraduate year. The Diploma of Education may not have been exciting intellectually, but it did prepare us for the rigid structures we would later encounter in the school system. Subsequently, when you taught beside other teachers without this professional training, the differences were obvious. We were taught how to teach, to engage pupils to be methodical in lesson preparation and to be intellectually disciplined.

Audrey Rennison had appointed me as the moral tutor in Duval College and this role was both confronting and engaging. I was responsible for the pastoral care of sixteen young women housed in a portable hut called Carramar, which had been relocated from the Snowy Mountains. Audrey Rennison was fair and unshockable. After I was married, she wrote a personal reference which she said I would need to get work in the United Kingdom:

> During Ms McCarthy's final year at Duval College, when she was still a student taking her post-graduate Diploma in Education, she was trusted with the care, as tutor, of a residential unit at the college, in which about sixteen young women were housed. They were an ill-sorted group, mostly first year students, who had by no means settled down to university life, and one or two rather immature and undisciplined students from more senior years. I knew they would give her a rough time of it and they did. But I had no other tutor available who combined her qualities of youth and maturity and I thought this may be the only authority the

> group may come to respect. It proved to be the case. And Ms McCarthy justified my faith in her. I think also, that she gained something from the experience.

I often think what a wonderful opportunity it had been to be responsible for a freestanding wing of college comprising young women.

In this last year at university, my friendship circle was changing. Our group of six best friends had started to fragment. One had left university to be married, which was very exciting. Another had dropped some subjects and managed to get a teaching job in a local private school to complete her degree. The four, including me, who remained became closer as we took on more responsibility at university life. All of us were in steady relationships, although my boyfriend had returned to Sydney.

My teaching friend managed to stay in touch. We would meet at the Union for coffee when she came for lectures. One day she seemed a little preoccupied, and when I asked what was worrying her she said she had a medical problem and she needed to see a doctor. She wondered whether I could borrow a friend's car and drive her to Guyra, a small town about thirty miles away. Having both a new licence and a friend with a car, I agreed. But I was shocked when she said she thought she was pregnant. I didn't know she was in a relationship with anyone. She was adamant that I was not to ask about the man or tell anyone else. I agreed, and we met the next day and took what was a tense journey to Guyra.

This was my first experience with unplanned pregnancy, up close and personal. So many fears and questions were spinning around in my mind. What would or could she do? I started to recall vague conversations about how things could be 'fixed'.

The woman who ran the local bookstore, for example, was said to be sympathetic to girls in trouble. Truthfully, I had no idea. But what were we to do? She came out of the surgery white-faced and crying. The doctor had established she was five-and-a-half months pregnant and there was nothing to do but have the baby.

We sat in the car and talked about what next. It seemed surreal. The doctor suggested she confide in her parents. But she was an only child and she thought it would break their hearts. She wanted to do this on her own. She didn't want to tell the father of the child, who was not part of her life. It's such an old story, and such a new story. Not one I had confronted before.

By the time we were back in Armidale we had developed one good idea: to contact a gynaecologist we had met in Townsville at another friend's wedding. We had spent a week with this person. They were part of the RAF Sydney University medical school. My first phone call elicited a positive and generous response. Of course, our friend must come to Sydney immediately. She could live with the doctor and his wife and children until the baby was delivered and then adopted. This was nothing short of a miracle. He would make arrangements for the management of her confinement.

Within days she left for Sydney, and I agreed to pack up her things for her parents to collect. I was still sworn to secrecy. The official story was that she had been offered another job. By the time her parents arrived, they knew of the pregnancy and constantly asked who her boyfriend was. I said I didn't know, that she had refused to talk about it. They kept insisting that as her best friend I must know. Obviously, they were hoping for a marriage. I assured them I had not been aware of any relationship.

After the parents had collected her belongings, a telegram addressed to my friend was delivered to the house. A telegram was an urgent communication. My friend asked that I open any mail, so I did. It was from my Sydney boyfriend, acknowledging that he was the father of my friend's child.

I was dumbfounded.

When I arrived back at the college I burst into the safest place I knew: the principal's office. Audrey Rennison listened to the story, let me weep for hours. She served brandy and coffee. I woke up the next morning in her apartment, on the sofa, wondering what I was to do. Perhaps it wasn't true.

Her advice was perfect: *First establish the truth*. I rang my boyfriend on her phone and asked him. It was true. He started to tell me the details. I really couldn't bear it. I remember asking whether he had told his parents. He said no. I extracted an agreement from him that he would ask his parents to offer her some financial support for the rest of her pregnancy.

When my friend realised that I had accidentally discovered the truth of paternity, she refused further contact with me. So now I had lost a friend, and I also had to work out what should happen with my boyfriend. Once again I took the advice of Audrey Rennison, who suggested that the whole affair could only be understood if he and I spent some time together and talked it through. After all, we had been incredibly close for two years. She suggested a weekend in Tamworth, away from Armidale. She would fill in for me at college.

My long-term relationship ended and that felt fine to me. It had been a profound experience for all of us. But of course life went on. I continued in my role as resident tutor at Duval, caring for my lively students. I did my first education practice, and had another few brief relationships. I started to think and prepare for the world post university. I was looking forward to a new life.

Holding secrets is always hard. But those times insisted on secrecy. And it helped me understand, for many years, how girls who had unplanned pregnancies just disappeared. One of the most beautiful, clever girls on the campus had done just that, and nobody understood why she had left.

My friend had the baby. It was so cruel that the beginning of a life in those days almost meant the end of a life for the mother. And it made me realise that my friend's experience could have been mine. An active sexual life for two and a half years, no contraception, meant that I had been truly lucky. She paid a much higher price than my boyfriend did. But it would be many more years before I thought about the baby again.

By the end of 1961, I was ready for my first teaching appointment. I had learnt a lot about life by now. The strength of family and loyalty. Like my mother's mother, who took us in at least three or four times. I'd understood how my mother had wanted us to be a regular, happy family, even when my father clearly was not up to it. And I could see that responsibility had weighed heavily on him and he simply couldn't cope. It made me understand how alcohol addiction is a genuine health issue.

I had lived away from home since the age of eleven, which had made me resilient and resourceful, with a strong work ethic. I had fallen in love, and I had been betrayed while in love. But, most of all, I was healthy, I had a leadership position, I had an amazingly wonderful education. For a country kid, life was looking pretty good.

I headed to Sydney to spend the summer holidays at the new family home in Roseville, where my mother now lived.

It was like coming home. What could be better? Twenty years old, living in Sydney, and finally having an experience of living with not just my mother but my siblings. I had barely lived with my sister Deborah before, and I was probably just a shadowy figure in her life at that stage. Kerry and I were closer, but he too had been away at boarding school, and was also coming home to attend James Ruse Agricultural High School. For the past years, home had been not so much a physical place as where my mother was. Now we had a physical place and a stepfather too.

CHAPTER 3

The best choice of all

It's good to see the school we know
the land of youth and dreams
To greet again, the rule we know
Before we take the stream

Cremorne Girls High School song

After four years at the University of New England, I had finished my studies. The summer of 1961–62 was the happiest of times. I was looking forward to my first teaching appointment. I had made a special plea to be appointed somewhere in Sydney so I could live at home with my mother, brother and sister. However, I was shocked to receive advice to report to Telopea High School in the Australian Capital Territory. I had never been to Canberra, knew no one there. It felt like I was being sent to Siberia.

I called the Department and begged for a Sydney appointment. The appointments clerk suggested I find someone who had compatible subjects and a swap would be considered. Serendipitously I ran into that person walking out of the Department of Education, and she was also looking for a swap. We knew each other from New England and we arranged the swap.

Day one of the school year saw me reporting to Cremorne

Girls High School as a graduate assistant level one. I was still only twenty and felt sure that the classroom would be my special place. I love the shape, smell and energy of schools. I had been a student since the age of four. I felt safe there. And writing this book now, during the COVID-19 pandemic, I am reminded how important it is for children whose home lives are in turbulence to have safe places to go. Places where teachers believe and understand them, and provide challenges, trust and confidence. I wanted to be that type of teacher.

I began my teaching career during the first year of an educational revolution—the implementation of the Wyndham Scheme that restructured secondary education in New South Wales. It determined that all schools would be comprehensive, rather than selective, and serve the children in the local area. This is something I profoundly believed in and still do. That single edict changed the entire school population for Cremorne, which had been a small school of five hundred girls and had long suffered from the dominance of North Sydney Girls High, the nearby selective academic school for the area.

The school had to respond to many disappointed parents whose daughters would have previously been assigned to North Sydney Girls High. They were concerned that Cremorne would be less intellectually rigorous and not offer the same academic opportunities as North Sydney. Many of these girls had parents who cared very deeply about their education, and many were immigrants from postwar Europe.

I belonged to the History/English Department, even though I would have been happier with History and Geography. Why did History and English have to go together? But you choose your fights, and I certainly wasn't in any senior position to do that, but it meant that Geography, my other love, was a subject I didn't get to teach for a while.

But I did ask if I could teach across departments, and I was counselled quite strongly that if I wanted to be a subject mistress I had to stick to the rules. I thought it astonishing that people would tell me in the first three weeks of my teaching career that I should be thinking of my future. I hadn't thought a lot about it. I had assumed that I would be a teacher for a few years, get married, have babies, and probably stop teaching.

In the July of my first year of teaching, 1962, I turned twenty-one. I celebrated at school with some of the girls in my fifth-year history class, who reminded me that they were already eighteen. I had to learn to teach differently to engage them. I couldn't pull rank based on years of experience. And I needed to recognise their own life experience was very different to mine—they were city children, I was a country child. I learnt with them, and it was exhilarating.

I worked hard night after night. I rarely got to bed before midnight, staying up reading history books and preparing lessons. First-year teaching is about finding the balance between knowledge of subject matter and enough emotional energy required to manage the class.

It was good to be living at home and getting to know my brother and sister again. Kerry attended James Ruse High School and Deborah was still in primary school at East Lindfield. My mother was generous with the loan of her car, as well as providing meals and space for me to work. I had a wonderfully productive year. I didn't warm to Geoff Lewis, my mother's new husband, though. However, he was the provider for our family, and for that I was grateful.

'First year out', as we used to say (when 'out' meant something very different), is the year after school when you learnt about work ethics and becoming a professional. The

Cremorne principal, Gwen Colyer, inspired fear, terror and respect. One of her more unusual habits was to walk around with a hairbrush and flatten any offending beehive-teased hairstyle—the fashion of the day.

On the other hand, she could be capable of extraordinary compassion. She was the woman principal of her times: hierarchical, authoritarian and determined to do the best as she saw it for her pupils. She was not impressed at the idea that the girls of Cremorne Girls High School were less competent or deserving than the girls of North Sydney. She was definitely the right principal for my first year.

The teaching profession—to the detriment of women, I believe—operated on seniority. As the most junior teacher, I was assigned the naughtiest class in the school: 2C. My girls were always in trouble. Lateness, rudeness, beehives, heavy make-up and truancy were the regular issues. In the class and house points competition, we were the school liabilities. I would despair about making a difference, while at the same time secretly thank Audrey Rennison for the experience of managing Carramar at university, where the girls were older versions of class 2C.

Teaching proved to be more than just History and English. I had my first encounter with an accusation of incest after one of the girls asked to see me after school. In a very direct manner, she said, 'Stop picking on "Jane", Miss. She just goes to sleep in class because she is so tired. Her old man roots her all night and she is exhausted. If she doesn't come to school she gets in trouble from the social worker, and if she stays home he is at her again. And you're not allowed to say I told you.'

My Diploma of Education had not prepared me for this. There was no training on how to deal with sexual assault, let alone incest—I barely knew the word. But I did understand that this girl was at risk and I was not prepared to leave her without a lifeline.

After a lot of agonising, I talked to the headmistress, who then helped the girl find another place to live so she could stay on at school. My respect for the headmistress grew from then; I could understand that, in her own way, she loved and cared for her students and would manage these difficult issues, which were so often invisible.

One day after a school assembly, where once again my roll class had featured as letting the school down, one of the ring leaders said to me, 'Miss, you know it's not your fault. We were like this before you came. You'll get a better class next year.' I told her, to her surprise, that I liked the class and I wanted to stay with them. I just needed some encouragement from them. And, slowly, it happened.

My roll class and I learnt to trust each other, and they became a cooperative part of the school. I loved them for their loyalty and support, and their ability to see right through the system, which was not always kind to them. And as I got to know some of the homes they came from and the issues they had to manage, which were not unlike some of the issues in my own life, I loved them even more.

This was a wonderful entry into professional life. With so many outstanding teachers at the school, the staffroom was a stimulating and friendly place. There were so many different female role models on staff. The young first- or second-year teachers. The married women with children who belonged to a permanent underclass of casual teachers—their lives classified thus because they had committed the unpardonable sin of interrupting their careers to marry and have babies and the benefits of permanent employment were denied to them.

And the single women in senior positions, like Hazel, our English mistress. She had planned an independent life and her retirement by the time she was forty.

Us younger teachers were fascinated by these single women, and we created fictions and fantasies about them losing their fiancés in the war. Otherwise they would have married, wouldn't they? Despite our professional education, it didn't occur to us that this might have been their choice. When we discovered our school principal went to Sydney Symphony concerts with a man, we were astonished. It flawed the stereotype yet again of single women having male friends. Most of us, implicitly or explicitly, were on the marriage track. I can recall no working mothers in senior positions. The demarcation lines were clear: eventually choices would have to be made between career and motherhood. I saw no reason to challenge that. The future seemed a long way away. In the meantime, it was exhilarating to be in a classroom.

Entering the teaching profession, first-year-out teachers were reminded that they were on probation and they would be inspected. We all prayed for a good inspector from the Department of Education. We knew that some were genuinely interested in young teachers and would be more inclined to work with them and give them positive feedback. I was lucky to have School Inspector Leo Payne do my inspection. On 3 December 1962, he wrote:

> Miss Ryan has shown pleasing development as a teacher in her first year of service. Both the principal and her subject mistress speak highly of her interest and enthusiasm for teaching, the good relationship she has established with her classes, and her ready participation in all school activities.

> Miss Ryan plans her lessons carefully, ensures the continuing participation of her pupils and strikes a good balance between oral and written work. Her supervision of regularly given written exercises is most conscientious.
>
> Miss Ryan has shown initiative in her successful use of the reading laboratories and is adept in the handling of such mechanical aids such as the projector and the tape recorder.
>
> It is recommended that her efficiency be determined as meriting the award of a Teacher's Certificate.

The Director General agreed and, on 17 January 1963, with my probationary period over, I was a proper teacher. I was thrilled. One of the senior women said to me, 'You will be a very good teacher and you may end up as a school principal.' I was not sure about that. It suggested being unmarried and childless. However, I was on a roll and happy.

Men and women at the time were paid different rates, and the equal pay campaign was a constant source of discussion in the staffroom. I cringe to recall how I initially accepted the argument against equal pay on the grounds that men who had to support wives and children needed the bigger pay packets. Phrases such as 'the rate for a job' were not in my consciousness. I thought I was well paid. And I was. Why did I need more? I listened carefully to the discussion in the staffroom, particularly to the views of those in the Teachers Federation. It was my first experience of a union and the constancy of political activity. I recall only one teacher, a new geography mistress, who spoke out about the justice of the equal pay argument. She urged us to support the Federation's case.

I tell this story to remind myself and encourage others to understand that with new insights, new information, and proper discussion, everyone is capable of change. I find it extraordinary that that's what I felt and believed. I could not have predicted that I would have developed the sort of autonomy I have later in my life. In my first year of teaching, there was no public persona Wendy Ryan. I was simply a graduate teacher living with my family and utterly absorbed in my work. Public sector jobs did not encourage a profile, except through the Teachers Federation.

I probably wouldn't have been a joiner without being invited. That has been a feature of my life. I like to be invited to dance. To join a board, to accept a challenge. I've never been good at presenting myself as the perfect candidate. Indeed, many of the roles I have accepted have been giant leaps of faith in myself and the asker.

During this time, I decided to buy my first car, and I found a pale-blue second-hand Mini Minor. I went to the manager of the local Bank of New South Wales. He refused the loan because I had no male guarantor.

'No father or brother?' he asked. Could I help it that my father was dead and my brother was seventeen? He strongly advised me against buying a car independently. I would probably get married, he said, and my husband would have one.

I changed my mind on equal pay overnight and borrowed the money from a finance company, refusing the salesman's invitation to dinner.

My old boyfriend reappeared. We went together on a holiday to Noosa in Queensland. I took my brother and sister along. It was a happy time, and at the end of the holiday he announced he was off to England to live. I waved goodbye from the wharf and said I planned to be in London in a few months, too. That couple of weeks in Noosa had lulled us into a sense of fantasy about resuming our affair. But, three weeks later, on a blind date, I met Gordon McCarthy, the man who would become the love of my life.

I was strongly influenced by my fellow teachers who role modelled such different lives. Two wonderful women who we considered much older, but were probably in their forties, were Jean Dunlop and Helen Johnman. They were avid readers, intellectual women with children, but had been made casual because of the system. And one book they suggested I read was *The Feminine Mystique* by Betty Friedan, first published in 1963. That book changed my life as I began thinking of women's lives as their own and not just tagged to a husband's.

The Feminine Mystique challenged all my assumptions about life after teaching as well, which at the time I saw as an interim activity, not a career, but a fabulous job all the same. The book provoked me to think about my mother's life and the lives of many of her friends. Their lives seemed nowhere near as full, varied and interesting as those of the women with whom I was teaching.

Curiously, many of my mother's friends whose 'husbands could afford to support them' felt sorry for women who had to go to work, or dismissed them as being rather too clever. This was not a compliment. It seemed to me that the working women were better off, generally happier, and generally better companions. They made a decision about the quality of independence in their lives and they chose to go to work, even under punitive industrial conditions that denied them superannuation and permanency. They were powerfully contrasting role models.

This was highlighted in 1963 when my mother announced that she was pregnant. She was happy about it. For her, a pregnancy consolidated a family. She had three children with my father and had still been a young woman when he died.

She had found a professional man who gave her a status and she wanted that relationship and status anchored by a child despite the pregnancy being difficult to achieve. I love babies, so I was perfectly relaxed about it.

What I wasn't relaxed about was her relationship with Geoff, her new husband. I thought they were ill suited. They had incompatible expectations. She wanted to be a creative homemaker and liked to think we would all sit down as a family for dinner. He liked to go to his club after work. He was a lawyer and a good one, I think, but I could never see them working out. Still, she was my mother, and if that was her choice I would support it. And I knew our family would welcome and love the baby.

I was astonished when someone asked me if I was embarrassed by it. No one today would question the pregnancy of a forty-one-year-old. I remember being shocked that anyone would think that back then. When Sarah arrived, she was welcomed wholeheartedly to our family and has been an adored part of it ever since. It doesn't matter she is twenty-three years younger than me.

Meanwhile, I loved the girls at Cremorne High, and still take pride in following their careers. There are many famous Old Girls—some I taught, and others who were there and part of the school community. Kathy Gee became Kate Grenville the wonderful writer, Pam Swain an ABC producer, Mary Vallentine an outstanding manager of the Sydney Symphony Orchestra for many years. Another Old Girl, journalist and writer Maggie Gowanlock, published a magnificent book on the school called *The Best School of All*. I was delighted to be asked to write the preface.

That book bears testament to the determination of principals and teachers that girls at Cremorne would have a quality secondary school education. Maggie captures the sense of a robust school community that encouraged ambition and success. Surely Cremorne Girls High really was the 'best school of all'! It was my first experience of a single-sex school, and I loved the vibe. I have a cherished photo of some pupils standing outside the church after my wedding and they just epitomise golden young womanhood.

I learnt as a teacher that respect has to be earned; that position is not sufficient. And I also learnt that command and control did little to motivate learning. I discarded it as a technique in 1963. My Diploma of Education, though, had not included any methodology about interactions with parents. At my first parents' night an elegant European father said, 'My daughter is going to be a doctor or a lawyer, and I don't want to hear anything to the contrary,' despite the school encouraging her towards another career as her IQ consistently tested below 100. I've never forgotten this family's tenacity and insistence that their daughter be given extra support to succeed. That left another memory in what I call my 'sixties imprints': given the right circumstances for learning, a person's ability to succeed is much wider and broader than we ever assume.

At Cremorne Girls High I also had my first contact with Aboriginal peoples' political struggle for recognition. When Faith Bandler came to the school to talk at an assembly, she had a profound impact on us. She remained one of my heroines, a person I met and got to know well later in life. The school magazine described her visit as follows:

> Mrs Bandler, who is a Torres Strait Islander, appealed to the girls to force a better relationship between the brown and white Australians, by breaking down existing prejudices.

> Speaking very fluently and charmingly, and in answering almost thirty questions asked in the senior assembly, we learned about the difficulties surrounding the Aborigines. Each state has different laws. For instance, privileges gained in Victoria where there are two thousand against one hundred and forty thousand in NSW cease to exist the moment the Aborigine crosses the border into another state. If you want to visit on reserve, you have to seek permission and you cannot be entertained overnight. Voting rights are given without citizenship rights. Families often have to travel with the father to seasonal jobs, the only ones available are from the irrigation area to the South Coast and then to the Central West. By doing so, the children's education naturally suffers. Often families on reserve haven't saved enough money to build a house elsewhere, but the white man's prejudice soon drives them back to the reserves. The pay for the Indigenous population is often only a seventh of the pay of a white man doing the same work. In twenty-one schools there is segregation in teaching as the schools are especially for Aborigines. This does not help assimilation. The Indigenous Australians only want to be treated as human beings. The protection laws of 1909 are no longer necessary. The usual arguments of dirtiness and untidiness and lack of education results from the conditions under which they are forced to live. Appreciation of their difficulties will certainly help us to understand and assist our Australian Aborigines.

It was a powerful message. Of course, this was before the 1967 Referendum that gave the Federal Government the power to make laws for Aboriginal people and to include them in the census. I was impressed that the women on our staff were concerned about social justice. And I remember feeling a sense of shame that when people had become engaged in Aboriginal Australian issues back at New England, partly through the leadership of Dr Russell Ward, I had not participated in the struggle. It was a turning point in my thinking.

As my days at Cremorne grew to a close and I made arrangements for my wedding and my planned three years abroad, I thought about my good fortune at having been sent to that school. It was a traditional school in many ways, one that aspired to academic excellence and resented the second-rate tag assigned to it by virtue of the nearby selective school, North Sydney Girls High. It's another 'imprint' on me from the sixties: I don't want to be second-rate. I don't want people I'm with to be second-rate. I don't want Aboriginal Australians, immigrants or refugees to be second-rate. And I certainly don't want women to be second-rate.

Cremorne provided wonderful role models of women leaders—intellectual women who quietly and firmly went about providing outstanding education. It was an all-round education and teachers were encouraged to take responsibility for other activities. I coached hockey and debating, and turned history excursions into an art form. My colleagues' gift to me was to ensure that when I left I felt secure that I had been a good and competent, though still learning, teacher, and could go on to teach anywhere. I asked the principal to forward details of my service, advising them that I was going to London to live with Gordon. And I also asked the principal to write a reference. She wrote as follows of my three years at Cremorne:

> I have known Mrs Wendy McCarthy, née Ryan, as a member of staff of Cremorne Girls High School. During this time, she was a teacher of English and History, taking students to honours standard in History for the leaving certificate

> examination. She showed keen interest in debating and under her guidance the senior team won the competition arranged for departmental schools in the Sydney and Newcastle areas in the State. In addition, Mrs McCarthy trained girls for a hockey competition on Saturday mornings and her organising ability was shown in arranging house functions. In all, I have found Mrs McCarthy an enthusiastic, energetic, and willing member of staff.

I was so thrilled when I received this reference. The principal was not a woman given to positive feedback. This meant a lot to me.

When I resigned from the Department of Education, I had to break my bond, which was a five-year teaching contract or £500. If after three years of service you were leaving to be married, as I was, the bond was waived. This benefit did not apply to men who had to repay their bond. I was pleased not to have to pay back the money. But on reflection I realised the structuring of those bonds was completely sexist.

I gave three years of service and walked out the door to be married. I had a new job now. The system assumed I had given up my career. So begins the cycle of women's broken careers. Where seniority determines promotion and superannuation is lost, our careers became bits-and-pieces careers. Women in the Teachers Federation fought many battles, but the clock ticks and potential leadership and authority are lost.

I did not understand any of this at the time, but I want young women to take a long view when they're considering their own careers. I was in my early twenties when I got married, and when I came back to Australia to rejoin the Education Department, my three-year overseas service and experience counted for naught.

CHAPTER 4

This is the story of a happy marriage

> The great marriages are partnerships.
> It can't be a great marriage without being a partnership.
>
> Helen Mirren

I had met Gordon McCarthy in September 1963. From that moment he became the most important person in my life.

It was a blind date—and not a very successful first meeting. But I was intrigued by him. As I write this, on St Patrick's Day 2021, he would have been turning eighty-one. And I realise that my fifty-three years of life with him represent nearly twice the number of years I have spent without him. And it does seem an extraordinary achievement to have spent that amount of time in a relationship. It was enduring, enchanting, entertaining, and a great love affair.

I never took it for granted.

I always assumed you had to work at a relationship. I didn't grow up in a family where long-term relationships were successful, equal, or to be much admired. I wasn't a young woman who was desperate to be married and have babies, either. Although I wanted to be married and have babies, I had a life with many relationships from adolescence—best boyfriends, a long-term relationship of two years at university, and then two years with no relationship except a slight reaffirmation of the previous one. In all these situations, I had been happy. I hadn't felt the need to worry about only being a bridesmaid and seeing my peers married before me. I had vague ideas about boyfriends or getting married, but I was so absorbed in my career. Besides, all the conventional people I was meeting just didn't interest me.

I wanted to find a partner for both my heart and my head. I was looking for a soulmate with whom I would build a family. I was quite prepared to wait to find the right person. I wasn't going to settle for second best. I also noticed that most of my major love affairs to date had been with men who were engaging rogues: charming, intelligent and witty, unreliable, unpredictable and unfaithful. Hardly life partnership material—and too much like my father, I realise in retrospect. Instinctively I knew I needed a relationship between equals, a partnership. I was confident that when I found the person I wanted to spend my life with, I would be making a serious commitment and forming a relationship to invest in.

I had finally moved out of home in 1963 when my mother and Geoff moved to Palm Beach to live, and I rented a bedsit in the same street as Cremorne Girls High. A friend had come to share my apartment for a month while she was finding a place to live. She asked her boyfriend to bring his flatmate to meet me. We had planned an early movie and supper. Like many young women of that age, we connived to make sure we were never left alone with new men we really didn't know. This felt safe.

There was an instant attraction. Gordon was different from any man I had met. But our first date could have easily been a disaster. He arrived late and disappeared early to catch his ferry, promising to call me.

He did call the next day and suggested we go to the cinemas to see Roman Polanski's first movie, *Knife in the Water*. It was September. I remember I wore a cream and caramel dress and jacket with matching shoes. Can you believe it? So often I remember events from the clothes I was wearing. I'm not sure this makes me a clothesaholic; I think my memory is simply enabled by the clothes I wore at particular events. Gordon, of course, remembered none of this. He checked the ferry timetables and coordinated the arrangements. Unfortunately, our ferries passed each other on Sydney Harbour twice. We made the late show and agreed to meet again for another date.

He was handsome, fun, cheeky and smart. On our second date alone, we went to dinner at Fiddlers Three, a local Cremorne restaurant. Three nights later, we were in bed and planning a wedding. Wisely, we kept this to ourselves while past liaisons were ended as graciously as possible—Gordon had a girlfriend in Canberra, and I had to settle the loose arrangement with the London-bound man. Once those ties were severed, we embarked on a wonderful love affair and started planning our future.

In February 1964, we told my mother we had decided to marry and planned to announce our engagement in March. It was at this time she announced that she was pregnant, and we couldn't possibly be married until after the birth in August. We agreed to defer until December—realistically, this gave us time to plan and save for a summer wedding, followed by an ocean voyage to London.

We became engaged. So strange and old-worldly it sounds. He arrived one day with an antique ring, a beautiful Russian amethyst with a diamond on each side. He thought diamonds were ordinary unless they were huge. As a Yass boy, he would spend his lunch times exploring Sydney and had found an antique jeweller, Ben Boulken, in Castlereagh Street. It was managed by two formidable and famous sisters who specialised in early Russian jewellery. The ring was referred to by some of our family as a second-hand ring. I adored it. Purple has forever been my favourite colour.

Being engaged for nine months enabled us to plan both our wedding and our trip overseas. I became very aware then that Gordon had many ambitions that I didn't. He had been dreaming about travelling the world, seeking adventure, although not with a wife. His enthusiasm for adventure was contagious. I was now looking forward to this adventurous life.

We carefully planned our wedding and accepted the financial responsibility. It was a traditional event. I wore a simple long, empire line silk dress in bridal flower. There were three bridesmaids, a pageboy, a bridal waltz and a wedding cake. My brother Kerry walked me down the aisle. I was twenty-three and Gordon was twenty-four. It seems ridiculously young today.

I love the rituals of weddings. In the fashion of the day, I departed the reception in a going-away outfit, which was a very pretty, pale-pink shantung coat dress, made by my mother, complete with a white Oroton bag and white slingback shoes. It could all be put on today and look perfectly appropriate.

I didn't promise to obey.

There were other unusual aspects. The photographs included the beautiful baby, my sister Sarah, who was four months old, and whose arrival had deferred the wedding. The major gossip between members of our families and friends was that Gordon wore a wedding ring. This was visible proof of unmanly behaviour, and I was advised by many that forcing a man to wear a ring would do me no good in the end. But it mattered to me as a symbol of commitment and equality.

After a night at the Newport Arms, we drove for an hour to collect a Halvorsen cruiser we rented for the first week of our honeymoon. An opportunity to enjoy our last Australian summer for some time. It was a wonderful first week of our marriage.

It is almost impossible for anyone now to understand the enormity of travel at the time. In a sense, we were leaving indefinitely because we were certainly leaving for another life with no end date confirmed. We boarded the *Fairsea*, a Sitmar liner, on 28 December 1964, bound for England, a journey that would take five and a half weeks. We took with us our suitcases of clothes, the money we had been given as wedding presents, and a total and utter belief that we could manage on our own. We knew no one on the other side of the world. There would be no one to turn to when things went wrong. We were on our own together, and it was powerfully exciting. The security blanket at the other end was Gordon's job as a chartered accountant with Cooper Brothers in London. I was confident that I would find teaching work, although I had nothing organised.

Our voyage was wonderful. We visited ports with exotic names and smells, and enjoyed street food in Singapore, Colombo and Aden. The stopovers ensured that we had plenty of time to explore. It began my love affair with Asia and Asian food.

Life on the ocean was all the clichés we might have imagined. Endless sunny days, Italian food, dancing, playing bridge for hours, time at our disposal to talk and dream and read. We made friends with other young couples doing the great journey across the world to our mother country. Because of the restrictions on the Suez Canal, we were bussed through the desert into Cairo and made the pilgrimage to the pyramids and the Nile. It remained one of the highlights of my trip—I still have the copper pot as evidence of shopping in the Cairo bazaar.

Travelling at this level was a spiritual experience of great rarity. For us there was the added adventure of a new marriage, and the feeling that we could do anything. We were curious about the rest of the world and wanted the experience of living on our own in a new environment. After the colour and movement on the journey from Australia, our arrival in England was a dull one. As we approached the southern coast, the sea was grey, and it merged into an endless grey sky.

At Waterloo station there were so many dark-skinned people, the colours of people from the Commonwealth, here in force and wanting their share of the action, but we were strangely disconcerted and unprepared. Did we think all English people were white? I suspect so. Within a week we didn't notice. After checking into a pub in Kensington, we went in pursuit of accommodation. We rented the basement flat of a handsome terrace house, 26A Bark Place, which was just off Queensway. At eleven guineas a week, it was expensive, but it was only a block from Kensington Park, and it was our first home together. We wanted to live with some style. And while the flat was short on sunlight, we decided that it did not matter as it would be only a night-time place for us. It was cosy and well equipped for entertaining while being close to the action in Central London. A bonus was that our neighbour Spike Milligan lived close by. Seeing him occasionally made me smile.

We had arrived at an extraordinary time. Winston Churchill had died while we were on the voyage over, and Harold Wilson and the Labour Party were in power. It was an exciting political revolution, the end of one era and the beginning of the other. A great time to start a new life.

Within a week, Gordon was at work with Cooper Brothers in the city and I was applying to the Greater London Education Authority for supply teaching assignments. Professionally, our lives were miles apart. His firm was busy seeking work with the new government, while wishing to maintain its Establishment origins and status. There were dinners at the Café Royal to introduce him to English professional life. I doubted that this would be part of my work experience.

Nonetheless, our marriage flourished in London. Weekends were completely different. There were no family commitments. We bought a green Morris minivan and equipped it with a bed made up of sleeping bags and a rubber mattress. Every weekend we were exploring the English countryside, sleeping in country lanes and byways, cooking breakfast on our little gas stove. We drank and ate in pubs, and talked to whoever was around. Some weekends we played golf at Richmond Park. We went out at least three or four nights a week.

We heard Andrés Segovia and Jacqueline Du Pré at Festival Hall, and saw the Harold Pinter and John Osborne plays *The Homecoming* and *Look Back in Anger* at the Royal Court. Ballet at Covent Garden, concerts at the Hammersmith Odeon, and endless movies. We loved those movie theatres where you could smoke the whole way through. We were like two little sponges absorbing everything as we ran around our new world. Hours in antique markets and shops collecting silver cutlery became a passion. Such a pity it does not go in the dishwasher.

While I lived in England, I learnt to cook seriously. I would thank a hundred times my friend and bridesmaid Amrey Commins, whose Estonian mother had extolled the virtue and dignity of good housekeeping. She saw no binary division between keeping a good house and professional work. Nor did the women I was meeting in London, who were both my professional colleagues and the mothers of our new friends and acquaintances.

Supported by our wedding present cookbook, *The Joy of Cooking* by Irma S. Rombauer and her daughter Marion Rombauer Becker, I developed into a good housewife and dinner-party hostess, things I still love doing. Quaint as it may sound today, I wanted to be a good wife and partner.

I am a great believer that breaking bread with people is a wonderful way to establish and explore relationships. As we travelled the world, we ate the local food and did our best to engage with the local people. I did have a couple of spectacular falls from grace, including my first English Christmas turkey, which turned green while cooking, as well as serving crustaceans to observant Jewish people (a faux pas I wasn't aware of). Almost every time it revealed my cultural ignorance.

London was the heart of the universe for European travel, and we continued to travel cheaply by camping. Gordon was obsessed with Scandinavia, and I came to share that passion. I was enchanted by the respect Swedes paid to children. Their best designers produced furniture, toys, schools and kindergartens. They were committed to the power of creative learning environments for children who were seen and heard. I found this inspiring and it changed the way I thought about teaching.

We were building the foundations for a happy marriage.

London—colonial teacher, corporate wife

When we left Australia, our experiences with political leadership was conservative. For so many years Robert Menzies had been Prime Minister and it was hard to imagine anyone else ever doing it. Britain's new leader, Harold Wilson, was a Labour man who subsequently went on to win more elections than any British Prime Minister to date. His mother had been a schoolteacher and he had a profound influence on the education system in the United Kingdom. His government placed a high priority on fairness and access in education. It abolished the eleven-plus examination and forced the merger of selective grammar and secondary modern schools into comprehensive schools. It was my second educational revolution.

By the second week of February 1965, I was assigned my first job. It was a long way away from the City Establishment. I arrived wearing my white kangaroo-skin coat, a wedding present from my husband. I caught the train to the Hackney Marshes to report as a supply teacher to the Hackney North Secondary School. The clerk at the Greater London Education Authority had assured me this was a good place, and they loved Australians. The school was three blocks from the station. Pretty well everyone was black, and I looked utterly ridiculous in my coat.

The principal greeted me by saying, 'Oh God, not another Australian. But I know you will be able to teach. What do you teach? Oh, it doesn't matter really. Take the Maths and the Religious Instruction.' By the time I had opened my mouth to explain that I was neither religious nor mathematical, she had gone. I asked one of the teachers in the staffroom about a text for teaching. One said that the students were all West Indian or Cypriot, and were not much interested in learning. She suggested I should read the Bible in Religious Instruction, and for Mathematics arithmetic worked well.

'What you do,' she said, 'is tell them they have £2 to buy their weekly groceries. These are the prices of the goods they are to buy and calculate how much change there is. That should take all the time of the lesson.'

I thought she was being facetious.

I went into my first class and introduced myself to scuffles and interested comments about my funny accent, how they loved my fur coat that they thought was made of rabbit. They were shocked to discover it was kangaroo. They just could not believe we killed kangaroos. It didn't seem that my prior teaching at Cremorne Girls High held much value here either. I went through the exercise as suggested in the staffroom and prayed for the bell to ring. For the rest of the day, I looked after other people's classes. Pretty sophisticated babysitting, but not much teaching.

My Religious Instruction classes were not a success. These fourteen-year-olds only wanted to colour in what looked like Sunday School comics. At one stage, I read something from the Bible and mispronounced Job, which sent them into convulsions of laughter: 'Don't you have a Bible where you come from, Miss?'

It was an environment without hope or success. Everyone had given up on these girls. Keeping them there until they were fifteen was a sufficient challenge. If they got a few extra life skills, it was a bonus. I decided to leave at the end of the week. I was so disturbed by the fact that these girls had such little respect paid to their learning needs. Meanwhile, some of the other supply teachers I had met told me that going to the Greater London Education Central Office meant you were always sent to places like Hackney, so it was best to just turn up at the Office closest to your home. I took their advice, and a week later I was at an interview at Gilliatt School for Girls at Fulham.

The principal, Miss Kindred, was welcoming and friendly. She said, 'I like colonials, they are usually very good at what they do. But I do want you to understand that this is an amalgamated school and part of the educational revolution the Labour party is implementing. We are combining a secondary modern with a grammar school to form a comprehensive school. Our task is to provide an all-round comprehensive education for the benefit of all girls.' This was a very good start.

The school was a place where everyone had a chance. A major objective was to get the first girls through A Levels and off to university—so few of the working-class girls were encouraged to aim for tertiary education. The teachers I worked with saw education as the only way out of the ghetto of poverty and under-realised opportunities. It was a great Labour experiment and the teaching force was dedicated to the task.

At the school, which was divided by a park and so existed on two campuses, I was frequently told by Miss Kindred that we had a very distinct philosophy at our school compared to others. We encouraged positive feedback. We didn't say no as a matter of habit to our girls—too many of them had lived their lives with people saying no to them. Society said no all the time. We tried to understand who they were and encouraged them in what they did, so that they could achieve. This was a new educational philosophy for me to think about, but it seemed a lot more promising than shopping lists and babysitting at North Hackney. I took the three-month temporary job on offer.

I discovered that the Gilliatt School had close connections to the British Labour Party. The Chair of the School Board, Mary Stewart, was the wife of the Foreign Secretary Michael Stewart. They both took a close interest in the school. They invited Gilliatt teachers to official sections at Whitehall and talked up the importance of teaching and teachers, with the new order being established by Harold Wilson's government. It was stressed to us that we were professionals leading a social agenda. I had not seen such political savvy and involvement before. And nor had I ever thought of myself as being or having any political significance.

Michael and Mary Stewart were a remarkable couple. As well as being the Foreign Secretary, he was a Fabian socialist and President of the Oxford Union. She would become a Baroness in her own right a decade after we met. They had no children. They believed with great depth and sincerity in the power of education.

After being at Gilliatt for two months as a temporary, I was encouraged to apply for a permanent position, which meant I would be employed by the school rather than the London Education Authority. They made it clear that they'd like a young colonial on staff. Someone had kindly pointed out in the interview that many of the girls at Gilliatt were from families who had been moved from the east end to the north end road at Fulham. This meant their attitudes and accents were not dissimilar to those people who had gone to settle in Australia, and that I would certainly have real empathy with them. I wisely refrained from commenting. This is when I learnt to hold my tongue. I decided the greater good would be to have a full-time job, be part of a school and to move into the school community life, and to belong.

This new restraint was tested when one day it was announced that Labour MP Anthony 'Tony' Wedgwood Benn would visit the school. He was admired by the teachers for being a great supporter of public education and there was great excitement in our staff meeting to discuss how to manage his two-hour visit. I was seen as an important part of the Tony Benn day. From Australia, a female, and a teacher, I offered a way of demonstrating how they accommodated colonials to be a part of the educational experiment of egalitarianism.

I understood that I had to live with this tokenism and turn it to advantage, even under extreme interrogation. Once it was mentioned that my degree could not compare to any UK degree because it was awarded by a colonial university. It begged the question of why I was being hired. They simply had never heard of the University of New England.

It was with mixed feelings that I advised the principal Miss Kindred, I had a problem with the Tony Benn visit. Gordon and I had been invited to Buckingham Palace for a Garden Party on the same day. The invitation came through Australia House as a complete surprise. It was policy to find Australians who would be pleased to receive such an invitation. It would be my first real introduction to royalty.

Choosing a Garden Party over the great Labour statesman seemed frivolous, but apparently not.

'Oh no, my dear Mrs McCarthy,' she said. 'This is not a problem. You have not been invited, you have been *commanded*. Of course you will go to Buckingham Palace. Your class will prepare their work and they can tell our Minister where you are. He will be thrilled to know.'

'Girls, we are so proud of Mrs McCarthy,' she said at the school assembly. 'She and her husband are going to Buckingham Palace to meet Her Majesty. Girls, what do we think?' It was wonderful news. Rounds of acclamations. I was the star. I had been chosen. And this in a Labour stronghold.

'Miss, you will see the flamingos, aren't you lucky, Miss! Do they eat off gold plates? Do you think you will see the children? What do you think the Queen is really like?'

Tony Benn had now become a marginal event. The hot topic for the next day is what I would wear to Buckingham Palace to meet the Queen. Should I wear a hat? What would she be wearing? Mothers from all backgrounds sent me their advice, and girls encouraged me to practise the curtsy.

I did not curtsy. I nodded my head when she stopped next to us. We were introduced as a couple from Sydney.

I did wear my going-away dress of pink shantung and prayed the weather would stay dry, which it did.

These were the years of Swinging London and Carnaby Street. It was also a time to marvel at the British welfare state, and its acceptance of the children of the Commonwealth. My classes had rarely less than ten nationalities in them. Eyes were tested, glasses provided if required, and teeth were straightened. Medical and dental services were established after years of neglect. Hot school lunches and school milk provided the basic diet. If anything was missing, it was sport and exercise, and this was about to be rectified by the so-called sporting Aussie, Mrs McCarthy, who was assigned to supervise rowing on the Thames.

'I can't do that,' I said. 'I don't row.'

Miss Kindred responded, 'But Australians can do all sports, can't they?'

'Of course,' I said, as I contemplated with terror the fragile craft I would be travelling on. I was astonished by the traffic on the Thames—the barges, boats, and ferries within six feet of our small rowing boats. The men who were coaching us would roar instructions. Somehow, we never capsized, and did we learn to row.

It was a happy school, and parents were encouraged to visit. Indian mothers who were worried that I didn't know how to make curry properly would send their daughters to school with freshly ground spices so my curries would taste just right. The West Indian girls showed me not only how to put on false eyelashes but how to straighten my hair too.

'First of all, you wash it, Miss, and then you iron it with the brown paper on top.' I desperately wanted my hair to be straight and followed their instructions carefully.

There were the breakthrough moments, just like there had been with my students in Cremorne. I suggested a school excursion one Saturday afternoon to see *Othello* at the cinema in the West End. On this, they said, 'We have never been to the West End, what is it like there?'

I couldn't believe it. The number fourteen bus went past the door, and it was a short trip to the West End. It was cultures away, and my girls did not think they had the right to be there. Social class was such a strong inhibitor of confidence and growth. They were not aware these opportunities were available to them too.

It was agreed that we would all go together, and there was much exuberance when we met at school at midday on Saturday. As we got closer to our destination, the noisy, over-confident girls became quieter. In the foyer, they were silent. One asked if she could touch the velvet curtains so she could tell her mum what real velvet felt like. We took our seats. I wondered if I was pushing them too far. But I underestimated the power of Will Shakespeare. Laurence Olivier's Othello filled the screen and brought them to tears. I reminded myself: *Never diminish your expectations on what kids can do.*

This was the first of many excursions. We learnt History and Geography together from books and expeditions—boat trips on the Thames and other tourist attractions at their back door. They lacked confidence in new situations, so I took this as a challenge.

Gilliatt School changed my professional approach to teaching. The philosophy of constant positive feedback was powerful and pervasive. Teachers were encouraged too, which made it a wonderfully supportive environment to work in. It aimed to break the cycle of negativity and it has worked for me ever since.

Australian teachers did well in London at this time. They were considered reliable and well-trained. Their earnings were tax-free for two years, which was a real bonus, and they were well paid. The holidays were better distributed than in Australia, and this offered me the opportunity for a long holiday, or a second job. And teachers in London were encouraged to get a second job. Experiencing community-based programs was well regarded, and many teachers worked abroad in holiday programs. It was very different from my Australian experience, where holidays were prized times to go to the beach. I decided to do what the Londoners do.

Before the end of the term, I went to see what was on offer. Within a couple of days, I was offered a job as Assistant Director of an adventure playground at Ravenscourt Park in Shepherd's Bush. I would work after school from 5 to 8 p.m. during daylight saving, and from 8 a.m. to 5 p.m. throughout the school holidays. I grabbed at the opportunity. Ravenscourt Park was only a couple of stops on the tube from our place, and working outdoors for a change was very attractive. I was longing for the sun.

Adventure playgrounds were invented by the Danes during the Second World War and had their origins in the creative-play movement, which recognised a child's need for adventure play. The first parks were in bomb sites, which kids chose as play spaces in preference to manicured parks, which are generally hostile to children. These latter sites would have

'Keep off the grass' signs on the very place that children wanted to play. The adventure playground movement, supported by the UK government, took part of that manicured space and dedicated it to a place that could be mucky and creative. An artist was appointed Director and I was his support. Just the two of us—and a brief to establish a creative adventure playground for local children.

Ravenscourt Park was an elegant and traditional English park, surrounded by a concentrated West Indian population, who lived in crowded accommodation nearby. Although we catered for children aged five to fifteen, we set about developing programs that would appeal to them all, and be inclusive and challenging. My colleague organised painting and craft activities, and I organised games and storytelling.

Our ambition was to build permanent structures of cubby houses and a flying fox. But every morning, when we came to open up, we found the place had been trashed. This happened for weeks. It was truly heartbreaking. Gordon McCarthy's carpentry skills were enlisted, and we started an ambitious ship, built around a tree, with a plank to walk. It was a daily race to get enough built to ensure it was too difficult to pull down. And to get enough boys to use the tools and make an investment in the centre.

One wonderful morning, we arrived to find the centre as we had left it. It seemed to be the management of a couple of the bigger boys whom we had previously suspected of the trashing. They told us they were minding it, and that their mums had asked for their little brothers and sisters to come along as well.

'Sure,' I said. From that day there was no further trashing. We ran a model park with our protectors keeping guard.

It was the year of the World Cup in London, 1966, and many summer nights were spent at the local pub watching the soccer—with little people from the park sneaking in with us, of course. It was a happy holiday working in a playground and getting to know the mostly immigrant families.

On other evenings, I turned up as the corporate wife with the bright young Aussie working at Cooper Brothers. In one place I was an angel, at the other I heard my career described as 'quaint'. Even the fact that I thought I *had* a career was considered quaint. People often ask why I refused to take umbrage at those remarks and the truth is I'm not sure, but I suspect I simply was not open to being patronised. Where I worked was far more real and part of the future, and I considered myself privileged to be a part of it.

I found I often knew more about parts of London than the Londoners I had dinner with. The classroom and staffroom of Gilliatt were a microcosm of London in the sixties. The teachers were upwardly mobile, regardless of their origins. The staff included the daughters of Welsh coalminers and the wives of middle-ranking public servants. The girls, with their invariably perfect skin, transformed themselves at the gates as they went to work after school in the new boutiques in Kensington and North End Road. English pop music brought us all together. It was a fantastic time to be in London. And as I went to work in my Courrèges boots and my miniskirt, I thought I was a perfect Swinging London citizen.

When I left London in the summer of 1966, I asked Miss Kindred for a reference. She wrote:

> Mrs McCarthy is conscientious, efficient and adaptable and teaches with a zest and enthusiasm which can also arouse in her pupils of all abilities so that good work and good discipline results. She is generous with her service for extra-curricular activities, arranging theatre and other educational

> visits and helping with games—especially in coaching a rowing crew and accompanying them to regattas, as well as taking full share of supervision duties in school. I am sorry that Mrs McCarthy has been unable to stay with us . . . as her contribution to this school has been greatly valued by her colleagues and pupils. She will be an asset to any school.

I wept as I read it. I thought it can never get any better than this.

School and life in London

I was separating further from my family at home and growing in confidence as both a corporate wife and professional woman. When I read my first letters home, they seem immature and more dependent on my mother's approval than I remember being. In June 1965, for instance, I wrote: 'Please hurry and write. I am getting desperate and can't afford to ring this week. It's horrible not hearing from you. I get so homesick and irritable and I am thinking of you all yesterday with Kerry going away to Vietnam.' My mother's fears had been realised. Kerry was conscripted in the first ballot.

I was quite accusatory if replies didn't come. I don't remember the intensity of those feelings, yet I knew my emotional wellbeing had improved. Gordon was calmer than anyone in my family and I did not miss the emotional seesaw that the relationship with my mother had become since I had left home. And I was constantly observing the way the other women I met ran their lives. I couldn't think of an Australian equivalent of Lady Antonia Fraser. And although I knew they had to leave the dinner table before the port and their opinions were not always acknowledged, I still saw women with infrastructure, public health systems designed for them, like the flying squad, which enabled them to give birth at home if they chose.

English women had a confidence about their place in the world. They assumed that they would have someone, like a community nurse, to help with their birthing at home. Whereas women in Australia had very little choice. Childbirth in Australia was medically controlled, and home births were not permitted. The au pair system in England was also alive and well. And many of the new mothers at the school had been au pairs themselves and knew the system when they hired young women to come work with them.

We left London in 1966 after Cooper's advised Gordon that he was being transferred to Pittsburgh in the United States. It didn't seem a very fashionable appointment; however, it was the United States, and we were curious and excited about living there. My first enquiries about teaching opportunities in the public system were depressing as the only responses to my letters came from Arkansas and Tennessee, both a long way from Pittsburgh. But the Pittsburgh appointment confirmed our decision to travel for as long as possible, and the firm was flexible about Gordon's start date.

In the August, we packed up our London house, bought our air tickets to the United States, and then set off for Europe until the money or our enthusiasm ran out. We had upgraded to a Volkswagen station wagon, making travel more comfortable. We intended to camp and only pay for other accommodation if the weather was too awful. So, for ten weeks we wandered around Europe. Visiting icons, sharing meals with young people like us who were exploring this part of the world.

In Florence, we found a convent where we ate lunch every day. In Paris, we stayed in a Left Bank hotel and came to realise our school French belonged to another country. We visited all the great tourist places and travelled through East Berlin and Dresden to our favourite city, Prague. I went to my first opera, *Aida*, at the Smetana Theatre, dressed in Bermuda shorts complete with binoculars. We felt at home. My self-consciousness about my ignorance of classical music and art began to weigh in, for here I met people who not only embraced the diverse range of interests but were honest about the gaps in their knowledge and learning. I was happy with this and dreamt of living like this forever.

But there were dark clouds at home. Kerry was in Vietnam on active service and my mother was distressed, especially when she learnt he was part of a major Australian battle—the Battle of Long Tan in 1966. From a distance, I wrote of my brother doing his bit and how good he would feel after it. How wrong could I be?

Pittsburgh—College professor, corporate wife

Inevitably, the money ran out and we returned to London to collect our goods and chattels with just a few days to confirm the arrangements for our move to the United States, where Lyndon Baines Johnson was currently President. During our first week in Pittsburgh, we were taken out to dinner by a couple of partners and their wives. They were hospitable and friendly, and we understood we were being checked out. I was offered useful wifely advice about where to live and where to buy Gordon's shirts—Brooks Brothers. I thought I'd stay with Bond Street.

Sympathy and surprise were expressed at our lack of children. Quick to see an opportunity, I confided in return that I was longing to teach and we weren't planning to have children while in the States. We expected to be there for a year. The fact that I had indicated support of parenthood seemed to help my case. It was then that one of the wives told me that the school they had helped establish had a temporary vacancy in the History department. While teaching was not exactly what the wives of Cooper's men normally did, perhaps I could help out?

Twenty-four hours later, I was meeting Sister Baptista, the Mother Superior of Fontbonne Academy, and Principal of the school. The school was new, and needed a university and college accreditation, without which it would not be the school of choice for middle-class Catholics. It had strong academic aspirations, and Sister Baptista was concerned the accreditation would be jeopardised without a demonstration of competency in all departments.

The teaching sister, who was Professor of American History and Problems of Democracy, was too unwell to return to work in the foreseeable future. I assured her I studied American history and was competent, offering my references. It was agreed I would start the following Monday. When Sister Baptista discovered I didn't have a green card, she assured me that God would provide, and meanwhile she would pay me as a charitable deduction—$300 a month. I was happy to be working.

As I was leaving the interview, she said she would like my skirts to be longer; I would be the only teacher not in religious habit. I could see the point. This was not Swinging London but deeply conservative Middle America. The skirts had to come down. So later that afternoon I was bought a little preppy baby-blue sweater and a knee-length plaid skirt, ready at my first day at Fontbonne Academy.

I was working in the Lyndon Johnson education revolution. My third education revolution. Fontbonne Academy was a school founded and funded by the wealthy Catholic community of Pittsburgh. It was a direct expression of a growing aspiration of Catholics to play a greater role in American society—the late John F. Kennedy had been the country's first Catholic president. In Pittsburgh, however, home of Mellons and Carnegies—both Andrews, who backed the foundations for the Carnegie Mellon University—the WASPS community ranked high and the Catholics low.

But the founders of Fontbonne had worked with the sisters of St Joseph, an intellectual order of French nuns that had two communities in the United States. I was the only teacher without a Master's degree or a doctorate. They were an extraordinary group of intellectually liberated female teachers. It was academically selective and certainly financially selective. A beautifully designed school. The best I have ever worked in.

It had marvellous modern equipment and light, airy classrooms. A contrast to the dark Victorian buildings of Gilliatt. For the first months, though, I missed the neediness of Gilliatt, the transparency of the girls who had so little and learnt to love learning, I think. Here, the girls seemed to have everything, and I wondered how I could add value.

The school community ate together every day. I would sit in the canteen, watching the girls choose between chilli con carne, pizza, hamburgers or good salads, and think again of my girls in London, eating grey mash potato with grey meat. Gilliatt girls would have killed for hamburgers. Fontbonne offered seriously good customer service. It assumed if you were to attract people, you would have to offer value, and these meals were all part of the package.

I had twenty hooded accreditors in my class during the first week of teaching at Fontbonne, in order to determine which college would accept Fontbonne graduates. It was intimidating. Each night, I would have to choose between cramming in more preparation or grabbing more sleep to ensure sufficient emotional energy, the constant dilemma of teaching. The school passed its accreditation with flying colours.

Sister Baptista was pleased with me and reported that the girls were responding well to my alternative way of looking at the American experience. She wondered if I would like to stay on—it seemed my predecessor was too unwell to return—the girls had told me she was an alcoholic and admitted to a special hospital. I said I would love to stay.

I was privately wanting to negotiate some extra money, but I didn't dare ask. I was grateful for the job, and 'Professor of American History' sounded great. Problems of Democracy, my other responsibility, turned out to be a flexible program of civics and sociology, for which we could discuss almost anything. The hot topic that year was whether women should work when they became mothers.

Sister Baptista had said a green card would be provided for me and, one year later, I received a three-year green card. The Lord—or rather Sister Baptista's application—had provided. Regrettably, by then we had decided to return to Australia, so I never did become a legal employee. Still, the Fontbonne Academy had welcomed me. I was given major responsibilities in the school. The welcome had also included Gordon. The parents opened their hearts and homes to us in a way the accounting firm never did. We were constantly surprised by the contrast of extraordinary conservatism expressed when I was asked whether I was a communist, and the great courage in taking a political stance about the role of the Church in achieving social justice.

We became friendly with some of the nuns and we were invited to have dinner in the convent. We ate a wonderful French meal complete with French wine from their excellent cellar. Probably the best meal we had in the United States. I was encouraged to visit Washington with the Bishop's Secretary, Jim Quinlin, to meet a History teacher at a Catholic college and compare notes. Gordon was invited to join me, which I thought was unusual.

It became clear when we arrived that Sister Baptista had arranged this meeting so that we could attend the Washington march against US involvement in Vietnam. It was then that I discovered the Fontbonne Academy looked after conscientious objectors. I found this confronting, partly because of my brother Kerry, and partly because I was so ignorant about the whole issue. I started listening to Catholic activists asserting it was our Christian duty to revoke the American and Australian involvement.

Who to believe and who to defend?

It was a deeply troubling time. I realised that for my brother in Vietnam, whose life was at risk, my platitudes and intellectual laziness were of no value. Subsequently, I completely changed my views on Australia's involvement in Vietnam. I moved from no intellectual position to strongly opposing Australia's involvement.

I taught my first sex education classes at Fontbonne. Sister Baptista said, 'I think the girls need some personal advice about love and marriage. Perhaps you could do it? You could have the girls for two hours and we will close the door in the gym. We won't listen.' I thought to myself, *that means they are going to listen*. When I delivered the lesson, I assumed from the flushed faces of a couple of my teaching colleagues that some discreet listening had occurred through the walls.

By then my moral and social status was so high that the following week Gordon and I were made official chaperons for the school prom held at the Pittsburgh Hilton. It was a swanky event, equivalent to university graduation in our country, and consumed hours of the girls' energy prior to the night.

My students at Fontbonne were confident and articulate. They ran many mock mini political campaigns, reflecting the politics of the day, and each semester they had to make a commitment to community work. In 1965, Lyndon B. Johnson established the Head Start program, designed to get low socio-economic children from birth to five years of age prepared for primary school. These girls, who had previously little or no contact with African Americans in Pittsburgh, became volunteers after school and during holidays supporting the centres. It was another moment that stayed with me forever and illustrates the significance of learning for that age group as well. Fontbonne's combination of commitment, vacation time, adequate resources and strong parental involvement provided the best teaching environment I have worked in. The way Americans express love of country was impressive, as was the ability to be critical when it was thought it was justified.

After a year, we decided to head for home. Gordon wanted some proper work as he spent much of his time in Pittsburgh reading American history in the Carnegie Mellon library and playing golf. His employers were not quite sure what to do with a colonial for the first six months. And we wanted to have a baby. Time to get off the pill and return home pregnant.

Sister Baptista had encouraged our parental intentions, but she told me she thought I would always be a teacher. That I must always find a classroom to work in. It was such a compliment. I was giddy with it. When I left, she handed me a reference that said:

> Mrs McCarthy is our loss and will be the gain of anyone who hires her. She is a real teacher in every sense of the word—a dedicated person who inspires youth with a sense of values and who helps each student to self-motivation. She is totally an unspoiled, gracious, and refreshing personality.

I knew I was fertile because I had had a pregnancy terminated in 1964 in Sydney. But as the months went by and I was not pregnant again, I became anxious. I had that little voice in my head that said, *You had your chance and you blew it, and this is your punishment*. Of course, the other voice could have said, *One unplanned pregnancy in four and a half years of unprotected sexual activity was hardly indicative of high fertility*. But when you start to focus on this, you are not always rational. And my knowledge of the statistics of successful pregnancy rates was zero.

I decided to consult a gynaecologist, who suggested that, if I wasn't pregnant in another two months, I should make an appointment with an infertility clinic. Two months later, I became the new patient of Dr Feingold Infertility Clinic, and was coming to terms with that word—*infertility*. A bad word. It was the opposite of how I saw myself or my future. I had spent years avoiding pregnancy. Was I now to spend years trying to achieve one?

Dr Feingold was just the no-nonsense man I needed. He took a medical history in the first consultation, asking the usual questions. I spared him the information about the abortion. He asked that Gordon and I come together so Gordon's fertility could be established. He suggested instant remedial action.

'Young lady,' he said, 'I can't see anything wrong with you. But in case you have tubal blockage caused by spasm, I will bring you in next week for a hysterosalpingogram. Then I want you and your husband to have sex every day, more or less at the same time, until you get home to Sydney in three months. If you are not pregnant by then, put your name on the adoption list.'

It was to the point and clarified the position. In pursuit of a pregnancy, I decided to forgo the Fontbonne journey to the Kentucky Hill Folk and join Gordon on a work assignment at Lake Erie. It offered us time to explore the area and, as 1967 was the Montreal Expo year, we decided to visit New England to attend the Expo and drive from coast to coast on Route 66. It was an amazing six weeks that reinforced my evolving view—America is the best and worst in the world.

It was hardly a punishment to spend these three months together, with pregnancy on the agenda as well as travel. Dr Feingold's words were treated seriously as we drove into various Howard Johnson motels, famous for low room rates and twenty-seven flavours of ice cream. Our diligence continued after we dumped the car, got a bus down to Mexico and landed in Acapulco. I threw up and dared to hope I was sick from being pregnant and not from drinking margaritas.

When we flew into Sydney from Acapulco in September 1967, I was overwhelmed by the beauty of the harbour and my love of the Australian light. But I was also feeling nauseous from the ache in my infected ears. I had finally had my ears pierced as an act of defiance before I got home. Retribution was two infected ears. Still, I had missed a period, so my first task would be to find an obstetrician who would see me immediately and establish whether I was really pregnant.

I was. It was a glorious moment.

CHAPTER 5

Coming home

> The quality of a mother's life—however embattled and unprotected—is her primary bequest to her daughter, because a woman who can believe in herself . . . is demonstrating to her daughter that these possibilities exist.
>
> Adrienne Rich

In Sydney, Gordon went straight back to his job at Cooper's, wondering how he would feel being back in the system. I was planning to resume my teaching career. I certainly wasn't ready to be a full-time wife on a limited income in a rented apartment in Kirribilli on Sydney's lower North Shore. So, it was back to the Department of Education to find a teaching appointment.

I arrived with new references and details of my experience. The interviewing officer was dismissive, explaining that overseas teaching experience did not count in New South Wales. He said that they had standards to protect and could not give credit 'to anyone who just walked in off the streets'. Despite six years' teaching experience, I would now be paid as if I was a graduate teacher. He offered to put my name on the casual list.

Surprisingly, after a few days, I received my notice of eligibility for employment as a casual graduate assistant. The rate was $20.84 a day. This could become $4250 per annum when I became temporary. As employment was dependent upon medical fitness, I did of course advise them that I was pregnant and would be perfectly happy to be appointed to a school that could confidently manage my departure in mid-April, as my baby was due in the first week of June. The rules were that one stopped work six weeks before the expected due date. I was asked to report to Mosman High in January 1968.

This was a gloriously happy year. Pregnancy, a soon-to-be mortgage, and a part-time job. It felt wonderful. Sydney was alive and jumping with the political issues—anti–Vietnam War protests, the Aboriginal Referendum, inquiries into corruption in NSW government—some of which we had been exposed to in London, Pittsburgh and Washington. We found new friends, renewed old contacts, and would play at house renovation as we prepared conscientiously for the birth of our first baby.

When I was house hunting, we had a $5000 deposit and Gordon's mother was happy to be our guarantor. We started at nearby Balmoral and moved around the water's edge to Balmain, when it was clear Balmoral was out of our price range. We wanted to be on a ferry route and close to the city so we would need only one car. We found our house at McMahons Point, near North Sydney. It was a large four-bedroom Edwardian place overlooking the water. We bought it for $22,000 and moved in on our third wedding anniversary.

We lived in McMahons Point for the next eleven years. It was a wonderful house with large rooms, a fireplace, crinkled glass sunroom that opened up to reveal extensive views over Berrys Bay, decorative plastered ceilings, newly polished floorboards. There was a downside. The kitchen and bathroom were grotty and, on Christmas Day, when our family came to have lunch with us, they were greeted with a plumbing crisis that needed solving when the bathroom taps burst an hour before. Fortunately, it made little difference to the cold tomato soup, the gazpacho.

McMahons Point was a significant choice. Our families thought we lived in a slum but conceded the house had promise. The Hills hoist in the garden, which was on street level, was not in 1968 an attractive Aussie icon to be treasured but an ugly bit of gear to demolish. Within a week of moving in, our neighbours—who were mostly elderly—called in to say hello and suggest we join the Progress Association, which was dedicated to improving the suburb. They were kind, helpful, welcoming and thrilled to have a young, pregnant couple living in the run-down suburb.

I joined the staff of Mosman High, my first co-ed school since commencing my teaching practice. The English History master, Don Brown, faced a dilemma staffing his classes: he was short of teachers. I assured him that as I was pregnant, I would fit in wherever. He assigned me to the senior History classes, so I moved back into the system at full speed.

My students were wonderful—lively, entertaining, smart. But the school had a poor reputation, probably because it was an area where many parents aspired to private-school education for their children. Shades of Cremorne Girls High and North Sydney, and so tragic.

I kept teaching throughout my pregnancy, and I kept deferring my departure because no replacement had been nominated. Until one of the boys came to me and said, 'You know, I dreamt about you having a baby in the classroom.' It was a timely reminder that I had to get out of the classroom and the Department had to step up to replace me. The kids asked if they could come to my house for lessons for the History extension. I agreed.

My obstetrician, Alan Bradfield, referred me to a physiotherapist in Crows Nest for childbirth preparation. Poss Beck, a leading physiotherapist, was a strong disciple of psychoprophylaxis (which is a method of childbirth without anaesthesia) and taught patients in pairs. My pair was a charming young blonde woman called Anna Murdoch, who also happened to live in McMahons Point and gave me a lift home if I was ever without our car. We bonded quickly and were both diligent about preparing for our first births.

We read endless labour reports, did our exercises, and dreamt about our new lives as mothers. We were utterly self-absorbed and never really spoke about our husbands. It was not until she mentioned Rupert was in publishing that the name Murdoch clicked. It's a gorgeous example of the levelling effect of childbirth. Sophie McCarthy and Elisabeth Murdoch were born six weeks apart at the same hospital, and the shared experience maintained a warm connection between Anna and me for more than thirty years.

I loved the physicality and sensuality of pregnancy. I loved meeting new people who were connected to these momentous changes in my life and with whom you established a level of intimacy as you discuss body changes and expectations. It was in a sense the beginning of a new way of relating to women. We were all in the same boat; we were all experimenting with new ways of birthing. I realised how ignorant I was having never studied biology or physiology. I knew so little about my reproductive system.

My first birth

I'm still amazed at how vividly I remember the experience of the arrival of my first child. On a Sunday night in late May, we were having dinner at the dining room table at McMahons Point. We still have that same table. We had friends over, the fire was burning, it was cosy. I had cooked moussaka, we drank red wine and finished off with port. (Sorry to all my friends and their children: we did drink during pregnancy.) The guests stayed late, the last leaving at about one o'clock, and we joked this was the last dinner party before motherhood, which was anticipated within two weeks.

Gordon and I crashed into bed, deciding to leave cleaning up for the morning. A couple of hours later, Gordon woke me with the news that the bed was wet, and my waters must have broken. I disagreed with him. I was feeling warm and sleepy, and I wanted to go back to sleep. I certainly wasn't interested in going to hospital. But he was soon on the phone and agreeing with the sister in a sort of conspiratorial way that it was time for me to go.

As we drove across the bridge at 4 a.m., I wondered if I would ever come back. Childbirth suddenly seemed like a long, adventurous tunnel that would change my life forever—as, of course, it did. But I suddenly wanted everything to stay the same. Perhaps I should just call it off. But when we drove into Camperdown, my mood changed to one of anticipation, and excitement at the thought that I was going to leave there as a mother with a baby.

The King George V hospital admission desk asked the obligatory question: my mother's maiden name. And then I was on the birth conveyor belt. The first stop: the euphemistically named 'preparation room' for the supposedly essential enemas and pubic shave. We don't do these now. Some brave women were already challenging those procedures, but on the list of things to argue about they didn't seem as significant as others. So, I watched as my labia were shaved, and practised my psychoprophylaxis breathing during the enema. It astonishes me today that women have their pubic area shaved to make it more attractive. Why anyone would want to be reduced to such a childish look is beyond me.

I can remember the enema, and the nurse saying it was essential so that I didn't dirty the bed. It just hadn't occurred to me that I would do that. Then into the labour ward, where the lights were bright, and there was the distinctive noises of rattling stainless-steel kidney bowls and bedpans—it was nothing like the films where people kept asking for hot water. Because my waters had broken, I was confined to the bed, due to the risk of infection. I was there for eighteen hours of contractions. Scrabble, backache and some boredom. When the time came to push, I sat up with two nurses supporting my legs. Dr Bradfield suggested Gordon go to the end of the bed so I could aim the baby at his wristwatch face. If I had been told to stand on my head, then I would have tried. But the face of the watch was the target.

And, at 9.10 p.m., in the world's most orgasmic rush, a six-pound five-ounce baby girl slid out. She was perfect. It was love at first sight. The three of us cuddled up and we told her that her name was Sophie, meaning dignity and wisdom. The joy, the sensuality, the power of being female that childbirth confers. To experience the brain and body so perfectly synchronised and the rush of profound love for a person you have just met feels like a life on a higher plane.

I was elated that I had managed a drug-free labour. And pleased that Gordon had not fulfilled the dire predictions of my doubting friends and my mother of fainting when exposed to my genitalia. He had been my partner. He was my partner and coach in the greatest event of our lives. I could never imagine giving birth without him. As the placenta was delivered, I wondered why so many people had counselled us that an awake and aware birth was not achievable. And that having one's husband there was not quite nice. I think it was one of the major bonding experiences of our lives.

After Sophie's birth, I had no desire to return to teaching. I wanted to be with her. The strength of love sometimes took my breath away. I marvelled at the social and family approval motherhood bestowed. We were suddenly 'a real family': a baby, a house, a cat, a dog and a mortgage. I was revelling in the sense of being Gordon's wife and Sophie's mum, which is not how I had been seen in the first three years of our marriage. Being a new mother in McMahons Point and exploring the local community with Sophie meant we got to know our neighbours and the local shopkeepers better. We were building a community. Attending the baby health centre was an interesting and regular political experience. There I met North Sydney community activist Carole Baker and first became interested in local government.

I was blessed with my neighbours, Jack and Dorothy 'Pank' Downes, a couple in their sixties who had lived in the house next door for over twenty years. They loved children. Sophie and I spent hours with Pank, who in true Australian tradition was known by her nickname, a reference to her Pankhurst family. She ran a home-based typing business. Following a career in the army, Jack was now a Commonwealth car driver. They became de facto grandparents to our children, all of whom adored them. It was a child-rearing community you dream about.

During this time, I was sharing babysitting with my friend Caroline Griffith, who had recently returned from England and whose son Andrew was six weeks older than Sophie. Caroline was studying law. Meanwhile I was learning how my community worked, and had enrolled in a pottery and sewing course. We minded each other's children one day a week. It was the model of childcare we continued to use as our families grew. Over the years, with my other friends Elsa Atkin and Antoinette le Marchant, we continued to look after each other's babies. Collectively, we raised eight children and held down part-time work. We had little choice as there was no day care and few kindergartens.

In what seemed an almost perfect world, I was surprised to begin feeling a little restless when Sophie was about six months old. It was the first sense that I might want to go back to work. When I mentioned it to Gordon, he said, 'Well, of course, you will go back to work. Why would you waste your education and skills?'

I could see no reason why one partner should provide for an entire household. We had always said we would share, and that seemed to be reasonable, although I had quite enjoyed being a stay-at-home mum. When I mentioned this to my mother and mother-in-law, I got very bad feedback. They couldn't imagine why I would want to work again. Both thought it lowered my social status. They questioned why I couldn't be happy at home with my baby, after all those years travelling and working. Well, it was only six years. And I was happy. But it wasn't enough.

I wanted other things to do. I see this now still playing out for young mothers. But I wanted us to have enough money to pay off the house, run a car and have a nice lifestyle without Gordon having to work himself into the ground. He wanted to be able to spend time with Sophie. I wanted a marriage that worked as a partnership.

Interestingly, it was Pank who thought I should decide for myself. And she provided me a line I have used so many times since: 'Whatever decision you make will be the right one, if you do your homework first.' So, it was time to find work.

After fruitless attempts with the Department of Education, whose offers were made early morning and required immediate acceptance when called to work that day, I decided to write to local schools and seek an appointment for a year. I had two responses out of twenty letters. One replied they had no facilities for women. But as luck would have it, the other was from Barbara Jackson of Wenona School in North Sydney, who recalled we played hockey against each other in Armidale when she was Geography Mistress at New England Girls School and I was at University. She agreed to my proposal—a three-and-a-half-day commitment taught in concentrated mode with the added assurance I would be happy to do excursions. I would teach Geography only, which was perfect.

At the end of that year, December 1969, Gordon left Cooper's and the accounting profession to work with Gordon Barton at Tjuringa Securities, as a financial adviser. I decided to end my casual teaching assignment at Wenona at the same time. I had been moving increasingly into the politics of my community. There were so many things to do there and I was high on it. Our next baby was also due in May the following year, and I was looking forward to the extra time with Sophie before our second child arrived.

Gordon started working on the takeover of Angus & Robertson, the Australian publishing house. Gordon Barton's company IPEC was a potential purchaser of the controlling interest of the British publisher William Collins, and we had many late nights while the game was played out. I loved listening in to the saga. Mergers and acquisitions still excite me.

IPEC was successful in buying Angus & Robertson, and Gordon was made Executive Director at the age of twenty-nine. He had been handed a huge responsibility. It was a complex business, which included retailing and printing, but was culturally dominated by publishing. When his appointment was announced, the first criticism levelled was that he was not a real book person. What would a chartered accountant/economist know about books, I was often asked. Being an avid reader did not help. But that was his battle.

Meanwhile, McMahons Point was under threat from high-rise development. At the bottom of the peninsula was the Harry Seidler–designed Blues Point Tower, where Gordon had lived when we first met. There were Seidler proposals for similar buildings along the spine of the peninsula. It was zoned industrial, and residential refurbishment was discouraged as we were to discover when we put in an application to the council to renovate our house a year later. But it was a perfect community, with a diverse and changing neighbourhood, corner shops, a friendly butcher who delivered your order and an active timber yard and boat-building business below us. We loved the energy of McMahons Point and loved walking around the neighbourhood. It was a good place to defend.

We both became strong members of the Resident Action group. We were on the fringe of 'Saving the Rocks', backing Jack Mundey's campaign, and saving McMahons Point became a seminal battle. Our passion knew no bounds. Pasting posters on telegraph poles in the dead of the night. Writing letters to the newspapers. And, with a group of women who had met at the baby health centre, running a council ticket led by Carole Baker to remove developers from the council.

The Resident Action ticket won control of the council and subsequently rezoned McMahons Point as residential.

CHAPTER 6

Personal is political

> Even when it is not pretty or perfect. Even when it's more real than you want it to be. Your story is what you have, what you will always have. It is something to own.
>
> Michelle Obama, *Becoming*

As Gordon rose higher in the corporate world, I continued to practise the fine arts of being a good corporate wife. It didn't seem a limited aspiration at the time. The excellent corporate wives in London and Pittsburgh had been good role models. I would have to do it differently, however, because I would be working and, by 1973, we would have three children under five. With the birth of Hamish in 1970 and Sam in 1973 our family would be complete.

Gordon and I were both active members of the Childbirth Education Association (CEA), which we were advised to join by my obstetrician. Its purpose was to give women autonomy and agency over birthing and lobby for the rights of fathers to be present at the birth of their children, the very thing that frightened people, including doctors. In a perfect world, births would be drug free if that was the mother's choice. What mattered is that you were active in the birth of your child with, as one wise friend said it, the woman rather than the doctor at the centre of the event.

I wanted to be part of the conversations about business, and I found that despite the advice that I should not talk about childbirth education over the dinner table with Gordon's associates it was still a hot topic. It was in childbirth education that I first found a public voice by agreeing to an interview with the magazine *New Idea* about my birth experiences. I gained confidence as I learnt to express my ideas about reproductive choices and fertility.

The *New Idea* article was driven by the Channel 10 screening of the childbirth film *Don't Cry Baby*, made to promote psychoprophylaxis—the method of conditioning pregnant women for drug-free childbirth through training in labour techniques and controlled breathing. Husbands were being encouraged to be involved. I found it deeply moving when a CEA member, Jenni Burton, delivered her first baby on the screen. Yes, the first frontal view was very confronting, but many other people were more than happy to make similar appearances. Such was our passion about making childbirth a normal part of our lives. I loved the film, and it was used as a teaching film for childbirth for years.

With its big, long sunroom, our house in McMahons Point became a hub for psychoprophylaxis classes. There were some fascinating women who came along. It resulted in better births, new friendships, with the women from different backgrounds being defined by their birthing wishes rather than their postcode and their husband's job. Our birth classes gave us new confidence about asserting our wishes.

It was a juggling act to be a wife, mother, and activist. I made an enormous effort to attend the after-work parties that Gordon was either hosting or attending. I deeply resented these parties—they were always held at crash hour in the home, when babies were being put to bed and meals were being prepared.

One memorable night, Angus & Robertson was hosting drinks for the publisher Sir William and Lady Collins. Of course, the event was at six o'clock. I raged internally when I received the invitation, even though I was pleased to be included. I put on my silk separates and my white Courrèges boots. When I arrived, I couldn't find Gordon, and was feeling left out and unsure. I considering turning around and going home. The secretaries were always extremely effective at either ignoring you or patronising you, while at the same time guarding their employers very, very closely, including from their partners and wives. It was so curious. And then somebody introduced me to Lady Collins.

Upon hearing I was Gordon's wife, she made a big fuss about how hard it was to make it to these events, which were so anti-social and so anti-family, and she was really flattered that I had come to meet her and Sir William. I thought I was going to cry with gratitude. I wanted to hug her and say thank you for the approval. Moments like that could focus me for weeks.

Women with these experiences understand the contrasting feelings of social vulnerability and mother power. That memory has always stayed with me, and I've really tried hard to ensure that whenever I went to other cocktail parties over the years, I gave support to new mothers or people who were just new to the whole deal of the cocktail party, which I think can be one of the most uncomfortable events in corporate life.

When our son, Hamish Gordon, was born on 6 May 1970, three days before Mother's Day, he was the best present. Fortunately, like many second labours, his was much shorter—eight hours instead of eighteen. We had the same hospital team and felt confident as we approached King George V at about eight in the morning. I was in the labour ward at nine, and he arrived at five. Definitely bound for an office, we thought, a nine-to-five baby. We were overjoyed. We wouldn't have minded if we had all boys or all girls, and we said gender didn't matter, but there was a sense of bliss at having both a son and a daughter.

The most notable responses to Hamish's birth, which I found a bit confronting, was the outspoken approval of the birth of a son. The entire community was pleased, and I was reminded how much we value male children above female children. Years later, I wrote a piece for the *National Times* on raising sons, and reminisced just how much approval is given to those who produce boys. And, by contrast, how much pressure can be placed on women who produce 'only girls'.

A couple of weeks after Hamish was born, I was already thinking about the next baby. I felt like earth mother who just hit her straps. For the next two years, I stayed out of the paid workforce and just enjoyed and flourished in feminism and community activism.

When asked to attend an Abortion Law Reform meeting on behalf of Childbirth Education Association, I agreed, despite feeling a little apprehensive. Abortion was always part of the choices of pregnancy. Some people found this incomprehensible. How could I be supportive of abortion and childbirth simultaneously? I saw no conflict. I didn't see the answer as complicated: if you supported choice in birth, it had to include whether or not *to* birth. But I still had not disclosed my own abortion. Instead, I spoke at the meeting about the matter in a more academic, right-to-choose sort of language. Although personal was political in terms of childbirth, I was not seeing those connections in quite the same way about abortion. There is always stigma about abortion, and I still wasn't confident about disclosure.

Speaking out on childbirth education, fathers in labour wards and abortion—all previously thought of as private women's business—seemed to me to be no different to my on-the-record statements on education philosophies, matters of censorship, public policy, or organisations like the ABC. Usually these comments were sought by journalist and I was happy to respond. There is little gained by not challenging the status quo for women. And during the early 1970s, as women found their voices, they found they could leverage the power of narrative and shared experience.

Revisiting my memoir offers me the chance to write about this as honestly as I can. In the past twenty years, many things have changed. As I look back over old photograph albums and my first public demonstrations as a first-year university student, I try to recall the exact circumstances when I agreed to march, dressed up as a pregnant woman, wearing a sign saying 'produce more scientists'. It was hardly a feminist statement because it didn't say 'produce more women scientists'. Who or what persuaded me to do this? I do not recall.

I learnt to be a feminist through reading the literature of Germaine Greer, Kate Millett, Robin Morgan and the newly launched magazines *Spare Rib* in London and *Ms.* in New York, while flush with the success of the breakthrough of fathers being permitted and even encouraged into the labour ward.

Not long after Gordon became Executive Director of Angus & Robertson, the head book-buyer asked me if I would like to be part of the 'poison testing group', made up of readers who offered opinions on new titles. The first book he asked me to read was *Sexual Politics* by Kate Millett. He said, 'A few people have expressed an interest in this, but quite frankly I think it's the boilersuit brigade. Read it for me and tell me what you think.' I was flattered to be asked, and took the book away.

I read it from cover to cover in two sittings and was entranced. I went back to him and said get as many as he could. He was aghast. He truly believed I would come back saying it was hopeless. However, he took my advice, ordered copies, and it sold well.

Not long after that, *The Female Eunuch* by Germaine Greer was published. Gordon Barton and Angus & Robertson launched the paperback edition at a Writers of the Year dinner at the Argyle Tavern in The Rocks. *Vogue* recorded the event, but the article does not quite capture the feelings of excitement and insecurity I experienced after reading the book. *The Female Eunuch* raised the ambivalence about the motherhood pathway for women, as though motherhood and feminism were binary. The book sang to me, but I was treading through unknown territory.

There has been no time in my life since my marriage that I haven't thought it is perfectly possible to be a strong feminist, a good mother, and a good wife. I wanted to succeed at all three roles. How could I keep it all together, I wondered?

Women's Electoral Lobby (WEL)

In March 1972, Beatrice Faust flew to Sydney on a mission to persuade Sydney activist women to support the founding of a women's political pressure group called the Women's Electoral Lobby. The people invited were all contacted through the Abortion Law Reform Association, which had been established by the Humanist Society in 1967, and we met at the home of its leader, Julia Freebury, in Bellevue Hill.

Helen McCarthy (no relation) and I went together, along with Hamish and Helen's second baby Claudia. We were committed to rigid timetables to collect Sophie and Helen's son Joshua from pre-school. We had a get-out clause.

The others present were postgraduate student Anne Summers; journalist Caroline Graham; women's activist Mavis Robertson; Joan Edwards; Victoria Green from Canberra, sociologist Liz Fell; Faith Bandler, my heroine from Cremorne Girls High but now representing the Federal Council for the Advancement of Aborigines and Torres Strait Islanders; Helen L'Orange, a local council woman; Helen Berrill, an independent candidate for the federal election; and June Surtees, a teacher. Helen L'Orange has since told me that Bob Ellis was also there. I have no recollection, which I find interesting in itself. All these women became significant public feminists.

Beatrice Faust spoke persuasively about an article written by Gloria Steinem in the first edition of *Ms.*, which started as a one-off insert in *New York* magazine, entitled 'How women see candidates for the White House'. It was based on a nationwide survey. Ten women in Victoria had looked at the questionnaire and developed one for Australia, and Beatrice hoped we would find supporters in New South Wales.

The small group in attendance were not especially well connected. It was hard to imagine we could find enough people in order to conduct interviews all around Australia. As she concluded the meeting, Beatrice looked around the room to see who was enthusiastic and who would coordinate it. Nobody volunteered. Some of those present were only mildly interested. Others thought it was too reformist and wished to stay with Women's Liberation, believing the tactics would only lead to superficial responses.

When the moment of truth came, almost by default as we seemed to have the least to do, it was agreed that Caroline Graham, who along with being a journalist also had four children, would be the convener of the group. Teacher June Surtees and I agreed to be deputy conveners. They were grand titles for unknown responsibilities, but the idea sounded right. We wanted to find an answer to the question: how did politicians define women's roles in Australia? As another election was eight months away, we didn't meet again until early June 1972, when we decided to call a public meeting to test interest in the idea of the survey, which would be the platform of the Women's Electoral Lobby. The survey questioned attitudes about our key issues.

The organisation already had its embryonic working title: Women's Electoral Lobby, or WEL. It became a great name for one-liners, such as 'get WEL' and 'WEL and truly'. We asked our own networks of friends and acquaintances who might be interested in joining. On 17 June, we held our first meeting at Women's Liberation House, 25 Alberta Street, at the Surry Hills end of the city.

It was a great success: over forty women turned up. The meeting soon reached a regular attendance of sixty-plus, and three country groups were formed in Armidale, Wagga Wagga and Taree. Finding interviewers was a challenge and eventually we did about one hundred and fifty using a Melbourne interview schedule modified by Eva Cox and June Surtees.

Membership and enthusiasm about being involved were astonishing. We were on a roll. Within two months, we had to move to a larger meeting space. We discovered a whole new network of women who wanted to be engaged in the politics of Australian democracy Our original five demands were equal pay, equal employment opportunity, free contraceptive services, abortion on demand, and free twenty-four-hour childcare. It is remarkable that we stayed with this list, and it continues to motivate us, albeit in different times. They are the foundation issues for women's equality.

Meanwhile, in July 1972, WEL member Anne Conlon had been preselected as a Labor candidate in the by-election of Mosman. WEL members were excited and enthusiastically offered support. A woman candidate at last. We decided to trial some of the strategies we had been talking about, such as public meetings and pre-polling of candidates. We held a Meet the Candidates meeting, where they were asked questions on their attitudes to women and their policies that had an impact on women.

The meetings were invariably packed out. It was exciting politics, grassroots-style. And it had great appeal in electorates where there were well-educated women, frequently working as teachers and nurses, and others who for whatever reason were no longer working. The meetings provoked laughter, despair and often shock at some of the extraordinary attitudes the candidates revealed towards women. It also demonstrated how far apart men's and women's political views and concerns were.

When the questionnaire was complete, we were further gobsmacked by views expressed by male candidates. My favourite remains the one from Sir John Cramer, the Member for Bennelong, who, when asked what a woman's most prized possession was, responded: 'A woman must be taught that virginity is the most valuable thing that she possesses.'

I'd have to say that those of us who had for some time been without that possession wondered what our residual value could be. Did he mean it? Was this true in Australia in 1972? It was so extraordinary that it simply gave us more energy to make sure that people like Cramer did not represent us. Unfortunately, in his safe electorate, he continued to do so for a few more years.

In the beginnings of WEL, we commandeered our kitchens and sunrooms, sitting rooms and verandahs as spaces to organise. They were the hubs-of-the-house. The first formal meeting of WEL NSW was attended by June Surtees, Gail Wilenski from Canberra, and myself. A photograph shows us sitting in my recently renovated kitchen. It was the place of high trust, women's ownership, dreams, and in a sense the power and control of the household. Otherwise, we commandeered our cars to carry our boxes, press releases and various children to demonstrations and deliver our messages.

During that time, I had my first radio interview and it was with Paul Lynch on 2UE. It was a talkback on a Sunday evening. As ever, I remember the event by what I wore: a green woollen shirt and a long black skirt. It was my confident, good-luck look for that year. I spent hours getting ready to make sure that I looked good—yes, I know it was radio, but I had to look good to feel good, and you never know who will see you. Despite this preparation, I had to stop the car and throw up from nerves. Then I stopped at a garage and bought some chewing gum in case I smelt of vomit. I got there pretending I was cool, calm and collected.

I always tell this story because it's important for people to know that nobody does this naturally. These performance skills are learnt along the way. You learn them first by agreeing to take the risk. Paul Lynch was known as a Catholic, conservative interviewer, but a decent human being. I did not assume he would be aggressively hostile, nor did I assume that he would be charmingly in agreement with what I said—no matter how I looked.

The interview went well. He seemed intrigued why a nice, young married woman like me would want to be involved in women's lib. I was confident in expressing my views about the impact of politicians on women's roles in society. Strangely, however, I was still in denial about identifying myself as a women's libber. I was very comfortable with the Women's Electoral Lobby, as it defined itself as reformist not revolutionary. But as I matured, I began to see things differently, accepting there would be no WEL without Women's Liberation. There was a middle ground in the way WEL took up the Women's Liberation demands. Perhaps the distinctive difference lay in the way each group thought they could be achieved.

During the 1972 election campaign, Prime Minister William McMahon, confronted by WEL and recognising it was a new constituency of women voters, was asked questions about childcare, contraception and divorce. McMahon, and many of his fellow conservative MPs, showed an outstanding lack of interest in these questions. Too late McMahon realised his error. Although he promised to hold a Royal Commission on the status of women—a popular, political response—he insisted he did not want to discuss abortion, birth control or equal pay. Fortunately, he didn't have to honour his promise because he lost the election shortly after to Gough Whitlam, who had promised to address these matters.

Sydney Women's Liberation nonetheless decided to hold a commission of its own. The emphasis was on women testifying to the actual conditions in Australian society, which had not been what former Prime Minister McMahon had in mind. It produced the most extraordinary and powerful narratives in consciousness-raising on a large scale. And it provided an opportunity to women to understand the difficulties and oppression suffered by women in Australia. It emphasised the primacy and problems of personal politics. Attended by more than six hundred women, sessions were held on women as sex objects, as workers, as mothers and as lesbians.

Consciousness-raising had already been taking place in small groups, where women explored their personal experiences in an attempt to see the patterns of their oppression outside the confusion of their own heads. Consciousness-raising was based on the idea that personal stories gave women power, and that transforming experience into narratives could build solidarity and sisterhood. The 'personal is political' challenged every existence of a private self, protected and separate from politics, and demanded that political action should be based on experience. It was situated in individual experiences and sought to transform the nature of politics. My own personal experience around abortion and childbirth became a political one, too.

WEL became recognised as pragmatic, reform-oriented feminism. We wanted results. We had a lesson plan/shopping list/political agenda and we worked our way through it. We used the opportunities the Whitlam government offered to achieve change and help define what change might be possible in the future.

WEL was focused on challenging the long-held views about how women voted. People had assumed that women were more politically conservative and merely duplicate their husband's voting patterns. It made sense to target women in different ways.

I reflected on this when I ran Kerryn Phelps's campaign for the Wentworth by-election in 2019. While on the streets handing out how-to-vote cards, I was surprised by how many husbands still assumed their wives or partners were voting as they did. It is a good reason to have a secret ballot. It is nobody else's business and I assured people there is no need to tell people how you vote. Enjoy the power of your vote.

The late Susan Ryan described WEL as the political bombshell of 1972, as it changed the nature of public debate by and about women. *The Age* stated: 'the election must go down in history as the first in which the average women is really interested, and much of this interest is due to WEL.'

Victoria and New South Wales had a healthy rivalry about who was the pre-eminent WEL, although a smaller group in the Australian Capital Territory was equally powerful. It was a dynamic movement that drew in women across the country, and there were branches of WEL in almost every state by August 1972.

WEL members interviewed politicians in pairs. What was fantastic about that is women became trained in political lobbying. It exposed not just ignorance but a dismissive lack of interest in how women voted. The responses generated great media coverage.

Within the WEL world, it was my job to manage the public relations and media in New South Wales. Eventually this grew into a much more significant role, especially when we were discussing how we would release the results of the national questionnaire. Of course, everything was unpaid. Within a short time, the national campaign became a new phrase in my lexicon.

I had done some publicity for CEA and lived near a few journalists, so I hoped that this would somehow transfer into skills for the WEL campaign. Surprisingly, it did. There is something compelling about the freshness of a new idea, the methodology, the influence, and the opportunity. Convention wanted us to think of these issues as personal and private.

We saw them as proper political issues that would enable women to be more active citizens.

On 2 December 1972, the ALP won the federal election with a margin of nine seats. It was my first Labor government as an adult and my expectations were high. WEL had been working on ideas we had hoped would become public policy. Part of the pre-election questionnaire was directed towards whoever won the election, thinking how they would employ the ideas that we were putting forward. Working on that policy before the election meant we developed strong bonds with the women we met who felt and thought the same as we did.

WEL crossed so many defining boundaries: geography, husbands, occupation, political allegiance, formal education. We could never have predicted how profound these friendships would be. In 2019, in the Pro-Choice campaign in New South Wales, many of us were back on the hustings to get abortion removed from the Criminal Code.

The seventies were a time when I have never been more brave, happy or determined. I was prepared to take the risks involved with speaking out, marching in the streets, and lobbying politicians. I loved the fact that I would go to meetings, play mum, develop press releases around town with the children in the back seat, attend more meetings at night, work on policy, return home. Gordon was the best husband and partner to have during that time. He always had my back. That doesn't mean he always agreed with me. But he believed in what I was doing. He found the energy of change exciting, as I did.

Meanwhile my mother and mother-in-law advised, 'Don't be bold. Stop drawing attention to yourself. Don't try and change things. This is the natural order of things. You will ruin your marriage if you speak out.' I heard it, but my experience was pointing in the opposite direction. This gave me a confidence and a voice that I hadn't had before. That inner voice continued to encourage me to undertake new personal challenges.

I wanted to tell everybody, and especially my women friends, 'Don't be sucked in and don't believe what people are telling you. You can be a parent, a mother and a worker too. If political men really value the family in the way they say they do, let's see the public policy response.' The evidence was clear: women's voices had been dismissed. Equal pay was but a dream. Access to education for women and girls was limited. Abortion was illegal and unsafe. And contraception was not easily available. WEL had plenty to do in order to remove systemic discrimination against women.

There was a marvellous moment in the early days of the Gough Whitlam parliamentary term. The federal election had been won, but some seats were still too close to call, which meant the Labor caucus could not meet to elect the full ministry. The prior incumbent, William McMahon, suggested to the Governor-General that he would act as caretaker until the election results were finalised. This was absolutely unacceptable to Whitlam, and within three days of victory he secured approval to form an unconventional two-man ministry of himself and his deputy, Lance Barnard. That maintained Labor's momentum before the 1972 Christmas break.

Those first three months of the Whitlam government saw the tapestry for the next three years set in place. Draft defaulters and paroled protestors were pardoned. Imperial honours abolished. The Schools Commission was established. And racially discriminative sports teams, like the Springboks, were not able to visit Australia. Whitlam reopened the Equal Pay case before the Commonwealth Conciliation and Arbitration

Commission, and on 8 December 1972, he not only removed the 27.5 per cent luxury tax on the oral contraceptive that had made it very expensive, but also put it on the PBS, reducing its cost to $1 a month.

To Australian women, this was a singular acknowledgement of their lobbying, planning, leadership, and in a breathtaking moment it changed the way we managed our sexuality. The Family Planning Associations and WEL had been lobbying for this tax to be removed.

Meanwhile, back in the McCarthy household, our family life was changing. In 1972, Gordon quit the Barton empire after a dispute about future management with the Angus & Robertson group. He took three months off to write *The Great Big Australian Takeover Book*, one of the first Australian titles on mergers and acquisitions, before starting his own consulting business.

Despite the worldwide support for biologist Paul Ehrlich and his Zero Population Growth group (which I found intellectually appealing), I wanted to have another baby. My friends mostly disapproved. Nothing could dissuade me. And while Gordon was working at home, I found another teaching appointment at Monte Sant' Angelo Mercy College in North Sydney, where I became the Geography mistress. It gave me the professional stimulus I needed. It seemed to help my fertility too—by the end of the school year, to the joy of the nuns and our family, I was six months pregnant and looking forward to our new baby. That summer was full of hope: a new government in power after years of conservative power, a new pregnancy, working in a school again, as well as for WEL as a volunteer.

In 1973, on 19 March, two days after Gordon's birthday, and a day before my brother Kerry's, Samuel Gordon was born. Gough sent him a telegram: 'Welcome SamuWEL'. He was a breech birth and arrived upside down, absolutely refusing to move into the regular birth position. A sign of things to come, really. The delivery with a different medical team was challenging. I missed the relaxed, wise and friendly coaching of Alan Bradfield, who had been hospitalised following a heart attack. Foolishly, I succumbed to the replacement obstetrician and the anaesthetist, who kept encouraging me to have some pethidine to relax. Their anxiety created tensions for me, and I wondered if they knew something about the baby that I didn't.

My birth classes concentrated on saying that breeches were best delivered by experienced mothers who knew how to push effectively when instructed. I could do this. But the power of those in control is omnipotent, and eventually I agreed to their wishes and like a good girl took my pethidine. It was a mistake. It made me feel groggy and less able to respond to instructions.

Sam was born with a concave chest and suspected green-stick fractures in his legs. Fortunately, at eight pounds, he was bigger than his brother and sister and his respiratory system seemed sound. He was whisked off to the intensive care nursery all the same.

When he hadn't been brought to me some hours later, I began to worry and went searching for him, despite having been told by the nurse to stay in bed because I had taken that wretched pethidine. I went down to the next floor, to the intensive care nursery, creeping into the lift when no one was looking, trying to find my baby. I opened the door and quietly moved in and who should I see but an equally guilty-looking man, Gordon McCarthy, searching for his son.

We found him together, and after assurances from the sister in charge he would be brought to me soon, I went back to my ward to sleep. Nobody told us our baby was to stay in intensive care—we had to be vigilant to find out what was going on.

The news got worse. As well as greenstick fractures, the paediatrician thought he had clicky hips, and a plaster cast would probably be a good idea. The thought of this little baby, lying in his cot for months in plaster, was totally unacceptable. I had only just finished reading about babies in Romania who stayed in their cots all the time, to the great detriment of their development. This was not going to be the story for my baby.

For the rest of the hospital stay, I listened carefully to the advice and, as soon as I was discharged, I went to my experienced GP, Tom O'Neil, for advice. He recommended double nappies, which seemed a much better idea than plaster. Whose advice to follow—paediatrician or GP? I stuck with the GP. Within six months the clicky hips had gone, but for the first year of his life Samuel had to wear orthopaedic boots. I found cute red and navy ones, from the English brand Start Rite. But when he got to wear his first sneakers like all the other kids, I couldn't stop weeping.

For the next six months, I fantasised about another baby and just decided to see if it happened, relying on breastfeeding as a contraceptive in the hope it would fail. Yes, we had three children under five, but I didn't feel I was over-extended. I was in love with this image of myself: earth mother, activist, newly discovered feminist. But after a year with no sign of pregnancy, I went back to Alan Bradfield to talk about fertility help.

We agreed to try Clomid to stimulate ovulation. Three months later and not pregnant, I decided to have a tubal ligation. It was a strange decision, people thought, for someone whose fertility was as unreliable as mine. But I had reached a point where I couldn't have my life controlled by an erratic menstrual cycle. I had to move on. Gordon was also beginning to feel the burden of supporting three children on one income. He thought that we had reached our parenting limit, and we should quit while we still had reserves of energy and finance.

I agreed.

A week later, I checked into King George V for the tubal ligation. The admitting clerk was not quite as friendly as he had been when checking me in for Sam's birth. He asked for written proof of my husband's consent for this operation. I explained why I thought that that wouldn't be necessary. It wasn't my husband being sterilised, it was me. The system went into chaos. They pleaded for Gordon's consent. But I stood my ground, and it was finally agreed that I would go to the operating floor and the doctor could decide.

Travelling along the corridor on the trolley, the same anaesthetist who had insisted on the pethidine at Sam's birth asked that Gordon sign the form. I said no. He responded, 'Wendy, this is very irregular. Nobody has ever been sterilised here without their husband's consent.'

'Well,' I said, 'I'll go down in history as the first woman to give her own consent.' As a family-planning worker many years later, I realised that this was not true; there were many secrets and lies about who had been sterilised without consent.

This was the end of the baby era. It felt right. To celebrate, I opted to stay overnight in hospital and, on the way home, I stopped off at Grace Bros. and bought a new bikini. Motherhood had given me bravery and courage I could never have imagined. After becoming a mother, I was never afraid, except for my children.

Women's options for pregnancy or not became one of my consuming interest throughout the seventies. I wanted to change the world. And I never doubted that with WEL's support I could.

The appointment of Elizabeth Reid in 1973 as the women's adviser to the Whitlam government was groundbreaking and caused endless media hype and speculation. For WEL supporters, it was a seat at the table and we believed the world as we knew it would be transformed. The conservative tabloid media, offering a free kick to trivialise women issues, quickly dubbed Reid as 'super girl'.

The United Nations had declared 1975 as International Women's Year (IWY) and sponsored the first World Conference for Women in Mexico 1975. It was agreed that Australia would send a delegation and Margaret Whitlam, Gough's wife, was asked to lead it. One of my favourite quotes from a speech she gave during IWY is:

> We must write our history, reform our language, keep our own names, live our own lives, redefine our god, make our own laws, learn to defend ourselves, command and get control of our bodies, and affirm that it is feminine to think.

I have these words printed on a tea towel and they stay with me. So wise and gentle.

Thousands of women took to the streets of Mexico City to demonstrate their commitment to improving the position of women during the conference proceedings. I would have loved to have been there.

By late 1974, WEL had an office and the necessary systems and was flourishing. But as much as I loved it, I was looking for a broader identity than being a WEL spokesperson. I thought that WEL needed new voices and I needed new challenges.

I began what I can now see is a pattern of my life. I am good at start-ups, but after the thrill of setting it up and making it work, I am really happy to hand it over to other people. Creating an organisation is a particular skill, and it is not necessarily the same skill as running it.

I wondered what I had to offer post WEL. My community activities had engaged me in passions and causes, and changed the way I approached the world. Creating a lobby group from the ground up had been a fantastic experience. But what was I to do now?

My life was rich and secure with motherhood and wifehood. I knew my community well and had many rich friendships. We were a thriving family, complete with Lucy, our wise black cat, Alice our springer spaniel, the McMahons Point community, new friends and feminism. What was missing?

I pondered this as I walked the streets of North Sydney during the next council election, where I was a candidate for local government. I was third on the ticket and I hated every minute of it. The thought that I could be a suitable candidate for local or any kind of government was unfathomable during that time. I liked to run the campaign, sell the team and its policies, but I hated having to sell myself. I am an issues-based person. I felt constrained by the party rules. I could not be part of those tribes.

I was proud of my association with the Resident Action Team, and full of admiration for Carole Baker's political skills. She subsequently became the Mayor of North Sydney. Today, in 2021, it gives me so much joy when I read the local papers to see that her daughter Zoë, Sophie's peer, is on the North Sydney Council and doing an outstanding job.

It was wonderful that I wasn't elected. Public office would not be my next career. I had begun to think about resuming teaching, which had been a part-time job of mine for the past six years. People were encouraging: motherhood and teaching go so well together, they would say; aren't you lucky you can teach part-time, earn some pocket money and still be a full-time mother; the hours and holidays are so good, so why not find a nice job in a private school like so many of your peers married to professional men? They seem happy.

But those women didn't change anything. Working with activist women made you examine everything you did. It demanded you use your publicly funded education to make the world a better place.

TAFE—Teaching grown-ups and dropouts

I felt unsettled. I wanted to have what I saw as a proper job. I didn't just want to be seen as someone who had little part-time jobs while raising children and running the household. All things I loved but, when Penny Hume, an ex-colleague at Monte Sant' Angelo, called to say she was teaching Geography at TAFE on the North Shore and there was a position available on campus she asked, 'Would you be interested?' I was.

This was a chance to teach second-chance students who were mostly adults. I hadn't been in the classroom since Sam had been born in March 1973, nearly two years before. The timing was perfect. Sophie was now in kindergarten, and I had a well-organised system of shared childcare for Hamish and Sam with my friends Elsa Atkin and Antoinette le Marchant. I jumped at the opportunity.

It was a part-time casual job, about ten hours face-to-face teaching of students who, for various reasons, had not made it in their years of compulsory schooling. They were a mixed group: ex-defence force blokes, pregnant schoolgirls, people wanting to change their professional lives, especially women whose parents had not valued education for girls. Their longing for second-chance education was inspiring, as was the TAFE system's effort to provide it.

Teaching adults was a whole new buzz. My hours gradually crept up until I was regularly teaching eighteen hours a week, which was the maximum face-to-face time for permanent staff. I could easily manage that amount of teaching, along with my family and other interests. A whole new career seemed to be opening up. I could see myself staying at TAFE. It was the most wonderfully flexible system of learning and, unlike the regular school education system, it could accommodate change—or so I imagined. I liked its quirky nature, and I would do anything rather than miss my evening classes. The commitment of those students was too strong to let them down.

So, when a permanent position to teach Geography became available, I applied with confidence. Some weeks passed and I heard nothing. I went to the senior teacher and asked him when the interviews were being held. He looked rather embarrassed and then said that an appointment had already been made: a nice guy with a young family. I asked why I had not been interviewed. Was there a problem with my skills as a teacher?

He assured me that I was a wonderful teacher, but this person was seen as more appropriate and more needy—after all, he had young children. Was I missing something? I wondered. Didn't I have young children? I already knew the answer: *It's different for men*.

I was stunned. I went and talked with one of the female teachers I trusted. She said, 'Well, the truth is, Wendy, you don't go to the pub on Friday night, everyone knows it. You go home to your family and that's not where you get the jobs. Grow up.'

Driving home that afternoon, I was awash with tears for the end of my teaching career. I cried because I really loved teaching and wanted to be a great teacher, and I cried for my naivety and raged that I didn't understand how the system worked. Getting ahead required more than being a competent teacher.

I knew I was on the way out of the profession. If I was not considered good enough to get a job as a permanent Geography teacher, I had a problem and I had better take note. I had to turn this into an opportunity and accept the unpalatable truth that I was at the bottom of the pecking order in the teaching profession. No longer would I make a virtue out of a career that fitted in to family life and assume that this was my only career option. The family would have to adjust to new rules. I was going to find the right job for me.

Could I put my theories about change being good for people into practice and reinvent myself? I still did not think in terms of having a career, but rather a series of jobs. It was impossible to imagine myself as anything else but a teacher.

I held on tightly to my determination to find something else to do. Checking the papers was of little value, and I felt very ill-informed about the opportunities available. A couple of attempts to place myself in a different occupation resulted in failure. I was even knocked back for a job as a tour guide on Sydney Harbour. It was further reinforcement that I was hopeless at pushing myself, despite seeming to be good and effective at pushing the issues I was committed to.

My International Women's Year was not going well professionally.

CHAPTER 7

Family planning: A bigger classroom

> If the women's movement can be summed up in a single phrase it is 'the right to choose'. Women must decide for themselves whether to have premarital intercourse, whether to do what mother said and 'save it for marriage' or whether to remain celibate. Women must be free to choose partners of their own sex, the opposite sex, or both. We must have the right to make the first move in a relationship or wait until we are asked. Motherhood must be optional, not obligatory.
>
> Beatrice Faust,
> *The Wit and Wisdom of Famous Australian Women*

I had to find another classroom and the opportunity arose out of my increasing interest in family planning, which brought together my involvement in the Women's Electoral Lobby, the Childbirth Education Association and the Abortion Law Reform groups. These were voluntary commitments, but they were a good fit, and they reflected my political and personal passion. I could see that education and health were the twin pillars for women to build fulfilling and independent lives.

I had to find a place somewhere and it almost definitely meant leaving my teaching hopes and ambitions. It was a time of change and I understand now how fortunate I was to be alive at that time, when everything and nothing seemed possible.

In their important history on birth control, *Populate and Perish*, Diana Wyndham and Stafania Siedlecky describe the times as a new wave of family planning. They wrote:

> The late 1960s and early 1970s were highly significant for family planning. The Abortion Law Reform and Women's Liberation groups in various states had brought the subjects of abortion and contraception into the public arena. The state Family Planning Associations were established in a more radical social environment than their forerunner the Racial Hygiene Association.

Feminist writers in Australia and overseas emphasised the right of women to make their own reproductive decisions and to have access to information about their own bodies. Germaine Greer wrote *The Female Eunuch* in 1970. Derek Llewellyn-Jones's book *Everywoman* appeared in 1971. In 1972 the WEL was founded in Melbourne and vigorously lobbied all political parties on women's issues in the 1972 federal election. Members became increasingly active in Family Planning Associations (FPAs). Population growth came to be seen as a global problem.

The growth of the family planning movement in the late 1960s was stimulated by all these factors. At that time there were only two FPA clinics in Sydney and in Newcastle. Professor Rodney Shearman in a report to the World Health Organization in 1967 said that:

> They are not permitted by the government to advertise their services in the lay press or in the medical press, or to place

> advertisements in the baby health clinics which are run by the Department of Health of the state government . . . the advertisement of any forms of contraception is still by statute, judged an obscene libel . . .
>
> *The Medical Journal of Australia*, which is the official organ of the Medical Association of Australia, will not accept advertisements for any form of contraception. It is the exception rather than the rule for any major hospitals that care for the public or clinic patients to have clinics specifically devoted to family planning, it is only in the last 6 years that the largest teaching hospital in Sydney—Royal Prince Alfred—has been permitted by the board of directors to give any advice to any patient on birth control.

An influx of doctors and nurses trained in England was another factor in the expansion of the movement. New staff and new volunteers brought fresh ideas and attitudes. One of the first of these was Vimy Wilhelm, an Australian nurse who trained in family planning while in Britain with her husband. She became President of Family Planning Alliance of Australia (FPAA) in 1967 and was one of the best-known figures in the family planning movement. She was virtually the full-time Executive Officer. She recognised the importance of achieving a high profile for family planning in order to gain official recognition and community support. She used her influence in academic circles to enlist the help of prominent academics, researchers and educators.

In 1968, she wrote in the FPAA annual report:

> the early protagonist of contraception little dreamed that such a movement would evolve from voluntary organisations born by benevolent ladies and adventurous doctors 'in

> pity of poor girls whom they see dragged down into old women by having one infant after another too quickly'. This Association continues to need the support of benevolent ladies and adventurous doctors since it is a charity in the true sense—it receives no government grant and is a self-supportive, non-profit making organisation.

While this was seen as a virtue at the time, it was one of the issues that so offended the new feminist movement, which saw no reason why doctors' wives and benevolent doctors should have to provide what they thought was an essential women's service.

By the early 1970s, the family planning movement had spread to all states with the establishment of state FPAs. Clinics and education facilities became part of the package with increased influence and interest of the medical profession. There was considerable community support. A survey in New South Wales showed there was a real desire for family planning advice even among Catholic women, and that only a few metropolitan hospitals and no country hospitals provided adequate advice.

In 1974 WEL members were encouraged to join and support the Humanist Society in its plans to take over the board of Family Planning NSW (FP NSW). When my WEL colleagues suggested I put myself up for election to the board, I agreed, though with no expectation I would be elected. But the WEL ticket won the ballot and took control of the organisation, and I was elected despite being on the bottom of the ticket.

It was my first board appointment, and I was excited and apprehensive about the task. It was agreed that as well as serving on the board of directors, I would join the Education

Committee. I had worked with the Department of Education and been a small part of the Whitlam government's *Girls, School & Society* report. Since I had managed the WEL media campaign, I also had good networks with journalists.

Meanwhile, I joined with other women's groups who were persistently lobbying the government for access to family planning services. This was successful and resulted in national funding for both women's health centres and family planning, which in a sense reflected the WEL–Women's Liberation nexus. Women's Liberation would take the new ground, the revolutionary position, and WEL would try to reform the existing institution. But both were shifting the paradigms of female sexuality.

The national lobbying campaign had been successful. The Whitlam government promised funding for family planning, but there were strings attached—there had to be a comprehensive federal body. The birth of this body was difficult and bitterly fought, but in 1975 the Australian Federation of Family Planning Associations (AFFPA) would be incorporated as the national body. Its task was to promote family planning, develop training and education at the national level, and participate in the central and regional activities of the International Planned Parenthood Federation (IPPF).

The FP NSW team set about restructuring the organisation so that it better fulfilled the feminist agenda of broad access to contraception, sex counselling, abortion referral and sterilisation. One of the first resolutions was that the consent of a spouse for any procedure carried out in the clinics would not be required. This was a powerful statement. It made the 1971 feminist demand to take the luxury cosmetic tax off the pill seem light-years ago.

After I had joined the board's Education Committee and the funds were secure, we advertised for an Education and Information Officer. We were surprised and disappointed when we did not find the right person and decided to readvertise. I remember saying to Barry Maley, the President of the FP NSW, that I couldn't understand why there were so few applicants for such a great job. His response was that I should resign from the board and apply for it myself.

Such an action had not occurred to me, but I thought it a great idea and acted immediately on his advice. This time two jobs were advertised: an Education Officer and a Training Officer. My friend Antoinette Wyllie and I decided to apply together, as parts of the job overlapped. Our children were similar ages, and our skills were compatible and complementary. We argued that we would support each other, as both jobs required evening work. However, we were also firm that our working day would have to fit in with our childcare. We would be leaving the office by 5 p.m. each day.

The day after the interview, our family plus my youngest sister Sarah went to the farm owned by our old Forbes friends, Bruce and Val McDonald, at Manilla in northern New South Wales, for a holiday. I tried not to think about the job, as I was not confident and of course knew nothing about my competition. As time went by and I heard nothing, I was sure I had missed out.

Then board member and feminist advocate Alison Ziller called to ask when I could start my new position: Media Information and Education Officer for the FP NSW. The peppercorn trees were singing; I had a new career. Better still, Antoinette was offered the Training Officer position. We were to begin in October 1975. My TAFE career was over. I had become a community educator.

The immediate domestic issue was the care of the McCarthy children. Sophie was at North Sydney Demonstration School and Hamish was at Lance Kindergarten, but Sam could not be enrolled there for another five months, when he turned three. It was Pank, our neighbour, who came to the rescue. She had a cousin who had a private kindergarten at Cammeray. After an interview, Sam was enrolled to attend five days a week.

Sam was a fairly typical third child—sociable, confident and familiar with the educational places attended by his brother and sister. I was sure he would settle in quickly. I was so happy and did my usual girlie thing—rushed out to buy some new clothes to wear. Oh, silly me.

On his first morning, Sam McCarthy screamed the place down and clung to me with the ferocious strength of children who do not want to be parted from their parents. I was astonished. This was the gregarious gypsy of the family, raised in the back seat of the car while I ferried Sophie and Hamish around. He talked to everyone.

Driving over the Harbour Bridge on that first morning, I could hear all the voices. They spoke of guilt, neglect, abandonment and emotional scarring when children were forced into care against their will. I wondered if I was doing the wrong thing and should have waited until he was three, which after all was only five months away. I tried to pull my head and heart together and decided to give him three months to settle in.

Sam protested for weeks, except when Gordon took him, when he waved goodbye cheerfully. Day after day, I would arrive to work emotionally fraught and turn to Dr Spock, or whomever I was reading at the time, to find a reassuring paragraph. Just as the partings began to improve, Sam got chickenpox. In fact, the five Wyllie and McCarthy offspring got chickenpox serially. Antoinette and I bonded even more closely as we struggled with temperatures, scabs, tears and our new careers.

These are testing moments for working mothers, when it all seems too hard. Then you remember the fun and companionship of sharing responsibility and taking professional pride in your work, and you find another solution. Had we not worked for an organisation that liked children and supported our efforts, we could have easily given up.

Earning money was heady, but money was not enough of an incentive because almost all we earned was spent on childcare. Whitlam's plans for childcare had not made any real difference, as yet. But I do remember the watch I bought with my second FPA pay packet. I felt so liberated—that extraordinary feeling of being a full contributor again and the independence associated with earning my own money.

And the job? It was heaven; better than I could have imagined. A chance to be the advocate for family planning and be paid to do what I had done as a volunteer. My head and heart were connected and, although I had much to learn about working in an office, I do not remember feeling daunted by the task. The arrival of the divine Collette Parr as my assistant prevented disasters on a large scale. We operated from a grotty little terrace in Chippendale, a place friendly to rats and cockroaches, and next door to the main clinic, which fortunately was hostile to rats and cockroaches.

Gradually, we built a team of educators, including Virginia Knox, Margaret Winn and some of the family planning nurses who wanted to become educators. Culturally, nurses were very different to teachers, yet Audrie Wray, a senior nurse, was one of the best educators. The education position had previously been a volunteer one and had been done well, but like most voluntary tasks it had not been given the recognition it deserved. I had a chance to build from the ground up to create and define the role.

From the beginning, I worked with the media, as my experience with WEL as de facto media manager had convinced me that would be the only way I would reach the broader community. In retrospect, my media skills were probably my most valuable contribution.

The Personal Development Program created by the NSW Department of Education for secondary schools was a world leader. The FPA, as a non-government organisation, was in a strong position to provide education in schools and train the teachers. I was the right person at the right time, able to develop close and trusting relationships with the Department. Sex education was in demand. The requests rolled in to run programs for teachers and pupils. And, yes, we were teaching about consent in the seventies. It is not a new concept: no means no.

Over the next three years, the FPA Education Unit ran programs in primary and secondary schools, university medical schools, psychiatric hospitals, colleges of advanced education, jails, hospitals, mothers' groups across New South Wales. Everyone wanted to talk and think about sex in a more public way. It was another amazing side effect of the feminist movement and was largely led by women and gay men.

Equally, the Royal Commission on Human Relationships, established by the Whitlam government to investigate the prevalence of abortion, provided a further opportunity for people to talk about their sexual issues and concerns. Submissions poured in. It seemed Australia was more than ready to express its views on personal political issues. The FPAs became reference points for many of these issues that would arise in our education programs about sex and sexuality.

The experience of becoming a community educator instead of a classroom teacher was powerful and liberating. Sometimes it was a daunting place to be. There were no role models to follow. The FPA had strong support from the Department of Education and I didn't want to betray that trust in any way. The variety of the work was astonishing. In 1978, I worked in Silverwater men's prison; Mulawa women's prison; Metropolitan Boys' Shelter, the remand centre for boys on Albion Street; the Sydney College of Advanced Education health course; and the Medical School at the University of Sydney, giving guest lectures to medical students.

The new opportunities and the buzz around the FPA was attractive to creative people. We saw them as our natural allies in community education, especially filmmaking. The first film I appeared in—*Getting it On* by Gillian Coote—was about condoms. We thought it daring and wonderful, and held regular public showings at our headquarters.

It was a coup when Film Australia agreed to make *Growing Up*, a series of six films about adolescent sexuality. The series was made by two young filmmakers, Phillip Noyce and Jan Sharp, who went on to international fame and glory. The films were aimed at teachers, trainees and senior students, and dealt with socialisation, patterns among teenagers, unplanned pregnancy and homosexuality. They won the Australian Film Institute Silver Award in 1978 for Best Documentary.

There were some calls, however, for the series to be banned from schools. Only a top meeting with the Minister for Education prevented it. Commonwealth politicians, including the Minister for Health, Ralph Hunt, Senator Shirley Walters and Senator Peter Baume, viewed the films. Senator

Walters was shocked, while Senator Baume thought they could be useful educational resources in the right hands. But a senior administrator referring to the films on homosexuality told Dr Stefania Siedlecky, the Commonwealth Family Planning Adviser, 'I see no reason for glorifying the abhorrent'.

Later, I collaborated in the series *Let's Talk About It*, which was directed at primary schools. It attracted similar comment from the vocal minority opposed to sex education in schools. Typical of the reaction was the petition that would be signed by twenty people and presented to Federal Parliament by Senator Robert Hill of South Australia in 1982. The petitioners considered the films advocated morally controversial behaviour, demonstrated serious moral and educational deficiencies, and were suitable only for in-service work with experienced teachers. They called for the withdrawal of both series in Australian schools and urged that no more funding be made available to Film Australia for the production of sex education films in conjunction with the FPA. In their letter to Senator Robert Hill, they asked for an examination 'of the Family Planning Association in health and human relations studies in Australian schools to be undertaken at an early date'.

From my point of view, it was wonderful to have an Australian product on these subjects after the endless stream of American audiovisual material. And the media was titillated and wanted sex education stories. When a commercial television network invited a British family planning doctor, Elphis Christopher, to be the guest on Mike Willesee's high-rated television show, I was invited on as one of the guest commentators.

I enjoyed my three minutes of fame. And, the next day, the phone rang with a request that I meet the editor of the *Sunday Mirror* to discuss the paper's sex advice column. The

Sunday Mirror was the tits and bum paper of Australia, and many feminists, including myself, had protested about it. Driven by a mixture of curiosity and a belief it could open up a whole new area of communication, I agreed to meet editor Gordon McGregor and feature writer Gus de Brito at the News Limited building in Surry Hills. As I went into the appointment, I thought: *Do I want to be associated with this?*

It was a short meeting. The offer was straight to the point: they wanted me to write their sex advice column. The letter supply was constant and they needed ten answers a week. The fee was non-negotiable and the deadlines were immovable. I asked for a day to think it through.

No one thought it was a good idea, except me. What I saw was an opportunity for us to reach a different audience. I found it staggering that my colleagues thought that writing in the *Sunday Mirror* was an absolute sell-out. But I thought family planning advice was for all of us, and being a reader of the *Sunday Mirror* shouldn't disqualify you from that service, particularly if you get accurate, impartial, sound information. To me it was a triumph to have an opportunity to reach a whole new group of readers and learn how to communicate with them. I agreed to write the column—and the truth was I loved it.

For the FPA, it was fantastically valuable because I could refer readers to our clinics, secure in the knowledge these people would be treated with respect. The big issue in this column was always how to negotiate sex in a relationship: 'Dear Wendy, I have just met this guy and he says if I don't have sex with him, he will go to my girlfriend. What should I do?' My response would always be how to negotiate contraception in a relationship.

It's hard for people to imagine how inaccessible the pill was back then. Many doctors would not prescribe it. Unplanned, unwanted pregnancies were a huge problem, as the Royal Commission on Human Relationships convincingly demonstrated in its report to the Commonwealth in 1977. Women were seeking control over their fertility. For Catholic women, it was particularly difficult to negotiate this moral dilemma with their faith, but they continued to come to our clinics for family planning services.

Being a sex educator, every day I observed extraordinary ignorance about sex and contraception. And this, at a time of sexual liberation, seemed counterintuitive. Recently, I spoke at a conference about my family planning years and mentioned that I was the *Cleo* magazine adviser on sex education for ten years. At the end of the speech, a woman in her sixties came up to me and said that my advice column had saved her from an unplanned pregnancy and a pretty ordinary bloke. I felt vindicated for all those letters I answered.

During that decade, the increasing number of young clients at the FPA suggested our community programs were working well. The emphasis began to shift from pregnancies facing married women to fertility, control and choice for all.

I lasted a year at the *Sunday Mirror*. I was sacked with an explanation that I was 'too serious'. Strangely, it was the same response given to me when I didn't get the job as a tour guide on Sydney Harbour. It seems that people thought straightforward information was not fun. My replacement at the *Mirror* was Jeanne Little, who the editor thought would make readers laugh about their sexual frailties. He thought this really would be the best response. I did not agree; I could see no fun in being a female victim.

It was some weeks later that Pat Dasey, the editor of *Cleo* magazine, rang and asked me to write their advice column. I loved the idea of a glossy magazine with a large readership of young women and accepted immediately. I found writing these columns a wonderfully grounding experience. Not many people have the opportunity to be trusted to conduct a public conversation with a wide readership. Despite its image as a women's magazine, *Cleo* was also read by men.

My *Cleo* years were considered by my children as my finest achievement. When the advance copies of the magazines arrived, the neighbourhood children would read them closely and say admiringly, 'Your mother doesn't know *that*, does she?' Of course, most children, as I discovered as a sex educator, think their parents never have sex.

This publicity meant the enemies of the FPA became more vocal. There were many conservative forces to deal with. Family planning was considered a threat to the traditions of the medical profession, and many male doctors were insulted at the suggestion that we would train them on the delivery of contraceptive services. After all, what would we know? Our answer was we listen to and trust women.

We would use the slogan Trust the Women in the 2019 campaign to decriminalise abortion in New South Wales. 'Just trust the women and listen,' we would say. 'You are not providing the service they need.' Our clinics were always booked out, and our phones rang for referrals to friendly doctors who did not patronise their patients and had a proper understanding of the contraceptive choices available.

Recently, I reread some of my *Cleo* letters to check if I would still give the same answer now. Turns out I would. There may be more product options today, but the real stories were about negotiating respectful relationships, finding information they could trust about contraception and family planning clinics, and exploring sexuality. As they are today.

Family planning stories are full of unsung heroines.

Advocates like Ruby Rich, and doctors like Dorothy Nolan and Stefania Siedlecky. Edith Weisberg, Sian Grahams, Sue Hepburn and Sue Craig. They offered leadership and risked their reputations with some of their peer group, particularly in rural and regional New South Wales, where the arrival of an FPA centre was often seen as a hostile challenge to the authority of the local doctors.

The most vocal opponent to the FPA was the Right to Life, led by the Reverend Fred Nile. How ironic it was that in 2019 he was still in NSW Parliament and part of a committee interviewing me about the Reproductive Rights Bill and my role as leader of the Pro-Choice Alliance. As I walked into that interview, I thought, *the more things change, the more they stay the same*. How is it that this man still confronts me about these issues?

I was often in the public spotlight and a visible target for the opponents of family planning. The attacks by Reverend Fred Nile became more and more tedious, and I learnt that confrontation was not the best tactic. I consulted my friend and lawyer, Helen Coonan (who later became a federal Cabinet Minister in the Howard government and NSW Senator). We discussed the advisability of taking legal action. As it happened, the threat faded. I had to develop a thick skin and stand my ground.

Since that time, the targeting from those groups has persisted. On at least three occasions when I have been appointed to public bodies, the letters have rolled in describing my wicked ways. The Right to Life, the Anglican Mothers Club and the Catholic Church remained on the Wendy McCarthy case.

In 1984, I went on to accept an invitation from Brother Ambrose Payne to be the guest speaker at the graduation ceremony at the Catholic College of Education. He ended his 21 March letter with 'the College looks forward to welcoming you'. But on 19 April, Brother Ambrose Payne wrote the following letter:

> Dear Mrs McCarthy,
> It is with deep regret and an acute sense of personal embarrassment that I write to withdraw the invitation. Under present College practice, the Principal is responsible for making invitations to address the graduation and reports the matter to Council. The Chairman has directed me, on behalf of the Council, to write and indicate that, while very much recognising your own undoubted capacity to speak as a Commissioner of the Australian Broadcasting Commission [well, they got that wrong, it was the Australian Broadcasting *Corporation*], this audience would be extremely hard pressed not to confuse this with other roles, most notably those in relation to Family Planning. The College is, in a particular sense, obliged not to confuse its public image in areas where divergent and opposed views are held.

As I transcribe this letter now, I am reminded yet again of the persistence of those opponents. During a friendly mother–daughter article about Sophie and me in the magazine section of the *Sydney Morning Herald* in 1996, there was a reference to my then position as the Chancellor of the University of Canberra, which produced a torrent of rage from one reader.

> Dear Madam Chancellor,
> May one enquire to the use and purpose of a picture of you, as if there weren't more interesting things to write about and take pictures of. Even Monica Lewinsky is more

> interesting than some write up about some Marxist crap CEO in Women's Electoral Lobby, or some female who's neither an engineer or a tradesman, who has been given Chancellorship of some university. I am not at all surprised that we got a Pauline Hanson and her One Nation. Ready to clean out all you Marxist lot, spending all our taxes on the ABC and those women conferences with those Family Planning Associations and National Trust and so on, to further that ultimate agenda, the Marxists, socialist, international of yours.

And so, it goes.

I wonder, *is this always the nature of public engagement?* These are yesterday's trolls and I am used to them. Does this scrutiny happen to other women? Yes, it does. For those who challenge the status quo will always be targeted and treated like a dirty joke. It has made me mindful and respectful of difference. Family planning and the women's movement provided wonderful training in conflict and crisis management partly because so many policy decisions were strongly contested and many of us were new to working in a structured entity.

In the public eye, I have had to find emotional resilience, just as in today's world public people are finding they must manage trolls on social media. Trolling is not new; it is just a different format—with a faster and easier distribution system today.

FP NSW was a turbulent corporate body, and between 1974 and 1985 there were three takeover attempts. An attempted takeover by the Right to Life was as dramatic as any corporate raid I have observed since. There is more at stake than money. This is the fascinating thing about for-purpose, not-for-profit organisations. They are about values, not widgets. Our attachment to the values that the FPA could represent was the bottom line.

The year 1978 was a stressful time in FP NSW. I was now a member of staff and we were feeling the tensions of a new board with many different ideas about what success looked like. People observing from the outside would have thought I was doing well, but in truth I was on the outer at the organisation. Seen as having too high a profile, too big for my boots, probably seen as too structured and not collective enough. There were many days when I turned my car onto the last street before the office and began to feel apprehensive and sick. I hated the conflict and disapproval. A part of me wanted to resign. But the other part of me said hang in there and go with dignity on your own terms.

You have to believe in yourself.

I applied to attend an international Planned Parenthood conference in Bangkok on Adolescent Sexuality. After a lot of negotiation with AFFPA, the federal body, it was agreed I would be the Australian representative. I was keen to share my experience in Australia over in Asia and the work we were doing with adolescents. It was a life-changing experience.

With our new films on adolescent sexuality, *Growing Up*, I imagined FPA would be a pacesetter. And, in a sense, we were. However, our films were culturally inappropriate to the needs and priorities of adolescents in Thailand, Malaysia and Indonesia. It was a wake-up call. It was my first visit to Bangkok, which was a steamy and exciting place. I fantasised that this could be glimpse of my future professional life and international career. I made many friends in Thailand, and their family planning programs were outstanding and supported by a United Nations grant.

The program leader was Mr Mechai Viravaidya, a true internationalist. He was Director of the Thai Family Planning program, Anglo–Thai, educated at Geelong Grammar and Melbourne University, and connected by marriage to the King of Thailand. His work in Thailand was already legendary and condoms were being called 'mechais'. Visiting his fertility clinics and observing his map of Thailand, which showed the location of the family planning health teams, helped me understand even more how family planning can be a matter of life and death, with access to services in rural areas needing to be run by locals.

At night, we went nightclubbing in the city quarter, where Mechai had established his instantly accessible vasectomy clinics and free colourful condoms. My experience suddenly seemed very limited, and I adopted Mechai as my new role model.

Flip the switch to 1996, in my role as Chancellor of the University of Canberra, I walk into the Summer Palace of the King of Thailand, where I will present an Honorary Doctorate to His Majesty, his first from an Australian university. The room is exquisite: pink and white silk sofas, courtiers in white silk uniforms. At the conclusion of the ceremony, His Majesty approaches me to shake hands. I had been told under no circumstances to do that. As he shook my hand he said, 'Mr Mechai is very sorry he can't be here. He tells me that you do very good work in family planning, and he sends you his best wishes. He is my major adviser on family planning and the HIV/AIDS problem in Thailand. I don't know what I would do without him.'

I wondered how many national leaders would speak on HIV/AIDS in such a situation and identify it as a problem. I remembered being the young woman in Bangkok in the late 1970s. How could I ever have dreamt I would be having afternoon tea with the King of Thailand twenty years later and Mr Mechai would be our point of reference?

Unexpectedly, back in Australia, an executive officer's job at the national FPA was advertised in 1978. It was the only other Family Planning job I could possibly aspire to. I knew I could not survive long term in FP NSW, even though I still loved the work. The departing CEO was a retired university administrator who wished fervently that family planning had nothing to do with sex and resisted all attempts to make the connection. He commanded little respect from the state bodies and he responded similarly.

Hearing of my confidential application, he strongly advised me to withdraw as it was a dead-end job. Anyway, I lacked the necessary administrative experience. I took no notice and hoped the election committee was done with retirees and looking for someone with new energy. There were a few candidates and only two were invited to an interview. The other withdrew at the last minute. Even so, I could sense that I would not be automatically appointed. I'd had feedback from the panel that I was too radical, too feminist and too outspoken.

I was offered the job for the less-than-princely salary of $12,000, some $4000 less than I was earning at FP NSW. Ignoring all professional advice about how to build a career—which says never take a drop in salary or make a lateral move—I did both. I did, however, negotiate that I would stay as a member of the National Women's Advisory Council, which paid a modest fee, and I could earn other income.

It was the best professional decision I ever made because it gave me some independence. From that point on I always negotiated similar contracts. The decision was based on instinct, survival and opportunity. The Chairman of AFFPA,

Professor Colin Wendell Smith, was a Quaker, a Professor of Anatomy and a true internationalist. He was a gentle man, and strategically and politically skilful. We were an unlikely and productive combination.

It was a wonderful time for me. There were so many opportunities to spread my wings and yet I had a wise person to counsel me. I was also within an organisation where I could lead and grow its responsibilities. Professionally, I had two major tasks and they related to money and education: we needed more of both. I worked hard to secure the Commonwealth funding for the FPA. It was always a tough call. And it was in that context that I first had direct contact with John Howard, the then Treasurer.

I had been advised by the Department of Health officials that the Family Planning funds would be cut because the Treasurer had decided that there was no need for the Commonwealth to be involved in direct funding; the states should accept that responsibility. I was furious, as was federal Health Minister Michael Mackellar, who was supportive of our program. I tried to make an appointment to see Howard, but his staff stonewalled it.

The McCarthy family had recently moved from McMahons Point to Longueville, and John Howard was my local member. So I decided to approach him as a Bennelong constituent instead. I made the appointment, and when I arrived it was obvious that other people had chosen the same route to reach him. Wayne Harrison from the Sydney Theatre Company was in the waiting room at Gladesville.

It was a productive meeting. Howard listened carefully as I put my case in the context of unplanned pregnancies and demonstrated the effectiveness of the program. I was impressed that he responded reasonably and courteously, and agreed that the Family Planning Commonwealth program would continue. The Department of Health officials, who were white-anting their own minister and wanted to bury the program, were furious.

I recall one conference referencing the double standards of some politicians in the abortion debate. Some would take the Right to Life position publicly, while privately would be calling me or others seeking a referral for a termination of pregnancy for a friend, wife, girlfriend, sister. We would always provide that advice confidentially. I felt the need to mention at this conference: if ever the women who now provided these services decided to blow the whistle, there would be many embarrassed people around.

The following day, the *Australian* newspaper announced that I was threatening politicians and was intending to publish the list of MPs who had used abortion services. Of course, I hadn't. I just wanted to remind them it is the height of hypocrisy to use services you voted against and then rely on the secrecy that surrounds them to protect you. More secrets and lies. I saw the same behaviour in the Reproductive Rights Campaign in New South Wales in 2019. Some of the same people as back then were speaking against a woman's right to choose, trying to prevent women controlling their bodies. The old-fashioned patriarchy at work.

Abortion has always been difficult for Family Planning. The FPAs were ambivalent in their support of the feminists' mantra of abortion on demand for fear of losing their funding. There was pressure on them to become abortion service providers as part of their high-quality clinical service, especially as early terminations were straightforward procedures. It was a vexed policy at the state, national and international level for FPAs.

The International Planned Parenthood Federation, of which the AFFPA was a sovereign member, brought together many nations that had lobbied for family planning to be a recognised human right. The issue of providing abortion services related to an intellectual debate about whether abortion was a contraceptive method and should be part of a service provided by family planning. The semantics of the debate were carefully constructed to enable the array of religious and cultural practices to remain part of IPPF. In Australia, the semantics of abortion were continually changing to accommodate the wide spectrum of beliefs, and the 'right to choose' eventually became the acceptable phrase in the late seventies. For the FPA, the responsibility to provide contraceptive education services was seen as an abortion deterrent. This offered an opportunity to take the moral high ground in the debate.

When Preterm opened as an abortion clinic in Sydney in 1974, FP NSW decided it would refer women there and abandon the idea of becoming a provider. A win all around.

From 1975, with the introduction of Medibank, all family planning services became eligible for rebates, including abortion and sterilisation.

Learning governance

When I am out speaking at conferences and public events, I am frequently asked how I built a corporate director life in so many different spaces. Grassroots, activism, governance, education, health, arts, media, heritage, and reproductive rights are some of the areas, and each has its story. Objectively, I can see the combinations look unlikely, and it begs the question of whether deep knowledge in a particular area is a prerequisite for a non-executive director, or whether there is real role for the specialist generalist, which is how I see myself.

When I began my corporate life, I was interested in how the art of governance was practised and finding out the difference between management and governance. Arriving in that club made me aware of the absence of women. It was another barrier to break down. This was a time before women were offered a seat at the board table. The Women on Boards lobby really happened post 2000.

In a working life, we are always looking for levers to pull and new ways of working to achieve personal and professional outcomes. I wanted women to achieve big results around change and public policy, where their experience and skills should be considered, and so I found for-purpose government boards effective and a good fit for my developing skills and curiosity. I hasten to say that I had no idea how to pursue this but, after my first board experience at FP NSW, I raised my risk appetite and said yes to new opportunities.

In the contemporary marketplace, women are developing careers as professional non-executive directors, which is a big leap since 1983 when the Hawke government opened statutory appointments to women. I learnt from all this that there was no new world of excellence in the boardroom and no reason for it to be populated almost exclusively by men. The issue was one of demand, not supply.

If someone had asked me in 1965, at age twenty-four and newly settled in London, what I would be doing in the next fifty years, I can't imagine that I would have said a key theme in my life would be one of corporate governance, words not then even part of my vocabulary. Our life then included a lot of businesspeople because of my husband's work. I was interested in the conversations at the dinner table and fascinated by the inherited sense of power and entitlement displayed by young men from Oxbridge, who assumed they would leave accounting for business. I never once met a woman in business. Wives and girlfriends were personal assistants, teachers or nurses, and usually didn't work after marriage.

I was learning by observations and conversations that a male in a professional firm in London was almost guaranteed a corporate director role later in life. This was the career path our friends expected. But it was not on offer for women, and having had no particular feminist consciousness at that time I had not been concerned about this. But I did notice.

In later years, I drew on these experiences as I realised being a company director or governor could be a key part of an activist life. If women could be the workers on the frontline or even managers in the middle, why would we not want a say in policy and determinations made by the board? We needed a voice at the table.

My professional life coincided with what has been a long battle to change boardrooms so that they reflect the communities they serve—a battle that is far from over. When I joined the workforce in the 1960s, a company board was still a gentlemen's club. A role on a board was seen as a prestigious and sometimes lucrative gift for the later years, and sometimes included perks such as an office on the premises.

Mystique was strong. Business was conducted in the discreet well-furnished boardroom via tablets of presumed wisdom in the form of the minutes sent to the management for executive action. In some boardrooms, members of management were invited to the boardroom to speak to their management responsibility but rarely stayed for other items on the agenda, unless the CEO of the board insisted they be present. In well-run boards today, and certainly the boards I chair, broader management attendance is encouraged. This applies to private, public and not-for-profit entities.

The time I spent in family planning profoundly influenced my career since marching in the streets as a young feminist. I often reflect on how naive I was about the risk I took in going on a board in 1974 with so little preparation. I really had no concept of governance or fiduciary duty. I was driven by what I wanted the organisation to do and my belief in what a group of like-minded people could achieve. Looking back, I can see I was in danger of thinking that I was there to manage rather than govern—so often the challenge for non-executive directors.

The OECD defines corporate governance as:

> involving a set of relationships between a company's management, its board, its shareholders and other stakeholders. Corporate governance also provides the structure through which the objectives of the company are set, and the means of attaining those objectives and monitoring performance are determined.

However, often the lines are blurred and in takeover situations, like the one that happened at FP NSW when I was on the board, it became important to understand the role of a non-executive director of the board. Fortunately, our then newly elected Chair, Barry Maley, understood the difference between management and governance. Directors were encouraged to be governors, which meant establishing broad responsibility for strategy.

At that takeover, the ousted directors were respectable, educated, middle-class and well-intentioned men and women, but few were up to date in their understanding of community attitudes to sexuality and contraception. The CEO was a Major General—who could be more respectable? The problem was one of perception. Could a man with no experience in women's health be an appropriate CEO for the Family Planning Association?

Tragically, FP NSW was forced into administration on the day the takeover was happening. The outgoing directors had determined the company was insolvent or likely to become insolvent, and they elected to appoint a voluntary administrator. By winning the ballot on who would be the directors, we had gained control of an organisation that was troubled. Being a director now looked less appealing.

We set about finding support for a bailout. The first call was to the Commonwealth government, then led by Gough Whitlam, which had included support for family planning among its election promises. I'd been part of the loose alliance of women's groups lobbying on the issue and was confident the government would not let the FPA fail. And indeed, they provided the support needed.

I didn't go looking for a role in corporate governance, but I saw an opportunity for change and holding organisations of significance to women's lives accountable. I had not really understood before Family Planning the power of the organisation to govern and direct change. Meanwhile I had a big job to do in establishing school and community sex education programs and building media networks. My eight years out of full-time work, raising and growing our family, and learning how communities worked, suddenly felt valuable, as did my WEL experience as voluntary media manager. I was excited to be back in a formal workplace. And my years in the NSW role provided wonderful community experience, which became a valued attribute in many of my future roles.

Not all boards of organisations are keen on their staff having responsibilities beyond their singular roles. However, when the NSW Minister for Education offered me a seat on the Higher Education Board, the body responsible for tertiary education in the state, AFFPA agreed that this was in line with its aims and objectives and agreed I should accept the appointment.

I had queried the Minister about why I was considered a suitable appointment (never do this!). If someone thinks you can do it, say yes and work it out later. His answer was, 'You have been to university and you know a lot about women and education. You can decide whether you want to be inside or outside working on changing the system.'

Case closed and I accepted the offer.

It was my second board role. I joined a group of seventeen men—mostly engineers and career bureaucrats. It was a statutory body, reporting to the Minister for Education. One of my first roles was to join the review team considering the case for nursing to become a bachelor's degree. The state government had decided that nurse education would be transferred from the Nurses Education Board to Colleges of Advanced Education from the beginning of 1985 and sought advice from the Higher Education Board as part of its review of higher education in rural areas as many of the colleges were.

It was curiously contentious, despite the increasing responsibilities of the nursing profession, who were primarily women. I found it hard to accept the idea that nursing should continue to be taught in what was effectively a trade/apprenticeship model. I still hear people wistfully ruing the day it happened: oh dear, beware of over-educating women. History records that during my time at the Higher Education Board, nursing did proceed to become a bachelor's degree.

Good board managers and non-executive directors work together for the good of the company. The government appointments have their own version of corporate behaviour and responsibilities and these in my experience are very clear. The nuance comes from the execution, but usually financial matters were managed at the central bureaucracy. The task is to interrogate and develop public policy or implement it. I find this tremendously stimulating and I learnt over the years a great deal about the limits and expectations those two roles had of each other. Sometimes, when I would be at board meeting as an executive, I learnt there are many ways to influence change through variable corporate entities. Subsequently, I became a great fan of board appointed, time-limited, issues-focused taskforces to assist the thinking of company directors.

What was common in all of them was learning that governance responsibility included respect for confidentiality, financial literacy, and collegiality. Chatham House rules applied, which meant that discussion held at board meeting could be discussed but were not to be attributed to the individual speakers. This encouraged openness and honesty and, in my experience, enabled people to ask questions which sometimes felt unaskable.

And more importantly, my experience in family planning was valued in all of the corporate roles I held.

CHAPTER 8

National Women's Advisory Council

> I do not have a quick fix. I have always believed that the continuing education of women and men was necessary to achieve their full potential, especially in public life, and thus contribute to this wonderful country of ours. However, education and reliance on evolution have not delivered political equality to women. It is time to consider other options, to consider new strategies.
>
> Dame Beryl Beaurepaire,
> 'Political equality for women: How and how soon?'

The National Women's Advisory Council (NATWAC) appointment was my first Commonwealth statutory nomination. The way in which it happened is worth telling as few people understand how unexpected and casual these approaches can seem. Most appointments would not be offered without the consent of Cabinet. Yet they can often appear to have no frame of reference. Every government offer I have had to date has happened in a similar way.

One July day in 1978, when I was teaching in a Family Planning program for nurses, my assistant Colette came into the room to say I was needed on the phone. It was unusual for her to interrupt me while teaching. As we went outside, she said, 'The man on the phone claims to be the Minister for Home Affairs and he insists on speaking to you.' My response was, 'Gordon McCarthy is playing a joke.' I had never even heard of a Minister for Home Affairs; however, if he was insistent on speaking to me, it must be important.

I picked up the phone. The answering voice was definitely not Gordon McCarthy but Bob Ellicott, Minister for Home Affairs in the Fraser government.

'Have you heard about the National Women's Advisory Council we have established? I would like you to be a member. Would you be interested?' I said I was interested, but what would I have to do? He replied, 'You will have to meet in Canberra and around Australia, and you would be advising the government on women's issues.'

It sounded like heaven. A public voice, a channel to government. I tried not to sound too eager while indicating my acceptance. I couldn't believe the Minister would just ring you like a normal person and invite you to do an important national job. I went back to the teaching program, told no one except Gordon, and waited to hear formally.

Some weekends later in Broken Hill, running a sex counselling program with Bettina Arndt and Dr Sue Hepburn for doctors and health professionals, I saw a tiny piece in the *Sydney Morning Herald*, which said the National Women's Advisory Council had been established. My name was there. I had read it in the *Sydney Morning Herald* so it must be true. Such are the processes of public appointments of those who are outside the loop of political parties.

But when my appointment was announced, I was told by the FPA board president, Professor Charles Kerr, that my salary would be docked for the time I was at NATWAC meetings. I felt I was being punished rather than supported. I protested that this was unfair, but to no avail. I knew I did my job well and my appointment to the NATWAC was a public testimony to the importance and significance of Family Planning.

NATWAC, which Prime Minister Malcolm Fraser established in 1978, was a classic example of how I could draw on my various experiences to have wide-ranging benefits. It was given a broad charter, and as we developed our program the supporting bureaucracy grew to assist us with research. It could be argued that we were always at the mercy of parliament agreeing to expand our budget, and we were, but that was a different tension to manage from others. As a result, we learnt to be fearless in putting our case to MPs. Skills that stood all of us in good stead.

The combination of working with the NATWAC and the Australian Federation of Family Planning Associations meant that I was always thinking nationally and meeting Commonwealth public servants—who until that time had been alien species and with whom I had little or no professional or private contact. I had a limited understanding of their political power. These were new relationships for me, and my ignorance was useful as I was not afraid to ask for advice. There was no script to follow.

Parliament House, now known as Old Parliament House, felt like a big boarding school for boys, where different codes of personal contact were accepted. I understood why politicians often seem to lose the plot when I wandered around those corridors of power. Their lives in Canberra were dysfunctional, and somehow it seemed to make them more aggressive about women's affairs and family planning, almost as though they had to prove loyalty to their wives at home.

There was often a tension around discussion on women's issues frequently prefaced by 'my wife thinks . . .' not dissimilar to Prime Minister Scott Morrison advising Parliament in 2020 that he had to consult his wife Jenny in order to understand female matters. I could understand it in the 1970s, but even then it was an inadequate response that assumed these were personal issues not political, and I certainly didn't think it should dictate public policy any more than a case study of one should.

What these issues had in common was the assumption that they were private rather than professional matters. Our challenge was to place them firmly in the public policy arena, and that required leadership from both ministers and the bureaucracy. Throughout this period my respect for the skills of the inscrutable bureaucracy grew, and my ability to research and present ideas improved. I had the freedom to speak out in a way a bureaucrat could not.

During my time as a member of NATWAC and CEO of AFFPA, MP Stephen Lusher's motion to remove family planning services benefits from Medibank in 1979 was tabled. This was a tough test for me. It was untenable to belong to a body such as NATWAC without persuading its members to advise the government to vote against the motion. If we were to represent the interests of Australian women, it would be unthinkable not to speak out. While I was agonising, the issue was raised by another NATWAC member, and in a short space of time we agreed to go public in our unanimous opposition to the Lusher bill.

Our leader and convener, Beryl Beaurepaire, persuaded Malcolm Fraser to delay the Lusher debate for three weeks, on the grounds that debating it in the house on 8 March—International Women's Day—was political suicide. This gave us breathing space to lobby hard against it. The women's movement went into action, seeking support, visiting their local MPs and speaking at public meetings to assist the defeat of the bill. The outcome demonstrated the extent of support for NATWAC leadership. I felt reassured my personal and professional convictions were shared by others.

It was an important victory for the National Women's Advisory Council. It also gave me a new level of confidence with the Canberra bureaucracy. I felt I had the backing of the government to pursue the Family Planning agenda, which I had never seen as radical; just sensible health policy. Without fertility control, women had no chance of being independent and playing their chosen role in our society. However, I was not so naive that I failed to acknowledge the opposing forces that persist to this day.

I realise in retrospect how lucky I was to be appointed to NATWAC. Recently I met up with Bob Ellicott. I was curious to find out if there was a methodology behind the selection of its members. Every member was told she was chosen as an individual, not as a representative of any group. I assumed that my appointment was related to Family Planning. Ellicott told me the Council needed someone from Women's Electoral Lobby, and WEL was considered the most significant women's lobby group: 'Your national role in Family Planning was important, we couldn't have a council without an effective communicator on these matters.'

Strangely, this is extremely gratifying to me now.

Several years earlier, in 1973, the Labor Party had appointed Elizabeth Reid as the first women's adviser to government. Gough Whitlam had responded to pressure from women's groups for better access to policy development by appointing her. The Fraser government had then made an election commitment in 1975 that it would continue the access through a national women's council in addition to maintaining the individual women's adviser position. But women's affairs had been moved into the portfolio of the Minister for Home Affairs. Bob Ellicott was given the responsibility of creating an appropriate body whose definition in its charter was to provide 'an effective channel of communication between women in the community and government'.

Lyndsay Connors, who was writing in *The Age*, thought the council looked conservative, and identified me as the only feminist. She thought that the lack of feminist representation was unfair given that feminists had created the new political consciousness leading to the very formation of the council. I acknowledge it was not a radical group, but it was a group to be respected for its broad base of experience and commitment to women's affairs, status, business, and community experience and expertise.

My appointment to NATWAC placed me firmly in national public life. Until 1978, most of my activities were based locally in New South Wales. Being appointed to NATWAC, now one of only twelve women reporting to the Prime Minister on women's issues, took me into a much broader place of leadership and women's affairs.

The first meeting was held in Canberra. I remember it vividly. Jan Marsh, Quentin Bryce and I sat together—clearly arranged by Beryl Beaurepaire. It was the beginning of enduring friendships. It is hard to think of my life before Quentin, as we have been close friends since that meeting.

We were organised, bossed and nurtured by Beryl, who was then Vice President of the Liberal Party's Victorian division. She stressed from the beginning that this was a lobby group (which is not a word the Labor Party would have used) and should not be seen as a creature of government or as window-dressing for the Liberal Party. Her political skills, her role modelling of leadership and managing conflict were remarkable.

Beryl realised that few of us knew the prime minister, so she arranged a meeting at our second gathering. She immediately took charge, dispensed with the pleasantries and focused on the discussion of improving resources for the council and its secretariat. She made it perfectly clear that she thought the current resources were inadequate. At one stage, she said, 'No, Malcolm, I don't think that's a good idea, I think this would be a better way, don't you?'

'Well, yes Beryl,' he nodded.

I am standing there thinking: *she is talking to the prime minister and he is doing as he is told*. He agreed that Minister Ellicott should fix our concerns. Mission accomplished and pleasantries resumed. It made a deep impression on me.

A levelling thought was that our sitting fees were at the same rate as the Pig Producers Board. Really, we would be on the same level as pig producers? The imagery wasn't good.

The NATWAC agenda was long and reflected the feminist agenda of the Women's Electoral Lobby: equal pay, maternity leave, access to family planning, the problems faced by migrant women, violence against women, childcare, Aboriginal women and girls, family law, isolated women and girls. We were able to commission research, and our research base was solid—it had to be for our credibility and influence.

In 1981, a paper commissioned by NATWAC on 'Financial Arrangements made by Husbands and Wives' reported on some exploratory Australian research. Meredith Edwards from Canberra College of Advanced Education conducted the research:

> It was in response to concerns raised on the relationship between marital power on the one hand, and family income and the employment status of the wife on the other. Husbands and wives were interviewed simultaneously but separately.
>
> The research tested the proposition that unrecognised poverty or 'hidden' poverty exists within households. This could be critical for getting children out of poverty.

The report showed that generally 50 per cent of families pooled their incomes, and women whose husbands managed the finances were more likely to have less personal spending money then their husbands did. A wife's chance of having a say in financial matters was greater if she managed the finances than if not. Women who earned their own incomes were likely to have more say in the total spending of family wages. So, when women were in paid employment, some of the husband's control was reduced. The report also revealed the value of paying family allowances direct to women and of not taxing husbands and wives as a unit, which in turn informed the government on tax and social security policies.

NATWAC offered wonderful avenues for networking and fact finding, and members generously gave their time and energy. We met in every capital city and many regional places in our effort to ensure that what we were pushing for was in line with the aspirations of Australian women, as well as in deference to the United Nations, who had declared 1976 to 1985 the Decade for Women.

When the mid-decade World Conference of the United Nations Decade for Women was planned for Copenhagen, Kath Taperell, the head of the Office of Women's Affairs, advised that NATWAC should develop the Australian agenda. Beryl Beaurepaire accepted this advice, viewing it as an opportunity to broaden the awareness and vision of Australian women. It might have also helped to divert attention from the tedious and troublesome Victorian group, Women Who Want to Be Women, who were aggressively anti-feminist and pro financial payments to homemakers. Their convenor, Babette Francis, managed to organise a media pass as a result of her writing in a small suburban newspaper, *The Toorak Times*. This was the realpolitik in Victoria, Beryl's home state, and it was making a lot of politicians nervous. A similar group in the United States, led by Phyllis Schlafly, managed to stop the passage of the Equal Rights Amendment (ERA) that, to this day, has not been passed by Congress.

This was the beginning of a long campaign against the so-called elitist women who were seen to be unhappy in their homes and out of touch with ordinary women—whoever they were. Petitions arrived in parliament insisting NATWAC be abolished. These conservative groups, frequently backed by churches, constantly expressed concern that the feminist influence was diminishing the status of women in the home and especially homemakers.

Déjà vu.

NATWAC decided to rise above the criticism and prepare for the Copenhagen conference by consulting widely with Australian women through regional and state conferences. This would enable Australian women to identify their issues and solutions, and prepare a plan to represent their views in Denmark. It was a high-risk strategy because it provided wonderful opportunities to vocalise criticism for the opposing forces. But the chance for women to have their say outweighed the risks. At NATWAC, we needed to test our assumptions that our activities enjoyed substantial support in the community.

Meetings were held all around Australia on the central themes of development, equality and peace, health, education and employment. Every time we turned hundreds of women away because of lack of space. In Melbourne, as the registrations reached four thousand, the meeting had to be abandoned as there was no venue large enough to accommodate these numbers. For Judith Roberts, NATWAC member in South Australia, a turbulent meeting at Christies Beach was a gruelling experience, and one that changed her life. She was a longstanding Liberal Party member, but until then she had not understood the passion that women's politics unleashed.

For me, the most reinforcing and surprising aspect of this work was that the council's views most often aligned with mine. Yet when the council was created, I—as the publicly declared feminist—was seen as the odd one out. I never actually felt that I was an outsider, but my feminist experience was notable in relation to the other members. I had a familiarity with the rhetoric around the issues.

I had rehearsed the discourse around fertility and women's education during my WEL years, and most recently at Family Planning. Now I was keen to examine the emerging issues that we were identifying around domestic violence and mothers with disabled children.

After all the state and regional meetings, the national conference was held in Canberra in March 1980. There were one hundred and twenty delegates elected from state conferences and more than a hundred representatives from women's organisations and members of the media. Interested individuals from Australia and abroad were invited to attend as official observers.

Minister Bob Ellicott opened the conference and stressed the importance of it as a means of providing government with a statement of priorities and aspirations from a wide cross-section of Australian women. At least some of us thought that we were having the definitive public conversation about the perception and definition of being female in Australia. This was being resourced and led by a conservative government; the results could not be dismissed as a Labor Party plot—a common theory judging from WEL surveys.

The council agreed the conference procedure should be based on consensus in order to foster a spirit of cooperation among the delegates, and to highlight, wherever possible, the areas of agreement. I found both the preparation and the debates exciting. We followed the UN rules of debate and hours were spent on the semantics. It seemed that every word had multiple meanings. Yet the goal was always to find common ground. So, if we reached an impasse, some members would form a drafting group to seek resolutions that the plenary could resume later.

These days, this doesn't sound so innovative, but in 1980 it was. And it has stood me in good stead ever since. From 2000 to 2019, when I joined international groups in overseas aid and development, the capacity to work in a large group, to find consensus across culture and diversity, became very important. I felt I was blessed to have this experience earlier in my career.

Beryl Beaurepaire chaired the plenary sessions with ease and firmness. She said in her opening address at the conference:

> The conference was part of the political process. A way of government hearing what women have to say. If all members of the government hear is that women are divided, they are likely to conclude there is no point in taking action

> and simply dismiss our recommendations. Division and confrontation is not in our interests. A victory for one faction, at the expense of another, be a loss for us all.

She steered the conference to a high degree of consensus. She led us to the view that we should stop thinking of platforms of demands as welfare but as human rights.

Taking time out from my job to do this caused some tension, but I argued it was in the interest of the family planning movement generally, and that I would be the organisation's advocate. I finally attended with my chairman's blessing. I chaired some of the sessions and enjoyed the buzz of activity and the energy put into the debate. The Family Planning Associations were happy for the preamble to the resolution on health to state:

> Health is a state of physical, mental and social wellbeing. It is not merely the absence of disease. The main determinants of the state of wellbeing for women include adequate housing, sanitation, nutrition, healthcare and welfare provisions, and the means of controlling their own fertility. Access to such facilities is a fundamental human right.

The supporting recommendations spoke of education in human sexuality and concluded that all methods of fertility regulation, including abortion with supporting counselling services, should be offered to women so they have the right to choose.

There was a memorable moment when Babette Francis from Women Who Want to Be Women began her speech with the statement, 'It is a well-established scientific fact that women's brains are smaller than men's.'

Evelyn Scott, a tall, charming, handsome Torres Strait Islander, rose to her feet and said, 'You used to say that about us.'

The draft document that emerged would be criticised for being both bland and radical. In truth, it was probably somewhere in the middle. Even so, *The Ballarat Courier* editorial wrote of militant feminists stacking the conference and asserted that Ellicott owed it to the women who had not burned their brains along with their bras to take no notice of the outcome.

Despite this advice, the conference outcomes provided the basis for the Australian document to be taken to Copenhagen. At NATWAC, we were optimistic that the Australian Draft Plan of Action was a good working document that enabled Australian women to move forwards.

Copenhagen was my first world conference. It ran from 14 to 30 July 1980. I was delighted to be chosen to attend the non-government forum as the representative of the NGO sector in Australia. I had my fare paid, but I had to cover all my other expenses. Jan Marsh was joining Beryl and Valerie Fisher, a very distinguished Country Women's Association leader, in the government delegation. Judith Roberts and other NATWAC members joined the forum with me, and fifteen other women who were assisted to attend.

Our bête noire, Babette Francis, managed to organise her attendance as a media representative. It did seem a bit of a stretch that *The Toorak Times* would normally cover such an international conference, but her presence was balanced by Lyndsay Connors from *The Age*, WEL member Rosemary Munday from *The Women's Weekly* and Janet Bell from the ABC.

Copenhagen had been one of the first holiday destinations

that Gordon McCarthy and I visited when we travelled across Europe all those years ago. It was different staying in the Hilton Hotel to the camping ground, but my memories were warm. It was a friendly and accessible city and I was excited to be returning. But on arriving I felt strangely insignificant. Suddenly I understood how small Australia was on the world scale and maybe I didn't have much to contribute.

The next day, on the way to the forum, we decided to hire bikes and travel like the Danes. That was fun and gave me a sense of adventure and wellbeing. I felt less like a tourist and more like an independent woman with a purpose. There were eight thousand women at this forum. It was overwhelming—a giant women's bazaar, heady to walk around and observe women of the world talking, talking and talking. And clicking over shared experiences, finding the same issues everywhere, in one form or another.

There were a few Australians women staying at the same hotel and we found ourselves bonding in the sauna. After a few conference sessions, we got smart and shared the daily coverage so we could compare notes at the end of the day. Our media team, excluding Babette Francis, were trying to cover the government conferences as well as the forum. But as NGO attendees, we had almost no contact with our delegates until Beryl, at the suggestion of Judith Roberts, began a series of daily briefings to bring the forum energy and ideas to the government delegation. Very few governments did this—indeed many of their delegations were all male, and not much interested in the issues, let alone the NGOs.

In the years since then, I have been to many places and many international forums where that is still the case, and I have always been especially proud of Australians who recognise the power and energy of the non-government organisations in our country, and who listen to others' advice and experience.

When I think about the Copenhagen summit, there are just so many wonderful memories. The reception of the Australian consulate, riding my bike around the city, spending my thirty-ninth birthday at the Tivoli Gardens, and the optimism of even the most oppressed women.

The goddesses were there in strength. Some known, others to be revealed, and aspects of women's life I had never considered were all on the agenda. Despite my privileged access to family planning literature, I knew nothing about female circumcision. It was at that conference that I heard about it, and I met the extraordinarily brave Egyptian doctor, the late Nawal El Saadawi, whose life I followed from then on. She spoke out in one of the health sessions about the practice. The stories were disturbing. While I understood the defence of religious traditions, I accepted it was a practice to be exposed and ended.

Janet Bell from the ABC and I persuaded Dr Saadawi to speak on the record about the practice and it was broadcasted in Australia. It was the beginning of a campaign across the world to end the custom. The conference also changed the terminology so that female circumcision became female genital mutilation (FGM).

It was in Copenhagen that I met the famous Betty Friedan, whose book *The Feminine Mystique* I had read as a young teacher. It was a moment to treasure. Each morning I read the daily sheets of activities to plan my day. One morning I discovered that the Women Who Want to Be Women from Australia were running a session about payment for mothers at home. It was billed as a major Australian presentation and I was determined to be there to defend our national honour.

I didn't want the rest of the world to think the majority of Australian women held these views. As fate would have it, the 4Ws were scheduled into the slot with a group from England called Wages for Housework, a front for the sex workers' union. The juxtaposition was wonderful.

The real thrill came when I walked into the room and I realised I was sitting two seats away from Betty Friedan and Bella Abzug, a member of the US House of Representatives, whose first campaign slogan was 'this woman's place is in the house—the House of Representatives'. I watched Betty's body language as she listened to Jackie Butler from the 4Ws. There was no need for me to defend national honour because, with one line, Friedan fixed the whole thing.

'Listen, sweetheart,' she said with her fantastic gravelly voice, 'you are only one husband away from welfare.' That fixed it. They were a disregarded group.

The 4Ws had a further brush with fame when the time came for our Minister to sign the UN Convention on the Elimination of All Forms of Discrimination Against Women. When Beryl and the Minister arrived at the ceremony, they were surprised to find Babette Francis and a small group of her supporters blocking their entry. They carried banners and chanted that signing this would be a betrayal of Australian women.

Ellicott was appalled, and the future for Women Who Want to Be Women was suddenly limited. From my point of view, it was a very satisfactory outcome. The Convention was signed, but the Australian government refused to ratify it on the grounds they would not get agreement from the states. Three years later, the Hawke government ratified it without reference to the states, with the view that it was national policy.

From NATWAC's viewpoint, Copenhagen demonstrated how much still needed to be done in Australia. But it also revealed that Australian feminists could play a role on the world stage, as indeed Jessie Street, Elizabeth Evatt and all the other women before them had done.

On 15 July, the term of the first council members expired. I was pleased to be offered a year's extension. Later on that year I accepted an invitation from the NSW government to be a member of the NSW Women's Advisory Council. I felt completely affirmed that I was on the right track.

CHAPTER 9

Consciousness-raising

One is not born a woman but becomes one.

Simone de Beauvoir

Gloria Steinem described the seventies as the decade of consciousness-raising—and it was as true for women in Australia as it was for their sisters in the United States. Consciousness-raising had been taking place for some time in small groups, places where women explored their personal experiences in an attempt to see patterns of their oppression outside the confusion of their own heads. But it was also a way of validating our personal experiences as political issues that needed attention.

Consciousness-raising was based on the idea that sharing personal stories gave power. That our narratives could build solidarity and sisterhood, and it sought to make the personal political. It situated individual experience and validated it within a larger social experience to transform the nature of politics.

While I was considering writing this book and swirling the idea around in my mind, I went to a lunch to hear Dr Michelle Arrow, an award-winning historian, at Macquarie University. I was interested because of the title of her book: *The Seventies: The personal, the political and the making of modern Australia.*

While I was familiar with most of what she had written, her take was refreshing and somehow or other it felt very validating for my claims about the seventies being the decade of consciousness-raising. I am writing from personal *and* political experience; she is writing from archives. It was such a happy coincidence.

Michelle Arrow said in her talk that, throughout 2012, she visited the national archives every week because 'I have found something extraordinary there. In 1974, Gough Whitlam's Labor government had initiated a Royal Commission on Human Relationships.' Indeed, and I knew the commissioners, and I was excited to hear it referenced. She went on to say that:

> . . . it was conceived as a way to investigate the prevalence of abortion in Australia but it grew much bigger than that. Underpinned by Whitlam's ethos of open government, the commission invited Australians to tell them what do you think about sex and sex education, abortion, family life, family planning, parenthood, childcare, women's rights and homosexuality.

These are my topics. These are my lived experiences. And I loved the validation that her book gave to so much of my life work, even up to the reproductive rights Pro-Choice campaign in New South Wales in 2019.

There were more than five hundred recommendations made to the Royal Commission. And when all the work of the commission had been finished, the evidence was archived and filed away safely. Years later, Michelle Arrow started opening those boxes and listened to the voices of mid-1970s Australia that spilled out of them. She writes of a public intimacy, which was a new way to talk about private life, and a new political strategy all at once. Women's liberation and gay liberation were built upon that core principle.

Family Planning offered a space to talk about sex education, sexuality, gender, family planning, contraception, domestic violence and homosexuality. It was one of the few places that not only permitted but encouraged those conversations. I still meet people who I remember coming to Family Planning for some of the film nights. It is here that we started a public discussion about sexuality and disability. This was then called sex education for the handicapped. Words matter.

Cleo had led the way as a magazine willing to talk about sex and within its pages I'd had a conversation with the public for ten years about these matters. Always personal stories and experience and seeking answers to seemingly unaskable questions.

There were negative moments in the seventies. The dismissal of the Whitlam government in International Women's Year was an extraordinary event. We'd had three years of planting the seeds of a feminist culture, and it was all due to change with the Dismissal. Yet it didn't. The Royal Commission on Human Relationships had still not filed its report when the Fraser government was elected but they made a commitment to implement the recommendations of the commission.

Of course, support for the movement didn't always come from progressive Labor governments. There were often uneasy alliances between social movements and governments. Part of the reason I wrote this book was to remember where the feminist spike for me came from. When people ask me, 'How and why did you become part of the changes in the sixties', the answer is always I didn't do it by myself. I did it with a whole lot of like-minded women and some good men in working towards a better and more equal world. And there were memorable moments that could be brought to mind if you were feeling despair.

Michelle Arrow recounts in *The Seventies*:

> For me one such moment occurred when a second Vietnam moratorium had been held [in September 1970]. The line-up of speakers at the pre-march rally were all male. The women demanded and won the right to be included.
>
> Kate Jennings wrote the speech at a 'boil'.
>
> The women were saying, give us our rightful place and they were saying, you are good for typing, tea making, scutwork and screwing.
>
> Her speech was so incendiary that none of the women would deliver it. So Jennings went to the University of Sydney frontline to deliver it. It has echoes of Gillard's speech in parliament—the great misogynist speech. I carry the images of both of those women, giving that speech.
>
> Jennings warned the crowd that she was a man-hating, bra-burning, lesbian member of the castration penis envy brigade. She excoriated the young men of the anti-war movement for the hypocrisy and myopia. Go check the figures, how many Australian men have died in Vietnam and how many women have died from backyard abortions? She was infuriated by the men's failure to see women's issues as political issues, 'You won't make an issue of abortion, equal pay, and child-minding centres, because they are women's matters, and under your veneer you are brothers to the pig politicians. All power to women,' she ended.

It was great theatre.

There was outrage after this speech. And there was much disquiet from the women because they had never really questioned the conviction of the men of the New Left to the fight for women's liberation. By drawing a line between soldiers dying in Vietnam and women dying of illegal abortion in Australia, Jennings insisted that women's private experience was as valid a subject for political protest and debate as the Vietnam War. For me this was a lightbulb moment. It explains why many of us came to the reluctant conclusion that men were not that interested in our stories.

Recalling the Jennings story, I am reminded of the connection to the Julia Gillard misogyny speech, but equally I am reminded of the reproductive rights campaign in 2019. In the end, women have always had to find their own voices about their own issues; they have to speak for their own rights. It is good if men support you, and it was wonderful in the Reproductive Rights campaign to earn the support from the seventy health professional agencies whose members were male and female, including the NSW Australian Medical Association.

In the end, you are on your own, and we need to accept that responsibility and make our own changes. Some of us did it on instinct, based on a developing sense of justice and outrage, fixing up past issues when we hadn't found our voices to sufficiently speak out. If we were to get the reforms we wanted, we needed to find our own voice and strategies. That would be the basis for female leadership.

For me, it has always been about head and heart being connected.

CHAPTER 10

Future directions

Without leaps of imagination or dreaming we lose the excitement of possibilities.

Gloria Steinem

The eighties began well for me, and 1980 was a watershed year. I was loving my role as chief executive of the national Family Planning body (AFFPA). It was time to leave the state office. Gordon and the kids were in great shape. We had settled into a new community at Longueville after leaving our beloved McMahons Point. I had been offered the *Cleo* column and was enjoying writing that and travelling with the National Women's Advisory Council.

I had the privilege of travelling Australia, listening to and meeting women from every conceivable interest group. I was fascinated by Canberra, despite people telling me how dull it was. I was meeting political activists, politicians, bureaucrats, and learning to navigate the system to achieve outcomes. This began my long love affair with Canberra, which I think of as one of the most liveable cities in Australia.

When NATWAC met in Canberra, Quentin Bryce, Jan Marsh and I walked the corridors of Parliament House and lobbied about the emerging NATWAC issues, particularly the ones we cared about. Beryl Beaurepaire was completely supportive of this, and she told us to: 'Go to the top, go to the ministers, put your case, don't spend your time starting at the bottom to work your way through. Go straight to the top, use the position you've got for the benefit of others.'

She took her responsibilities very seriously and used to worry about us a bit, because we smoked, and we liked drinking and running up and down the corridors of Parliament House. She didn't want us to be seen in the wrong company, although she never specified exactly what that meant. She was worried that we would be led astray. The realities were rather different.

Despite the endless dinners in Parliament House dining room, trying to persuade anyone who would listen to us the virtue of our views, we were not easily led astray, and we were all in rock-solid relationships. When we were talking together, we were mainly talking about children, husbands and building confidence in our friendship, managing the social disapproval we encountered as feminist mothers who wore lipstick and smoked. We loved staying in hotels and having room service, even if it was only a sandwich. Sounds pathetic as I write it, but Quentin had five children and I had three. There were not many solo eating opportunities for us at home.

In my role at AFFPA, which was a member of the International Planned Parenthood Association, it was my duty to ensure that Australia supported family planning services in its international aid program. Two days after my return from the Copenhagen conference, I received this extraordinary telegram:

> You are invited to join a select group of next generation Australian opinion leaders at a residential conference on future directions for our country.

Dates: August 10–14
Venue: La Trobe University
Major sponsors: The Age and Commonwealth government
Organisers: Australian Frontier
Emphasis on group discussion towards agreement. We urge you to reserve dates now. Details and documents will follow, for information call—

I was beyond flattered to be thought of as an opinion leader and a next-generation leader.

Before I had time to treasure the telegram, documents had arrived describing the expected commitment at the Future Directions Conference. In order to encourage consent, they revealed that broadcaster Phillip Adams; David Armstrong, CEO of the new Australian Bicentennial Authority; senators Susan Ryan and Gareth Evans; and Sam Lipski, the radio commentator, had all previously been invited—and only Phillip Adams hadn't turned up.

The rules were clear: it was mandatory to stay for the entire four-day program. This was a very big ask. I had only been back from Europe for a few days. It seemed a bit unfortunate to ask Gordon to hold the family fort again and so soon, and I wasn't sure AFFPA Chairman would be too enthusiastic about me being away from the office for another week either. Who would I go to first? Why did I always have to ask a man what I could do? I decided Gordon, my husband. While reluctant, he agreed. Fortunately, Colin Wendell Smith, my Chairman, also thought it was an opportunity I shouldn't miss.

Later, I reflected how lucky I was that two people whose consent I required gave it so graciously. And I am always loyal to people when they give me room to move, and it is something I have always tried to do when I am in the consent-giving business.

I had to prepare a five-hundred-word statement setting out what I saw as the major problems and challenges facing Australian society in the next fifteen to twenty years. I found this terrifying. I was still not comfortable writing. I thought of all the experienced people whose words would sit beside mine, and wondered what on earth I would write. In the end, my piece reflected my passion about the shifting definition of being female. In the conference book, the quote next to my picture reads, 'By taking over decisions about population size, family size, succession of heirs, women are challenging nationalism and challenging the power structure, whether religious or familiar.'

On Sunday 10 August, I caught the plane to Melbourne. The first person I met was David Armstrong. We had been at university together, but we had seen each other only once since 1961, when I had left New England. The plane was full of people attending the Future Directions Conference and there was a nice buzz in the cabin as we chatted throughout the trip. David had left academic life and was fired up about his new appointment.

The conference was a life-changing event. A heady mixture of carefully planned isolation from the outside world for four days and four nights. And the opportunities to let your mind range over previously unexplored ideas with a group of animated and diverse people. I began to believe that these concepts could become reality.

What was especially confronting was that, even in this group of future leaders, women still had to confront plain, old-fashioned sexism. On day two, some women, including me, decided to call a women's meeting. The announcement caused a flurry, so we agreed that anyone (that is, including men) could come, but they should understand that we women would be managing the agenda.

Despite the rumbling, almost everyone attended, and Susan Ryan, Helen L'Orange and I explained what we thought was missing from the discussion, and how ignorant of and resistant to the basic tenants of feminism we found these men to be. It was as though the last decade had not happened. Males kept reverting to alpha type, dominating the conversation and dismissing alternative perspectives. It turned out to be an interesting intervention with the pay-off being better male behaviour and interaction for the duration of the conference.

I have done this a couple of times since. Most memorably at Third International Conference on Health Promotion in Sundsvall, Sweden, in 1991. Again, a group of women, including Gertrude Mongella (who was later the UN coordinator for the Beijing Women's Conference), started describing the inability of the traditional males to understand either female or Aboriginal peoples' views. Or even to think that they should. So we called a women's meeting and changed the momentum of the conference. It was an effective strategy to monitor those men who already got the point, and manage the ones who didn't. We were not suggesting we would form a breakaway group; we simply needed a breakthrough in the proceedings, so our voices were heard.

In moments like those, I've often wondered, why do I need to become a monitor for male behaviour? Why don't I leave well alone and settle for a quiet life? It would be easier. But I've worked hard to find a voice. And I want to keep it and use it.

Opportunities to build friendships and networks, and to think differently, don't often come as well orchestrated and managed as the Future Directions Conference. And those networks have survived in various forms to this day. The conference was also my introduction to scenario-planning, a technique where you think about the different scenarios that may occur and how you will respond to them. I have used scenario-planning many times since.

There were five scenarios-planning sessions offered at the conference:

1. Connection with the Asian Region
2. Growth of High Technology
3. Growth in Knowledge-based Industries
4. Feminisation of Australia, and a belief that 'they' (that is men) would not change the world
5. Convivial Equity, which imagined a shared definition of the future where power and responsibility were shared in pursuit of the greater good.

Of the hundred and fourteen participants, thirty-five, including me, were attracted to the Convivial Equity scenario. It reflected a very Australian vision, which many of us have since pursued.

It is now forty years since that conference. I realise how prescient it was. The five scenarios have all occurred in one way or another.

The session inspired us to take responsibility as we had to run the session ourselves. People who attended that conference still find they are working on the same issues in Australia. Most have provided leadership and added value to Australian society. The experience gave us an extraordinary optimism that we could effect change.

On the way home, I was chatting to David Armstrong again and he asked what I would do when I left Family Planning?

And I said, 'Oh, I haven't even thought about leaving Family Planning, why would I do that?' I was enjoying my role at AFFPA. He asked if I would be interested in working at the Bicentennial Authority? If so, he would send me a couple of job specs, work that was going to happen there, and in particular the management of the NSW celebrations.

I sent in a resumé and expressed an interest in the position of State Manager. David called me and said, 'Drop by and we will just have a bit of a chat about it, and see what you think.' I arrived thinking I was going for a background chat, which turned out in fact to be a full-scale interview. I remember wearing a black woollen dress, with buttons down the front, with two buttons undone at the bottom. I did have black stockings on, but it was not a dress I would have worn to a normal interview situation.

The all-male interviewing team asked the predictable questions about my work and were clearly somewhat disconcerted by the fact that I considered myself appropriate for this job. One of them asked if I had had ever worked in an office before? Another commented about the level of travelling in the job and wondered how I would manage with 'all those children'. He explained, 'One of the reasons my wife doesn't travel much with me is that she hates leaving our children.'

I was so gobsmacked it was a full minute before I could respond. I channelled Joan Bielski of the WEL, who always says, 'Never lose your cool, because a case study of one doesn't prove anything', before I replied, 'I think you will find that I have been travelling around Australia, in the Pacific, South-East Asia, and I have recently returned from being part of the Australian contingent at a world conference in Copenhagen for two weeks. There is no indication in my life that being a parent who travels is a problem.'

But he persisted.

'Yes, but there will be a lot of pressure on you in 1988. How will you put up with the pressure? You will have to be at functions every night, and out at things every day, and working at weekends, and by then your children will be adolescents.' And then he said my favourite line—'as my wife says'—'they need you more then, and you just wouldn't be able to leave them or they would get into trouble.'

At that, I did the worst thing possible and argued back. I said, 'I don't think there is a problem, but I'll face it if it comes up. My husband and I are both parents and we share bringing up the children.' This obviously was an inflammatory statement. I left knowing the job was not to be mine. As it turned out, that was a good thing.

I had not handled the interview well. Worse, I didn't put in a formal complaint. The successful candidate was a male with a scouting background. He lasted about three months. Perfect revenge.

My two referees were David Moore, the chairman of the Anti-Discrimination Board, and Dame Beryl Beaurepaire, convener of the National Women's Advisory Council. Both were quizzed about my ability to do the job because of 'all those children'. I was wondering at this stage if I had lost some—I only had three. I had never thought of them as a problem; perhaps for this committee they were the convenient excuse. As it turned out, the interview and referee checks became a case study for the NSW Anti-Discrimination Board.

It is very typical of those times to recruit from what they thought were the standard, Establishment institution—defence, church, army, scouts. All the people who maintain the status quo. The appointment of Quentin Bryce as Governor-General in 2007 was a remarkable change.

I was considered risky. Maybe it was the fear of change. Some of my friends think it was just the fear of females. In the early seventies, when we did the takeover of Family Planning, the person who was then running the national office was a Major General. What on earth were his qualifications for family planning? Even the International Planned Parenthood movement placed a great deal of reliance on men from the Establishment, such as the defence forces. It is a pattern that keeps repeating itself, even to this day. It keeps women and those who are different out of a whole range of activities and responsibilities.

Despite my new restlessness, I continued working in Family Planning, very happily. I applied for a couple of jobs to test my market skill, but rarely did I see a position I was interested in. Despite my experience as a teacher, a member of the Higher Education Board and the Education Commission, I was unsuccessful even when applying for jobs in education. A pattern was emerging.

I needed a broader portfolio. I liked to be many things at once: someone's wife, someone's mother, an executive, and non-executive. And the Future Directions Conference had achieved exactly what it set out to do: create an opportunity to clarify and acknowledge my energy and ambition. Something I had never done before.

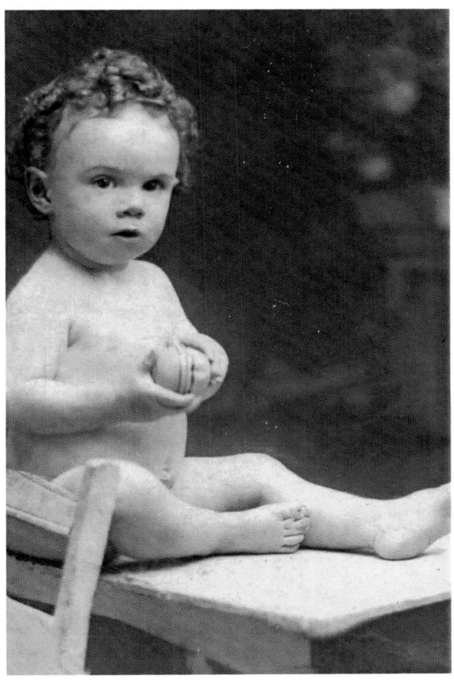

My father, William 'Bill' Rex Ryan, as a baby, 1916.

My mother holding me at my christening in 1941—my clothing was handmade by my Nana Taylor.

My mother and her best friend, Joi Rudwick, in Orange, standing by the table set for my sixth birthday, 1947.

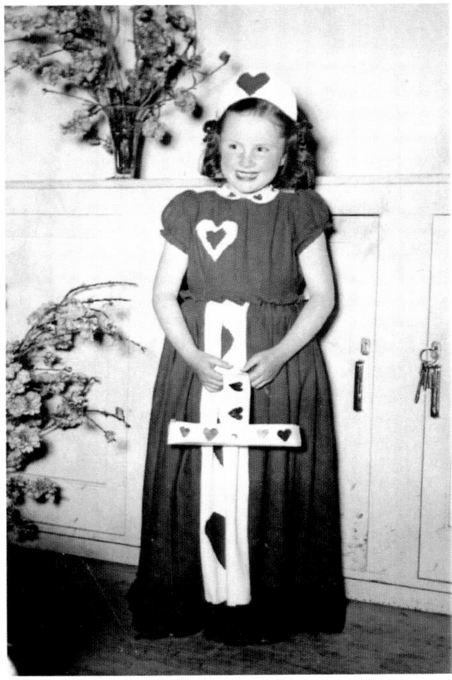

Me in fancy dress as the Queen of Hearts, for my sixth birthday party, 1947.

From left: My brother Kerry, me, sister Deborah and father at the Forbes Show, 1954.

University of New England Hockey Team, 1959. I'm second from the left, in the front row.

The day I graduated from the University of New England, 1961.

With Gordon McCarthy—the love of my life—on our wedding day, 1964.

A tender moment captured while Gordon and I were camping in Greece, 1967.

My brother Kerry in Vietnam, 1967. His birthdate was drawn in the conscription ballot and while on tour there he survived the Battle of Long Tan in August 1966.

Gordon and I chaperoning at Fontbonne Academy's prom held at the Pittsburgh Hilton Hotel, 1967.

Early Women's Electoral Lobby meeting with Gail Radford, me and June Surtees, at my house in McMahons Point, 1972.

At home with my new baby Sam and toddler son Hamish clinging close, 1973.

From left: My daughter Sophie, my youngest sister Sarah, and my sons Hamish and Sam, enjoying their iceblocks at the Walgett baths, Christmas 1975.

First formal gathering of the National Women's Advisory Council, hosted by Prime Minister Malcolm Fraser (fifth from right), 1978. I am third from left.

Me, Eve Mahlab and Alma Morton at the Tivoli Gardens in Copenhagen at a reception for delegates to the mid-decade World Conference of the UN Decade for Women (1976–1985), 1980.

Launching *Choices* for the national Family Planning body (AFFPA), supported by the Family Medicine Program, 1980s.

Visiting China with Australia–China Council, hosted by the Chinese government, which provided us with long black vehicles and drivers, 1984.

With Prime Minister Bob Hawke at the wrap-up party for the Australian Bicentennial Authority staff, 1989.

Receiving my Order of Australia Award at Government House, 1989. From left: My daughter Sophie, husband Gordon, me and my mother, Bette.

Making the cover of *ITA*, 1991.

CHAPTER 11
Black Friday

I am prepared for the worst but hope for the best.

Benjamin Disraeli

Friday, 13 February 1981, was a day to test all reserves of prayer and superstition. I am inclined to stay in bed when Fridays and the thirteenth day of the month coincide. Friday the 13th of February 1981 is the touchstone day for our family. We were never the same again.

We'd had a gorgeous summer holiday, which included a week in the January on a houseboat on Myall Lakes. We probably just looked like a regular Aussie family, with three children, having a relaxing time. Gordon had moved from being a corporate consultant to joining one of his clients as an investor, and then to Managing Director of Wolseley Castle, which was a manufacturer and supplier of powder detergent and other domestic cleaning products. It competed with Unilever, Colgate and a few other Australian companies with a share in the market.

I was a busy working mother, my children were happy and doing well, and I had defied the notion that working mothers damage children. But during the holiday, Gordon had been slightly short-tempered, and this continued when we returned to Sydney. He was sweating a lot at nights. Being intolerant of illness, we dismissed the idea there was a problem and put it down to too much sun and not enough fish.

The children returned to school. I returned to work and, on 12 February, I flew to Young where I was speaking at a dinner, to be followed by a morning tea in Temora the next day. As a member of the NATWAC, I thought it was really important that I made a big effort to give women in regional and rural Australia feedback about the Copenhagen conference. I had my expenses paid and was encourage by Beryl to reach out to as many women as possible, especially country women.

I had an appointment to talk to my daughter Sophie's headmistress about her progress at school. The meeting had been scheduled around my return from Temora, midmorning, Friday the 13th. Gordon and I joked it was Black Friday and wondered what she had done.

The plane back to Sydney was a twelve-seater with no toilets and no in-flight service. I sat down next to a Catholic priest and we started talking. He had been staying with his family after a long illness and had spent some time confiding to me about his fear of flying. He then began throwing up and convulsing. I thought he was having a heart attack, but with no flight attendants, nurses or doctors on board, there was little we could do other than make him as comfortable as possible. As his seating companion, the task fell to me.

The pilot radioed ahead and was advised to keep flying to Sydney, which was about 90 minutes away, where they would have an ambulance waiting. There were about a half-dozen people on the flight. We were strained, white-faced and feeling ill from the nauseous smell of vomit and the anxiety of our newly acquired friend, the priest. I stayed to help when we landed. We touched down with preferential landing rights and were met by an ambulance with people from St Vincent's Hospital.

My legs had turned to jelly and I made an instant decision that after visiting Sophie's school principal I would take the day off and have a sleep. Sleep is one of my main refuges. I rang the office to say this was a bad day and I would not be in until tomorrow. I then made my way to Wenona at North Sydney. We talked about Sophie, the future of Wenona, and I went home to Longueville.

I just finished making lunch for myself and was preparing to go to sleep to erase the dramas when Gordon walked in to say he had been out for lunch and felt really sick with pains in his abdomen and chest. He thought he might be having a heart attack.

I called our GP, who arrived about an hour later. Dr Lele examined Gordon and said, 'This is not good news, Gordon, you've got a very inflated spleen and I am not sure what that means. It is now late Friday afternoon. Take things very quietly for the weekend, and I will arrange an appointment at North Shore Hospital with the professor of surgery on Monday. But as you have many doctors living in your street in Longueville and some surgeons, I suggest you call one of them to have a look at you.'

By 5 p.m., Bob Perrett, one of our surgeon friends, arrived to examine Gordon and pronounced that things were very black indeed. Gordon's spleen was enormous. The sweating he had been having suggested a problem with his immune system. He should take things quietly over the weekend before he started what would be a battery of blood tests and further investigations next week.

As a family planner, I had an extensive network of medical practitioners who could offer honest advice. I sat on the phone seeking this and possible diagnosis. We were in shock for most of the weekend. The C-word kept floating around and a gut tumour had to be high on the possible list. Gordon was referred for a CAT scan and blood test by the professor at Royal North Shore Hospital, who repeated the new mantra 'this is a very bad story, but we can't offer you a diagnosis yet'.

The hospital CAT scan machine was broken and the alternative machine had a four-week waiting list, but eventually I found a private one. With a growing sense of unreality, all we could do was put one foot in front of the other and keep life as normal as possible for the children. Gordon had the CAT scan and blood tests on the Tuesday.

I had a Higher Education Board meeting scheduled on Wednesday, and Gordon wanted to check in to his office. We decided to divert ourselves in our work, rather than sit around wondering in a parlous sort of way what the verdict would be. I was tearful as I kissed Gordon goodbye and we headed off to work.

At 5 p.m., I was called out of my Higher Education Board meeting to take a call from our GP, who spoke very calmly. He said the diagnosis was conclusive. Gordon had chronic myeloid leukaemia. His white blood cell count was extremely high and the prognosis was grim. Leukaemia to me seemed like a death sentence, but I had only ever thought of small children having it, not grown-up men. Perhaps the doctor had made a mistake. Could the blood test and the CAT scan really show that so clearly?

Dr Lele said not to tell Gordon I knew his diagnosis when I got home. It would be best for me not to be the messenger. I should just go home as usual, feed and bath the children, and sometime after 8.30 p.m. he would arrive to give Gordon the results. I felt very unsure and shocked about this but agreed to follow his advice. I felt as though I was just a robot and would do anything I was told.

I returned to the meeting, numb. And someone back in the meeting asked, very kindly, if I was okay. Remember, I was one woman alongside sixteen men on this board. The kind question started me sobbing and shaking. The men were astounded and probably distressed. After a few uncomfortable minutes, while I blurted out the story, they moved into crisis management. It was magnificent. One of them would drive me home as I was in no state to drive. Another would follow in my car and collect the driver. We had concocted stories in place if Gordon arrived unexpectedly and started asking questions about my inability to drive home.

I arrived home safely, played mother-provider, and cleared the top floor of the house of children. Our GP arrived at 8.45 p.m. and we sat down to hear the news. We listened intently, even with our sense of disbelief. Gordon said, 'How long do I have?' And the doctor said, 'I think about six weeks.'

That didn't seem like a very long time. As he was leaving, he repeated his message, 'Plan for the worst and hope for the best.' It has been my mantra in life ever since. He said responses to treatment were variable, and while the odds were not promising, Gordon was now a case study of one—another mantra to hold on to. We went to bed, unable to speak, emotionally exhausted and curled up together.

My brain went into overdrive as I started planning the funeral. In the next few days, we found our way to Dr James Isbister at Royal North Shore Hospital. He told us that although with childhood leukaemia there were significant improvements in treatment, little progress had been made in adults. There were only two examples in the local case studies of people who had survived more than ten years. Ten years sounded like a lifetime compared with six weeks.

As our GP predicted, within a couple of days Gordon had dismissed the six weeks as ridiculous and said, 'Well, he's only a GP, he wouldn't really know.'

Gordon kept a diary while he was in hospital. He gave it to me when he came out. But I couldn't bear to read it. Because I wanted him to be part of this story, and to have his own voice, I did read it as I was writing this chapter, and I want to include some of the extracts here:

> Unless you have a prior knowledge of blood cancers, all of them sound like the one-word leukaemia. The mind is not able to comprehend the differences between acutes and chronics, lymphoblastic and myeloblastic, granulocytic and lymphocytic. They all end with the same crunch, *leukaemia*. The prognosis offered by the haematology specialist at North Shore was guardedly optimistic or professionally hedged. Whichever way you cared to read it. They couldn't really tell you what caused it, they can't be sure. Is there any treatment? Yes, but the results are unpredictable. Can I go back to work? Yes, but you may feel sick from the treatment and have less energy than before. My immediate reaction to the diagnosis was to go home to Longueville, close the curtains against the summer sun, and play Shostakovich symphonies on full volume. I did that for two days. And during that time, I considered the likely causes of the disease, the possible effects and the time I had left. I read as many books as I could borrow from medical friends but most were uniformly obtuse and positively unhelpful. A common note on my complaint was to the effect that a cure was unknown and death could be expected within a few years. Removal

of the spleen, which usually became diseased, was standard procedure. I resolved not to consult medical dictionaries and encyclopaedia again.

By Friday the 20th, Gordon was on his way to hospital for an indefinite period, with a bag packed with new pyjamas. It was the same day as the Lane Cove Primary swimming carnival. A horrible, rainy, grey day. And when we dropped the boys at the pool and said good luck, tears were streaming down Gordon's face. He said, 'I hope I'll be back here to see you swim later on today, or next week when you get to the district finals.' Both the boys were good swimmers and we were worried that all this distraction would interfere with their performance. Sophie was coming with us to hospital. I hated leaving the boys with no family, but our darling Pank, their surrogate grandmother from our McMahons Point days, who by now had moved to Lane Cove, was there with a lunchbox for the day, as well as special treats. She would cheer them on and make sure they were warm.

At the hospital, a couple of the doctors suggested that Sophie should wait outside. We said no. Our doctor, James Isbister, supported my view. It was better to have her there, knowing what was going on, than sitting outside worrying about it. Gordon was to be put on a cell separator to separate his red and white blood cells and remove his excessive white cells. It was the standard procedure for an enlarged spleen. When they attached him to the centrifuge machine, he looked suddenly smaller. Sophie and I managed by being mesmerised by the technology. It was just like an old-fashioned cream separator I had grown up with.

The centrifuge machine takes the blood through a catheter in one arm, spins it around, until the red and white cells and other components separate. The unwanted whites are bagged off, given to someone else, and the rest is returned through another catheter into the other arm. In a few hours, Gordon's white cell count dropped from 450,000 to less than 20,000—normal being 7000.

Victory. We might avoid the surgical removal of the spleen.

We had assumed he would be staying at the hospital indefinitely. But there were more surprises when Jim Isbister said, 'I think he is better cared for at home. We are giving him some heavy doses of chemotherapy; you are so close to the hospital so you can take him home. And, if there is a problem, it's a quick trip back.'

Amazingly, at the end of the day we were there to pick up the boys with their swimming ribbons, and we all went home together.

It was a very tough couple of weeks. We set about planning for death, while hoping for life. All our affairs were revised so, if suddenly I was to be the sole parent and provider in this family, I would be well informed about all the business deals in which Gordon had been involved.

Gordon's care for us had always been wonderful and it was well reflected in the arrangements he'd made. I would be able to manage financially. We talked through with the children what all this might mean. We decided to live each day as it came and assume the best would happen. Gordon was determined that he was not going to die yet—and emotionally, if not intellectually, I believed him.

From 1981 to 1988, our family would live with leukaemia. Gordon would have chemotherapy every couple of months and/or as required for those seven years. We learnt when Gordon needed medication. He would often be cranky and irritable and easily stressed. We respected that he did not have the same energy now, but that wasn't so bad—moderate energy levels for him were energetic for others. His legs would ache, and he could no longer play tennis or golf. He was delighted, however, that he had the perfect excuse never to come to a cocktail party or anywhere else where he had to stand for long periods of time.

He would need an extraordinary amount of sleep and began changing his lifestyle by taking Wednesdays off and going to our farm at Berrima, which became our lifeline. Three hundred and sixty acres with a river frontage on the Wingecarribee River where we bred Red Poll cattle and scratched about in the dirt. There was no moment when we were assured that he would be better, no silver bullet.

Gordon and I had to find new life rhythms in our relationships throughout these years. We had a regular relationship with Royal North Shore Hospital, where Gordon attended the blood-collection clinic. He had oral chemotherapy in variable doses, roughly alternate weeks. We already spent most weekends with our children down in the bush, and we lessened the expectations of each other's attendance at business-related social functions. We decided to have our best working lives separately and a family life together. Social life had to fit around that. The cocktail scene would not miss us, and we would not miss it. The truth was that we loved our family more than the social life that was on offer.

I kept up my work at Family Planning and my involvement with the Higher Education Board, the Education Commission and the National Women's Advisory Council. I needed that other focus in my life. It was my way of coping. For Gordon, coping was spending more time in the country and otherwise getting on with the jobs he wanted to complete just in case he did die.

We all cope differently with grief and shock. After his initial diagnosis, I suggested talking to a grief counsellor. Gordon was thunderstruck and said he would just go to the bush more, but if I needed someone like that, go ahead. I decided against it as I thought we could work it out together.

His business strategy was to build a factory and expand our detergent business, Wolseley Castle. To do this, he needed to again investigate what was happening in the rest of the world. So, our first venture, after the diagnosis, was a trip through the United States and Germany, looking at chemical plants and trying to decide what would be the best plan for Wolseley Castle. He wanted to make this a state-of-the-art business/factory for detergent manufacture.

The timing of the trip was difficult. His mother was dying. And we had made the decision not to tell her that he was ill. How do you tell your mother you have received a terminal sentence? It was too hard. We visited her in May, three months after Gordon's original diagnosis in February 1981. And really it was to say goodbye. She died a week after we left, and by agreement we did not come back for the funeral. That was painful as we both loved her.

It was not possible at Gordon's age to have a bone marrow transplant at that stage of the cancer—the odds of success weren't good enough. People too often died as a result of the procedure. Gordon kept a close eye on the research and probabilities. He worked it out like my brother Kerry worked out the racing guide.

After passing the initial six-week diagnostic milestone, Gordon did as Dr Lele predicted and questioned his skills. After all, he was only a GP, how would he know anything about leukaemia? Of course, that changed as his condition progressed. But Royal North Shore Hospital was given the credit and Gordon followed their counsel carefully. A moderate smoking habit was out, stress was out, sleep was in.

Our only frame of reference was Michael Daley, the ABC science reporter who was diagnosed with this identical leukaemia and was being treated at the same time as Gordon. We met when a friend got us together for dinner. Michael said, as a scientist, he wasn't giving up smoking, drinking or changing his lifestyle. Gordon declared that he would do what the doctor suggested to survive, and if that meant some lifestyle changes, so be it. Michael died a week after our dinner. We were shocked. And devastated and frightened that it might happen to us. We hoped that Gordon's moderating his habits would be rewarded.

During these stressful times, we had to make other decisions about life after Gordon. The first one was to decide where Hamish would go to secondary school in 1983. I was in panic mode because I was concerned our sons would grow up without any male role models. There were no male grandparents, and my only brother lived in the country far from Sydney. Gordon's only brother also lived in the country. And it bothered me, at the time, that our sons would be raised almost entirely by a woman and become disconnected from the world of men. A world they would need to know something about. And there simply wasn't enough human energy for me to cope with three children, a job and an ill husband.

I checked out a couple of schools and went back to Knox Grammar, where I had run some successful family planning programs in the mid-seventies. I spoke to the headmaster, Dr Ian Paterson, who assured me that Hamish would be carefully cared for if I would like him to become a Monday to Friday boarder. It seemed a good solution, and in 1983 he started at Knox as a weekly boarder. Three years later, Sam did the same as a year seven student.

With these arrangements, it meant our family was very disciplined by the idea that we all worked and did our own things during the week, and at the weekend we went to the farm together on Friday nights if there weren't sporting fixtures on the Saturday and Sunday, with the boys back to school on Monday morning. It worked really well. Meanwhile Sophie continued as a day girl at Wenona and finished schooling in 1985.

Chronic illnesses are difficult to handle for families and friends. Some friends disappeared overnight, and some came back later. Others worried the illness was contagious. And, of course, there were the ones you love the most, who are there for the good and the bad times.

By October 1984, the new factory was finished and was to be opened by Senator John Button. I had arranged for the children to come out of school for the day. The McCarthy family was scrubbed up, full of pride, as the helicopter landed with Senator Button and his adviser Phillip Clark. My ABC colleague and Chairman Ken Myer and his wife Yasuko had joined us for the day we had been anticipating for two years. It was probably the only factory attended by the Chair and Deputy chair of the ABC.

I had been told by the Acting Chairman of the Bicentennial Authority, where I was now working as General Manager of Communications, that I could not have this day off because Prime Minister Bob Hawke was coming to visit the staff of the Authority. I explained that I had a prior commitment: I was a partner in a state-of-the-art factory opening in the western suburbs of Sydney. I was not missing this event. I had invited Senator Button, who was after all the Leader of the Senate, to do the honours. I said I would call the Prime Minister's office and explain it was a long-standing appointment and offer my apologies.

I was advised by the Chairman of the ABA and two cabinet ministers that this was the end of my public life. I was to do what the Prime Minister told me. I refused. I reckoned my marriage would likely be a longer relationship than my employment with the Bicentennial Authority. Against all the advice (and shouting and some threats), I attended the Wolseley Castle opening and returned to the ABA office at 4 p.m.

Writing this I reflect on the experience of Christine Holgate, CEO of Australia Post, being verballed by the Prime Minister in Parliament and wonder how it keeps happening. Why is this okay?

The sky did not fall in, and Bob Hawke's visit had been spectacularly successful. I had not met Bob Hawke at that time. When I finally did, his first line to me was, 'Oh, you're the woman who prefers her husband to me?' I agreed that this was the case.

The new Wolseley Castle plant was an impressive, modern, computer-controlled system. It would relieve Gordon of some day-to-day responsibility. He decided to reduce his working week to four days, while he considered selling or floating the business. When he was made a good offer by Clyde Industries, he accepted it. The sale liberated him from the daily responsibility of running a business. It enabled us to pay out our mortgage, renovate Longueville, buy more property and develop the cattle breeding.

In 1986, Gordon took up residence at our farm in Berrima and became a full-time cattle breeder. Some of our friends were astonished; I was deeply offended when asked if this move meant we were divorcing. No, we were living separately in order for all of us to survive, and to come back together again. By 1988, Gordon was weary of chemotherapy. He had to listen to the medical science, which told him that each year twenty-five per cent of chronic leukaemia converts to acute. He wrote in his diary:

> Suddenly, the entire picture had changed. The major business obligations had gone. And I was free of personal debt for the first time in thirty years. The children are now five years older, and over the possible trauma of losing their father. Wendy was on the board of the ABC, and a general manager of the Australian Bicentennial Authority, and quite secure in her own life at the same time as sharing mine. I decided to reverse my normal life and spend four or five days a week with the cattle and weekends in Sydney, or in the country with the family. After a fishing trip to North Western Australia in August '86, I became a resident cattle breeder at Berrima, determined to build the best Red Poll stud in Australia. This seemed entirely possible when we made a clean sweep of all championship ribbons in the breed of the Sydney Show in 1987. It was almost possible to forget about Myleran, the drugs, and the blood tests, in the idyllic surroundings of the Southern Highlands.

Despite all this, Gordon needed to re-examine the bone marrow transplant option. First of all he had to check out if his brother or sister, who had offered to be donors, could be a good match. At forty-eight, Gordon was already on the age margin of acceptability for a transplant. And now there was a sense that we were running out of time. In his favour, however, was his good general health, his brother's good health, and the professionalism of the medical team at Royal North Shore Hospital, in whom we had great faith. His brother's tissue type seemed to be a perfect match. Looking at the odds for a successful transplant, he decided to prepare for the operation. His major Bicentennial activity would be a bone marrow transplant in late 1988.

Sometimes when I got up in the morning and looked at my day, I felt I had a thousand balls in the air, and knew that if they came down in the wrong sequence we would all disappear. It was both easier and harder when Gordon moved to the country in 1986 as I had one less person to think about day to day. Yet there is a profound loneliness that arrives when you lose your daily companion, and there is no one there to share the day's stories and events. I had accepted the appointment as Deputy Chair of the ABC, and was surprised and offended again when friends said why wouldn't I stay at home and look after my sick husband?

When I think of those years, I remember productive and domestic years of adolescent children, school activities, early nights, and sitting at the dining table writing three books on sex and family planning. We all learnt to live one day at a time.

As Gordon's diary notes, reflection was a part of that:

> Today is Tuesday, November 22nd, 1988. Twenty-five years after the day they killed JFK. I've been riding the Honda around the cattle for the last time for at least a month. Checking final details with my dependable manager, who will cope easily in my absence. The old news reports of that day, twenty-five years ago in Dallas, continue to draw old memories from my mind. Tomorrow I am due at Royal North Shore Hospital for a bone marrow transplant and an early meeting with the psychiatrist.

On 23 November, Gordon was admitted to Royal North Shore Hospital for the transplant. We were greeted at the reception area of Ward 12D and immediately sent off to radiotherapy for initial planning. This involved various radiotherapy specialists, consult X-rays and CAT scans, and deciding how best to blast the leukaemic cells in the spleen, and then the entire body. It was determined that he would have two doses in the spleen, and six doses of total body radiation over three days.

We were both very quiet as the assistant drew lines all over him. The cleaners were still sterilising his room. As I write this, in the middle of the COVID-19 pandemic, I am reminded yet again of his month of being barrier nursed, the constant sterilisation of the room. We left and went out for our last meal together and talked about the children, in the way people who have been together for twenty-five years can.

As Gordon went off to ward 12D, he was to be isolated for up to four weeks. I couldn't take anymore and so I left, glad of the need to be in Canberra by 6 p.m. to open the new Australian Science Museum, a major Bicentennial gift. I had been asked to do it by the chairman, Jim Kirk.

The next morning, I felt very agitated knowing Gordon was starting the radiotherapy. But when I reached the hospital, I was amazed to find that he looked fine, had ridden the exercise bike and was typing his diary entry for the day. Two days later, it was a different story. Massive doses of chemo had begun, and the nausea seemed to overwhelm him. A few special friends and family were allowed in after agreeing to be gowned, masked and booted.

By 29 November, his immune system had been destroyed. His brother Alfred was in the ward next door, ready to be the donor, and it was all systems go. I wanted to stay the night because there was one final king hit of cyclosporine to be dripped into him, and I could see he was fading. The body cramps were excruciating, but he wanted me to go and come back for the transplant tomorrow. He wrote in his diary:

> The protocol for today says bone marrow harvest BM and infusion and cyclosporine. This is D day in the ultimate. My brother's bone marrow attempting to take root in my body, which will attempt to repel invaders, if I have a skerrick of my own immune system left surviving. All that radiotherapy, all the chemo, has been designed to kill my leukemic cells, and to eliminate my immune system to avoid it rejecting the graft. Quite a day for both Alfred, who goes into theatre for two hours at 9.30 am, and for me, waiting to see if I get some bone marrow to replace what I no longer have in operating order. And then we wait days and weeks to see the new marrow growing in my body . . .
>
> I have been mentally preparing for it for almost a year, and it is like being on a moving belt waiting for the next inevitable step in the process. You can't get off and you can't go back. Even if the chemo and cramps bring on times you wish you could crawl back into the womb, I have done a whole ten kilometres on the bike to try and break up the cramp problem before tonight. It may make it worse but I need the exercise to push air through my lungs and blood through my heart and body . . . My own formula for the next three weeks will be exercise, food, water, and writing, plus ABC FM. I can survive well on that mix.
>
> Mid-morning, Dr Chris Arthur arrives through the door of 12D9 with two ordinary looking blood bags full of the creamy red goodies from Alfred, because we have similar tissue types and similar blood types, there was no need to strain any of Alfred's blood components off at all.

> I get the lot. Marrow, reds, whites, platelets, etc. In a short time, the first big bag is hooked up in a drip. They give me some anti-allergy Phenergan and steroids in the drip, and away we go. In less than an hour, the first bag is gone and the second is hooked up. I have my life-creating potential marrow back again after a new week of body whacking therapy. The deed is done. Time alone now will tell us of the result.
>
> We soon hear Alfred is out of the anaesthetic after his two-hour general, where they sucked the marrow out of his pelvis and sternum by large needles and syringes. What an amazingly simple procedure, but what a lot of technical, chemical, and human back-up, to make the transplant work. And to make sure I don't expire from something simple like a common cold. The lowest point of my white cell count will not be recorded for a few days after the transplant as my old cells are still dying and the new ones have not yet grafted. So, there is a crossover point.

On 1 December, after Alfred's bone marrow had been harvested, I walked into Gordon's ward with the doctor and watched as he hooked up those two bags of warm marrow and they started dripping it into Gordon. It all seemed so simple. Within three hours, Gordon had turned from grey to pink. We waited to see if his body would accept the marrow and graft. He was as high as a kite and convinced he was cured. He sat up and wrote a long letter to the *Sydney Morning Herald* about capital gains tax, insisting I post it on the way home. It wasn't published. I checked that Alfred was okay and left for home, exhausted.

On 20 December, Gordon came home weighing seventy kilograms and looking like something out of Bergen-Belsen, and with an immune system that could just tolerate being out of hospital. He was desperate to be home for Christmas—and he was. The family photographs of Christmas 1988, I can't bear to look at it. A totally hairless man, bony and grey, sitting at the table, glad and grateful to be there, but exhausted and irritable.

Here is Gordon's diary of his last day in hospital:

> As a token of protest, I have not ordered any hospital meals today . . . One, because the better my tastebuds get, the worse the hospital food tastes. And two, because I won't be here after midday. My final meal is Robin Sexton's apple crumble, plus bread and apricot jam, plus juice and tea. Luke takes out my shoulder skin biopsy stitch and I am all ready to go. The packing up after four weeks is a slight anti-climax. To the nursing staff it is a normal event. To me it is the beginning of the next stage. I ride a final five kilometres to take the score to six hundred kilometres in twenty-seven days.
>
> I am ready to go. Wendy arrives at about midday and Elaine helps with the carrying. After two trips, we are loaded and ready to go. Then we are gone. We drive to Longueville. It seems strangely green, compared to four weeks ago when everything was so dry and burnt. The arrival home is like returning from an overseas holiday. No real changes that are obvious except for the colour of the grass. We unload, have lunch, and unpack. It is not one of the great homecomings of my life. Rather the last piece being placed in a four-week jigsaw puzzle. Where you knew it was only a matter of time before all the pieces were fitted into place.
>
> The humidity is a shock after the air conditioning of the hospital, but I become accustomed to it during the afternoon. I read, have a sleep during the afternoon, and at dusk

> go for a walk with Sophie and the dog down Mary Street to the Longueville wharf. On a humid evening, looking back to the city, this is a view you know will always be worth preserving. The water, the boats, the trees and houses of Woolwich and Northwood, surrounded by the evening sunset. This is a good place to start one's second life.

This was a really tough time for our kids. They were twenty, eighteen and fifteen—and, frankly, sick of it all. And although never unsupportive, they found it hard to manage the dominance of it. I accepted that and knew they had to find their own way of coping.

Amazingly, Gordon was back on the farm within four weeks, and though told not to have contact with animals while his immune system was low, I have no doubt he had his hand up a cow delivering a calf some weeks later. I was so proud of the way Gordon managed this. He stands as one of the lucky ones. A reminder it is possible to survive cancer.

Chronic illness is a huge experience for a family. It's a bit like how, if you have an alcoholic in the family, everyone carries the repercussions. If someone in the family has cancer, it's always there. You become part of a club you didn't want to belong to. I lived for years with Gordon's funeral planned in my head. Every time there was a crisis, I replayed it and prepared myself for the inevitable. It was an enormous relief to let that imagery go. There is a life post leukaemia, and within a year Gordon was leading an active and full life again. By 1996, he was technically cured.

CHAPTER 12

Eight years with the ABC

> On 1 July 1983, the Australian Broadcasting Corporation came into being. It was like and unlike a church, a theatrical company, a newspaper business and, on a drastic view, an asylum run by the inmates. Its singular nature had destined it to be a field of contest . . .
>
> K.S. Inglis, *Whose ABC?*

The ABC was my first big board. It catapulted me into a different national role. Even today people ask me how I came to be appointed to the ABC. There is a sense of disbelief that a teacher, community educator, family planner and feminist activist could know anything about being an ABC director. Who did I know? Had I been a broadcaster? Did I belong to the Labor Party? Who was my tribe? Which club did I belong to in order to have this entrée?

The truth is, no one could have been more surprised than me to be appointed to the ABC Board. I was totally flabbergasted. Never in my wildest dreams had I thought of myself as a Director of the ABC. However, I knew to take my own advice—say yes first and think about it later.

There are many versions of my appointment to the ABC Board. Here is the real story, which I share because this is the way appointments are often made. There is no reliable manual.

One Sunday night in 1983, the phone rang in Longueville and the caller identified himself as Senator John Button, a man I admired but had not yet met at this point. He said, 'I would like to have this conversation in confidence. Many people have suggested inside and outside the ABC that you would be a very effective and appropriate director for the new broadcasting corporation.'

I said I would keep this in confidence, and I would be interested in accepting such an appointment. As I finished that sentence, there was a piercing scream, as Sam fell over the only one-bar radiator we have ever owned. I made sure he was okay and returned shakily to the telephone to finish the call with the Leader of the Senate. Afterwards, I immediately confided in Gordon, who said, 'But what would you know about broadcasting? Someone is playing a joke.' I was not entirely impressed with this response.

Senator Button had asked me if I had read the Dix Report. I had not read all of it, but I certainly had read the summary and I understood the general intention that the ABC should become a corporation rather than a commission, with guaranteed independence and triennial federal funding. The Dix Report of 1981 had been commissioned by the Fraser government in 1979 and implemented by the Hawke government as the national broadcaster approached its fiftieth anniversary. The inquiry found that:

> The ABC is now nearly 50 years old, and in the last decade its record has faltered. However, this has not been entirely the fault of the organisation, nor of any individual or group within it. The ABC has been led into changes which have ended nowhere, such as the experiment with access radio; on the other hand, it has remained aloof from other directions

> of obvious change, such as multicultural broadcasting. It has stood on its dignity and independence when pressing priorities cried out for attention.
>
> It has tried to maintain an idea of Australian society after that idea has undergone change. Its energies have been sapped by often bitter industrial conflict. It has not only slipped from the forefront of change but threatens to be eclipsed by it. The ABC has become slow moving, overgrown, complacent, and uncertain of the direction in which it is heading despite the efforts of many talented and dedicated people who work for it.

The review urged fundamental change, making 273 wide-ranging recommendations on the future objectives, powers and policies of the ABC. It urged the ABC to become more innovative and competitive, and to do more to market itself. It recommended that, while maintaining quality programming, 'the organisation must become more entrepreneurially minded, it must overcome its distaste for the commercial'. It also required that the ABC embrace cultural and demographic diversity, stating that the 'ABC has a duty to provide programs to Australian society as a whole and its constituent community element'.

While responding positively to the offer from Senator Button, I could hear the little doubts jumping around in my head. Could I do it? Was I good enough? What attributes and skills did an ABC director require? Their only manual was the ABC Act, which not surprisingly I did not have on hand.

As he closed the conversation, John Button asked that I respect the confidence of his request, but said, 'You can assume we will be making you an offer.'

I immediately read the Dix Report's executive summary.

I thought I could see a place for me. I was ABC-literate and friendly. I was politically aware and understood the need for change. And I already had a reputation as a change agent in education, health and women's affairs. I reminded myself we women are fifty-one per cent of the population. I was not risk-averse. I thought I could do it. I would not be a micromanager.

I was familiar with the ABC; it had been part of my life for as long as I can remember. I knew quite a lot of the journalists. I had been an unsuccessful applicant for the job of Director of Education at the ABC quite recently, I had been a guest commentator on the dedicated women's radio program—*The Coming Out Show*, usually discussing contentious feminist and family planning issues. The program provided a platform for discussion around concerns like the age of consent, which was being changed in the seventies. It was hard to get that discussion anywhere else in the media. It was a pioneering program with a devoted audience. Listening to the show was the highlight of my Saturday afternoons.

I was confident I would learn on the job.

A couple of days later, I was called by the Secretary of the Department of Communications, Bob Lansdowne, who asked me if I would be willing to be considered as ABC Chairman or Deputy. I said yes. He said, 'Well, you will certainly be appointed to the Board, and it is now a matter of whether you will be Chairman or Deputy.'

I got off the phone, my head spinning, thinking, *you might have overreached yourself there Wendy, what would you know?* But the other part of me was saying, *jump in feet first, then steady yourself, you will be able to do it.*

The next day I had a phone call from a friendly National Party MP I had met at the Future Directions Conference. He told me I was definitely on the Board with the blessing of the Coalition. This was important to me as all appointments were to be approved by cross-party agreement. Sadly, that is no longer the case.

A couple of hours later, Bob Lansdowne called and congratulated me on being appointed the Deputy Chair of the Australian Broadcasting Corporation. He advised me that Kenneth Myer, the scion of the Melbourne Myer family and Myer retailing business, would be the Chairman. Ken had recently declined the invitation to be the Governor-General. He was a mature, experienced and wealthy business leader with a love of technology and great national and international networks. I was looking forward to meeting him. We both had a head start with our passion for the ABC.

I was now in a documentary without a script. But nothing beats being invited; and I am still that girl standing on the side of the school dance waiting to be asked and relishing the thought of being chosen while at the same time hearing my mother's words, 'don't be bold'. I was forty-one, a feminist, a change agent, wife, mother, Executive Director of Family Planning Australia, member of the NSW Education Commission, member of the NSW Higher Education Board, *Cleo* columnist, and now Deputy Chair of the ABC. I was torn between joy and terror that I would be out of my depth. But I had said yes, and for the next eight years I was Deputy Chair and devoted to my role.

The entire Board had been replaced and for the most part the headlines were positive, but it soon became clear that many of the senior managers were resisting change. The chairman, by contrast, was *impatient* for change. The ABC I joined was a place where women were not visible in senior management and only two of the fifty members of the Senior Officer's Association (SOA) were women. They suffered from the idea that this was okay. There were few women's voices on air. It's hard now for people to remember that no woman read the news, but trust me, such was the case.

My advocacy had to be for the advancement of women in the corporation. My female colleagues on the board, Jan Marsh and Sister Veronica Brady, decided we should work together to establish Board policy to structurally assist women. For example, all interviewing committees would have a female member, and all jobs were to include a female candidate. We supported work-based childcare and insisted that all new ABC buildings would make provision for this. This strategy was supported by the Board and provided a policy framework we could work with.

This remains a good learning thought for young women coming onto boards today—get strategic with your colleagues when you are trying to change the system.

In August 1984, the Board and management held a two-day meeting to agree on some future directions. Out of that came the ABC's first corporate plan: a secretariat created to assist the board and management with implementation. The Chairman encouraged each of us to take ownership of particular issues. A good example was Dick Boyer, who was committed to writing a philosophy of the ABC, which resulted in a publication, *The Role of the National Broadcaster in Contemporary Australia*. It powerfully spelt out the national broadcasting commitment to expanding the range and experience of being Australian. It recognised the ABC's pivotal role in that task. It remains relevant today.

A key role for the chair is to bring the directors together and work in a collegiate way. It requires trust and leadership. Board business takes time and consideration. Ken found meetings irritating because he wanted instant outcomes.

A good example was his commitment to having a staff-elected director on the Board. When advised it would take time to select one, he said, 'You want a person on the Board you choose one today or there is no spot. I am the Chairman of the Board and that is how it is going to be. There is no time to wait and I want someone now.' Tony Bond was selected.

I had a much higher tolerance and regard for process, and would try to keep him buoyant, as did other board members. Every time we had a meeting in Sydney, Ken and I would walk around Hyde Park at lunchtime and sometimes visit the ground floor of David Jones department store. It was good to debrief the morning's meeting, get some fresh air and let him check out what DJs were doing as they were Myer's competitors.

These board meetings could run for ten hours and in the interests of health a walk in the park and a cruise through a beautiful shop with a pianist playing was the perfect switch-off. Ten hours is a long time to be in a boardroom without respite, especially if it is a two-day meeting with a Board dinner overnight.

Building trusted relationships with my colleagues is always a priority for me. In highly functioning boards there must be trust between board and management. This does not preclude dissent or argumentative discourse. In the best boards, the relationships within the board, and with management, are complex. It must be strong and trusting but distant enough so that it does not impact independence and the role of the non-executive director.

Relationships with stakeholders are also crucial in enabling good governance and board effectiveness. Our stakeholders included the Australian community and the Commonwealth Parliament. I rarely met a person in my time as a director who would refrain from advising me how best to do my job and serve the Australian community. I always saw this as a measure of trust and ownership of the ABC—something to be cherished, not resisted.

The Chairman insisted we use an executive search firm to manage the process. This was outside the experience of directors, but Ken was persuasive and said the price doesn't matter, broadcasting is part of a global communications revolution, and we must look for the best person in the world, who may or may not be Australian. It doesn't sound so unusual now, but it was big thinking back then. Nobody really argued against this, fearful that they might be seen to be a small thinker. But most of us had concerns that maybe an Australian would understand our culture better. This is now the conventional way to appoint directors and senior executives.

After hours of interviews, discussions and media beat-ups, Geoffrey Whitehead from New Zealand was appointed. He was the only candidate with skills in broadcasting and broadcasting management in an international environment. He had work experience in the United Kingdom and New Zealand and was a cleanskin who owed no political favours and no internal broadcasting favours. It was a unanimous decision after the second interview.

When I called Michael Duffy, the Communications Minister, as the media announcement was being released, his response was, 'Geoffrey who?' I explained. 'Well,' he said, 'that's a surprise. I wish you the best of luck and hope you've got the right person for the job.'

The first challenge on our watch was in May 1984, when Geoffrey Whitehead was on leave. A dispute over the screening of a *Four Corners* interview in Papua New Guinea offended the PNG government. At issue, the ABC's political independence. The PNG government complained that a visiting ABC television crew held a meeting with self-styled OPM (Free Papua Movement) leaders, which was directly contrary to directions from government. And this was in contravention of Papua New Guinea's security interests. The government requested an explanation and wanted assurances there would be no repeat offending. And, just as an extra, they hinted the ABC correspondent in Papua New Guinea, Sean Dorney, might be expelled.

The Acting Managing Director, Stuart Revill, assured the PNG government that the film would not be used. For two weeks or so, the issue became a cause célèbre. The media generally condemned the ABC for caving in to such a request.

When interviewed by the media, the Chairman responded, 'We are not dealing with a simple domestic, Australian issue. A lot of people in Australia live in an unreal world. In most countries where I travel in Asia, the media is totally controlled by the government. What I am saying is, if you want to get into those countries, whether you like it or not, you have got to follow the rules set by those governments.' This was a really inflammatory statement for the journalists.

At our Board meeting when the matter was being discussed, Stuart Revill outlined the reasons for his decisions, and referred to documents that most Board members had not seen. When the vote came, five directors—Dick Boyer, Bob Raymond, Tom Molomby (by now the staff-elected member), Veronica Brady and I—voted to run the interview on the grounds of the independence of the ABC. We believed the ABC must be free to report the news without fear or favour. Four directors wanted to suppress it. We decided to sleep on it. It was a groundhog moment.

The next morning, we were advised that Geoffrey Whitehead and Stuart Revill had offered their resignations.

Ken Myer said that if they weren't here, he would go too. And although we had agreed on confidentiality, it seemed that Geoffrey had been told that other executives would withdraw their services if he went.

We deferred the final decision and agreed to hold a special crisis meeting in Sydney. The majority of the Board held firm. We were not persuaded by the argument that if we didn't back the management when we think they have made an error of judgement then there would be a revolution. It was Ken's first defeat on a critical issue, and it was a bitter blow. Our relationship suffered a little on this, and I realised few people had ever challenged him.

Geoffrey Whitehead and Stuart Revill withdrew their resignations. We expressed confidence in the management, but we never quite regained the early trust and camaraderie. My own internal revelation was that I must find my courage to stand my ground when my fundamental beliefs are threatened. And I must never allow myself to love the role so much such that I would not be able to let go of it.

There would be many challenges to Board authority. On one occasion, I spoke to the Melbourne Law Communications Association, and described the old ABC management as 'ossified, insufficiently oriented towards product, and lacking diversity'. The SOA promptly banned me from being a member of the top-level appointments committee. The next day, Geoffrey Whitehead telephoned me with the news that SOA had passed a resolution insisting that I be called to account for my comments, asserting that these comments made me an unfit person to sit on any interviewing committee. How ironic! Today those comments would qualify me to sit on interview panels.

The SOA had already indicated their opposition to the idea of affirmative action for women or minority groups.

I accepted the invitation to attend their meeting. I walked into a threatening atmosphere. The hostility was palpable.

I sat at the back of the SOA meeting room for a couple of minutes before I was called up to speak. I spoke about my vision and made it quite clear that I cared more about the ABC than the SOA, and I would always want the best person for the job. It did not mean SOA members would be at a disadvantage when it came to recruitment. In fact, I did not see any reason for membership of the SOA to be an inhibitor.

The in-house newsletter *Scan* recorded that I offered an unreserved apology. It's not as I remember it, but I let it go. I don't know that they ever rescinded the resolution, but I kept on interviewing, and they kept applying for jobs, and some were successful. But quite simply, a public broadcaster that failed to reflect the community it served was in trouble. My role as a governor/director was to protect and grow it.

Perhaps, in hindsight, I am sounding more confident than I had been. And although the atmosphere was electric and scary, the truth was I had felt sure of my ground. If they wanted to be part of the new ABC, they had to change. I was not prepared to be bullied, and it gave me a resilience that I have exercised in subsequent boardrooms since.

Conservatism was not the prerogative of the SOA alone; the unions had also arranged their work practices to keep the ABC a fortress. One of the most extraordinary things was to discover that the ABC was still recording on film, despite having available the video cameras used in the Commonwealth Games in 1982. Because they didn't agree with management about their use, those cameras were in storage, gathering dust and becoming obsolete.

We decided to bring the issue to a head. We talked to our Minister, Michael Duffy, and Ralph Willis, Minister for

Industrial Relations. I was told to pull my head in by a couple of very senior bureaucrats. We talked to our unions and still made no progress. Ken and I went for one of our strolls in Hyde Park, where he said, 'I am just not having that equipment sitting there unused at public expense.' I agreed. It seemed that the rest of the world had moved to video but us. And in places like Tasmania, it meant that the commercials would always get the drop on the ABC, which had to fly film in.

Finally, Minister Michael Duffy called a peak meeting of the key players, and I heard that the thought of the Board, not the unions, turning the screen black helped refocus people's thinking. Thanks to the leadership of ministers Duffy and Willis, settlement was reached.

I remember thinking at the time that it was like being back with the highly educated nuns I taught with in Pittsburgh, who, in respect and obedience to papal decree, ate fish on Fridays. When the Pope ruled that meat could be eaten on Friday, fish was immediately passed for meat without a backward glance. Here, the rules changed and any attached principles disappeared. The ABC union cave-in to use video camera to shoot the news was not a matter of principle. I wondered what all the angst was about.

In July 1984, we launched a magazine, *Look and Listen*, which was a joint venture between the ABC and an independent company. It described itself as more than a program guide. In the first edition, I wrote the following piece of my twelve months as a director:

> It doesn't seem like a year—well not really. It's reminiscent of the experience of motherhood; I waited twenty-six years, and immediately I became one, I couldn't remember life without children. The arrival of an ABC directorship was

rather more of a surprise than my first pregnancy and when the pressure is on, I can at least console myself that, unlike the children, the directorship can be returned. However, the ABC and I have bonded very quickly; the toys and artifacts of ABC directors have joined those already in my place; at last count they included a VCR, a telephone answering service, two floor to ceiling bookshelves full of paper and a constant stream of cardboard cartons on their way to the shredder. The soft swishy thud of heavy-duty envelopes at the front door every evening is part of the daily ritual. It's rather like a security symbol and reminds me that paper and policy have their place in ABC affairs. I must not assume that evenings are just for programs: that was my life before June 30, 1983.

Accepting a position on a public board is always a risk. Being a non-executive director of the ABC has a higher risk component than other directorships I've held because of the high visibility of the Corporation. Everyone is an expert on the ABC and more than ready to send you chapter and verse on every issue. Motherhood statements and advice are available everywhere. The Board appointed in June 1983 is a most disparate group of individuals. Their common features include intellectual curiosity and successful careers. In practice this means everything is questioned, nothing is accepted at face value. This can be disconcerting, irritating and probably tedious for senior management who may have seen boards come and go. So, what is different? Can this board claim any special considerations, are the differences real or cosmetic?

The legislative changes made in the establishment of the Corporation should not be underestimated. Although in some ways a deficient Act—for example, the clauses on investment and borrowing are restrictive; there is a belief that the removal of the ABC from the control of the Public Service Board will ultimately be seen of great significance to the operation of the Corporation. In symbolic terms the legislative changes herald a new opportunity for an independent broadcasting authority. The ways in which the Board interprets and defines the new Act will influence broadcasting in this country for many years. What a privilege it is to be part of it.

The group dynamics involved in moulding a corporate policy group or board out of such individuals and under a new Act are complex. The background music was confusing—high approval and expectations from the wider community and unprintable descriptions from some inside the ABC community. Moreover, of all Board members only Jan Marsh and I knew each other and had worked together. To a professional human relationship educator like myself the possibilities for failure were enormous. It was with this background that we met for the first time on June 23—sight unseen, task not clearly understood and only one established interpersonal relationship.

Our first act was to include an interim staff member as a Board member and to record our view that the Board should always include a staff-elected director. The ease of that decision was a good omen, the first meeting's chemistry was marvellous. Clearly this Board was to be a working board willing to be accountable and take risks. The collective view: that the ABC had lost its centrality in our national life; that there were signs it was sinking into apathy and demoralisation bound us to a commitment that the ABC must become again the leader of broadcasting in Australia. It is the single goal which dominates the strategy of the Board.

However, boards can handle only so many concerns at one time. In our first year we've moulded ourselves into a corporate entity. We've increased our numbers midway through the year to include the Managing Director, Geoffrey Whitehead, and Tom Molomby, the Staff-Elected Director. Both of these appointments are significant in the composition of the Board. The skills and talents have been invaluable in the establishment of priorities particularly because of their experience at the cutting edge of broadcasting. Probably the most important priority decision was our acceptance of the fact that we have to make some sacrifices now for a healthy future for the ABC. We cannot afford to be diverted by the multiple bushfires whose resolution becomes de facto policy.

The major restructuring of the organisation has been an important part of the strategy. We've ignored the advice of the chairman of Bendix, William Agee, who described most corporate planning as belonging to the school of 'Get me through the next election or the next board meeting' in favour of the long-term approach. Although all ABC directors except the Chairman and the Managing Director have three-year appointments and a short-term expedient approach may induce a warm inner glow, we're settling for a better future and some long-term strategic planning. To encourage people to believe that the best leaders are facilitators and not order givers may be the contribution of non-executive directors who are very involved in the affairs of the Corporation, but conscious of the fine line between non-executive status and public accountability. If that could be achieved it would be in line with sound, successful management practice theory throughout the world and would equip the ABC to face the next 20 years more in charge of its destiny.

> Setting an agenda for change and announcing it publicly involves a high degree of risk because it raises high expectations from the community and accentuates failure. However, it is unreasonable to expect staff to be more adventurous and risk-taking if boards don't do the same.
>
> The bottom line for both remains responsibility and accountability.

It was a tough and exhilarating time in my life—and I loved it. I had resigned from the Higher Education Board and the Education Commission to concentrate on the ABC, Family Planning and my own family. There was no time or energy for anything else. Back then, Gordon's health was still variable, he needed a lot of sleep. I organised family life around an early dinner. When everyone else had all gone to bed, I would read my papers, watch ABC television, or write books on sex education. I published three in the eighties. It was wonderful to legitimise my life with television. We watched wall-to-wall ABC. And, of course, the children were incredibly impressed when the ABC provided superior audiovisual equipment, including a VCR.

Being a director of more than one board meant that I had to be well organised and read my board papers carefully. There is nothing more insulting and disrespectful than to sit at a board meeting where your colleagues have not come prepared.

At the end of 1984 I went on to resign from both AFFPA and my *Cleo* column to also become General Manager of the Australian Bicentennial Authority (ABA). It was a big switch and marked the end of a decade of community education. I was reinventing myself. I felt that the ABC and the ABA fitted together well. They were both in pursuit of what it means to be Australian—something that has been of continual fascination for me. I wanted some synergies in my professional life and generally that combination worked well. Other people had different views.

One morning I woke up to read a nightmare headline across the front page of the *Sydney Morning Herald*: 'McCarthy Double Dipping', or words to that effect. The story exposed the fact that I was paid by both the ABA and the ABC. As far as I was concerned, these facts were in the public domain and it could hardly have been news. I got that wrong.

For a seemingly endless period in 1985, the Bicentennial Authority was attacked politically. In my combined ABC/ABA role, I too was under constant attack. On 21 May 1985, Senator Peter Rae from Tasmania spoke at the Senate Estimates Committee about the ABC and particularly the *Four Corners* program where outstanding litigation between then Premier Neville Wran and the ABC had been settled. He began with me, quoting from a letter written by Clyde Cameron, a retired member of Parliament:

> Isn't something going to be done about Wendy McCarthy being permitted to draw a salary from the Australian Bicentennial Authority while at the same time being paid a stipend as Deputy Chair of the Corporation?

Senator Rae continued:

> . . . the question which another number of people have raised is—is it reasonable that someone who appears to be receiving a remuneration tribunal of $13,564 per annum as Deputy Chair of the ABC should also receive payment as a fulltime member of the Australian Bicentennial Authority?

Senator Grimes, the Tasmanian Minister for Community Services, responded on behalf of the government:

> Wendy McCarthy did get a stipend. Mrs McCarthy, who I must admit seems to have raised great interest amongst opposition members whilst being employed by the Authority, raised the matter of that remuneration with the Authority. As I understand it, the Authority raised it with the Public Service Board. In light of what Senator Peter Rae has said, I wonder what is the difference between someone who is employed in a private legally limited company who receives a similar stipend from the ABC and Mrs McCarthy? Or is it just that the opposition has a hang up about Mrs McCarthy?

Hansard records from this session detailed questioning about my *Cleo* magazine contributions, my role in hiring Geoffrey Whitehead, and a claim that my books on sex education were sold in ABC bookshops—untrue.

I immediately rang Minister Michael Duffy and asked what on earth was going on? When I accepted the Bicentennial Authority job I was Deputy Chair of the ABC. What had changed? I had been assured by the Office of the Attorney-General that an appointment to a statutory authority was not in conflict with my governance task at the ABC, which had an unusual structure as it had been constituted as a company rather than a regular statutory authority. I saw no conflict of interest and I would not have taken the ABA job if I had. To have this revisited on the front pages of the media sometime later was both humiliating and enraging.

Duffy's response was: 'The Silver Bodgie [Hawke] says you can't do both.' My response back was: 'If I have to choose between the two then I will stick with ABC because it is more important than the ABA, and that is my decision.'

'No Wendy, you don't understand. The Prime Minister wants you to stay at the ABC, but you can't be paid for it.'

I refused to accept that proposition and asked him to convey that message to the Prime Minister, with whom I had no contact. In fact, I had not actually met Bob Hawke at this stage.

He rang back fairly quickly to tell me that under no circumstances was I to consider leaving the Bicentennial Authority, it had been through too much trauma and I was the most stable and reliable person there, apart from Jim Kirk the Chairman. The Prime Minister would accept the advice of the Attorney-General's department and I could continue in both positions.

I was very happy and pleased I had stood my ground. It is a telling reminder that slagging women in public life is not new. I have written about this in my first memoir *Don't Fence Me In* but had decided not to include it in this book. But Julia Gillard, Christine Holgate, Julia Banks, Kelly O'Dwyer, Sarah Hanson-Young and many other women have since received this constant drip of hate and questioning about our capacity. I need to acknowledge this, so people understand that what is happening in 2021 is not new, just worse. Worse because we have been here before and thought this could never happen again. A reminder to constantly stand your ground.

The years between 1983 and 1986 at the ABC were volatile and confronting. This was in part due to the extraordinary energy and vision of the Chairman. It was a restless energy, focused on his commitment that the ABC should be both more Australian and more international. The end of the Chairman's term was painful and unexpected. On 30 April 1986, we were at a Board meeting in Elizabeth Street and our chairman was a troubled man. As we started what was clearly going to be a tense meeting, I was sitting in my usual position next to him and I could feel the pressure increasing. A couple of times he muttered to me and I kicked him under the table—code to keep cool. He was in a rage because the staff-elected director, lawyer Tom Molomby, was asking questions that Ken believed reflected negatively on his chairmanship.

This was the persistent hangover of the Whitehead/Molomby dispute, on which Justice Beaumont had ruled in Molomby's favour the previous November. The dispute concerned access to papers covering a range of issues. Geoffrey Whitehead had refused to give Tom copies of advice he had provided to the Chair and myself, and it had developed into a legal battle, with Tom taking Geoffrey to court for access. The resulting case established that a director is entitled to any information he or she requires. The ABC Board had to pay costs. Molomby was vindicated, Whitehead was in trouble and Ken was deeply upset.

The matter had been a painful and unresolved issue at subsequent Board meetings, and cast a shadow over our proceedings, despite the Chairman trying to move on. As this meeting progressed, Tom kept asking questions, until suddenly, with a look of white rage, the Chairman slipped his chair back, stood up and said, 'I don't have to sit here and listen to this!' and walked out.

I went onto automatic pilot. I knew that the ABC Act stated that in the absence of the Chairman, the Deputy Chairman shall preside at the meeting (Section 22(4)). I didn't look up or acknowledge the departure; I just acted as though it hadn't happened and proceeded with the business of the day. I couldn't really think what else to do, though I knew I had to get the temperature down. It was an instinctive response. The Managing Director then left the meeting, presumably to try and locate or placate the Chairman, but I knew in my heart that Ken meant it. He had had a gutful and he would not be back.

I felt so sad that it had come to this. The beginning had been wonderful. I have thought about this often. This was a job that Ken Myer wanted but had to be persuaded to do. He adored the whole business of communications and was in love with the technology and the ideology of public broadcasting. He wanted to be a broker between Japanese public broadcaster NHK and the ABC, and he had the networks to achieve this. Walking out that door must have been one of the hardest things he ever did.

We met that night and talked, but he was adamant that it was over. It was one of the few things he'd done in his life where he'd failed to get the results he wanted. He loved many people at the ABC, but he just couldn't take any more of the frustrating process.

After Ken's departure, I continued to act in the role of Chairman, something I'd done frequently in those first years. When the Chairman was overseas, for instance, the Deputy was in the chair. Invariably it seemed there would be crises when he was away. I learnt to ring Tokyo and other parts of the world with ease to get hold of him. In retrospect, it was a fantastic experience. I knew I would be able to chair a significant board.

While I was acting in this role, Minister Michael Duffy and I had various conversations about the ideal ABC Chair and Board. We did not discuss names but generic attributes. The government felt it had taken a huge risk with Ken Myer, and they were constantly surprised and often outraged by his obsession with technology, his outspokenness and of course his independence—the very things that made him in many ways so ideal for the job. They were also, by this stage, dismissive of Geoffrey Whitehead, and they blamed Ken for his appointment and for what they saw as an unrealistic view of the ABC about its place in the world.

Of course, this is not a new story. Governments who appoint ABC boards fall out of love with them very quickly. It's the nature of the task and relationship. When Duffy rang me to say that Cabinet had decided to appoint David Hill as the new Chairman, and that his appointment would be announced within a day, I was surprised. But I needed to be out of the caretaker position. It's not an easy role, and I had a lot going on at the Bicentennial Authority.

David was duly appointed, and within a very short period of time he became critical of Geoffrey Whitehead, to whom I was still loyal. In fact, David was dismissive of much of the management, referring to Radio National as bomb-throwers. He wanted change and immediate outcomes, objectives we all shared.

Some Board members were quickly restless with his style of corporate governance, yet most of us could see he had passion and flair and a wonderful analytical mind that went to the heart of the matter. The comparisons between David and Geoffrey were stark. Geoffrey was increasingly trapped in that terrible zone of isolation that happens when trust and communication disintegrate between the managers, the CEO and the Chairman. So much of corporate governance is about relationships.

I was torn between feelings of despair and responsibility, and I was coming around to the view that the Board would have to act when David Hill said to me, 'Geoffrey has to go. He no longer has the confidence of the staff and the external stakeholders.' In my heart I knew this was true, but I protested he should have more time. I have learnt in subsequent moments that it's best to act early. The terrible tragedy for Geoffrey was that he failed to engage the hearts and minds of the organisation. In an interview, he presented as a confident man who knew a lot about broadcasting and management. Now, he was battered, defensive and isolated in a volatile, political environment.

After discussions with the Board, David and I were given the task of telling Geoffrey the time had come for him to go. It was a truly hideous moment. He had counted me, until that moment, as someone he could rely on, and I felt like Brutus, unable to give him any warning that the axe was about to fall. This is when I learnt that board solidarity and confidentiality are crucial.

After hours of negotiation, Geoffrey's departure was organised. I went home feeling sick, thinking how bizarre it is that one's professional life can descend into a discussion about keeping a Ford Telstar. It was a sad and ignominious ending to a great experiment. But, like most wicked problems, there are consequences. Solving this problem just created others: Who would be the managing director? How would we go back to the market?

We agreed we knew where most of the talent was in Australia—it was only three years since we had interviewed and headhunted around the world. Most of us thought we should find an Australian to do the job. Cultural hostility had worked against Geoffrey. We were committed to what we had done to date, so we needed someone who could come in and manage that approach. I was given the task of sounding out David Hill's interest for the role.

We had a series of phone conversations in various parts of the world. He did not want to have an interview with the Board because he felt they had seen him in action, and if they said no at the end of an interview it would be impossible for him to be Chairman. I agreed with that. After a great deal of discussion with the Board, we made an offer, and he accepted the position of Managing Director.

I rang Michael Duffy to tell him we needed yet another Chairman. His response was an atypical silence. I asked that for his next appointment he look for wisdom and experience as a chair. He later offered the position to Bob Somervaille, who was experienced in the communication portfolio, having chaired the Overseas Telecommunications Corporation and Telstra. It was a good choice. He came with a wise experienced legal head and many years of experience dealing with government, corporations and legal practice.

David, Bob and I worked together very closely as a team. We talked about things together and separately, and seemed to complement each other's skills, despite our different ways of looking at issues. Although having already been the Chair, David hated Board meetings when he became the CEO. He always sat next to me and was only energetic when he was giving his report or when someone brought the ratings in. I'd watch his brain ratcheting around, making sense of the information. The day was lit up if it was good news and went black if it was bad. In today's boardrooms those distractions are replaced by mobile phones, which are far harder to manage from the chair.

David's tenure was a creative time at the ABC. He was pushing back the barriers—questioning, analysing and looking for the money in every 'hollow log', as he'd done so well for Neville Wran some years before. If the Labor government thought they'd got a pussycat because he was a protégé of Wran's, they were mistaken. He argued on behalf of the ABC with almost every minister in Canberra. When the ABC funds were threatened yet again and we ran the 'eight cents a day' campaign, people finally did understand that David put the ABC first. The government hated the campaign, especially Gareth Evans, who was by then Communications Minister.

It was a risky process, but the Board generally felt that their decision to appoint him without advertising the job had been more than vindicated. I remain of that view. And it has happened in other boards I have been on. Mostly quite successfully.

Most of the experiences I had on the ABC Board prepared me for future board roles. Eight years is a long time with Aunty. When I left the ABC, the childcare centre in Ultimo was named after me. And the Board room after Bob Somervaille.

Funny that.

In 1991, I attended the opening of the new ABC Ultimo Centre by Prime Minister Bob Hawke. It felt strange. I was a guest after being a major player for eight years. It was a great way to end one of my major public roles—a role I loved. I felt both proud to have been part of this extraordinary organisation and sad that I was no longer a formal part of it. But it had been time to leave. I had learnt by then that there is always an optimal time to separate from such a commitment, to recognise my best work had been done, and that it was time for someone else to assume my role.

The Ultimo Centre was a state-of-the-art broadcasting building where radio and television were co-housed, the culmination of Ken Myer's dream to ensure the ABC had fit-for-purpose buildings, along with my dream of an in-house childcare centre. How surreal it was to read in 2020 that the

Ultimo building was to be rented out as a result of defunding by the Morrison government. Subsequently, the decision has been made that the ABC would be relocated to Parramatta. I can only hope there are some next-generation dreamers and doers who will find a way to claw back the central position of the ABC in Australian life. Why would we want to discard the public broadcaster, loved and trusted by eighty per cent of the population? Public broadcasting is not a role for the market.

It is hard for me to accept that the ABC's future may not be one of continuing growth and development. It is something I did not want to learn. What I know is there is no board that taught me more about governance than the ABC. It was a new governance model when I joined and there was much to be learnt as we made the new structures work. Being asked to be a steward of a public authority is a statement of trust and a great privilege.

I learnt that passion and purpose carry you through dark and enlightening moments, and to be an effective director you must be committed to continuous learning, otherwise you are not governing properly and caring for your entity.

The media and broadcasting world of 1983 is today barely remembered or recognisable, but the fundamental reasons for its existence remain true. But re-reading then Prime Minister Bob Hawke's speech at the opening of the ABC Ultimo Centre on 22 June 1991 reminded me of the achievements of the Board I joined:

> This ceremony marks, without doubt, an historic milepost in the story of the Australian Broadcasting Corporation, one of the enduringly respected institutions of Australian culture and, in many ways, one of the abidingly great institutions of Australian national life.

We are not just celebrating the opening of a new building as magnificent an achievement as the Ultimo Centre is.

We are celebrating the survival, and indeed despite all the dilemmas and challenges of the 1990s the continued improvement of Australia's independent, non-commercial, publicly owned broadcasting service.

Today's ceremony tells the people of Australia that their national broadcaster remains the dynamic and creative force that has done so much to shape Australian cultural life.

It tells the nation that the ABC is flourishing as never before, because it is succeeding as never before in being a quality non-commercial broadcaster that reaches out to embrace the overwhelming majority of the Australian people.

The Ultimo Centre is the end product of a successful and effective process of consolidation, a micro-economic reform that represents savings worth millions of dollars a year.

Mathematicians take note: twelve into one does go. This one building replaces 12 separate ABC offices scattered throughout Sydney and in doing so it provides the best accommodation that corporate management, ABC radio and the Sydney Symphony Orchestra have ever had.

If we want an example of Australia as the 'clever country', it is right here. Because this building is fitted out with state-of-the-art equipment, including the highly advanced acoustics in the Eugene Goossens Hall and the largest installation of touch-screen technology by any broadcaster anywhere in the world—international-best technology developed by an Australian firm.

So, my first task today is to congratulate everyone who has been involved in the vast and complex process of designing, constructing and fitting out the new building and of managing the move into it.

I recognise achievements like this don't just happen. They are the result of careful and deliberate strategic planning—planning which has been made more possible by the stable funding environment in which the ABC now operates.

The triennial funding guarantee instituted by the Government in 1988 has been a success because it has given the ABC flexibility, with a stable and predictable bottom line . . . Let me add, once more, that the Government believes the ABC must and will remain free of commercial advertising and sponsorship.

We recognise that the ABC's strength, and the basis for the enormous reservoir of goodwill that exists in the community for the ABC, is its non-commercial style and its capacity to be an independent provider of news and information.

In an industry where broadcasters are too often blamed for appealing to the lowest common denominator, the ABC is still the quality alternative.

And what is just as important, this quality alternative does not mean that the ABC is forever locked into serving a narrow elite of the community . . . In the same way, the radio revolution at the ABC has seen a dramatic expansion of the audience without any loss of quality.

In the country, millions of Australians who used to have only one ABC radio station now have a choice of three: Radio National, their local regional station and ABC FM. And Triple J is now broadcasting to every capital city and to Newcastle.

Let me add that the ABC's international news reporting remains one of its greatest strengths. At this time of historic and exciting change around the world, it is vital that Australians be well informed and that they be informed by Australians, and from an Australian perspective.

Whether it be in the United States or the Soviet Union, in Europe, the Middle East or our own region, the ABC's news bureaus are reporting the world with insight and great expertise and we are all the beneficiaries of that.

The number of international radio and television awards that the ABC is winning is further proof of the ABC's commitment: to quality. And this international recognition is being matched with increased overseas sales of ABC programs and increased revenue from co-productions with foreign broadcasters.

And talking of quality, I want to make special reference to the Sydney Symphony Orchestra. As you know, Hazel spent ten days touring the United States with the SSO in 1988, culminating in that fantastic concert in Carnegie Hall. You already have a lot of fans, and you won a lot more on that tour—many of them in the United States and one of them who lives with me in the Lodge.

It is my hope, and it is certainly Hazel's, that these new facilities will enable the Orchestra to continue to make great music and we are looking forward to hearing you play shortly.

So, in all these respects, the ABC is delivering the goods repaying in full the half-billion-dollar investment made by the Australian tax-payer each year. At the same time, and without compromising the ABC's political and editorial independence, it is important that the ABC be finally accountable to its audience the taxpayers who support it. I welcome the fact that the ABC has set up an independent Complaints Review Panel . . . The maintenance of full public funding for the ABC is a significant commitment in the current economic climate and it is one which has helped the ABC stay strong.

And that in turn has ensured that your audiences can still rely on you for quality news, information and entertainment.

And whether they live in the capital cities or in provincial towns or in the bush, whether they listen to the radio or watch TV—that is what they get.

That is a particular credit to Bob Somervaille, Wendy McCarthy and to their Board, and I join Kim Beazley in thanking them for their energy and dedication over these years, and in welcoming the new Board members . . .

Three decades later, I can't imagine our prime minister would make this speech.

We have lost a lot.

CHAPTER 13

The Bicentenary

> A national festival is an occasion to refine and rebuild the national character.
>
> Narendra Modi

In 1980 the Australian Bicentennial Authority (ABA) was established to plan, fund and coordinate projects that emphasised the nation's cultural heritage. The Act included a clause to enable the Authority to be wound up on or before June 1990. This made it an unusual entity and it certainly focused the employees who were trusted to do the job. I read it carefully before I joined the team.

David Armstrong, CEO of the Authority, had called and asked that I consider joining the executive team as General Manager. I reminded him of my previous humiliating interview, and responded, 'I am not sure I want to do that.' I had been a tenant in the ABA building in George Street for a year and had come to know the Authority and its people. He persuaded me this was a serious role and I agreed to an interview.

I was concerned that I had to leave Family Planning to take the role, leaving something that was so utterly worthwhile and going to what some of my friends described as 'a white wank'. How could you go and fabricate fantasies about Australian life and history, and ignore the facts that the Aboriginal people were sidelined? I did struggle with that, but I decided that 1988 was going to happen anyway, and I wanted to get inside the tent to influence it. If we did it right, we could make the changes that might help us expand the kind of Australians we wanted to be.

I attended my last Family Planning meeting in October 1984. I had worked in Family Planning since 1975, nine years in total. I don't easily leave roles I love. But I was to commence my new role as General Manager at the ABA in January 1985 and was planning a three-month break between engagements. A new professional relationship requires a rested and clear brain to give it a chance of success.

Again, I was going to be doing a start-up job but this one had a sunset clause. The possibilities seemed endless. Better still, I had a proper professional salary, superannuation for the first time, and a company car. After the not-for-profit sector, the quasi-public sector looked good.

Within a couple of days of joining the Authority in January, I was aware from the feel of the place that things were not as they seemed to be from the outside. Since my recruitment interview in August, a team of consultants had worked with the managers and organised a restructure. I couldn't actually see any role for me now. I asked David what that meant. 'Oh,' he said in a very sort of airy-fairy way, 'we will think of a title, community relations or something like that. We don't have a budget yet.' The alarm bells started ringing. By the end of the first week, I could see that my first task was to find a proper role.

I had that ghastly sinking feeling that I had actually been hired as a bit of window-dressing. It was a huge shock. I had a view about myself that I was a competent person, with a strong track record on policy developments, social- and cultural-change management in education, women's issues, reproductive health and media. I felt demeaned by the suspicion that I had been hired as the token female.

One of the first people I met was Gaye Hart, who had been working as a consultant and had now been employed as Director of the Community Program. The management language of the place was bizarre: directors were of lesser rank than general managers, who reported directly to the chief executive. It was clear there were going to be some major territorial decisions to make. Gaye and I seemed to have similar expectations about our roles, with the differential that I would be more involved with the media relations.

I was raging inside: *What the hell was the difference between community relations and the community program?* Well, actually, no one had thought of this. I seriously considered leaving after the first week. I wondered how I could have made such an error of judgement.

When I first visited the Authority, it had been a complex, serious and exciting organisation. I had been working in the same building for eighteen months and thought it had the resonance of the convivial equity scenario of the Future Directions Conference. David's view and vision had been compelling, and my interview with John Reid, the Chairman, had been reassuring. However, there was a sense of smugness and superiority, as though everyone in there was right, and the people outside were stupid for not understanding and trusting what they were doing. I recall one of the general managers saying to me, 'It is going to be a fun ride, Wendy. It will be first class all the way and a serious appointment at the end.' I was shocked that we all travelled first class. When I said that I didn't need to travel first class in Australia except to faraway Perth, I was seen to be letting the side down.

At the end of the first week, David assigned me my first major responsibility: the management and coordination of the state and territory offices. He explained it was the national game that mattered, but we had to put up with these meetings, and it would be a good idea to organise and manage them. They were gathering in Melbourne the next day, and he asked that I get on a plane immediately and run the meeting.

I was trying to work out the game plan. I had moved from running an organisation modelled on Australian Federation, with a fine balance between the six state and two territory members in the national office. The Australian Federation of Family Planning Associations office barely existed in its own right. It was the sum of the parts, and member states either allocated, or agreed to, the work agenda. Success was not possible without the member states having confidence in the national leadership, and believing they got value out of their membership. I found the patronising tones and conversations at ABA about the state members something of a surprise.

The Melbourne meeting was a fiasco. Little resolution, few shared understandings, and an excessive amount of expensive food. Lunch was the major event, followed by dinner in an overpriced restaurant. At the end of it, we retired to the Windsor Hotel in Melbourne—we stayed only at the Windsor—where another round of drinks was ordered. I was already beginning to feel that I was about to join God's police because I didn't want to keep on partying. It was a classic case of mixed expectations.

The group wanted a program laid out for them to implement, but there were no lines of accountability, and no sense of leadership or direction. Most of them had little interest in changing the social agenda. They were a very conservative group and suspicious of centrally controlled programs. They certainly did not want to discuss Aboriginal people, ethnicity or women, and saw themselves as reinforcing the status quo. This would be a rather chauvinistic celebration of the great success of white Australia. If David was going to make the Authority any kind of change agent, he would have a tough job getting any support from these people.

The ABA staff were encouraged to think they were different, specially chosen, and weren't really the same as public sector employees. The facts said otherwise. They resisted the constant questioning of Commonwealth public servants regarding the plans and costs of the program. At least one of the managers was fond of saying it would be unveiled in due course, when the Authority was ready.

The election of the Hawke government in 1983, and the shift of the Bicentennial Authority responsibility to the Department of Prime Minister and Cabinet (a change welcomed by the Authority), brought with it a much tougher bureaucratic regime. The Department considered the ABA a maverick and was determined to bring it to heel. John Reid was enraged and put pressure on the senior executives at a time when they were patently unready to deliver anything more than some recent well-researched intentions.

People called me within weeks of my joining the Authority to say how pleased they were that I was there to get the place moving. It never occurred to me that that was my role. And it seemed a little unfair to think that I would be changing everything in the first week. Board members Phillip Adams and Ranald Macdonald called to say they were concerned about David's stewardship and thought he should be counselled to lift his game.

Sometime later, I went to breakfast with some friends and was told by a bureaucrat from the Department of Prime

Minister and Cabinet that I had political enemies in the senior team, including at least one who was on the ABA interviewing committee. I was surprised. He had given no indication that he was anything other than supportive. I filed it away.

On the other hand, I was noticing that as the political pressure increased my colleague Robert Maher, General Manager of Marketing, wanted to handle all of media relations and did not want to involve me. That wasn't all bad as far as I was concerned. I didn't want to buy into old battles. But I resented being excluded from decisions with consequences I may have to manage. I wanted my seat at the table and my share of responsibilities.

My role remained positive with David Armstrong during this time. I had been appointed General Manager of Community Relations, and sometime later this became Communications with a much wider brief. I was to look after media relations, internal newsletters, information of public affairs, and coordinate affairs of the states and territories. I know we were inventing on the run, but that often happens, and I could see the General Manager of Marketing was clearly threatened by my presence. Clarifying our roles and responsibilities was vexatious as the Board was putting pressure on him to deliver a marketing program of some certainty. When he was to leave later that year, Catharine Retter, who had been appointed as Marketing Services Manager, would become Director of Marketing and responsible to me.

As often happens when consultants come in and work in a somewhat defined space, and then leave with no thought of executing the plan, the Bicentennial consultants had an issue that I had to confront head on and straight away. There were silly recommendations that would only enhance the separatism of responsibilities. One such example was that every division was to have its own media staff. I refused to agree.

Meanwhile, the people I knew and trusted in the media were saying the honeymoon period would soon be over and slating the ABA would be fair game. They saw it as arrogant, with no sense of accountability to the public who paid for it, and there was a lack of information in the public domain.

The Authority needed to find a trusted voice. Di Buckley, who had worked in organising the 150th anniversary of European settlement celebrations in Victoria, was recommended. She had all the skills, and I offered her the job. It was one of the best appointments I made. Fortunately, I made it at the right time as before long we were in political freefall. I needed her political savvy and strategic thinking.

The ABA Board became increasingly dissatisfied with its management. Gone was the bipartisan approach. It divided on straight political party lines and was outraged over Prime Minister Hawke's attitude to it. The resignation of Ranald Macdonald, citing 'an acknowledgement of a difference in approach', was an unexpected blow. The Chairman tried hard to keep it together. But the 'please explain' from the Prime Minister's Department was soon in the public domain, and the media had a field day.

Ranald Macdonald was a highly respected media identity. He had been the instigator of the Future Directions Conference and I had a great admiration for him. My view was that he was driven by his sense of public duty and outrage. He accused the Authority of waste, overstaffing and an inappropriate style of management. He cited the first-class trips to secure the participation of the Tall Ships as a waste of public money. He had lost all confidence in David Armstrong's ability to lead the organisation effectively and said he didn't want to spend his life as director defending an organisation that had attracted so much hostility for what he thought was indefensible behaviour.

The crisis forced the organisation to the realisation that it lacked public credibility. And when crisis management becomes more important than program design and planning, organisations are in danger. I was asked to put together a plan to manage public opinion. Di Buckley and I presented a strategy to the Board, which we thought quite impressive at the time. On re-reading today it looks pretty basic. Then again, the issue was pretty basic.

David was under serious pressure. Although he had surrounded himself with people of his own choosing, he was increasingly isolated and alienated within and outside the organisation. He had delegated much of his day-to-day management responsibility to Robert Maher, whom he considered an effective manager. The plan was that David would have more time to represent the Authority publicly, which meant he had to travel, which of course caused more criticism. But the marketing program was under scrutiny and found wanting, and the General Manager was being held to account. He was finding public management very stressful as he had arrived with a large reputation and a belief that he would be able to show the public sector how to do Marketing 101.

The Board met on 15 and 16 August 1985. John Reid was summoned to Canberra to meet Prime Minister Hawke, who put strongly to him that the best interest of the ABA would be served by terminating the services of Dr David Armstrong. John did not raise the matter when he returned to the Board meeting. However, by 22 August, David Armstrong had resigned, and damage control was the top priority.

With seemingly breathtaking speed, we had lost a chief

executive. A few days later, the general manager of marketing left. John Reid insisted that the terms of the settlement were to remain confidential. He said to me, 'Only two people know this—the chief executive and myself. It is best that you don't know as you are going to have to manage the media, and you can say honestly you do not know.' And I am thinking, *oh my god, this is not a private organisation.* I had been around the ABC long enough, and Family Planning, to know that there is no such thing as a secret in public life.

I counselled whoever would listen that they would be better to be upfront about the terms, but to no avail. David Armstrong's departure was high farce. A media conference was called so the Chairman could announce it, while David exited through the garage and went to the north coast to hide.

Di Buckley and I rehearsed with the Chairman before he went into the conference. There were probably sixty media people present, including prominent journalists Peter Bowers and Richard Carleton. There were a couple of ambiguous questions and answers, but our Chairman was cool.

On 13 September, I was with John Reid outside the Senate, where he was to be asked to disclose the terms of David's settlement. As we stood in the corridor I said to him, 'If I am to handle the media, I think the time has come when I need to know these details.' He handed me a copy of the document, which I could see was political dynamite, although not unreasonable from David's point of view.

Things got a lot worse before they got better. By 26 September, the Prime Minister had sought and received John Reid's resignation. John Utz, a member of the ABA Board, was announced as interim Chairman.

Morale was at an all-time low and the loyalties of the staff were fragmenting. At least half of the people in the

ABA thought the departures of David and John Reid were unfair. Desmond Kennard, the Director of the Travelling Exhibition, said, 'You get up in the morning, listen to the news, and then go to work wondering if you still have a job.' My prior experience, however, put me in good stead to stay calm and manage the anxiety and surrounding turbulence day by day.

It is moments like this for working mothers that you value having other responsibilities at home to engage you. Your single focus is rarely your job. You have to compartmentalise, and for me home was always the safe place. I knew that if I had to leave the Bicentennial Authority because of those dramas it would not be the end of the world. I still had other responsibilities as Deputy Chair of the ABC. And Gordon still needed a lot of support managing his leukaemia during these years.

Many times, I asked myself the question: *Why do I really want to stay here?* I have come to the conclusion that it was all part of my pursuit to understand what it means to be Australian. When I lived in London, the first question was, where do you come from? Other questions then follow. Who are we? Who do we want to be? The ABC was the perfect place to ask that. As a history teacher, you question it. And as an expatriate, you are asked all the time: Tell me what Australia is like. This was another chance to make a difference to the questions and answers about Australia.

In mid-November 1985, Jim Kirk was appointed Chairman of the Authority by Bob Hawke. I hadn't met Jim, but he came with a strong record of community interests and affirmative action. He was the Executive Chairman of Esso, which had been the pacesetter in the private sector around affirmative action in the 1970s, famous for putting women on oil rigs in

Bass Strait. I was looking forward to meeting him and was pleased that the government had chosen an external person with no baggage. He was also the man who designed the Esso advertising program, 'Put a tiger in your tank'. It seemed like he had a sense of humour.

He was a tough taskmaster, and his first action was to bring all the managers together to review the organisation. We prepared budgets and were asked to justify all proposed expenditure and every individual program. He encouraged peer-group feedback—which was quite threatening. Throughout the process, which continued for some days, decisions were made at the end of the sessions about which program would stay and which would go. There was plenty of space to talk during this, but once the decision was made, you were wasting your time if you tried to get Jim to change it. You had your moment, and then you had to adhere to the party line.

At the end of those couple of weeks, he said that he would become an Executive Chairman, so the Acting Chief Executive, Robert Maher, was to return to his previous position as Deputy, and responsibilities for program management were reallocated. Depending on your perspective, Gaye Hart and I came out of these sessions as winners.

Since my arrival at the Authority with a vague portfolio, I had moved from community relations, to communications, to marketing and licensing, and now the responsibility for the Tall Ships and the Travelling Exhibition, the two big ticket items. I was really excited. Gaye Hart became the General Manager of Programs with the responsibilities for the arts, Aboriginal education, and community-based programs.

As part of the damage control, I started writing again. In December 1985, the following piece appeared in the *Women's Weekly*:

When I told my friends and colleagues that I was going to work for the Australian Bicentenary, their reactions varied from astonishment to utter disbelief. 'You must be mad. Who cares about a two-hundred-year anniversary of European settlement? And what does Australia have to celebrate anyway?' they asked. People kept stressing to me that Australians were not people who showed their feelings, who would be able to express a national pride. When I said that my task was to get sixteen million Australians involved in 1988, people shook their heads and said, it can't be done.

Perhaps the sheer size of the task was one of the reasons I took the job. It was, and remains, an enormous challenge, irresistible because of that. More importantly, I took the job because I think it's worth doing. The possibility of setting aside a year in the life of a nation, for people to look back at yesterday and look forward to tomorrow, is a rare opportunity. The timing seemed right. I wanted to be part of the proceedings. In 1972, when I became excited by involvement in women's issues, the crucial issue was always defining the role of women in society. The Women's Electoral Lobby helped by taking women's issues into the political arena, and during the decade of women the process has been accelerated and developed. I have had many opportunities to be involved in the movements of social change, or more simply, finding out where one fits in the scheme of things. In my case, I was particularly interested in where women could be. In many senses, it is logical for me to look now at what all Australians feel about who they are, and where they fit in their country.

My years spent in Family Planning, talking to women, men and adolescents about important and intimate aspects of their lives, and my experience at the ABC, have convinced me even more that Australians, regardless of their heritage, are looking for a definition and an understanding of what it is to be Australian. Being Australian is not only the flavour of the month in the US, it is also high on the agenda here. We do have a sense of national pride. Knowing who you are and where you come from and what your values are will lead you to a national identity. I'm optimistic.

So here I am, general manager of Communications and Community programs of the Australian Bicentennial Authority. And I would like you to know I am optimistic. I believe all Australians are coming to the party. It is a BYOI party—that is, bring your own ideas, and it lasts not for a day but a year. There will be hundreds of opportunities to find the event or celebration that will suit you. Although you bring your own ideas, the Commonwealth Government has agreed to be the major sponsor. They have committed $166 million for a national program of events and activities, which works out around $10 a head. The corporate sector, state, territory and local governments are all making their contributions on top of that.

It is going to be a big party. You might choose to run in the round Australia relay, watch the vintage and veteran car rally, sing in the big top at the Australian Bicentennial exhibition, watch the military tattoo or the air show, or have you thought about hot air ballooning across Australia, or writing your local history? At least contact your local Bicentennial communitive and find out about the plans in your area. If you want to watch it on the telly, or hear it on the radio, we can arrange that. Or better still, you can. Ring your local radio station and check their Bicentennial coverage. The year 1988 will be fun. We will all be there, warts and all, the knockers, the tall ships, the sad, the

> happy, the historians, the politicians, the entrepreneurs, the community leaders, the do-gooders, the people who hate the do-gooders, but it will be a great party. And most importantly, it will be remembered as the year which helped us work out who we are and what we are today. The time to be proud of our yesterdays and optimistic about our country's future.

Of course, this provoked many of my enemies, particularly as I was organising the major advertising campaign and the board had approved $10.5 million to be spent on it. Ron Casey, on radio 2KY in May 1986, became hysterical:

> Well, I noticed in the latest edition of the *Bulletin* that our Bicentennial Authority, headed up by Jim Kirk, is about, are you ready for it, to spend $10.5 million in advertising to boost public awareness of the Bicentenary. Just imagine that? An advertising campaign to tell us that we are going to have Bicentenary celebrations in 1988, 10.5 million bucks. Imagine what you could do with hospitals, with so many things in our community today. And that brings me to another festering sore that I have tried to eradicate, but I just can't get out of my system, and that is the very high profile of Mrs Wendy McCarthy. Now, Mrs Wendy McCarthy is the general manager of the communications and marketing with the Australian Bicentennial Authority. And you would think if they were going to spend $10.5 million to market and communicate with the public, that would be a full-time job. But it ain't. Wendy McCarthy is a deputy chairperson, but I call her Chairman of the ABC. Now the ABC has just had Myer resign, walk out in a huff, and he has gone back to Japan to eat some rice. And Wendy McCarthy is now the Acting

> Chairman. Wendy Chairman of the ABC, and the ABC isn't travelling well. And here, we have got Wendy, boss of the ABC at this stage, boss of marketing and communications for the Bicentennial Authority, and she is also a very happy housewife who keeps the family clothed and fed, strike me lucky. I wouldn't say exactly the ABC is a raging success and I wouldn't say the Bicentennial Authority is a raging success, and Wendy McCarthy has her finger in both pies.

These comments put me under pressure and made me more determined that the advertising program would be successful. I invited a hundred prominent Australians from all walks of life to donate their time and speak out for Australia and the Bicentennial celebrations. It required extensive negotiation with park rangers and tribal elders. It was agreed that we could shoot the commercial at Uluru because the market research kept telling us it was one of the top-five icons in Australia, and politically it was neutral territory. Travelling with, and caring for, a hundred large egos with extraordinary energy was fun. Our guests included Carla Zampatti and Kathy Lette, ABC broadcaster Norman May and long-distance athlete Cliff Young. It was a very diverse group.

The central piece of the Bicentennial celebrations was the Travelling Exhibition, sponsored by BHP for $6 million, the largest sponsorship in Australian history. It was based on a concept that had been tried in America, of the moving road train taking the celebratory story of American settlement to the American people.

Daryl Jackson, the well-known Melbourne architect, had won the design competition. The concept was looking shaky when it was realised that the Jackson design meant the exhibition had to be custom-built from the ground up. Existing circus pantechnicons were not suitable. The construction was vexatious, but the intellectual philosophy, theme and content were even more so. When the curator, Dr Peter Emmett, developed six themes for the display modules, anxieties eased about the viability of the project.

The new Chairman was terrified we could not deliver and the exhibition was put under excruciating scrutiny. In February 1986, it got the green light from the ABA Board. It was enormously difficult to manage, despite clever, experienced people doing it, such as Desmond Kennard. But the most interesting thing that I reflected on during this time and since then is how often that governments try to do major projects and just repeat the mistakes of the past.

The operating style of the ABA aggravated many potential stakeholders, including truck manufacturers in Australia, who were offended that we wanted custom-built pantechnicons. It reflected adversely on their stock and their ability to win a contract, so of course they complained. Similarly, ABC concert music, the biggest entrepreneur in the world, was rejected in favour of the West Australian Festival to recruit and manage visiting orchestras. Yet ABC concerts had been touring orchestras and performers for fifty years and doing it well. I always felt a slight modicum of responsibility that this was to punish me, where people made it so obvious that I had to be very careful about crossing a line, as if I had any personal gain.

When we looked for sail training to participate in the Tall Ships race, we were accused of paying little attention to the Royal Australian Navy and Foreign Affairs, at least in their view. It was as though we were reinventing the world, and all previous expertise was disregarded. As happened with SOCOG, the Sydney Organising Committee for the Olympic Games, and exactly as I see of people trying to build submarines today. It is this reluctance to pick the best out of the past. The ABA selected a new typeface, as it considered none of the current ones were appropriate and they had to be abandoned.

Buying a fight with Foreign Affairs by visiting another nation to negotiate a tall ship was, however, extremely dumb. There was barely a minister in Cabinet who didn't berate me at any given opportunity about the way the Authority treated Foreign Affairs. Similarly, the ABC would be telling me that overseas orchestra people kept ringing them and asking, who are these people? Should we trust them? Why aren't we travelling with you?

These were real undercurrents and tensions in the Authority—and Jim Kirk understood them very quickly. The staff didn't want to use the conventional channels, and they thought they could do it better their way. Sometimes they forgot it was public money. If the public could not see their vision they said, it was the public's fault.

The exhibition had a dress rehearsal in Ballarat in late 1987 after a training course at a nearby army base. It was not exciting. I became very apprehensive about its preparedness. Then, on New Year's Day 1988, the exhibition was formally opened in Albury. Prime Minister Hawke and his wife Hazel were there to perform the honours, as was the Chairman of BHP, Sir James Balderstone, and his wife. The weather was dark and threatening, thunder was crackling. The Prime Minister's plane was late. And the waiting children were beginning to fidget. The rain started bucketing down, water swirling on the ground.

In the performance space, there were some little girls dressed as swans and cygnets. I was transfixed as the little feathers on the girls were slowly dripping and floating down their bodies while they bravely tried to continue with their show. A perfect Aussie scene.

The initial response to the exhibition was worrying. Crowds were way below estimates and far too small for a free event. Yes, there was a technology buzz from interactive computers. People who loved trucks adored the Kenworths, and the film in the Big Top was a knock-out. But there was a sense of confusion. And perhaps a slight emptiness when people left. They weren't quite sure what they had seen. So, we went back to the arguments we had been having about signage. Curators didn't think we needed them; we should let people respond without direction. But the Chairman told me, 'There will be signs, Wendy, go fix it.' And I did, asking Daryl Jackson to design them.

At that stage there was a very small PR component to the exhibition. I thought it should be larger although the manager of the exhibition thought it was not required. But I looked at the coverage in Ballarat and Albury and watched the reactions of the visitors. I knew we were in trouble. We needed a community-awareness program, and fast. By the time it got to Adelaide, it was almost a dog. Volunteers and local performers were essential to the show, but many of them did not turn up in South Australia. The attendance numbers were shocking. I persuaded someone from the central communications group to go on the road for the rest of the year and run the public relations and community program. I thought the exhibition had no chance of survival unless it had an aggressive marketing campaign so that people had some idea of what to expect.

After Kalgoorlie, the next stop was Perth, where the Queen and Prince Phillip would be attending. We needed some drastic surgery. Jim told me to get on the road and stay there, until it was working. I took my mother with me and flew to Perth to prepare for the Royal opening. Somehow, miraculously, the changes worked and the exhibition team got it all together, making Perth a success. This was the second time I had had a personal exchange with the Queen and the Duke.

I noticed that the Queen's private secretary, Robert Fellowes, was very moved. I asked him, 'What is it that has affected you so?' I so vividly remember his reply: 'I saw Bradman batting.' It was my first insight into the awe and reverence that men have for Donald Bradman—his batting made grown men cry.

Later in the year, ABC Radio Sport, as its major Bicentennial contribution, released *Bradman: The Don Declares*, a documentary series of eight one-hour programs produced in conjunction with ABA and featuring Norman May as the interviewer. It was described by ABC Journalist Alan Marks as a story that demands the full attention of all Australians. Jim Kirk of the ABA and Bob Somervaille, Chairman of the ABC, had a private lunch with Sir Donald to celebrate the release of the series. They told me meeting the Don was one of the biggest moments of their lives. I felt really happy for them, if not a little mystified by such men's business.

By March and April, the exhibition was bedding down—and on its way to being successful, thanks to the road team who just consistently backed each other and worked around the clock to ensure good coverage. The plan to engage the local people in the curation and presentation in their area had been a good one. It was probably never quite what people hoped it would be, but it did represent a shift in the way we portrayed and thought about the Australian identity. It assembled objects and images, and let them speak for themselves. For the more than million visitors, it was an exhibition of its time and would not easily be forgotten.

The Travelling Exhibition was the major land event. The Tall Ships was its counterpoint on water, in recognition that we are an island continent. Twenty-one countries had accepted our invitation to join the Parade of Sail on Sydney Harbour planned for Australia Day 1988. It was modelled on a similar event that had been a great success for the American Bicentenary. These ships were sail training ships for young people.

David Armstrong and Robert Maher were keen on it from the beginning. They saw it as an opportunity to celebrate diversity of our relationships with other nations. They hoped it would shine a light on a new view of multiculturalism. It would recognise the unique nature of Australia as an island continent, and our relationship with the sea. Its enduring legacy was the sail training, an adventure and character-building opportunity for young people. The announcement that the British would be offering us a sail vessel as their Bicentennial gift confirmed the Authority's intention to proceed with the event.

The Parade of Sail, a feature of the Tall Ships event, was to be a spectacular sight in Sydney Harbour. It had the ability to provide the magic that stays in people's imaginations—the aspiration of every event organiser. It seemed it would be a good event, yet it created conflict and division throughout the Authority because of the persistent request of the First Fleet Re-enactment proponents, in particular from historian Jonathan King.

The First Fleet Re-enactment supporters saw the Tall Ships event as a meaningless, empty event. They lobbied for the Tall Ships money to be allocated to them and were ably assisted by the conservative think tanks around Australia, who wanted a much more British celebration, with recognition of our Anglo connections.

As a nation we continue this argument to this day. Who owns our history and who will teach it? The ABC at the time was a similar battleground with many of its viewers just wanting constant BBC reruns.

Most of the management of the Authority, however, still believed the Tall Ships was the appropriate event to celebrate in Australia in 1988. That it should not just be a celebration of the arrival of the Europeans. It was a view I shared. I found the First Fleet group irritating and distracting. I recognised the skill of their persistence, though, as they manoeuvred their vessels into a potentially embarrassing position with the United Kingdom, and secured funds in the end from both the New South Wales and national offices of the Authority.

I decided to miss some of the formal events on Australia Day to be on the ground with my family. On the night of 25 January, I had taken a room in the hotel opposite our office in The Rocks. Gordon and I had been to the Tall Ships Captain's Ball. We found Sophie and Sam asleep in the room, and a message from Hamish saying he would join us in the morning.

I was very anxious about whether the public would turn up to the event, and I desperately wanted the whole family there to see it. We went to bed after I checked the sky for rain. At about 5.30 a.m., I woke to the noise of a soft but regular sound. My instant interpretation was that it was raining and I rushed to the window. It was not rain but the sounds of Aussie feet in sneakers and thongs coming to the party. I wept. And I thought back to my *Women's Weekly* article: 'Just come and be part of it.'

Many of the staff felt that they had been let down by the First Fleet component—they felt it was inappropriate. Their worst fears were justified when they saw the leading First Fleet vessel sailing into the harbour with the Coca-Cola logo on it, and not a sound of objection from Ron Casey. However, the 2.6 million spectators on Sydney Harbour that day did not give a toss about the internal politics of the event. It was a day no one would ever forget. And the flags of twenty-one nations were flying for Admiral Roth Swan, who managed the Tall Ships event with his small team—it was a triumph.

I always downplay my achievements, but I do realise, in retrospect, what an enormous event it was. It is so difficult from the outside to appreciate what an intense experience it is to plan a major national event. It is project management with a high risk. You don't get a second chance; you have to deliver on the day. There are no options. And I think it left a legacy and began many new careers in staging public events, which we do so well in Australia.

Probably we gave too little consideration to the political tensions between the states at that time. Western Australia, South Australia and Victoria had all celebrated their sesquicentenaries during the 1980s, and were not so enthusiastic about the Bicentenary. New South Wales saw itself as the showpiece and the natural theatre—a cause of great resentment from other states. In hindsight, it was a wonderful decision that the World Expo went to Queensland rather than New South Wales. It was a huge logistical event.

I was surprised by how much I enjoyed the planning, the project management, the organisational overview and the compelling communication task of encouraging people to work together. I often refer to it as a one-night stand—a one-off, intense experience. You work on a fast track and collect an amazing array of skills. You learn to put the show on the road. People applaud or criticise. You have to live with rejection and success. At the end of the experience, there is no particular reward. The rewards are the process as it happens, and then the show. You also have to accept that you are not necessarily recognised or are given an opportunity to get the next big gig. Few people at the Bicentenary were offered the opportunity to be involved with the Sydney Olympics, for example.

I'd learnt to take each day as it came when Gordon got sick. It taught me a lot about management style, business and life. Now we talk about mindfulness and being in the moment. I learnt to live in the moment in 1981—that skill has never left me. I reminded myself every day to plan for the worst and hope for the best.

I give my best to things I commit to on the grounds that this is now, and this may be all there is. The same is true if I am giving a speech, committing to a task, or writing a book like this one. Some people felt they weren't as well rewarded for their work at the Bicentenary. Others launched fabulous new careers from there.

The Bicentennial Authority position gave me an entrée into many of the boardrooms of corporate Australia. Jim Kirk and I had done endless lunches at the Authority and visited many boardrooms, always with the Bicentennial video and a story to tell. I now realise how important that was in building my credibility and my capacity to stand up and speak to a group of people. Not that different from a classroom.

We encouraged Business Australia to be involved without necessarily sponsoring events. Essentially, we were building relationships and trust. After the charges of extravagance, we were unlikely to get big lumps of money anyway from other sponsors. This was a publicly funded government event; it was not appropriate to spend excessive time fundraising.

Working with Jim was invaluable for me. The perspectives of this successful, corporate, mature male were an important part of my professional development. And I would like to think this forty-year-old feminist activist, who happened to be a good manager, was useful for him in return. In any event, it was creative and productive. And I had a close working relationship with the then Chairman of the ABC, Bob Somervaille, at the same time. He was a similar age to Jim, and was wise, doughty, and very experienced in a very different style. I am grateful for the opportunities of having worked for both of them.

One of the great successors of the Bicentennial celebrations was the arts program. And again, writing this now, I reflect on the dire state of our current federal arts funding. When I joined the Authority, I was astonished to find there was almost no role for the five state-based ABC orchestras (all the orchestras were owned by the ABC back then). I had to be careful I wasn't seen as having a conflict of interest, but I was concerned that the ABC should play a pivotal part in the Australian experience. I enquired why this wasn't so. I was told the Authority wanted great orchestras like the Vienna Philharmonic or the Chicago Symphony Orchestra—and the ABC orchestras weren't up to scratch. I was enraged and offended by this.

It was a great honour when the Sydney Symphony Orchestra was invited, in recognition of our Bicentenary, to be the guest orchestra on United Nations Day in New York in 1988. I appealed to Jim Kirk for some funds to support it, but the management of the arts program was adamant they would not provide support. To this day I do not understand their position. I hope it wasn't just as silly as punishing me. In any event, they didn't get funding but, fortunately, a generous sponsor, Epson, provided the orchestra with some sufficient funds to undertake its US Bicentennial tour.

Mary Vallentine, the General Manager of the orchestra, suggested I travel with it and assist with the marketing and

PR. It suited my experience and I couldn't think of anything better. The tour was to take place in October and November, and since all the Bicentennial events would be over by then, it was agreed that I would be the major communications consultant for the tour. The ABC Board thought it was a good idea, but Jim Kirk was so concerned I would have a conflict of interest that I was forced to take leave without pay from the Bicentennial Authority. I thought this unreasonable as the invitation was acknowledging the Bicentenary, but I knew when to stop arguing with Jim. After all, it was only ten years earlier that the Chairman of NSW Family Planning had been telling me I had to have my pay cut in order to work with government.

Also travelling with the orchestra would be Hazel Hawke. I had suggested to Mary Vallentine that Hazel, a person whose musicianship was sound but unrecognised, would be a very appropriate ambassador. After all, presidential wives did these sorts of things. I raised it with the Department of Prime Minister and Cabinet, who returned in horror, 'No, no, no, it is not possible, there is no precedent.' My response? 'I'm sure you will find one.'

Four days later they did, and Hazel became the SSO's travelling Ambassador. It was a wonderful opportunity for her. She was a great Ambassador, and because we had the Prime Minister's wife travelling with us, the orchestra and the tour were enhanced in America's eyes.

For Hazel and me, it was an enriching time in our relationship. A twenty-eight-day tour with fourteen performances. Travelling with any band is probably wonderful, but this one was special. Mary had an American specialist consultant, Margaret Carson, who managed the marketing and PR in the United States. We met each other by telephone and got to know each other through fax—a pre-internet world. While we were in the States, she would handle the US media, and I would manage the Australian, and we would liaise before committing one of our team to an interview.

I'm now eighty. Back then, I thought of Maggie Carson as old, and she was only in her *early* seventies, but she was impressive and she has always remained in my mind as a great role model. She knew everyone and everything we needed to know. She had managed Leonard Bernstein, former US president Harry Truman and conductor Michael Tilson Thomas. She was a wise woman and it was a privilege to observe her in operation.

The Washington and New York performances included Joan Sutherland and Richard Bonynge. It was astonishing to see the American audience's rapturous responses to both of them. I was anxious to read what the *Washington Post* critic had said. Maggie was quite relaxed; she said, 'Wendy, this is America—don't read it, just measure the paragraph inches.' The measurements stacked up. The orchestra was travelling well.

When I first became involved in the tour, I had rung Rupert Murdoch and asked if he and Anna would host a reception for the orchestra after the Carnegie Hall concert. This was a follow-up, really, of my and Anna's friendship during those early childbirth education classes, along with an offer to visit whenever in London, which I had done. They were now living in New York. They agreed and hosted a wonderful reception in the penthouse on the 57th floor of the Le Parker Meridien hotel. Unlike our other hosts, the Washington Embassy, the Murdochs recognised the need for real food after the performance and provided Thanksgiving turkey.

There were so many special moments on the tour. The UN concert, meeting Javier Pérez de Cuéllar, Secretary-General of the United Nations, eating in Carnegie Deli late at night, lunch in The Russian Tea Room, sitting at a table next to Kathleen Turner, going to the Opera at the Met, travelling in provincial America and finding heritage treasures, the amazing concerts and concert halls in Las Vegas and Chicago, walking along the Potomac Canal with Hazel and Ros Dalrymple, the wife of our American ambassador, the reaction to Australian composers Carl Vine and Peter Sculthorpe.

And, of course, the music. For me, fourteen concerts in twenty-eight days was heaven.

I spoke regularly by phone to the family and knew when I got to Hawaii for two days' rest that I had to get my energy together: I would soon be facing the big moment in our family life. Gordon was now firmly booked in to have his bone marrow transplant. We had agreed he would go to hospital when I returned. But when I rang from Hawaii I was told he was already in hospital. When I rang the hospital, he had already discharged himself after a preliminary catheter insertion. This was not part of our agenda. Nothing was meant to happen until I got home. I felt powerless, bewildered and extraordinarily anxious.

I was so tired that when I lay down on top of the bed I went to sleep and didn't wake for sixteen hours. By then, the world did look a little calmer. I rang Gordon, who was surprised I was panicking. He explained, 'I have just gone for the Hinckman's catheter,' which allows for the insertion of a drip, and it would be all systems go when I returned.

By January 1989, there were few people left at the Authority. Jim asked if I would stay on with Bill Fairbanks to wind it up. I agreed. I needed a year to draw breath out of the public eye, and I wanted to think about a new career. So, in a systematic and organised way, we collated papers, evaluated audited programs, and made sure that our resident historian, Dennis O'Brien, had the information he needed to get on with the Bicentennial book. We finalised the accounts and endowments of the Multicultural and Youth foundations.

It was a good year to reflect and slow down, especially as Sam was in year eleven, and Gordon was adjusting to his new immune system. In mid-1989, I was invited by the Minister for Health, Neal Blewett, to chair the National Better Health program—a commonwealth initiative to focus on health promotion and advocacy. It was a broad-based program and offered an opportunity to bring the states, territories and commonwealth together, with the aim of spending health dollars more effectively on disease prevention.

It was a three-year commitment and it returned me to the world of health after an absence of five years, amazing as they were. It gave me some sense of a future and where I might be for the next decade, and I felt very secure about all the skills I had acquired during my time at the Bicentennial Authority.

CHAPTER 14

Multi-tasking

Yes, you can have it all, but not all at the same time.

Madeleine Albright

By the end of 1989, life had become calmer. I was busy closing down the Bicentennial Authority, a task I found satisfying. I am still a teacher whose lesson plan says beginning, middle and end. And we don't often get a chance in public life to tie up the pieces, put them in boxes and archive them. That is what we did now.

Gordon was back at the farm after his transplant, and apart from a mean dose of shingles, seemed to have only positive side effects. Hamish was in his second year of Arts at Mitchell College of Advance Education (now Charles Sturt University) in Bathurst, Sophie was doing extra subjects at the Australian National University and thinking about an Honours year, and Sam was living at home, managing his year eleven.

Quentin Bryce came to live with us, and it was wonderful to have her here with Sam and me. We had a lot of fun together. It made the change in Gordon's and my life much more bearable. For her, it was good to live with our family as living alone in Sydney, away from her husband and children, would have been very lonely. Since our days together at NATWAC, I doubt that a week would pass without a conversation and shared experience, which made it easier for her to slip into our family life.

One would wonder now to think of the intransigence of a government that insisted the Sex Discrimination Commissioner needed to be based in Sydney. Most weekends Quentin went home; otherwise, she, Sam and I lived as a little trio in Longueville. We had many parties. It is hard to believe that when we were selling and moving out of Longueville in 1993 and 1994 Quentin was still there. What a testament to friendship that we could live together, stay in love with our husbands, keep our children out of jail, manage some major public organisations, *and* remain friends.

But back in late 1989, I was wondering what to do next. I was interested in the whole concept of being a rescuer for an organisation or doing another start-up. Preferably a not-for-profit in strife and too important not to save. Strangely, one found me. It all seemed so accidental.

My ex-colleague, Gaye Hart, and I went out for dinner one night and talked about what our post-Bicentennial life could look like. We met up with another friend, Deborah Marr, who had started the executive search arm of Pannell Kerr and Forster, an accounting firm. When asked what I had in mind, I said I hadn't the faintest idea, 'All I know is I want to be the chief executive of an organisation with good values.' It just came out spontaneously, so things were clarifying in my mind. I wanted to grow a business. I was confident that I could do that. I was still chairing the Better Health Program and was Deputy Chair of the ABC. I was not unemployed, but I knew that my role in those places was as a non-executive chair/director, not a manager.

I agreed to meet Deborah the next day and talk about my prospects. We met at her office, and while talking a brief for a job arrived. I looked at it and thought, *this is my job*. It was the role of CEO of the National Trust of New South Wales.

A community-based, not-for-profit statutory body committed to promoting and conserving the natural and built heritage of the state. It was established in 1945 by Annie Forsyth Wyatt and committed volunteers who wanted to protect heritage under threat, including native bushland. It was a trusted and loved organisation. However, in 1988 the NSW government had sacked the Board and placed it under the control of administrator Martin Green.

His first task was to decide whether it should be liquidated or managed out of its $2million debt. Martin had decided to advertise the role and see if anyone out there was interested. My eventual appointment reflected a strategic decision by him to try trading out of the debt. It was a déjà vu moment from the Family Planning Association in the 1970s. It looked like a perfect challenge to me—financial crisis, good values, respect for history, community-based membership, and a determined love of Australian heritage. An absolute dream job. I was familiar with the National Trust and like many history teachers of my era had become a member in my first year of teaching. I expressed my interest formally the next day.

Two weeks later, I was invited to an interview. It didn't start well. I arrived at the Trust headquarters at Observatory Hill and was met by a charming woman who said, 'We are very pleased you are an applicant for the job. Would you like to meet all the staff?' She had been the executive assistant of the previous manager. There were only six staff present at the time, but I was completely nonplussed as I belong to the school of people who believe that job applications are confidential. I didn't want to meet the staff as a potential applicant until I had the feel of the place. It was clearly too late to be concerned about that. I found it really unprofessional. However, disregarding the loss of privacy, I proceeded on my guided tour of the building and tried to be pleasant while I was in fact upset.

I could see all the signs of an organisation in despair. Offices were hoarded up and there was no sense of openness or trust. It seemed like a collection of tiny fiefdoms inhabited by unhappy people. I was not surprised to read the following Saturday that my candidature for the job was disclosed in the *Sydney Morning Herald* by Sydney columnist Leo Schofield.

I've had some really unusual interviews, but this is one of the more curious ones. There were three people on the interview panel: one remained relatively neutral, one became quite enthusiastic, and the other was exceedingly hostile. The latter was a woman I had never met before and in whom I provoked a strong sense of antipathy. I found it very confronting. I left the interview thinking, *I really could do this job and I would love to, but I doubt that it is going to happen*. I comforted myself on the drive home by thinking that maybe not that many people will want it as they will see it as a dog. So, it was somewhat of a surprise when it was offered to me.

We sorted out the terms and conditions of my contract quickly, and it was agreed that my starting date would be January 1990. As the salary was modest, it was agreed, as had been the case since my time at Family Planning, that I would continue my existing work on other boards.

On 28 December 1989, two weeks before I started at the National Trust, an earthquake devastated Newcastle. As I drove from our farm at Berrima to Sydney, I was listening in disbelief to the radio reports. It did not occur to me this would have an impact on my new career at the Trust.

The earthquake introduced me to the Trust in action. Their dedicated volunteers were concerned about the effect on the precious heritage of Newcastle, and they were attempting to identify, record and assess the damage done to the most valuable buildings. Not everyone in Newcastle thought the Trust teams were helpful. Many of the city officials saw them as interfering and not understanding that the best thing that could happen to Newcastle was an opportunity to get rid of this old stuff.

This was an important crisis for me to manage during my first weeks of the job. It went to the heart of the Trust's existence as it offered an opportunity for people to examine what heritage they valued. It introduced me to some outstanding volunteers, including Colin Crisp, a heritage engineer who could structurally conserve anything. He would quietly take the council engineers through the reasons for saving them. I can think of no building where his assessment was wrong.

A high priority was to start raising money. And this is where I learnt to love the game of fundraising. I interviewed seven fundraising organisations and selected Everald Compton's firm. His approach was systematic and disciplined. It involved the establishment of a foundation led by prominent people. I invited Bob Hawke to be one of the leaders, three days after he had been ousted as Prime Minister by Paul Keating, conscious of the fact I was offering him an unpaid job and asking for a financial commitment. I stressed to him that we valued his name and association. I wasn't asking him to attend endless meetings but open doors occasionally.

Bob Hawke rang me back the next day and said, 'You've been very persuasive. I've always supported Australian heritage values. Hazel and I will make a donation to the Bush Regeneration Program and I will chair the foundation.' To his credit, he was always helpful and available in providing access to people I would have not otherwise been able to reach.

It was important that the foundation leadership was politically even-handed, so I then invited Rosemary Foot, a former Deputy Leader of NSW Liberal Party, to co-chair the foundation and play an active role in its governance. She agreed and did a superb job.

An unlikely but successful combination.

I was determined to persuade the government to support the work of the Trust. There had to be financial recognition for its role in caring for so many places in the public domain. The former premier, Neville Wran, had created the Historic Houses Trust as a government-supported agency, partly because of the fights he had with the National Trust. It felt like petty retribution and not in the interests of good heritage management.

Martin Green and I worked together managing the Trust for eighteen months. We researched and analysed the organisation and selected a management team. In the short term, life without a board was wonderful. I think of it as my extended Whitlam–Barnard period—a time when I could implement change pretty much when I wanted. It was a privileged opportunity to get the systems and the people right.

I thought the constitutional structure of the Trust was clumsy and had too many government appointees. After discussions with government, we agreed that this was an opportunity to ensure the Trust's governance structure would be appropriate for the twenty-first century.

In July 1991, the first Trust elections in three years were held and a new board was put in place. The administrator's job was finished and the Trust's headquarters at Observatory Hill were refurbished thanks to Premier Nick Greiner. A big change was the status of the Chief Executive, who was now a Director equal to all others, unlike previous Trust executives, who were treated as staff and told to come and go from meetings.

When Paul Keating in 1992 announced the One Nation program, I was on the first plane to Canberra, and within a short period of time we had a grant of $1.5 million, on a dollar-for-dollar basis. Sometimes in these campaigns, there is just one moment where you can grab success. We were on a roll.

I loved my time working there—so many happy memories. It was the first time in my family life that I could please myself about my working hours. When I took the job, I announced to the family that this was my time to consolidate my career by putting it first and that would mean there would be food in the house, though I would often not be home until eight-thirty or nine in the evening. Much of the Trust's advisory work was done by volunteers and they would meet between 5.30 and 8.30 p.m. I thought it was important that I should attend. The S.H. Ervin Gallery, owned by the Trust and one of Sydney's better hardworking galleries, had regular openings that I attended.

It was under the competent management of Dinah Dysart when I arrived, but I persuaded her to take over the management of all the Trust properties. Her deputy, Anne Loxley, was appointed as the Gallery Director, an outstanding young woman who brought a fresh energy and intellect to the gallery. Various Trust members called to advise me she was too young. I thought she was just what we needed—a wonderful curator and scholar—and she has since become a leading national and international curator of community-based arts projects.

One of her spectacular coups was to bring an Aboriginal community from Central Australia to Sydney. Their work was hung in the gallery, which had been transformed by tons of red sand from the Western Desert. They sang and danced as part of the performance. It was astonishing. One morning, when I was driving in, I saw the surprised expressions of one of our members as she watched the woman in front of the campfire, which they were burning just outside of the entrance to the gallery, applying paint and ochre to her bare breasts. Red sand on the gallery floor was one thing, this was another. But there were no complaints.

I loved the scholarship of the Trust. The intellect that was applied to artworks, historic collection and property interpretations. It taught me not to jump to quick conclusions about whether or not to save a building. It was a studied, proper process. Vigorous debate was part of the daily working life, and it was a very stimulating environment.

I continued with my existing portfolio of roles and responsibilities. I learnt to be adept at piggybacking my interests and networking between them. My ABC Deputy Chair appointment ended in 1991, and my Better Health Chair position in 1992, and I thought I would be happy to focus on a single activity. Yet, in 1990 and 1991, when I was travelling to conferences on Better Health in Singapore and Sweden, these experiences just kept reaffirming how much I loved the big picture, and how much I liked to work nationally and internationally.

When Ros Kelly, the Environment Minister, among other portfolios, asked me to be part of a four-member panel to review and resolve Australia's intractable waste rubbish problem, I was concerned the President of the Trust, Barry O'Keefe, may not be pleased if I accepted another appointment. However, the government had supported the Trust through the One Nation funding, and I did not want to find myself in a politically difficult decision by appearing to be uncooperative. Barry agreed I should join the panel.

We held consultations in various Australian towns where waste management was a significant community issue and no one wanted a high-temperature incinerator. It was a very divisive political issue. At our public meeting in Moree, over one thousand people turned up. I was back in the eye of the storm.

The Independent Panel on Intractable Waste, headed by Professor Ben Selinger, was expected to look at technology around the world. The itinerary included Cincinnati, Bay City, Detroit, Basel and Paris, all of which had developed new technology in waste management. Meanwhile, we had an issue in Cobar in central western New South Wales, where the locals were also saying no to an incinerator. We were met at the airport by demonstrators wearing black shrouds. The local people wanted to discuss the matter when Nick Greiner's plane arrived at the same time. He just said, 'Go and speak to Wendy about this.'

One passionate man started putting the case against the incinerator to me. He said, 'Nick thinks I am dumb because when we were at Riverview School together, he was the top of the class and I was the bottom. But I know more about the science of this than him, and he has to listen to us. We know that children are being born with deformities when near a high-temperature incinerator.'

The Chernobyl, Bhopal, Exxon Valdez disasters had all left a legacy of mistrust about corporate safety and scientific truth throughout the world. We no longer believed governments and corporations who tell us what is good for us. The arrival of the internet, and the capacity to research, learn and understand information makes communities strong when they decide to fight the peer-reviewed science.

In the COVID-19 crisis, we are seeing much pushback against the scientific evidence. It is the most intriguing aspect of community consultations. Communities can find alternative evidence very quickly in today's world and it is hard to shift a fixed opinion. When I reflect on the matter, I look at the climate change movement, which in a sense is a larger version of the community debates we were having. I realise we have made progress on waste management but not much. Governments are not leading on these issues. It is one of the deeply depressing things about that time in my public life.

Our solutions for intractable waste in Australia did not include a high-temperature incinerator but an eclectic mix of streamed waste types. We presented the final report to the Australian New Zealand Environment Ministers Conference and were congratulated for our creative work.

By 1991, I was feeling restless. I now understood this pattern in my life: I would feel I had made my contribution and it was now time to move on, especially if I wanted another executive job, which I was unsure about.

Despite my enthusiasm to work hard and long, the hours at the Trust were becoming tedious because of the expectations, fostered by myself, that I would be at events at the weekends and four nights a week. I was running out of energy. The financial targets I had set had been met, the fundraising was well on target, and we had the benefit of the substantial estate of Dr Thistle Stead, a conservation pioneer who established the Wirrimbirra Sanctuary at Bargo. I felt it was time for someone else to take over the Trust and secure its future in another way. I wanted to run my own business; I couldn't imagine what it would be.

Before I left the Trust, I arranged for Prince Charles to open our newest property, Merchant's House at The Rocks. It was a coup for a republican to snag the Prince, and for many Trust members it was a thrill, although some hated admitting it. I had been contacted by Michael Ball, an advertising man, to discuss a visit to Australia for Prince Charles, who had wanted to improve his profile here and test the republican sentiment. His marriage to Princess Diana was already in trouble, and while her star shone, his media coverage was constantly negative. I suggested to the Prince's private secretary that we enhance his image in the built environment by asking him to speak at a gathering sponsored by the Trust. We knew he would feel comfortable with us, and this became the plan. However, protocol and politicians got in the way. So, in the end, it was a short visit to the official opening of the Merchant's House instead.

Gordon and I were invited by His Royal Highness to a private black-tie dinner at Admiralty House on 25 January 1994. There were about twenty guests. Some of them had connections to the Prince going back to his school days. It was an unexpectedly pleasant evening. I sat next to the Prince and I found him a lively and engaging dinner companion.

My four years at the National Trust had been satisfying. There were victories, including the Trust Act of 1990 and the long fought-for introduction of tax incentives for the restoration of heritage buildings. And disappointment in losing the Trust's right to comment in the Central City Planning Committee on the redevelopment of heritage buildings. And there were many wonderful exhibitions at the S.H. Ervin Gallery, which belonged to the Trust. It remains a favourite place in my heart.

I was happy when the *Sydney Morning Herald* heritage writer, Geraldine O'Brien, wrote that during my four years as Executive Director the Trust had made its way back from the edge of extinction. As I moved on and left the people I had worked with, I felt a sense of sadness but also exhilaration at the thought of a new adventure. Best of all, my successor was my friend Elsa Atkin. I knew it was in safe hands.

The opportunity to chair the Australian Heritage Commission was a second chance for me to stay in this arena—the macro world of the National Trust. It included Aboriginal culture and heritage as part of its portfolio. I was honoured when offered the job by Senator John Faulkner in 1994.

The Commission, established in 1975, was a statutory authority for a Register of the National Estate, the list of natural and cultural places that records the sites Australia holds dear. There were more than 12,000 sites listed on the inventory, ranging from Kakadu to cattlemen's huts in the Monaro to the Afghani mosques in the Northern Territory. I think of them now as our national family photos. When we lose them, we ache, because they give us a sense of place and remind us of our heritage. They become the benchmarks for heritage places to which we subscribe.

The Commission was a distinctly Australian response to heritage conservation, and its establishment was supported across party lines. Country Party member Ralph Hunt, a farmer and future minister, said at the national reading of the Bill in 1975:

> The environment, and for that matter, the national estate surrounds all of us, it belongs to all of us. It is not for the monopoly of any one man. [Did he even think of women?] However, it is not the monopoly of any one generation, one group, one party, one government. It is ours to pollute, to destroy, to desecrate. Or it is ours to value, to preserve, and to protect, to hand on to the next generation.

Seriously, can we imagine a National Party member saying that today?

My appointment to chair the Heritage Commission was time-limited to 1998. I like the discipline of these appointments but there is often a dilemma when the government changes and you wonder if the new minister would like to appoint someone who might share their political views. When the Coalition replaced the Labor government in 1996, as much as I loved my role, I decided to offer my resignation. I advised Senator Robert Hill, the new Minister for Environment, that I was willing to exit quietly if that was his wish. I have done that subsequently when this situation arises. To my surprise, he asked that I stay on. I agreed that I would stay until the end of my term in 1998, and somehow that clarified the agenda for me. I had been given a clear assurance that I could get on with the job without political interference.

I wanted Australians to feel emotional about heritage, to feel it in their heart so much that they would fight for it. And I wanted to test the connection between what was on the register and popular views about heritage. In 1997, we ran a competition called Places in the Heart, where we asked Australians to describe their favourite heritage places in no more than a hundred words. It attracted nearly three thousand entries. A further great result, from my point of view, was that ninety per cent of the places nominated were already on the register.

Natural and cultural environments come together with social values to give us our sense of place. The integrated approach of the Commission was reaffirmed, and the register was validated. But I had plenty of heat. The proposed listing on the register of the Holsworthy army area provoked strong feelings and became a hot political issue, as it was being considered as a second Sydney Airport site by the Coalition government. All the usual accusations followed, such as I was a Labor apparatchik stopping the government from getting on with business. By then, I really was not fussed by these things. I had a clear mandate to get on with my statutory responsibilities. And the Commission members were united in our views.

Holsworthy was an outstanding place, and the Department of Defence had cared for it very well. The local land council invited the commissioners to visit Aboriginal sacred sites there. They guided us through exquisite and pristine bushland and convinced us that our intensive investigative and assessment system had been right. History records that Holsworthy did not become the site of the second airport and is now listed on the register for its natural, historic and Aboriginal heritage. And, of course, the wonderful thing about these battles is that when they are won, people care even more because they become de facto owners of the public estate, which is what we all want as conservationists.

During my time at the Heritage Commission, a single gunman killed thirty-five people at or around Port Arthur historic site in Tasmania. The date was Sunday, 28 April 1996. The site was on the Register of the National Estate, and most of the murders took place inside the Broad Arrow Café. The majority of people killed were day tourists, although some worked and lived in the area. Like most Australians, I was deeply shocked. It is impossible to comprehend such a massacre in Australia.

The morning after, Sharon Sullivan, the Executive Director of the Commission, and I started thinking about what this could mean from a heritage point of view, and how we could best contribute to the situation at Port Arthur, which was now closed. Compared with a loss of human life, the idea of heritage could have seemed trivial. But my experience after the earthquake in Newcastle convinced me that neither massacres nor earthquakes should be followed by obliterating the evidence of the disaster, no matter how painful. We need our memories, and our sense of place is assisted by evidence.

In a radio interview on 7ZR Hobart, I responded to calls to remove all traces of the Broad Arrow Café by saying that by doing so you won't obliterate the pain; it won't take away the memories, and the gross inhumanity of it may not be remembered in the right way either. We have to have a bit more time. It is hard to speak over the pain barrier, no one can understand that better than the victims and their families as well as the staff, the people who were there that day, who were confronting its horror. At the Commission, we wondered if all these interests could be brought together—survivors, witnesses, heritage managers, local residents and more.

Two weeks after the event, Sharon and I visited Port Arthur, and at a media conference called for a delay on the demolition of the Broad Arrow Café, pending a mature appraisal of historical and cultural significance. Against all the emotional odds, we persuaded the Tasmanian Premier, Tony Rundle, to agree.

Even two weeks after the event, visiting Port Arthur was a scarifying experience. I could feel my gut heaving as we walked around the café. At its best, Port Arthur had been full of poignant memories. And I remembered how moved our family had been when we had been tourists there in 1988. But this was really different.

The outstanding results of the Port Arthur tragedy was the decision by then Prime Minister John Howard to transform our gun legislation, and secondly to create a grant for a new interpretation visitor centre. Today the memorial garden dedicated to the thirty-five people murdered at the site on 28

April 1996—then the world's worst mass murder by a lone gunman—is spare, beautiful.

Shielded from the rest of the Port Arthur site by a row of native trees, it includes a reflection pool and the gutted walls of the Broad Arrow Café. There is little signage, just the names of the dead on an elegant wooden cross, repeated on a stone, and some engraved poetry by the late Tasmanian writer Margaret Scott. A small plaque at one entrance has a short statement about the 'devastating violent crime'. There are few details, and the gunman is not named. As a place of quiet reflection, the minimalist approach works. The garden is deeply moving. But the discretion is not just an aesthetic choice. It is also a response to the needs of the historic site's nearly two hundred staff, and the local community.

Another huge plus of being with the Commission was working with Aboriginal Australians, especially fellow commissioner Bill Jonas. Hearing his perspectives, taking advice from the people in our Aboriginal and Torres Strait Islander unit, and being exposed to Aboriginal ideas about wellness and heritage were transforming. It made me sad to think how I had been denied knowledge about Aboriginal people during my schooling. In 1995, an event held at the Aboriginal Embassy site, at the parliamentary triangle in Canberra, to mark its recognition as a site of significance, attracted wide media attention and many visitors. But people are fearful of being different, and ignorance highlights those fears. The public comments were so often deeply racist and confirmed for me it was the right action to take.

In my last year as Chair, the Commission listed some special places: the North Sydney Olympic pool (where the McCarthy family had learnt to swim) and the Homebush Bay Wetlands (once called swamps), the site of the 2000 Sydney

Olympics. It was the year the Commission's authority to identify Australia's national estate was upheld in the High Court; it would have been a landmark victory, one which I could ill afford to lose as fighting in court with public money is extremely high-risk.

On 29 January 1998, my last day as Chair of the Heritage Commission, I addressed the National Press Club, on the theme 'Heritage: Who benefits, who pays?' I was nervous despite my ease with the topic. It took me ages to look at a recording of it, and when I did I was reminded of the loyalty of friends and family, including Sam, his partner Farida, and Hamish, who came to lend support. Anne Summers, my frequent walking companion, and her partner, Chip Rolley, were there; as were Don Aitkin and Meredith Edwards from the University of Canberra, where I had been elected as Chancellor in 1996; and old colleagues from NATWAC, Evelyn Scott and Monica McMahon. And, of course, the team from the Commission whom I valued so highly. And best of all the ABC was the broadcaster. It was a satisfying way to end my involvement.

But the postscript is painful. Shockingly, in 2007 the Register of the National Estate was closed; phasing it out had begun in 2003. It was a great loss for the protection of Australia's natural and cultural environment.

CHAPTER 15

Women's business

Nothing has ever been achieved by the person who says it can't be done.

Eleanor Roosevelt

Feminism is not the property of the women's movement. It is a state of mind. It is democracy in action. I'm going to prove that you can run a business with feminist principles and make money.

Sandra Yates,
The Wit and Wisdom of Famous Australian Women

In December 1993, Gordon and I decided to explore Malaysia and Singapore in a casual way by travelling on the local buses to places we hadn't been. The Cameron Highlands, Ipoh and Penang were on the list, and these places could all be done comfortably on local transport as the spirit moved us.

The trip offered a chance to test Gordon's health and capacity for international travel after his bone marrow transplant. Wolseley Castle, his detergent business, had been sold and he was concentrating on the cattle, moving from stud to beef production, and feeling confident, positive and ambitious about becoming a more significant beef producer. We found again that sense of freedom that travel always gives us, and enough quiet time to talk about our future without the anxiety such discussions had provoked pre-transplant. We also loved reconnecting with Asian culture.

We had been thinking it was time to sell Longueville. I wanted to move to the inner city. I was ready for a more urban life. Longueville had been our family space for seventeen years, but the family was changing and we no longer needed a six-bedroom house. Quentin was still living with us, as was Hamish, but Sophie and Sam had moved out, and Gordon spent most of the week at the farm.

A week before our Malaysia trip, I had found a house in Darlinghurst I wanted to buy. A beautifully renovated heritage place in a cluster of buildings that once serviced the Darlinghurst Gaol. It was due to be auctioned while we were away and I could not persuade Gordon to do an absentee bid. When we returned, we drove past to check if it was still on the market. It was and we put in a bid immediately.

I am not one for keeping property that is not used effectively. There was no sense in me living on my own in Longueville. It would be the end of an era. The end of our family living together as a unit. I would no longer be seen as the security symbol, earthed in a special place to which everyone returned. And all that was hard to let go. There is a lot of status with this. But intellectually and financially, it was the right thing to do. We would now have two spaces—our log cabin near Berrima and our smaller place in Darlinghurst, if we could secure it. Which we did.

Moving to Darlinghurst meant that Gordon took our dogs, Ruby and Otto, with him to the country. I missed them enormously. And then we started to have them week about. But there was no longer the energy of children living in the house. I was really on my own. And, it became my first home office.

Meanwhile, the National Trust's lawyers, Price Brent, suggested I might like to join their practice as CEO. They needed to make a lot of changes. They found it difficult, as most partnerships do, to create the transformation they needed. They asked me to become their Chief Executive and I agreed to start in February 1994. I would work a four-day week as I wanted some time out to develop other interests in my office at Darlinghurst.

Gordon and most of my friends counselled me strongly against working for Price Brent, saying I would be bored, I shouldn't do commercial things, as a not-for-profit sector was my habitat. But I was bugged by this idea that I was never recognised for being a good business manager. The assumption that the skills I had in managing not-for-profit entities were non-transferable was deeply offensive. I liked the idea, too, of being a non-lawyer running a legal practice. The media did as well and kept writing up that I was the first female non-lawyer in Australia to run a legal practice.

The media was encouraging when I began working at Price Brent, a medium-sized commercial legal practice, with coverage in *The Financial Review* and *The Australian*. And the future sounded interesting. I was trying hard to believe my own PR. Well, in fact, I believed it. Very big mistake. It was a good barrier to knock down. And the world did not end.

Before long, I knew I had made the wrong decision. I had disobeyed my fundamental decision-making process—I had made it with my head, rather than my heart. I should have known better. I had fallen for those feelings of inadequacy when people downplayed my career to date. So, here I was with good people, well paid, in a downtown office with parking . . . *What was wrong with me? Isn't this what I wanted?* Well, no. However, I would not be walking out.

I knuckled down to make sure that I did the best possible job for them.

Essentially, I had been hired to make changes they were finding difficult to manage. They wanted a smaller partnership base, and probably no longer the one they had in Melbourne, but the partners just could not agree on the leadership or direction of this change. It was hard for them to think corporately, despite their best intentions.

I observed and listened for a few weeks. I was really amazed that every solicitor had a separate office, where he or she dictated into a machine whose tape was dispatched to the typing pool. This assumed as little interaction with the work team as possible. Each solicitor was territorial about clients and would not think it unusual to refer them to other practices rather than another partner. This seemed to be against all the rules of marketing and teamwork. It was really an uneasy coalition of consenting adults, based on someone's idea of a gentleman's club.

I thought this might be fun after all. They knew they needed to change, or they wouldn't have hired me. The first building block was in place. My observation and analysis of the problem, together with my private awareness that I would not be there for a long time, probably made me braver or more brutal, depending on one's perspective. By September 1994, the Sydney–Melbourne partnership was demerged, the banking and financial arrangements were reorganised, the offices renovated—which involved relocating for three months—partner numbers were reduced to those who earned the requisite annual income in billable hours, and the firm's name had changed. I learnt to chase and collect debts. Once I realised that well-known names ran up huge accounts and continued to play golf on weekdays, I had no reservation whatsoever in calling them and reminding them of their debt.

In July 1994, I was invited to join a group of one hundred Australian businesswomen attending a seminar in Singapore, joining another hundred leading Asian businesswomen. The meeting was subsidised by Telstra and the Australian government and was a glamorous affair at Raffles Hotel.

Any idea that Australian women might feel sorry for their Asian sisters was quickly dispelled. We were in the company of leading women entrepreneurs who were confident, well-educated and wealthy. They also had a domestic arrangement unknown to most Australian women. I sat next to one woman at a dinner and she asked me how many servants I had, expressing surprise when I could only account for a weekly cleaner.

'Oh,' she said, admiringly, 'I think you Australian women are so strong. For my two boys, I have two maids, a cook, a chauffeur, and my mother runs the household.' I knew that being strong was not really a compliment.

Despite my misgivings about working for the partnership, I found the change of pace professionally satisfying. Another really interesting part of it—and this is something that had bugged me forever since—is that overnight I was described as a businesswoman rather than an activist or a feminist. This was none of my doing, but a reflection of the times and my role in a commercial business.

In professional terms, I was no more, nor less, into best practice than I had been at the Trust or as a non-executive director at the ABC. The difference was the perception people had between a not-for-profit, for-purpose organisation and a commercial partnership or business. Business had become fashionable for women. People thought they were paying you a compliment describing you as a businesswoman. Male colleagues expressed approval at my new role, and of course I enjoyed that. At the same time, I did not want to devalue women working in not-for-profit. I felt very conflicted.

My identity was shifting, but I never thought for one minute that there was any conflict between being a feminist activist and a businesswoman. I could not see myself working in another corporate position. I needed to create my own professional environment. It would be eclectic and opportunistic.

Setting up my own

Towards the end of 1994, I decided I no longer wanted to work for the partnership; I would tell Price Brent that I felt my mission was accomplished. I would find someone to replace me. Looking around, I could not see any new executive roles I could be interested in. I began thinking of setting up my own business. As a first step, I would register Women's Business and Corporate Good Works as trading names for McCarthy Management, our family company. I still own them.

Call it serendipity, but shortly afterwards I noticed an advertisement for expressions of interest to run a series of training programs for women attending the United Nations World Conference on Women in Beijing. This had to be Women's Business, and I decided to express my interest.

My first shot of working at home was in 1995. I loved the idea of managing my own time and space and being without the emotional responsibility of employees or family. Our Darlinghurst home was a place to nest in and develop for

Gordon and me in the next stage of our lives together. I felt as far as my income was concerned that I was flying by the seat of my pants, but I was prepared to take that risk.

A breakthrough came when Women's Business won the contract for the Beijing Seminars. Not long after that, I was invited to chair the Australian Heritage Commission as part of a three-year appointment, commencing on 30 January 1995.

I was going to be able to pay for myself. I didn't need to go to anybody's office.

Unexpectedly, I was also invited to be the Executive in Residence at the University of South Australia's International Graduate School of Management. I had no idea what it entailed. But, true to my usual form, I said yes first and thought about it later.

I would have a key involvement in public policy in heritage, education and women's issues. The Leightons bid team I had joined for the licence of the Sydney Casino had been successful. Beating Kerry Packer for this was very satisfying and it meant I had a commercial directorship as part of my responsibilities.

My wish to have an eclectic portfolio was coming together.

In January 1995, Women's Business ran its first seminar for women planning to attend the Beijing Conference. My ex-Family Planning colleague, Margaret Winn, had agreed to join me in running the seminars, and we asked Sophie to work with us part-time.

Sophie was working at Liverpool Health Centre four days a week in research. It was wonderful working with my daughter. I felt so proud of her competency, her style and her generosity. I offered her a Beijing airfare as part of the deal and felt excited that this was something we could do together. I had written to another ex-Family Planning colleague,

Lorraine Williams, who lived in Shanghai, and planned to visit her for a few days.

The Beijing Seminars took us around Australia. Kathy Townsend, the then head of the Office for the Status of Women, predicted that they would be popular. I was less sure, but she was right. Our task was to prepare the participants to contribute to the Forum dialogue and be China-sensitive and aware. To enable that, in each location we found a China expert to provide reliable and contemporary information about Chinese culture. We ate Chinese food during the seminar and insisted on chopsticks as part of the learning. We had some extraordinarily funny moments chasing rice grains.

These women were amazing and were determined to be educated and participate actively in local and world affairs. One Aboriginal woman in Alice Springs worked as a cleaner by day and studied at night with the 'University of the Air' on the ABC. She and her husband were equally committed to this learning and recorded television programs in preparation for what she called the other side of the desk she currently cleaned. When she couldn't deal with the chopsticks properly, she went home to practise, and returned the next day chopstick-perfect—an educator's dream.

The bush telegraph worked effectively. We spent no money on advertising. And we were invited by women in Papua New Guinea to go to Port Moresby and hold a pre-Beijing seminar. We said our usual twenty-group size would be appropriate and were overwhelmed when more than fifty women came to do 'the women's business with their sisters across the sea'. One could only marvel at their tenacity. They walked miles to prepare themselves for Beijing. They were acutely aware in Papua New Guinea, at that time, that the gains that women had made in the previous ten years seemed to be slipping away. We said goodbye and see you in Beijing to continue our work.

Boarding the Qantas flight from Port Moresby after the last seminar, I was feeling tired and triumphant. Margaret and I reflected on the universal struggle of mothers to improve the opportunities for their daughters. It was a major issue for participants. They were angry that even primary school education was barely accessible for most of their girls. I flashed forward to an image of Sophie, Margaret and me in Beijing, three generations of women connected through values and long friendship. I was so looking forward to Sophie meeting my PNG friends.

Sophie's story

On the plane, I decided the time had come to read *Paula*, my Mother's Day gift from Sophie. I had four straight hours ahead of me. I had already read all of Isabel Allende's novels and I was looking forward to her first memoir. I was engrossed from the beginning.

Paula, Allende's twenty-nine-year-old daughter, is in a coma, the cause of which is unknown. The prognosis is grim and the medical advice is to keep her comfortable, but Allende is warned to have no expectations that Paula will survive as the person they knew and loved. Her mother cannot accept this and sits beside her bedside, trying to reach her. She recounts family stories and retells Paula her own story in the unsuccessful hope this will reach her consciousness and activate her mind. It's a powerful story of her mother's love and I identified strongly. Paula was Sophie's age when she died.

I was sobbing as I finished it before we landed in Sydney. I was feeling unsettled and wondered how I would respond to such a situation. Would I think of a similar technique? The power of the storytelling was strong. But I wished Sophie hadn't given the book to me. I needed to call her and check she was okay. She was, and we agreed to meet at the Korean bathhouse the following Sunday.

While we were there, she told me she was feeling tired and not quite herself. I offered a mother's clichéd advice—more sleep, less alcohol, less coffee, fewer parties and more exercise, even though I did know she ate and exercised sensibly. I mentioned that her grandmother, Bette (formerly known as Audrey), and I both suffered from a rumbly gut and it was probably her genetic predisposition. We talked about plans for our trip to China. It would be our first grown-up adventure together and we were excited about sharing it.

We enjoyed our time at the bathhouse, and the next day I left for Adelaide as part of my contract as Executive in Residence at the University of South Australia. I was flying via Melbourne where I had some work, and I would get to the Adelaide Hilton late on Monday night. On Tuesday morning at six, the telephone woke me. It was Hamish.

'Don't worry, Mum,' he said, 'but Sophie is in the emergency ward at St Vincent's Hospital. She has been haemorrhaging from the bowel. If you call immediately the doctor on duty will take your call and explain what is happening.'

My guts turned to water. I moved to automatic pilot. I called the Hilton desk and asked to get me on the first flight to Sydney while I talked to the emergency ward. The news was shocking. Sophie had dangerously low blood pressure and had lost a lot of blood. Nobody seemed to know what was wrong with her.

Her friend Rob was at the hospital; he was with her when it happened. He and their other housemate David managed the ambulance journey and hospital entry with great skills. He assured me that he and Hamish would stay with Sophie until I got there. The doctor was being noncommittal, other than to say it was dangerous. I was in the air by 7 a.m. It was the longest trip. And all I could think about in the air was Paula and Isabel. *Was that gift an omen to prepare me for this? Would I find Sophie unconscious?*

Before getting on the flight, I left messages for Quentin, Sophie's friend Heidi, and Gordon, asking them to be there at the hospital. Unbelievably, not one of them was at home. I was talking to answering machines and becoming hysterical. When I reached the ward, I found her weak, barely conscious, and wired up to everything. Her blood pressure was all over the place. She kept bleeding from the bowel and there was still no diagnosis.

She was scared and so was I. I wondered what star we had crossed. I was overwhelmed by the powerful feelings of fear and love and determination that this was not to be a rerun of *Paula*. The pain was white hot. I felt like a new, vulnerable mother all over again.

The days blurred, my family and friends rallied around, the diagnosis term was Crohn's disease, which I had never heard of. It is a chronic inflammatory bowel condition but manageable if Sophie could get through this crisis. When the diagnosis was confirmed, she asked me to find out what it meant for fertility—she wanted to be a mother. I was reassured by the specialist.

As Sophie began to stabilise, there was suddenly a setback, and she was returned to intensive care. I called my mother and Quentin. It was too much for Hamish who started spinning and left. My sister Sarah, who was six months pregnant, arrived in the waiting room with chamomile tea. I thought I wanted to be on my own, but I was really grateful she was with me. A young man who had collapsed in the City-to-Surf Fun Run the previous week had just died and his family, who had been camped in the waiting room, were packing up and talking to me about it. They wished me luck as I left. I was becoming superstitious and thought this was another ominous sign.

I wished Gordon was with me, but he had the flu and couldn't come in. I was furious that he thought I could manage this alone. It was a really hard night. Sarah stayed with me, and we went in and out of the ward until the nurses suggested we try to sleep in the waiting room. Sophie was asleep. But there was death in the air, and I didn't want to leave her. The surgeon was still working, but we had agreed that surgery was the last resort. Few Crohn's sufferers get through life without it. But I was hoping Sophie could survive this attack without surgical intervention.

When the surgeon went home, I was reassured the crisis was over. The medical staff advised us to go home too, and a security guard insisted on escorting Sarah and me to the car. It was 4 a.m. and he was worried about our safety in Darlinghurst. I didn't dare tell him I lived around the corner.

In all the drama, there were memorable and tender moments. Watching Hamish and Sam massage their sister's legs when they were grossly distended and swollen from fluid retention and arguing about which was the most effective way to massage. The relief on her face when the physician assured her that her fertility would be okay. I was so glad. I wanted my children to love children. And when I took her home and put her in my bed, that overwhelming feeling of safety and gratitude that Sophie's story was not to be the same as Paula's.

I counted my blessings that we are an intact, family unit, with loving friends who helped us through. The mother–daughter gig did not happen in Shanghai, and Sophie has still not met the women from Papua New Guinea. We played out our survival in Darlinghurst and the fifty thousand women who gathered in Beijing did not include Wendy and Sophie. But my daughter survived. And that was everything.

She's a businesswoman now

In the first six months of 1995, as the Executive in Residence at the University of South Australia, I spent three of the agreed six weeks at the Adelaide Hilton. It was like being on sabbatical, really. Reading articles that I had saved up for years and talking management and business at the University and the Casino—it seemed like the perfect portfolio.

Women's Business was successful. And work was coming in. But how much work did I really want? The phone call that my daughter was in Emergency brought home that nothing matters more than the safety and wellbeing of the people you love.

The seminars had also been successful, but I continued to find it difficult to hustle for business. I always reflect on my upbringing and the mottos: *Good girls are not bold girls; Nice girls wait to be asked to dance; Don't be pushy for yourself* . . . These can be seen as a disadvantage in business. But there was one instance during this year when I ignored those refrains and made a successful career move that improved my portfolio and income.

I was in residence at the Management School in Adelaide when I was called by AIC, a conference company, to endorse and approve a female management consultant they were planning to bring to Australia for a series of seminars on being a successful woman in business. I read her resumé and the proposed program, thinking, *this is ridiculous! Why do we need an American woman to tell us how to be an Australian woman in business?*

I took a deep breath and called them back to say that I would neither endorse the consultant nor the idea. Why wouldn't they ask an Australian woman to run the course? The young woman on the phone was astonished.

'Well, who would you suggest?' she asked.

'Well, I could do it,' I heard myself say. After all, was I not now being described in the Australian media as a businesswoman?

'Oh,' she said, 'well, send me your resumé and we will discuss it further.'

I didn't really expect to hear from her again, but I sent the resumé, feeling both elated and anxious that I actually dared to put myself forward. I had read the texts, had the experience, and I wanted to be back in teaching mode. I am still a teacher—I just work in different classrooms. I thought the worst outcome was that they would say no. I could live with that. But after a few days, I was asked to prepare a short draft outline about what I might teach. This was accepted, and in a surprisingly short time I was on the circuit with a glossy A4 brochure extolling my skills. I would soon find out if I was worth anything in the marketplace.

I was.

For the next three years, from 1995 to 1998, I ran seminars in Sydney, Melbourne, Canberra, Auckland, Singapore and Wellington. Usually, the groups were limited to twenty. And until the day before the event, I would have no idea of their composition. The age range of participants could be twenty years, and the occupational experience base was broad. I focused on generic executive leadership for women, but we spent a lot of time working out how to maintain a balance between their professional and private lives.

I just loved working with these groups. I loved the rush that comes when you try to turn them into a group, and the trust that builds up so that they share their experiences and help solve other people's problems. Some, of course, wanted a how-to manual, but that is training not education, and manuals can be found on the internet. I prefer learning through narrative. Women's stories are a powerful and reaffirming format for such learning. They help provide the script for the documentary we live in as we challenge old ideas about business and where we can contribute.

The conferences took me full circle. I was back in front of a group, only this time it wasn't history or geography or sex education, but business. It still meant thinking on my feet, and homework preparation. And for three years it was an important and satisfying part of my portfolio. Then one day, in mid-1998, I thought, *I don't want to do this anymore, I'm talked out, I need a break.*

When I created Women's Business, I had no clear vision. Various friends had helpfully suggested that I create a brochure but I couldn't imagine what I would put in it. I liked the sound and the provocation of its name. Much of the work I had done in the last four years had been concerned with finding pathways for women in executive life. The AIC conferences, numerous speaking gigs, corporate in-house seminars, and the servicing of the group Chief Executive Women (of which I was President in 1996) have all been part of the process in defining Women's Business. I remain of the view that most business is women's business; we just haven't been seeing it that way.

Because I was leading a portfolio life, I had every opportunity to follow my heart between 1995 and 2000. I loved the flexibility of this work and there was definitely no turning back. What it enabled was an opportunity to respond to contemporary events if I wanted to be engaged; I had no restraints imposed by employers. I could be myself and choose my roles. I could spend time campaigning for the Australian Republican Movement. As I did.

Brian Babington from the Heritage Commission and I talked about what was next for both of us as our terms were coming to an end. I was going to work on the State of the Environment Report in 2001. My years at the Heritage Commission had given me a heightened sense of the importance of Aboriginal issues and history. I wanted to persuade corporations to support reconciliation. We agreed that Corporate Goodworks would be a good banner for us. The essential proposition was to find funding companies to match their desires to do good works in the community. It was a pacesetter for its time and many other businesses spiralled out of it.

I had been working in Citigroup doing a cultural analysis for the CEO, who was concerned about the paucity of women's promotion through the ranks. Brian Babington and I decided to build on this and put together a proposition around a reconciliation program for the bank under the auspices of Corporate Good Works. Even as a non-executive director the situations I had encountered in this area required a high level of financial literacy, and significant experience in mergers and acquisitions, which I had been doing since the Family Planning days, albeit in a different sector to Citibank.

I was amused when some of my friends described me as going to the dark side by looking at this end of business. The truth was, putting Family Planning NSW into administration back then wasn't because of disputes between nurses, doctors and patients but because the place was badly run and going broke. So, it seemed to me, through Corporate Good Works, we could bring together the financial disciplines of good businesses, and the ideas of many people thinking around fairness, justice and using business skills for a better way of implementing change. And, in particular, looking at the issue of reconciliation between opposing sides.

Working from our Darlinghurst residence, all the roles I had been taking on were consuming. I had been consulting at Citibank and was the Executive in Residence at the University of South Australia. I also become a director of Plan International Australia, a child sponsorship agency, because I had a yearning to work internationally. I had worked in London and Pittsburgh, and in Asia and the Pacific in Family Planning. This was an opportunity to work with underprivileged children and their families. Quentin and I both agreed to join the Plan Board around the same time.

In 1996, I had also become Chancellor of the University of Canberra. Up to that time, there had only been two women Chancellors in Australia: Dame Roma Mitchell at the University of Adelaide and Dame Leonie Kramer at the University of Sydney. I had first joined the University Council, at the invitation of Kim Beasley, in May 1992. In the time since leaving the Higher Education Board in New South Wales in 1983, I was not especially interested in the politics of higher education. The compelling reason to agree was that Don Aitken, the Vice-Chancellor, had been my friend and mentor all those years ago at New England. I thought he was one of the best Vice-Chancellors and was having a real impact at the university.

I acknowledge I liked crashing through these barriers, but I was having some moments of imposter syndrome. *How could this be happening? Would I be taken seriously?* But I decided it was only another boundary, and I was comfortable with governance in a way that many academics aren't.

Some weeks after being offered the Chancellor role, I was in Melbourne at a management conference where the speaker was Sir Adrian Cadbury, a prominent businessman from the United Kingdom. In response to a question about the number of women on boards, he made a strong point of saying that if he was looking for women to appoint to boards, he would be looking at health and education experience as the women in those sectors had long experience in managing or governing complex bureaucracies and health and education systems. It was music to my ears.

I stayed in the role of Chancellor for ten years, being re-elected by my colleagues every two years. The role is a creative leadership task, and I liked the opportunity for policy input into the higher education sector. A Chancellor is a figurehead, a mentor to the Vice-Chancellor, and ultimately responsible for the proper management of university affairs.

There was a lot to be done to improve the governance, but there was huge resistance to the idea that a university should be in any way corporate. The Vice-Chancellor was fond of saying that universities are really a collection of craft unions who stay together for their common good. The Councils or Senates were large and clumsy; the lines of accountability were unclear and significant authority lay outside the control of the Council. The role of the Academic Board was sacrosanct. It was a time when universities were competing for international students and grappling with diversity at every level—student, subjects, government relations and competition. It was a tough time for the higher education sector and the beginning of the major international student push.

Meanwhile I loved the happiness and ritual of graduation ceremonies that came with satisfaction, optimism and pride that they had made it. Our graduations moved from the gymnasium to the Parliament House Great Hall. In my time I conducted eighty-eight ceremonies. They were special.

Star City Casino

On 12 December 1997, the *Australian Financial Review* ran an article with the title: 'A suitable job for a woman', and opened with: 'Wendy McCarthy wonders why so many people have a problem with her—a woman, God forbid—being a director of a gambling den . . .'

One of the hottest tickets in Sydney in the last few weeks had been to the opening of Star City. Being a Director, I was asked by various people to arrange an invitation or two. My male colleagues on the Board were similarly approached. However, the requests to me were inevitably followed by comments and questions about how someone with my background could possibly be a director of a casino.

Expressing opinions about the suitability of my role as a director of a casino has not been confined to such direct approaches. At a recent cocktail party, one of my friends was taken aside and asked to explain my fall from grace. (It was apparent that her responses were not important as the questioner had an established position that he was eager to share.) At Star City, I was apparently acting outside my image as social reformer and betraying my supporters and prior roles: Family Planning, Deputy Chair of the ABC, Chair of the Heritage Commission, CEO of the National Trust, Chancellor of the University of Canberra. These are good and suitable jobs for a woman like me, but God forbid a commercial board *and* a casino. How to explain it?

Not long after at another public event, a prominent ABC broadcaster, in noting and lamenting my absence from the organisation, referred to my successful time as Executive Director of the Trust, before adding that that, of course, had been before I went to the casino. It sounded to many present as though I had embraced a new outlandish cult, even though I had been in the National Trust job while also Board member of the casino without serious consequences. But why was this a matter for public comment?

Then there is the tendency to delete reference to this directorship when introducing me at public events. For instance, some months ago, at an international meeting of women entrepreneurs, I referred to the casino as a new employment option for women. A powerful and wealthy woman from Indonesia asked if I knew that gambling was forbidden by Islam and that this must be bad for my reputation. I discreetly decided not to mention the Indonesian gamblers who frequented the casino.

It seems that we are creating a new stereotype. Women can do some boards and statutory authorities, but don't mess with the big time. These are not suitable jobs for women. If some are chosen, it will be because of safe, specialist skills like law and accounting, not the more convivial, broad-based perspectives that identify many good company directors. Such attitudes defy logic and make restrictive assumptions about gender.

The truth is I accepted the invitation to join the casino board when it was a small entity making a bid for the casino licence. I liked the idea of working with Leightons, whose skills I had admired during the construction of the ABC building at Ultimo. I love creating and growing people and business. And I thought it would be fun to challenge Kerry Packer, especially as he was such a fine strategic player. Moreover, this would be a business for the future and would attract many young people. They needed a work environment that protected and developed them. I could contribute to that.

With my experience as a resident-action activist, I could help paraphrase the concerns of the local residents whose world was to be physically altered by the construction of the casino. Add to that, the excitement of a commercial business and the challenge of designing a casino in the Australian idiom. It seemed like a great opportunity.

My professional life has been dogged by advice about appropriate professional career decisions. But there is a perversity in my character which resists being stereotyped no matter how caring those around me believe their motives to be. Why do people not counsel my male colleagues about their Star City director roles?

Have we implicitly decided that some directorships should not be available to women? A casino is a people and money business. Why deny fifty per cent of the population the fun of building a business from the ground up and the opportunity of developing a career in the entertainment business of the 1990s?

Philosopher Charles Handy, who specialises in organisational behaviour and management, writes of the eclectic portfolio and the mix between professional and voluntary responsibilities. Perhaps that notion could replace the more restrictive notions of what is a suitable role for a woman who is interested in and curious about the changing definition of being Australian? And could we just occasionally be relieved of the role of God's police?

CHAPTER 16

An international life

Wherever you go becomes a part of you somehow.

Anita Desai

There is something special about living through a change of century. It encourages us to take stock. What was the best of the twentieth century? What do we hope for in the new century? It's a big New Year's Eve—a time for new resolutions for a new century.

In 2000, all my portfolio responsibilities included international activity. I was Chair of Plan International Australia, a child-focused overseas aid agency, and quickly became its nominee on the international board based in Woking in the United Kingdom. I was also Chair of the Advisory Committee of the World Health Organization Centre for Health Development (WHO Kobe Centre), a role I had accepted in 1999.

Chairing an international board of such significance was exciting, and in a sense a measure of long relationships. When people ask me how I could have ended up chairing a board in Japan, I respond that it is all about trust. The background story goes like this.

In 1976, when I was working at Family Planning, our Medical Director, Dr Sue Hepburn, was offered a speaking role in Tokyo at the International Meeting of Obstetricians and Gynaecologists to talk about maternal health and welfare. She was given two tickets and offered me one in return for helping her prepare her paper and slides for the event. I jumped at the chance.

While in Japan, we spent a week getting to know the people in the Japanese Department of Health. Our host was Dr Yuji Kawaguchi, the Director of Maternal Health and Welfare in the Japanese government. Our presentation was well received and subsequently we travelled with Dr Kawaguchi to meet many of his colleagues and supporters. Subsequently, he became the Deputy Director of WHO in Geneva.

We all stayed in touch with Yuji, who married an Australian woman and often visited Sydney. In the mid-1990s, he asked if I would be interested in chairing a new WHO Advisory Board that was being set up in Kobe, Japan. The WHO Kobe Centre was established in 1995 by the WHO Executive Board as a global research centre, and it is one of only two centres based outside Geneva that remains part of WHO's Headquarters. Its establishment, post-earthquake and -tsunami in Fukushima, was supported by local corporations, including Kobe Steel, as it was seen to be a prestigious centre. Effectively a public–private partnership—a new model for WHO.

The WHO Kobe Centre's role was to support research, capacity building and information exchange. It also responds to local interests and needs, utilising international knowledge and experience where appropriate, as well as drawing on local and national expertise for global application. Yuji had missed out on the role of Director-General of WHO and the Kobe Centre became the consolation prize.

My colleagues, highly esteemed international leaders in their field, included Dr Louis Sullivan, Director-General of

Morehouse College in the United States, and Dr Kenneth Kaunda, the first President of the Independent Zambia. It was an amazing three years, with some spectacularly good work done on health promotion and disease prevention. One of my close friends from the early days at Women's Electoral Lobby, Helen L'Orange, who had gone on to have a distinguished career in the status of women affairs, joined me for a year or so as a consultant. At various times, other Australians worked with us too.

The Centre convened significant conferences and published research on oral health, reproductive health and women's health, the health of cities, special studies on diabetes, ageing, and various chronic diseases. I found myself on the overnight flight to Kobe many times. Apart from reimbursement of expenses, I received no payment, but the rewards were significant and being a volunteer in these roles was highly regarded in the countries I worked in.

Plan International

I joined the Plan International Australian Board in 1996 and Plan International Board in 1998. Plan is a global, independent development and humanitarian organisation, and even back then it was operating in seventy-five countries, with the aim of achieving a just world that advances children's rights and equality for girls. As one of the oldest and most experienced organisations in the field, Plan knew there was nowhere where girls were treated as equals. Plan works beside children, young people, supporters and partners to tackle the root causes of the injustices facing girls and the most marginalised children.

Plan began by providing food, accommodation and education to refugee children whose lives had been orphaned or displaced by the Spanish Civil War. Its founder was John Langdon-Davies, who conceived the idea of a personal relationship between a child and a sponsor—a model that puts the child at the centre. This remains the core of what Plan does today. It is a truly outstanding organisation.

The Australian office of Plan International ran overseas programs supporting children in more than twenty-five countries, using the particular methodology associated with Plan, which was the sponsorship program that encouraged a relationship between the sponsor and child. Plan addresses the immediate needs of children dealing with poverty, inequality and disaster, working to empower children and their families in the long term. It is committed to the rights of the child, and it recognises the power and potential of every one of them. We had the backing of Australians who wanted to see a fair world for children and equality for girls. It was a wonderful, inspiring organisation to work with.

In 1998, I became Chair of Plan International Australia. At the time, it was not travelling well. We were in default on the internationally agreed costs that could be allocated to marketing and communication. I thought the rules were too restrictive. After much reflection I called John Stuckey, the CEO of McKinsey Australia, and asked if he would help us pro bono. I could see we were headed for disaster. We were running out of cash and not following the international marketing protocols—which we saw as totally inappropriate for us and impossible to achieve.

The advice John Stuckey gave us was tough. He said to me after our meeting that he would provide a couple of smart young staff as interns pro bono, but that we probably wouldn't be able to achieve the necessary reductions. I was determined that we would. We hired a new CEO, Ian Wishart, and followed a very disciplined plan that helped Plan Australia to get back on its feet financially.

During my twelve years with Plan, I led a lot of change. The relationship I built with McKinsey in Australia I took worldwide. They worked with Plan International on its new look and governance structure. It was fantastic to work on such a big palette. And being a volunteer in an NGO of that size meant there was lots of opportunities for me to do hands-on work that the existing management knew it did not have the capacity to do.

I can't imagine how many hours I spent on Plan business—probably the equivalent of a year's work. I remember travelling forty hours for a meeting in Santiago and then on to Albania, distances not even imaginable by my European colleagues. In 1998 I was part of the aftermath team to Hurricane Mitch, called the deadliest Atlantic hurricane in over two hundred years. In Tegucigalpa, the capitol of Honduras, I worked with a film crew covering the devastation to use the footage to appeal for funds to rebuild the schools.

In Sri Lanka, after the 2004 Indian Ocean earthquake and tsunami produced unimaginable destruction, Plan Australia played a significant role in reconstruction. There is humility that comes with knowing that you could return to your home safely, and a sadness that once the cameras had left these communities will be on their own.

Plan focused on the needs of the children. I think of a little poignant moment in a school in Sri Lanka, maybe eight days after the deadly tidal wave, and the girls have their hair styled into thick plaits. We decided the best strategy was to get kids straight into school, as it was the safest place for them to be.

They are wearing white school uniforms and you think, *how is it that the mothers get their boys and girls to school looking the way they do?* You would have to have the hardest of hearts, and the narrowest of minds, not to feel for those parents trying to do the best for their children. It is motivating and connects you to a common humanity.

Plan returned to Vietnam after a long absence, and the Australian Board went to visit for a week. It was an immersion program and a very effective way to receive feedback that could inform our support for their national policies and learn. The Vietnamese cabinet comprised many who were graduates of the University of Canberra; some had been there during the Colombo Plan days, and they were keen to meet our Board and share their insights into the experience of the country as it moved out of communism to controlled capitalism. My two sponsored children at that time were in Vietnam and it was a moving moment to meet them and their extended family, observe their enterprise and energy as a result of their being given a bit of a hand up.

From 1998 to 2009, Plan was a continuing thread in my life. My children sponsored children too, as did many of my friends, and it kept us in touch with the rest of the world. It introduced me to the writings of Nicholas Kristof, who now writes for the *New York Times*. It took me to meetings in New York boardrooms, to the King of Spain, to palaces, and to shocking urban slums and pop-up baby health centres made of corrugated iron, with water dripping down to keep them cool, but all done for love and the life of children.

When he was about six, my grandson's teacher asked me to speak to the class about Plan. She said that Elias told her I looked after all the children in the world. I thought that was just about the nicest thing. I did go and talk to the class, and

I reminded myself why I could never have been a teacher in primary school—thirty minutes with twenty-five wriggling five-and-a-half year olds is a very different prospect professionally to thirty-five minutes with twenty-five adolescents. I'll take the latter any day. But it was good to see Elias being proud of his grandma for looking after all the children in the world.

The Plan International Board also took me all over the world. When I left Plan in 2009, it was with great sense of affection and respect for the organisation, and a sense of privilege that I had the opportunity to take such a leadership role internationally. I was the Vice-Chair internationally for six years.

I sometimes wonder how I managed to sustain my role in Plan. But when I was offered the International Chair, even with extra support, I realised how far away Australia was from the rest of the world, and how much that distance matters. Being monolingual and twenty-four hours away from Europe I thought it would be too hard. I declined. I was sad about that, but it was the right decision.

I miss Plan. It was an international conversation. I remain friends with many of my peer group from then. I can find someone to have dinner with even now in Stockholm, Copenhagen, Helsinki, London, New York, Los Angeles, the Hague, and pretty well anywhere in the Netherlands, Japan and Thailand. And the miracle of it all is that Plan is modest and voluntary and totally committed to its purpose to improve the lives of children

Writing about Plan during the COVID-19 pandemic, I feared for the impact and implications for the lives of women and children worldwide, especially in Africa, where you could see the infections rising and the roll-out of a vaccine delayed. The work is never done, the millennial goals have not been reached, but there was improvement through Plan. You become a footnote in history for your contribution. You have done your best and you have been part of a common humanity.

That is enough, after all.

Pacific Friends of the Global Fund

In 2008, I expanded my international program by becoming the Chair of the Pacific Friends of the Global Fund. I knew that I would be leaving Plan in 2009 because I had introduced the rule that no one can be on the board for more than nine years. I wondered if—and how—I would replace it.

Ever since I did my first overseas job in Fiji in 1978, I always wanted to be part of the way Australia did international aid and development. I wanted a seat at that table. And I really wanted it as close to the frontline as possible. I knew that I would not be able to be a full-time executive, but I could be an enabler, helping people in those countries to find their voices and making sure they got what they needed, often through Australian aid.

In 2000, the idea of a global fund was discussed at a G8 Summit in Okinawa, Japan, at the time I was working at the Kobe Centre. As Kobe was part of WHO, we heard about the ideas expressed by Kofi Annan, then the Secretary-General of the United Nations, who said, 'When I first mooted the idea of a global fund, people said I was dreaming. I love dreams. It always starts with a dream.' And so, it did.

The Global Fund to Fight AIDS, Tuberculosis and Malaria was created in 2002. Its mission was to invest the world's money to defeat these three diseases in whatever way possible. Cure or control.

The Global Fund, as it says on its website, 'arose from a wellspring of grassroots in political advocacy, coming face to face with the imperatives of global leadership. AIDS, TB, and malaria are all preventable and treatable'. But solving the problem requires the commitment not only of world leaders and decision-makers, but also of those working on the ground to help the men, women and children living with these diseases.

Bill Bowtell, who has had a long history in HIV/AIDS policy, was really interested in this program. He wanted Australia to be part of the Global Fund. He asked me if I would chair it, and he would become the CEO. Geneva welcomed the offer of Australia to lead the Pacific contribution. These things don't usually happen quickly, and it wasn't until 2009 that the Global Fund in the Pacific was launched in Sydney by Governor-General Quentin Bryce.

Our media release said: 'The Global Fund warmly welcomes the launch of Pacific Friends, a new advocacy organisation, founded in order to create and sustain visibility and awareness of a global fund across the Pacific region. And to build political and financial support for the organisation, and the fight against these three diseases.' I had bypassed the AIDS epidemic in my work—by the time I left Family Planning, the worst thing we thought you could get was herpes. I was pleased to be back in this conversation/discussion and advocacy role. I could see opportunities to connect Plan, the Fund and Kobe Centre. My Plan contacts would be valuable.

Hansard records Senator Marise Payne welcoming the formation of Pacific Friends of the Global Fund:

> It is a very important new initiative in the fight against three terrible diseases which cause extraordinary suffering and

very significant numbers of deaths in our region particularly, which is a matter of great interest to this organisation.

The Global Fund to Fight AIDS, Tuberculosis and Malaria was established in 2002 as a unique, global public-private partnership dedicated to attracting and disbursing additional resources to prevent and treat HIV-AIDS, TB and malaria. It was developed after the action of the United Nations and, in particular, then Secretary-General Kofi Annan, who called for the creation of a global fund to channel additional resources to fight those three diseases. The UN General Assembly committed to it and, soon after, the G8 endorsed and helped finance it. It was launched in 2002, and the first round of grants was then approved to 36 countries. Since then, the global fund has become the main source of finance for programs to fight these three diseases. In fact, it has committed more than $15 billion in 140 countries for prevention, treatment and care programs. It is designed to be a new and better approach to international health funding. It is a partnership between governments, civil society, the private sector and affected communities. It works in close collaboration with other bilateral and multilateral organisations, supporting their work through substantially increased funding.

The global fund benefits very much from the work of the friend's organisations, and this one hopefully will be no exception. It is chaired by Wendy McCarthy and includes amongst its number Andrew Forrest, the Rt Hon. Helen Clark, Professor Tony Cunningham from Westmead Hospital, the Hon. Michael Kirby, Dr Nafsiah Mboi from the Indonesia National AIDS Commission and Sir Peter Barter, the former health minister of Papua New Guinea, to name just a few. It is a group of very determined people

> who are committed to ensuring that it does an effective job in its advocacy. I am very honoured and very pleased to have been invited to join this group as one of the inaugural Pacific Friends of the Global Fund.
>
> It would not have been possible without the support of the Lowy Institute for International Policy or the Bill & Melinda Gates Foundation. The support of the foundation in particular is beyond invaluable; it is almost incalculable. The Pacific Friends is based at the Lowy Institute in Sydney. Its inaugural executive director is Bill Bowtell, known to many of us in this parliament. He is also the Director of the HIV-AIDS Project at the Lowy Institute. I know Bill, I know his commitment and I know he will do an outstanding job. The work of the fund is in all of our interests and worthy of our strong support. It is a very important regional initiative and one of which I am delighted to be a part. I thank the inaugurators of the Pacific Friends of the Global Fund for that opportunity.

Pacific Friends was one of the strong voices communicating to donors the importance of financing the future of so many people in the Pacific region. Bill and I were a good team. We managed to receive support from the Bill & Melinda Gates Foundation through a grant worth almost $1 million. The Gates Foundation had been a long-time supporter of the international fund. The President of the Bill & Melinda Gates Foundation's Global Health Program says, 'The Global Fund is one of the best and kindest things people have ever done for one another. It is a fantastic vehicle for scaling up access to effective tools, and it has already helped prevent millions of unnecessary deaths.'

When we used to have our World AIDS Day function,

it was always fun to do something dramatic. One of our more spectacular moments was to have Bono on World AIDS Day, with a lit-up Sydney Harbour. The photographs tell the story—Prime Minister Julia Gillard, NSW Premier Kristina Keneally, and Chair Pacific Friends Wendy McCarthy. A dream, really. Three women doing their best and a night with Bono—such fun, and effective.

There were other memorable moments at Pacific Friends. The Bono concert, the World AIDS Day launch at the Opera House by the Governor-General Quentin Bryce, with Sir Elton John performing. The use of music and celebrity was a key part of Bill's skills in bringing people around the world together, and it is something that I have always admired. Not just to stay in the prescribed box that says this is overseas aid and development, therefore deadly serious, people die. But to say there are many reasons for celebration.

People are better off than they were twenty years ago—malaria and AIDS are very much on the decline. And because the arts are so important to the transmission of messages, artists can tell their stories, and particularly since the first AIDS concerts in the 1990s with Bono, Bob Geldof and Elton John. Gaining access to these people was a great benefit to the cause and kept reinforcing the message.

In 2009, I visited America as the Chair of the Pacific Friends of the Global Fund and I sent the following note home of my experience:

> The UN General Assembly is meeting this week so the Global Fund decided to take advantage and hold its meeting in parallel. The big names are in the US this week.
>
> Last night I went to a cocktail party hosted by Mr Peter Chernin, ex-CEO of News Corporation; Dr Barry Bloom,

ex-Harvard Professor of Public Health and current advisor to the Global Fund; and Mr Tom Freston, high-profile NY businessman. The guest of honour was Mrs Carla Bruni-Sarkozy, wife of the French President. Beautiful home, beautiful paintings and beautiful people. I watch approximately 100 people who were there mingle and talk and recognised many—Rupert and Wendy Murdoch were there offering their support to the Global Fund. Michel Sidibe CEO of the Global Fund, Queen Rania of Jordan, Jeffrey Sachs an American economist, and of course Madam Bruni, who in her pumps and sleek dress managed to look incredibly chic and French. People applauded her decision to be the HIV/AIDS ambassador for women and children for the fund.

It was fascinating to hear Peter speak about the Global Fund as the most efficient business proposition. He said, 'I come to this from the point of view of business and I see an efficient investment, I see measured outcomes and I see change and my initial interest was in malaria and I have watched that very carefully and I can see the difference. As we move towards the replenishment cycle, I want to urge people to encourage their governments to continue to support the Global Fund and ask that the private sector continues its support.'

Being New York, there were 3 cocktail parties. I managed 2. I left that cocktail party to attend the next one at the Millennium where the Gates Foundation and the Global Fund had hosted a small group for the Pacific Friends of the Global Fund.

Professor Jeffrey Sachs arrived and spoke passionately about the efficacy and commitment of the fund and the need to not be complacent because, in his words, 'this is as good

> as it gets in development' and any suggestion that we do not increase and continue would mean it's like going backwards again. It is extraordinarily important that we keep this kind of pressure on.

I stayed Chair of the Global Fund until 2014, when, again, I applied my rule of not staying too long. I could never pretend that after five years with the Global Fund I had found the politics of Geneva, and in particular the meetings of Geneva, easy to deal with. But I found ways to be effective, and to connect people. And to support Australia's aid program take its money and its ideas to the rest of the world.

All these international roles required changes in my domestic life. An international career is not easily compatible with a domestic family life. There needed to be flexibility; it was just a matter of how we organised it.

CHAPTER 17

Our family and the 21st century

> To love what you do and feel that it matters—how could anything be more fun?
>
> Katherine Graham,
> the first female CEO of a Fortune 500 enterprise

Our family was in a happy place as we moved into the new century, despite a residual sadness I had about the failure of the republican referendum in 1999. I had been looking forward to starting the twenty-first century with a clear plan for Australia becoming a republic.

In March 2000, my memoir *Don't Fence Me In* was published. It was an emotional day for me, at many levels. I was thrilled and proud to be a real author. I had already written or edited five books. But this was different, it was personal, it was political, and it was my story. My memoir.

The weeks before it had been published, however, were painful. My mother thought it was a vanity project and asked that she not be mentioned in it. Seriously? How can I have just arrived without a mother? She hired a lawyer to stop the publication. She claimed it was made up, but she could never really identify what part of it was untruthful. The publisher offered every opportunity to discuss her concerns, but to no avail. I had to go very deeply into myself to think about whether I would stop the publication. That was the moment I decided I was not going to be bullied. My mother asked for a couple of changes, which I agreed to. I didn't want to offend her, but I wanted to tell my story.

The day of the launch was a very happy one. I chose the S.H. Ervin Gallery at the National Trust, which is the old Fort Street Girls High School, and a space with many women's stories in it. It was a contented place for me during my time at the National Trust. My dear friend Quentin Bryce launched the book.

Phillip Sametz from ABC Classic FM and the conductor and director of the Mell-O-Tones sang 'Don't Fence Me In'. There was a fun moment when my friends formed a queue and kicked their heels up while singing along. We all thought we were The Andrews Sisters. I wore a fabulous purple suede suit. We had scones, tea and coffee, and sold over a hundred books. It felt good.

My mother didn't come to the launch, and she forbade all the children and grandchildren from attending any events connected with the promotion of the book. Fortunately, most of them ignored the instruction and celebrated with me wherever I turned up in a country town, or somewhere near them. An unexpected bonus in the months following the launch was the number of relatives who made an appearance when I was visiting regional New South Wales. Family I didn't know much or anything about, and I had never met. My mother didn't like my father's family, so we never had anything to do with them, although I was very close to my Nana Ryan. Cousins came out of the woodwork, bought half-a-dozen books, gave me their contact details and sent

Christmas cards. I learnt that Crohn's disease was in the family.

Meanwhile we were looking forward to the Sydney Olympics in September. I had been working closely with the Lord Mayor, Frank Sartor, for two years, chairing the Look of the City Committee. I was also a member of the Olympic Urban Design Panel and the Olympic Public Art Committee. It was a great experience and I was looking forward to being a tourist in my own town.

As it happened, the Olympics was a glittering event. The weather was perfect, the sun shone, the harbour sparkled, Sydneysiders were generous, kind and thoughtful to visitors, the new train system to the Olympic village worked, and everything looked beautiful. It was a heady time. No Australian will ever forget the moment that Cathy Freeman entered the Stadium.

The newly pregnant Sophie and I watched the hockey grand final together, which Australia won. Hockey is a shared love, and that game remains a little cameo in our lives.

Turning sixty—post Olympics

By late 2001, our new farmhouse had been built and I could see another life emerging. A satellite went on the roof under one of the new federal plans to encourage people to start business in regional Australia. I created a beautiful office space in our home, looking out to rolling paddocks with cattle grazing. I started a garden and improved my cooking, and became a fetishist of fresh food—I think I always was. And, once again, the dining room table became the centre of the lives of our friends. I can't think of how many campaigns, introductions, long lunches and dinners have since been held at that table.

But after six months of commuting and occasionally checking into the visitor's room at the Women's College where Quentin was at the time Principal, I realised it was good and fun for everyone else—*oh, yes, Mum and Dad are back home together again, so lovely, so romantic*—but it actually wasn't that good for me, which was quite a revelation. I had gone into that spiral, which so many women do, of trying to please everyone in the family, returning to being Mother Earth, pushing the career behind. I was nearly sixty! Time to retire. *But why?* I finally asked myself. The nuclear family has graduated from home. *What was I doing and how was it going for me?*

I needed to acknowledge that driving up and down the highway wasn't much fun when I had to do it two or three times a week. I'm a people person. My business is all about people, I need to talk to my clients. I felt I was living in a car or out of a suitcase. I had imagined Gordon and I would be having cups of tea in the afternoon when he came in the from the paddocks, which turned out to be a dream—he was ready for a Scotch and an early supper, and I was usually on a conference call.

So, before the dream became sour, I had to decide whether this was the life I wanted after sixty. The answer was an unequivocal no. I wanted an urban weekly life, with a country weekend, and I accepted that Gordon wanted a country life with an occasional city weekend.

As by now we had sold our Darlinghurst home, we agreed I would find a one-bedroom apartment in Potts Point to rent. I needed to do this to discipline myself to not turn it into another home. It was a place where I operated my city life and increasing business travel, particularly the international work.

And so, for the next fifteen years, I commuted. I would travel to the farm on Friday afternoons, listening to Richard Glover and the Friday Show on ABC radio. Coming back on Sunday nights listening to FM and my other favourite Radio National talk programs.

We rediscovered the weekend. Within a year, the farmhouse at Mundi Mundi was well established in the new rhythm of our lives. It was Gordon's favourite home and as permanent occupier he was the primary caretaker. It became a happy meeting place for family and friends for seventeen years.

It was perfect. We took up cycling. Weekends were dinners together and a movie, some shopping on Saturday maybe, or a bike ride, friends to lunch or to stay overnight. It felt like a charmed life. We were finally honest that I really didn't need a social handbag and nor did he. I put the ribbons on the cows at the Sydney Easter Show when he won, which he did often, but by and large I wanted the ribbons for myself. I wanted to do other things.

These arrangements challenged some people, who would ask my friends if Gordon and I were still married? Yes, we were. We were just designing our marriage differently. I learnt to operate and reflect on what it is to be a woman of sixty, effectively on my own.

In January 2001, Elias Green was born. He was perfect. I became a grandmother. Everything else faded from view. The rush of love when this little boy was born to Sophie and Tony was something totally unexpected. Like a second chance at love. His birth gave me a renewed sense of purpose and wellbeing, just like motherhood had. I began feeling confident and purposeful about the future.

Some of my peers were giving up work to look after the new grandchildren. I had no intention of doing that.

However, I needed to think through how I could be the best grandmother to this family. I offered to be the first emergency call and, if required, would drop everything. But I would not be ending my professional life to be a grandmother any more than I ended my professional life to be a mother. We decided the biggest gift we could give to Sophie and Tony was to move into their house when necessary to let them go on holidays without their children (yes, more followed), secure in the knowledge that we would care for them.

Some very wise woman said to me when I first became a mother, 'Just remember you married your husband, not your children.' Does it sound hard? Maybe it does to some. But to have a healthy and strong marriage, in which to raise children, requires time alone with one's partner. It is the great gift of grandparents to be able to give parents that time. We wanted to do that for Sophie and Tony.

In July of 2001, Elias Green attended my sixtieth birthday He was six months old. We celebrated at the Clock Hotel, then owned by the Green family, and had sixty guests. It was great to look around the room and to see the many diverse faces from different parts of my life.

In September 2002, Lara Green was born. Our first granddaughter and more love to be part of. Happily, she met her great-grandmother, Bette, who died just a couple of weeks later—circle closed. As weak as she had been at that time, I could see my mother's joy when Sophie walked in with her baby girl. I wanted to yell at her and say, *Mum, just let it go, and say how proud you are of all of us. We are here, four generations.* She was in charge of that moment and she could not give us the feedback we craved. After Lara, there was Aidan, another September baby who sadly my mother did not meet.

Over the next ten years both Hamish and Sam were

married—wonderful and happy events. Sam's wedding to Aline in Italy 2012 brought the Aussies and the Germans together. Their son Luca was best boy and some months later Freya was born. Our world was full—five grandchildren.

I carried those babies with me in my heart when I found myself in strange countries as I travelled the world with Plan. And I remember a moment in Delhi in India, in what was a terrible slum, entering a new daycare centre Plan had opened by walking over foetid water on shaky wooden structures. It was a day of searing heat, and the centre had corrugated iron for walls and the roof, a little gap in between to get the air through. And lots of little babies lying like a zipper, head to toe. Its existence, though, meant that mothers could go to work knowing their children were safe.

I picked up one little girl. She was the same size as Elias. I said to the carer, 'How old is this little girl?' She was one. Elias was three months at the time. It reinforced my commitment that every child should have the opportunities in life that Elias was having. The right to nutrition when the brain and body are developing. The right to health care. All the offers promised by the Convention on the Rights of the Child. The Rights my grandchildren enjoy.

I thought of the photographs of my grandchildren digging in the dirt, looking at kangaroos, riding in the tractor, sitting on the motorbike—the luckiest of children. I remember one of my grandsons explaining to his class at show and tell that his grandfather had a couple of tractors and a few motorbikes, his little chest exploding with pride at the excitement of a grandpa who could do all these things.

It reaffirmed my determination to keep working for all the other grandchildren of the world. Being part of Plan seemed the best way I could do that.

CHAPTER 18

Money for our causes

> There could be a powerful international women's rights movement if only philanthropists would donate as much to real women as to paintings and sculptures of women.
>
> Nicholas D. Kristof

Finding money for women's causes has always been challenging. Few of us are individually wealthy and many of us are not much interested in fundraising. We are so used to giving our time to community matters that we have come to believe that this is enough. It is not. As I learnt at the National Trust, we have to be financially numerate and responsible. There are no shortcuts, and we must back ourselves as men have always done.

Back in 1995, I had been approached by Rosemary Foot, Deputy Liberal Leader, to chair the Royal Hospital for Women Foundation, I agreed. Rosemary had been so supportive at the National Trust. There had been a huge community swell of anger and protest when the NSW government announced that the Women's Hospital at Paddington was to close. People from all over New South Wales petitioned and protested. The central concern was that there would be no women's hospital in the eastern suburbs, where I now lived.

Royal Women's had a fine tradition of service and research,

and finally the state government agreed to relocate and rebuild the hospital at Randwick. The funds allocated were insufficient and the community was asked to assist. It really was a disgraceful proposition.

We initially set a fundraising target of $5 million. When our feasibility study by the Everald Compton's team suggested we could probably find $10 million, we doubled the target. It was a great project, lots of fun, and two years later we had achieved our target.

Although I acknowledge with gratitude the donors were mostly male, the askers were women. It was steep learning curve as we became bolder and bolder in our requests and preparing our proposals. All the team got over their angst about asking for money, as it was for good causes.

When the target was achieved, I left the Foundation. I had done my job and there were other people who were happy to take over. It was my second major fundraising project and it reminded me how I do love that chance to match values with funds. It also was a warning of the future and the reliance on philanthropy and community fundraising for what were provided without question by government.

The magical outcome of this campaign was that women in the eastern suburbs had a place to birth near home. It reinforced my belief that if the idea is good enough, you will eventually find money to back it.

The Sydney Community Foundation

The establishment of the Sydney Community Foundation seemed like a good idea at the time. In 2003, I was asked by Lynette Thorstensen from the NSW Premier's Department to support it. I agreed because I thought it would be easy to find a team of people to be part of it. In fact, it was a struggle.

Lynette now lives in France, and unsure of those early details of the foundation I asked her to send me her story. Her response is as follows:

> My first contact with the idea of establishing the SCF was in 2003, a meeting with Bill Downing of United Way Australia, and Heather Kent in my office at the then NSW Premiers' Dept. (I held the role of Director, Social Development and Environment—and I was also Director of the *Strengthening Communities Unit* in Premier's Dept.)
>
> Heather and Bill were aware of the successful operations of community foundations in the USA and Canada and thought that the model might work well in Sydney.
>
> I was struck by Heather's persistence . . . I felt pretty certain that I would have a lot of difficulty persuading the political operatives of Premier's office of the potential of such a Foundation without a convincing result from a feasibility study. This funding was found for the study from contingency funds in my *Strengthening Communities* budget, and a grant from the Myer Foundation.
>
> A board was established, initially chaired by Graham Bradley, with Wendy McCarthy appointed as Deputy Chair. (I am pretty sure I approached Wendy on behalf of the Board about joining—I could think of no one better!) Other original Directors included: Heather Kent, Christopher Breach, Elsa Atkin, David O'Connor, Neville Roach, Bill Downing, Bob Sutton, and myself representing NSW Premier's Dept.
>
> Alex Smith replaced me when I left Premier's to take a role at IAG.

I think it is fair to say that the Foundation got off to a pretty sluggish start. Sydney-based businesses were slow to engage, partly because promised connections from the recently retired business folk on the Board took some time to materialise. Wendy had privately warned me that retired captains of industry are just not the same as those at the height of their power and still actively engaged in their roles!

However, the SCF was launched on the 24th March 2004, but it was not until Wendy took over as Chair in 2006 that SCF really began to make progress. Wendy's inspired move of establishing and launching an SCF sub-fund, the Sydney Women's Fund (SWF), proved to be a watershed development, and in fact, at that time, the SWF rapidly became the strongest pillar of SCF.

Typically, Wendy put in a vast amount of work, mobilising her phenomenal network of senior women across business, government and the community sectors. The recruitment of Lucinda Brogden to the cause was a stroke of genius and Lucinda remains to this day joint patron of SWF, along with Wendy.

The initial donations to the Women's Fund were generous and it was no accident that in 2008 the fund was launched by then NSW Governor, Marie Bashir, at a very well-attended and high-profile event.

The launch of the SWF substantially raised the profile of SCF and led to a number of other sub-funds being established. Perhaps even more importantly, this period involved a careful examination of the role of the SCF, a clearer articulation of mission, and new and more compelling ways of attracting donors.

When Wendy left the Foundation in 2009 after five years . . . , handing over to Ros Strong as the incoming

Chair, the SCF was in infinitely better shape both financially and in the genuine work being carried out by its Directors. I think it is fair to say that Wendy left to Ros a Board that finally had a clear and thorough sense of its mission.

I wrote in the Sydney Community Foundation Annual Report 2009:

When we created the Sydney Community Foundation five years ago, we were optimistic that the Sydney community would support us. We had examples of other international and Australian cities where community foundations were flourishing and the idea of a foundation was compelling.

The first research indicated a level of community support and it is that which we have sought. It has been challenging, but as I write this annual report for the 2008–09 year we can finally reflect that we have become an established part of the Sydney donor community.

Sydney is a great city. Many of us who live here flourish, but the statistics tell us that is not the case for others and we still have a significant level of poverty in our community. As a public philanthropic foundation, the Sydney Community Foundation is well placed to assist donors who want to invest in the Sydney community by giving now and for the long term. It offers an opportunity to support a range of causes in their community that they care about so that Sydney can be a great, socially inclusive city.

Through the hard work of a lot of people, the SCF has engaged a number of donors, built the endowment fund and delivered $270,000 to the community of Sydney. Support has been provided to grandparents, school children, families who want to save energy, young Indigenous radio stars, basketball players, people with a disability, young people living in inner Sydney who are at risk, and women and babies escaping domestic violence. The establishment of the Sydney Women's Fund recognises the importance of investing in women and their families.

Below is Heather Kent's recount of her time at the Sydney Community Foundation:

I first heard of community foundations due to listening to a radio interview with the CEO of the Vancouver Community Foundation, when visiting family in Vancouver. I was so impressed by the concept that I wanted to get involved with a like-minded foundation back in Sydney . . . only to discover there wasn't one.

It took 1.5 years, a few research feasibility studies, grant support from the Myer Foundation and Premier's Department, as well as mentoring from the Melbourne Community Foundation, to see the Sydney Community Foundation launched in 2004 by then Premier, Bob Carr. At the launch, the SCF granted $50,000 to Midnight Basketball and Council of the Ageing's 'Grandparents Raising Grandchildren'.

Over the next 5 years, the SCF focused on attracting and assisting donors who wanted to invest in their Sydney community by giving now and investing for the long term to build an endowment fund. We engaged donors to support a range of causes in their community that they cared about, including school children, people with a disability, young people at risk, connecting seniors with primary-age children, and environmental-education community projects.

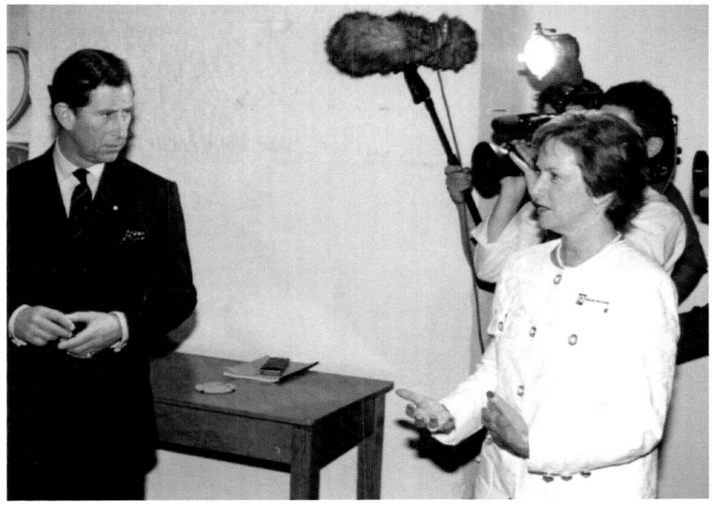

With Prince Charles at the opening of the National Trust's newest property, Merchant's House, at the Rocks, 1994.

My brother Kerry (right) at his favourite place: the sales yards in Walgett, 1994.

As Chancellor of the University of Canberra, I was delighted to confer an Honorary Degree on Susan Ryan (left), 1999.

Two of the best: Gordon McCarthy (left) and Michael Bryce at our farm at Berrima, 2000.

At Charles Sturt University, when Linda Burney (centre) was awarded her first Honorary Doctorate, 2002. With us is Jennice Kersh, from Edna's Table (right).

Visiting Sri Lanka after the 2004 Indian Ocean earthquake and tsunami, when I was Chair of Plan International.

Formal portrait at the conclusion of my term as Chancellor of the University of Canberra, 2006. Photo by Louise Lister.

Being a guest speaker with Susan Ryan (right) at a celebration for the Women's Electoral Lobby (WEL) at Sydney Town Hall, 2007.

Marking World AIDS Day at the Sydney Opera House with NSW Premier Kristina Keneally (second from left) and Prime Minister Julia Gillard, with members of the U2 band, Adam Clayton (far left), Bono (second from right) and The Edge (far right), 2010.

My seventieth birthday, celebrated with friends and family, 2011.

In Vietnam, my Plan sponsor child shows me a letter he has written to me, 2011.

At a shoot for *Boss* magazine in the *Financial Review*, when Goodstart was founded, 2012. *Financial Review*

The World AIDS Day Pacific Friends Official Party held at Government House, Melbourne, 2013. I am in yellow, front row, far left. Photo by Sharon Walker.

With Mike Finch, the General Manager of Circus Oz, at a function in the Spiegeltent, Melbourne, October 2013. Photo by Ken Leanfore and Jacob McFadden.

Circus Oz Gala Night in Melbourne. From left: Tom Davis, Matt Wilson, Quentin Bryce and me, October 2013. Photo by Ken Leanfore and Jacob McFadden.

Speaking at a function when I was the first woman inducted into Women's Agenda Hall of Fame, 7 March 2013.

Our fiftieth wedding anniversary, with our children Sam, Sophie and Hamish, 2014. Photo by Naomi Hamilton.

In those early years, the SCF held numerous symposiums and enlisted the support of community peak bodies to discover emerging issues in areas such as homelessness, ageing, youth and refugees. This helped us guide the donors to specific needs/projects in the causes they cared about.

In supporting these early grant recipients, the Foundation was funding new and unknown grassroots programs, as community foundations are about providing the seed funding for projects that meet emerging community issues. Many of these early projects progressed to grow nationally across Australia.

I look at how embedded the SCF is now in the Sydney community. Having a fulltime CEO Jane Jose has improved its capability and status compared to those humble beginnings and struggles in the first 5 years. I enjoyed my SCF time immensely in helping the foundation to move towards occupying such a unique place in the Sydney community.

My special giving place is the Women's Fund, which Lucy Brogden and I established in 2007 in sub-fund of the Community Foundation. Sydney Women's Fund has been at the forefront of gender-lens grant-making to grassroots charities supporting women and girls across the Greater Sydney area for over ten years now. It is designed to shine a light on the 'forgotten' suburbs and communities in the most disadvantaged local government areas and help reduce social problems that government or community service providers cannot effectively tackle alone. Our local and gender-focused granting seeks to bring together resources needed by the community to support the changes they wish to achieve.

With SCF and SWF support, we've seen one social enterprise become seven, providing employment to people in need; a business skills class become a retail shop; at-risk youth become the first in three generations to finish school; young girls saved from prostitution and empowered to make better life choices; young boys coached away from gangs and taught how to have respectful relationships; long-term unemployed re-skilled; refugees, tortured and traumatised, gently supported to recovery and a new life.

CHAPTER 19

A girl, a priest *in loco parentis*, a bishop and a governor-general

During my secondary education at Forbes High School I lived in the hostel adjacent to the school. Hostels were created to encourage education for children from rural families who lived away from schools and whose parents could not afford to send their children to city boarding schools. St John's Hostel in Forbes was an integral part of the local community. It was co-educational—there were twenty girls upstairs, twenty boys downstairs.

The girls lived in a dormitory of bunks on a long verandah. We didn't choose our bunk companion but usually we were put with someone who was in the same year as us at school. In my case, I shared a bunk with Beth, a girl from Condobolin. We became friends. Her parents, like mine, wanted their daughter to have a decent secondary education. And although the hostel was more affordable than a Sydney boarding school, it still was a significant part of a farming family's income to send their children there. Even as children we understood and valued that.

During my four years there, Don Shearman and his wife Faye lived in the hostel as the custodians *in loco parentis* for the twenty-eight children aged eleven to eighteen. Don and Faye were only a few years into their marriage and seemed to be very much in love. 'Padre', as we called him, introduced us to classical music and we shared all domestic duties. It felt like a big happy family; we admired and loved both Don and Faye.

There were rules that could never be broken. One of Padre's was when the 'Oak' was on his study door, he was never to be disturbed, not under any circumstances. He told us that the Oak, a little square block of oak timber, was a tradition begun by Oxford and Cambridge dons. When the dons wanted extended privacy to interview students or for study, the Oak would be placed on the door. We accepted and respected this rule.

But enforcing such a rule offered Padre the perfect opportunity for grooming someone, and that is what happened to Beth. I often wonder how it was that the young girl in our dormitory could have been sexually abused without any of us knowing. How could that have happened right in front of us? But the truth is, I wouldn't have even been able to imagine such a thing happening because I was completely naive. Other students were privately received in the study with the Oak on the door, myself included. Once Padre called me in and congratulated me for winning a race, another time it was to speak about my father. This was all perfectly normal and so I would never have been suspicious about my friend going into that study for a while.

One day Beth just disappeared. She was expelled. There were stories. It was said that she had been 'promiscuous'—I had to go and look up that word. None of us could make sense of it. Her parents had come to collect her and we didn't hear from her again.

At the end of 1956 I had to leave the hostel as my family lost our farm. I finished school in Tamworth and lost touch with my Forbes connection.

In 1981 I visited Temora for a speaking engagement and Beth was in the audience. I hadn't seen her for twenty-five years. She told me an extraordinary story. She asked if I knew that she and Padre, as I still called him, were having a relationship when she was at school. Of course, I'd had no idea, and told her so. Beth told me their relationship had resumed many years later, when she was an adult. She'd hoped she and Padre could have the opportunity to have a life together and they were planning to meet at Wagga Wagga to talk about the future. She showed me the letters and gifts she had received—amethyst and jade crosses, pendants, jewellery—all with the promise they would be together one day.

I was completely shocked. Yet I believed her and asked that we stay in touch. I received a couple of cards from her over the next few years, one to say she had left her husband and another to say she was living in Adelaide and seeking an apology from the Brisbane Anglican Diocese for the sexual abuse she suffered at the hands of Don Shearman, now a bishop.

We met face-to-face again in 1995, in the street outside St Vincent's Hospital, where Sophie was desperately ill and where Beth's son Paul, who had leukaemia, was also very ill and later died.

She spoke then about her frustration in trying to engage with the Archbishop of the Brisbane Anglican Diocese, Peter Hollingworth, seeking an apology for her abuse by Don Shearman, who'd gone on to serve as Bishop of Rockhampton and then Grafton. Hollingworth rebuffed her, and this deterred her from taking any further action until 2001. Meanwhile Shearman, now retired, had permission to officiate in the Brisbane Diocese. Beth asked that this be taken from him. Hollingworth declined to do so.

On 18 February 2002, the ABC broadcast an episode of *Australian Story*, called 'The Gilded Cage', on then Governor-General Dr Peter Hollingworth, who was under pressure to resign following his unsatisfactory handling of sexual abuse cases within the church when he was Archbishop. He was interviewed by Rafael Epstein and he admitted that he could have done better in dealing with sexual abuse.

Rafael Epstein introduced the program by saying, 'The Governor-General has a simple reason for his refusal to resign.' Hollingworth then came on and said, 'If one Governor-General felt forced to resign on an issue like that one, who in the future would ever take on the Office? I mean who could say there's nothing in my past that mightn't come out unexpectedly?'

But that was not the end of the matter. Things were about to get much worse for the Governor-General.

In the *Australian Story* program, he'd been asked about the abuse of a young girl in the student hostel where I'd boarded at Forbes. His reply included these words:

> The genesis of it was forty years ago and it occurred between a young priest and a teenage girl who was under the age of consent. I believe she was more than fourteen and I also understand that many years later in adult life their relationship resumed and it was partly a pastoral relationship and it was partly something more. My belief is that this was not sex abuse, there was no suggestion of rape or anything like that, quite the contrary. My information is that it was rather the other way round.

There was a collective gasp from women all over Australia, shocked by the inhumanity and ignorance of these remarks.

This man was a trained social worker, who had access to any information he required. There was no excuse for his cluelessness and victim-shaming.

While the identity of the woman was suppressed, I knew it was Beth.

My mother called me and said, 'This could not be true. You should say something but make sure you don't disclose your name and draw attention to yourself.' I pointed out that if I was to call ABC radio, I would have to identify myself. She reluctantly agreed.

I went for a long walk early next morning to help me decide whether to intervene. I decided to speak out.

I called ABC Radio on 20 February and said I would like the opportunity to speak about the matter. I had lived in the Hostel in Forbes and I would like to talk about it and defend the woman involved. Within an hour I was being interviewed on radio 2BL.

As I came off air, I had a call from Kerry O'Brien asking me to appear on the *7.30 Report* that evening. I agreed. In neither interview did I mention Beth by name.

* * *

On 11 May 2003, Peter Hollingworth stood aside from his role as Governor-General and resigned later that month. In 'The Gilded Cage', a chapter from *Behind the Scenes: Australian Story* (ABC Books, 2003), story producer Helen Grasswill wrote:

> In February 2002 the then Governor-General of Australia, Dr Peter Hollingworth, created a national crisis by comments he made on Australian Story about the sexual abuse of a woman by a priest. These remarks were a major

> cause of his eventual resignation as Governor-General—ending one of the most controversial episodes of Australia's vice regal history.

The appointment of Hollingworth as Governor-General by Prime Minister John Howard had been controversial. As Helen Grasswill told me:

> In secular Australia, to appoint a clergyman as Governor-General had been a contentious issue from the outset. There were those who were bitterly opposed to the church–state nexus, believing the two should always be separated. His choice of title was tricky—Bishop? Mr?—eventually settling on Dr when a 'Lambeth Degree' was bestowed upon him by the Archbishop of Canterbury, 'in recognition of his past work'.
>
> Overnight he became Dr Hollingworth.

The fact that he had been appointed by a conservative Prime Minister to represent a monarchy in the aftermath of a controversial and unsuccessful referendum on whether Australia should become a republic seemed like a slap in the face for many Australians. There was also anger that the opportunity to appoint a woman had been ignored.

Helen Grasswill's fascinating insights in 'The Gilded Cage' describe the ABC's decision to pursue and tell the story of the Hollingworth controversy. Dr Hollingworth had advised Helen in the lead-up to the story being aired on ABC TV that he'd spoken with the bishop at the centre of the storm and expected him to release a statement to the media that would 'clear it all up'. Articles appeared in the *Sydney Morning Herald* and Brisbane's *Courier-Mail* naming Bishop

Donald Shearman, though not the woman. Bishop Shearman echoed Dr Hollingworth, rejecting the term 'sex abuse' and was similarly equivocal about the girl's age.

The day after the *Australian Story* program aired, various stories ran in the media, many somewhat hysterical. It was a couple of days later that attention turned to the one comment that Hollingworth and many others believe triggered his final downfall.

Initially, as the *Australian Story* team had predicted, opinion was divided over his remarks about Bishop Shearman and the girl, with the most forceful comments coming from those who agreed with Dr Hollingworth. My own part in the story was included in the book by Helen Grasswill:

> It was in this climate that, on Wednesday, 20 February, prominent academic and businesswoman Wendy McCarthy spoke out strongly. Wendy, it transpired, had not only been a boarder at the country hostel where the abuse by then 'Padre' Shearman took place, she'd shared a dormitory and bunk bed with the girl. Apart from confirming that the girl was indeed underage, Wendy revealed that Padre Shearman was married at the time of the abuse and also the warden in charge of, and taking parental responsibility for, the children at the hostel. I was gobsmacked—in other words he was both an adulterer and *in loco parentis*! As well, I'd discovered that Donald Shearman was nearly thirty at the time—considerably older than I had been led to believe—and I would later learn he already had a child.
>
> The Governor General released a statement in answer to his critics, stating that 'Retired Bishop Shearman had sex with a girl about 15 years of age when he was a young curate some 50 years ago'.

> He [Hollingworth] acknowledges that the then Padre Shearman was supervising the hostel where the girl was resident and says he does not condone and has never condoned Shearman having sex with her. Noticeably, however, he falls short of directly acknowledging that Shearman was *in loco parentis*, nor does he acknowledge 'sexual abuse' or carnal knowledge as a criminal offence. More glaringly, he omits to mention that the so-called young curate was already married—and had a child—so had therefore committed adultery as well. He does not apologise to the woman . . .
>
> Wendy McCarthy's comments had thrown more fuel on to what was fast becoming the Hollingworth pyre.

On Thursday 21 February, three days after the broadcast, the Governor-General gave a doorstop interview at Yarralumla about what he'd said in the interview:

> On *Australian Story* on Monday night: 'I answered a question. I think I didn't hear the question properly or something like that. It gave the impression I was a) condoning child abuse, sex child abuse, and secondly that I was really talking about a girl. I thought I was talking about an adult relationship. And I want to make an unreserved apology to the woman concerned and to the whole of the Australian public. That was not what I meant and I realise that particular little segment has been picked up and used on the media yesterday.'

His words, 'I didn't hear the question properly or something like that', could not have been more inflammatory. The ABC released the unedited camera tape. The unanimous view of commentators was that he had been represented fairly.

As Helen Grasswill reported:

> Dr Hollingworth had met the woman at the centre of the controversial case only once, in 1995, when he was archbishop and she had come to a mediation in Brisbane wearing a purple bishop's shirt and an episcopal ring, both given to her by Bishop Shearman after he renewed contact when she was an adult. It must have made a considerable impression.

He wrote a letter of apology to the woman on 1 March 2002. He resigned from his office on 28 May 2003 after the release of the inquiry report, which censured aspects of his handling of sexual abuse complaints while Archbishop of Brisbane.

* * *

In 2005, Helen Grasswill later produced the two-part *Australian Story* series 'The Gathering Storm', in which Beth identified herself publicly. It was her story. I supported her during this time and worked with her to get financial compensation from the church. Her life had been devastated by Donald Shearman's sexual exploitation and subsequent betrayal. I learnt more than I ever needed to know about sexual grooming.

Beth has not forgiven Dr Hollingworth for what she saw as his abandonment of her. Don and Faye Shearman are no longer alive. Don Shearman never apologised for his behaviour.

CHAPTER 20
Our bodies

> No woman can call herself free who does not own and control her own body. No woman can call herself free until she can choose consciously whether or not she will be a mother.
>
> Margaret Sanger

This is as true today as it was when Margaret Sanger, the founder of Planned Parenthood in the United States, said it. For women throughout the centuries, ignorance about our bodies has had one major consequence: pregnancy. Biology was our destiny because our bodies are designed to get pregnant, give birth and lactate, and until recently that is what all or most of us did. The birth control movement and the advent of the oral contraceptive changed that in the second half of the twentieth century. It also increased our interest and knowledge about our bodies and health.

The publication of the Boston Women's Health *Our Bodies, Ourselves* in 1970 was groundbreaking. It began a worldwide movement about women's health and what it meant to be female, and we began believing that we could truly control when or whether we would have babies. We would claim that this knowledge made our pregnancies better because we chose them, our parenthood better because it was our choice, not our destiny.

Most of us knew little about our bodies and our reproductive systems. The knowledge has given us a larger life space to work in, an invigorating and challenging sense of time to discover what else we can do. It has meant changing laws and practices that make us unhealthy and taking responsibility for our health.

Body education is core education. Our bodies are the physical bases from which we move out into the world; ignorance, uncertainty—even, at worst, shame—about our physical selves create in us an alienation from ourselves that keeps us from being the whole person we can be. Women of my age grew up encouraged to think of ourselves as the weaker sex, needing to be rescued or saved, not admired for our physical strength. That imprint takes years to shake off, and even today the ideal norm for women comes from unrealistic social media and glossy magazines. Women's bodies are valued as ornaments. Men's bodies are valued as instruments.

Learning to understand, accept and be responsible for our physical selves gives us confidence and energy. We are better people and live better lives when we are stronger. Gloria Steinem wrote recently, 'I often think that female human beings are more ourselves before we are ten or so, before gender expectations kick in and perhaps again after we have reached the age of having and raising children.'

Our bodies have their own agenda, and we need to know how to manage those rhythms and changes. For some girls, puberty and the onset of periods can be a shock. Access to privacy and sanitary products can be limited. She may think she is sick. She may stop being active at a time when her body is changing and unknowing how this is managed. During the years I wrote the *Cleo* magazine column, I was very aware of the taboos around puberty, the fears about accidents and erratic bleeding, not to mention period pain.

The visibility of breast changes and body hair can be embarrassing too. Young women are told they are not attractive to men unless they have a Brazilian—for those of older years who may not know, this means shaving or waxing their pubic hair to look prepubescent. I'll just leave you with that thought.

What on earth are we doing? It is at puberty that girls are most likely to become vulnerable to the cruellest of all diseases: eating disorders. I am well aware that young men are also vulnerable, but nowhere near the rate of young women. The legacies of bulimia and anorexia linger for years. When their bodies let them down, girls often decide to cease being physically active and lose the security that comes with bodily autonomy.

Our bodies are designed to have children earlier than later and the deferral of children is complex. It is about finding the right partner, decisions around the costs of having children, career development. Timing is everything. After thirty-five, fertility declines and if we need IVF treatment, being able to manage the costs and flexibility required can be tough. And then when you have a child, there is pressure to appear normal again when in truth you have had a profound experience and need time to settle and establish your new life. You are a mother and that will never change.

The feminists of the seventies fought for maternity leave to give those who came after us an income and time-out with the right to return to work. The first beneficiaries were women in the Commonwealth Public Service who in 1973 were provided with twelve weeks' paid leave. By 2020 eligible employees, those who are the primary carer of a newborn or newly adopted child, get up to eighteen weeks of parental leave, which is paid at the national minimum wage. There are many ways to manage these benefits, which are also available to men. As a new mother planning to take time out I comforted myself with the thought that we live five to seven years longer than men so there was time available while we grew into our new roles.

Good men settle into the rhythm of parenthood but they don't have to deal with women's next challenge: menopause. I cannot remember any discussion about menopause around the kitchen table where many of these matters are shared. It was secretive. I was so lucky to be working at Family Planning then and have access to new thinking and treatment. The symptoms of menopause often manifest in the night sweats, waking up in the middle of the night with drenched sheets. Or we turn bright red and sweat at a work meeting. It seemed mystifying and confusing. My worst menopause memory is bleeding unexpectedly when in a white suit and incapable of moving until the room emptied. These moments are beyond our control and embarrass everyone.

During this time, women have conversations to reassure themselves that they are not going mad with mood swings. The uncertainty and lack of control over our bodies in menopause can take us through to our middle-to-late fifties before we are back in charge.

Years ago, I presented a paper at the World Menopause Conference. I was startled that almost all the presenters were men. Very few had a lived experience, and very few of the lived experiences were given any credence. One man I raised this with dismissed my words by explaining it was all about science. It is also about drugs, money and control. Many of my peer group took hormones to escape the symptoms, as I did. It was a considered choice.

Female ageing is not without its liabilities. The urologist who cracks the management of urinary tract infections (UTIs) should receive a nomination for the Nobel Prize from women post sixty. Just when we thought we were free of biology, here come the UTIs. If men of mature age got UTIs there would be a campaign to find a successful management regime.

I know there will be people, I can hear them now, saying how inappropriate it is to raise these issues in a book that looks like a nice, safe political and personal memoir. But we *are* our bodies. We need them to work with and for us. Ignorance is not a virtue.

Post menopause, a new world awaits—free of some of the female constraints. No need for contraception, no periods, often a better sex life, and time to pursue our interests, unless we are homeless and poor. Not, fortunately, like the ad that ran in a US medical magazine in the 1970s that depicted a harassed middle-aged man standing by a drab and tired-looking woman. The drug advertised was to treat menopausal symptoms that bother him. HIM? This image of menopause as an affliction that makes us a burden to our family and friends still resonates with my peers.

It can take a while for true heroines to emerge in the world. People whom you can really admire. And I have always thought women can't be seen in that way until we are post-menopausal. Nonetheless older women can offer our younger sisters, at the very least, an honest report of what we have learnt and how we have grown. And how our trajectory of growth has been so different from that of our mothers and grandmothers.

I have never lied about my age. I used to be quite pleased to think I was the youngest person in the first year of university at the age of sixteen; it made me sound smarter than I was.

And even as I went through the decades of birthdays, I was very conscious of the fact that once you have outed yourself on age, you can never pretend. It enraged my mother, as she did not want people to know her age.

Nigella Lawson wrote a beautiful piece when she turned sixty, saying how she hated birthday parties and she had to come face to face with herself, saying this is what sixty looks like. But, most of all, it was about how she lived to be older than her mother, and she felt that that was an important statement to make. She said, 'You see, the thing is, I have turned 60, when I say it, it sounds strange enough, but when it is written down, I find it very odd indeed.' I agree with her view in that what age looks like is shaped in one's childhood. So, when I say the word *eighty*, I don't think it's someone who looks like me, I still think it's someone with a grey bun, which is absolutely ridiculous. Particularly now, as I am letting my hair go grey, I may well end up with a grey bun. But I think I am different.

There is a lot to be said for getting older and some wistful moments about the loss of youth—what is the alternative? Not being here. My mother died at eighty and I am excited about turning that age. But I can't control it. I have to go with the flow. I'll use all the tricks I can—scrape the skin cancers off my face, wear clothes I love, and dance. Always dance even in the privacy of your home. I recognise that there is an agility in the body that is not there that even all the exercise in the world can't change. And I am less risk-averse. I just feel I can go with the flow when I don't have anything planned and opportunities arise, I can say yes or no. And I can change my mind.

I now live alone and one of the things I have found in the last five years is that I love to be on my own and make decisions about what I want to do. I feel anything could happen.

Recently I did something quite reckless for me by going to Singapore to meet Michelle Obama. She was speaking at a conference and Karen Beattie, CEO of The Growth Faculty, sent me the flyer and offered me VIP status and five minutes with Michelle one to one. I accepted and asked my friend Elsa to join me. Michelle was engaging one to one and in the auditorium professional, witty and poised. Her hair had returned to Afro curls. It was our last travel before COVID-19 hit. And worth every dollar. I would not have done that five years ago.

My message to young women is: respect your body, look after your health and keep moving; stay curious and keep learning and meeting new people.

Currently Australian women's life expectancy is eighty-five. For men, it is eighty and a half. Don't waste a day.

CHAPTER 21
The things that make us

The more that you read, the more things you will know.
The more that you learn, the more places you'll go.

Dr Seuss, *I Can Read With My Eyes Shut!*

Changing business/changing careers—people ask me how I had the confidence to do it.

I have always been a reader. For as long as I can remember, reading has sustained my life. I feel sick if I don't read at least one novel every ten days. But I also read management texts, newspapers, Twitter and Facebook. I have a deep curiosity about what goes on in the world, so it's three newspapers a day. But I also have a longing to bury myself in a book and move to another place.

As a little girl, I read stories of heroic girls like *Ann Thorne—Reporter*, *Anne of Green Gables*, *Verity of Sydney Town*, *Veronica at the Wells* and endless stories of girls at boarding school who seemed to be called Hilary. Denied Biggles I followed the adventurous Worrals and always stories about horses—*My Friend Flicka* was a favourite. By late primary, I was reading adult books that came into the house. But to avoid arguments about whether they were appropriate, I would swap the dust jackets.

Before I went to secondary school, I was reading about the Kokoda Trail and *Reader's Digest*, newspapers that came with the mail three days a week, David Jones and farmers' catalogues and farm guides. It was not discriminating; I just read everything.

Reading was always approved in our house, and during a childhood without the distraction of television, but with the distraction of turbulence in the home, reading was a safe place to be. At Garema School, apart from looking after the little ones and listening to ABC broadcasts, I read all the books that came my way. When I first started teaching, I had to introduce a new reading-effectiveness program, SRA, which was a speed-reading program, and I found it really exciting to do. And, so, I can now read more and more.

I probably read less in high school because I slept in a dormitory and you couldn't read at night, while our days were strictly organised. I was then, for the first time in my life, enjoying team games. And reading was more directed and compartmentalised. Although I did think many of the school texts were silly and babyish. And then of course there were university texts, which were neither silly or babyish, but challenging and became my new reading habit. When I was a teacher, I went to sleep next to history and geography books. Always reading into the early hours of the morning, and I loved it.

When I started reading about feminism and the women's movement, all the other books were moved out of the way. I was riveted to the idea of women's writing and the universality of women's experiences. Georgette Heyer was moved aside for real life.

At the beginning, it was polemical and needed to be discussed with friends. Particularly new friends and companions in the United Kingdom and the United States. I had started the feminist reading in Cremorne Girls High School with Betty Friedan, but I graduated to women as experts, such as Sheila Kitzinger, who was telling us how to birth, and of course, Germaine Greer, whose *The Female Eunuch* challenged us all for many years. Our stories as women replaced my need for fiction, and I consumed them voraciously. I have continued to read women's writing since.

Gordon would always have on his side of the bed books about management and money, which I thought rather dull. However, when he wrote a good one—*The Great Big Australian Takeover Book*—I became interested and vicariously enjoy the world of business.

And somewhere in the middle was a zone of books we shared—Australian fiction, politics and social commentary. At Family Planning, the books were all about sex. I had access to books not always available in bookstores, and I had to read them for professional reasons—doesn't everyone say that? Books on sexual theory and technique were dominant for a while, but we got over that, and the need for fiction was reasserted.

Somewhere in the late eighties, I found myself absorbed in management texts, as the books moved across the bed. By the nineties, the bedside authors included Charles Handy, who talked about the building of an eclectic portfolio, and I realised he was talking about my type of career: a nonlinear career. Handy legitimised the nonlinear careers for women like me. Not for the feminist reasons, but for the good business reasons, and because it suited the time we lived in, even now. We live longer and linear executive careers may be unsustainable and unsatisfying.

There was one major omission in my business reading. Women were invisible. And writing this book and checking contemporary texts has surprised me how often it remains the case. Our experience is passed over, perhaps not noticed.

Handy's description of the portfolio career gave it virtue and dignity, despite it looking rather messy in my case—education, media, family planning, national event organiser, heritage/conservation custodian/manager . . . Where does it all lead? The truth is, I don't know. I followed my gut instinct. I was and am a curious person. Why does this all have to lead somewhere? Isn't it enough to be doing it and enjoying it? Making a contribution and changing some of the things that need to be changed? That's what I do.

I was increasingly interested in seeing the world through a business lens. Running the management workshops and being the Executive in Residence at the University of South Australia encouraged this. I was consumed by filling the vacuum in my business knowledge. The confidence I gained from this enabled me to have a very clear instinct about risk management for myself, as well as the organisations I engaged with.

I was developing a profile as a woman of business. Sometimes I still felt like an imposter. I was President of Chief Executive Women while living in Darlinghurst. There were business lunches every other day, speaking at business seminars—and, in a sense, making it up as I went along. I learnt that many women were shut out of these positions because they weren't confident enough to say yes to opportunity unless they were perfectly trained.

We never are. We always learn on the job. Just as men do.

Food

People think that reading, food and clothes are all trivial. They simply are not. They tell us a lot about ourselves, about our values, about our confidence; they tell us about the company of strangers, the conviviality of sitting at a dining room table; they tell us about the trust you have when you invite someone into your house—the same people that I trust to do business with.

My interest in cooking started with my mother's interest in food. She had never prepared food for a family before she was married. She became interested in a well-set table—I think it was her time in Goulburn more than any other place, where she met people with money and style. Photographs of her at the time show a very beautiful, glamorous young woman who was clearly attractive to the local grazing fraternity. And when my father was away during the week, I am sure the little dinner and cocktail parties that she went to gave her the opportunity to see a much broader range of lifestyles—plus, she had some domestic help for the first time.

She had a very strong sense of personal, innate design in the way she arranged her clothes, the houses we lived in—the most modest of houses would have her touches of colour, a cushion here or there, curtains she had sewed, and always interesting food. I do have a recurring memory of my father's meal on top of an aluminium saucepan to keep warm because he hadn't come home in time for food, though that may be a relic of the late forties anyway, where mothers ate early with children. In any event, my mother became increasingly interested in cooking. And not the baking kind of cooking her neighbours and peers were interested in.

I find it fascinating that my daughter and daughters-in-law bake. I don't bake much. My mother didn't bake much. She couldn't have cared less if she never made a sponge cake. Although she liked a good fruit cake. Her interest was in having food on the lunch and dinner table that was interesting and nourishing. I remember when I ate my first capsicum, and excitedly told her about it. She had just started eating capsicum herself, she reminded me. I think I was eighteen, so she would have been thirty-six.

She lived for a while with her friend Ruth Watson in Killara, whom she had known in the Goulburn days. Ruth was a wonderful cook. And as I later did, my mother watched other women in the kitchen to get a feel for food, prepare it, take it to the table, and enjoy it with friends. That was so charming.

We never had wine, for example, at our dining room table, and we always ate in the dining room—if there was one. But we would sit at a proper table, mind our manners and eat our food. All of it. I still feel the need to eat everything on my plate. It has left me with an enduring love of family dinners, having people over, sharing a bowl of spaghetti, a BBQ meal, a roast chicken—all the traditional dishes and special dinners when I would plan and prepare for days. Food is relationship-building, nurturing, loving. I started cooking on my own when I was at university as our college had a kitchen. Spaghetti bolognaise and Indian curries were my best and favourite foods at the time, as well as anything with mashed potato.

When I first lived in Sydney, I became friends with Amrey Commins, who subsequently was a bridesmaid at our wedding. I was enthralled by her Estonian approach to the preparation of food. I would love to watch her in the kitchen preparing Russian-influenced food—blinis with vodka was a standout. It was hard to find a good delicatessen in those days, but she would track down providores. I still use the cookbook she gave me as a wedding present—*The Joy of Cooking* by Rombauer and Becker. It has fingermarks all over it, the paper is turning brown, but it remains the standard that I use as a reference.

Travelling for me is always a culinary experience. I am interested in street food—the food that reflects the culture of a place. And the simple food with distinctive culinary approaches, such as how many ways we can do rice or potatoes, how many greens we can chop into a salad, how many ways we can cut meat. Living in America, I became addicted to chilli con carne and Mexican food. When I travel, I always buy a cookbook to reinforce the memories.

Our first house in McMahons Point was the place where we had a lot of parties. The Childbirth Education Association had its meetings at our kitchen table. Women's Electoral Lobby Sydney was put together at our kitchen table. A photograph of Gail Radford, June Williams and myself is a reminder of the time we spent together, and always around the kitchen table. It is where great ideas are nurtured, permission is given, failure is allowed.

I am thrilled that all my children love cooking, and they are good at it. I sent them into the world with a capacity to do that, and to care about it. I didn't give them particular recipes but they knew that if they tried cooking, the rewards would manifest.

So, what's the basic? The roast chook. On the internet, you can get a thousand recipes on how to roast a chicken. Roast chicken whole is still my favourite dish. It signifies happiness and warmth in the house, a sense of conviviality. Or you can buy chicken in pieces and cook it. The news that there is more rice and pasta sold than potatoes today, I find fascinating. My background is Irish, so the potato is always my first choice. But I do love pasta and rice.

If you love food, you will find a way. And don't be frightened of the domestic arts. I understood—early in my single life at university, as a young married woman—the preparation and serving of food gives you a power base in the family. The kitchen is a powerful place to rule from. It's the hub of the house. So, I encourage us all to be our own survivors, to raise our children to have the survival skills to wash themselves, cook for themselves, pick up after themselves, clean their living spaces, accept the opportunity to be educated—I am sure it leads to a better life, and more fun.

I remember, while doing the enquiry into intractable waste, a small team of four of us went to Paris, looking at what was happening with high-temperature incinerators. Our host for lunch took us to Boffingers, possibly one of the most beautiful traditional French restaurants in Paris. Strangely I cannot remember the menu but I was struck by the richness of the food and the amount of cream in every course. It was a beautiful meal but not nouvelle cuisine. Sadly, it was a one-off, as we did not award the French company a contract, while acknowledging their high-temperature incinerators did work well. But that trip reminded me of the number of deals in the world that are done over food. Never underestimate the power of breaking bread across the table. It is a sign of equality and respect that we should all treasure.

I love having people eat at my dining room table. I've had the same dining room table since 1971, so there's a lot of stories etched into that table. It is a very seductive kind of table to pat and stroke. The wood came out of the harbour in front of McMahons Point, where we lived at the time. Gordon made the table himself, without a nail in it.

I look back and reflect on the sharing and caring, the discussion of ideas, during those years in Longueville, especially when Quentin was living there with me. And none of our friends minded being asked for dinner twenty-four hours in advance. They could come or they couldn't. We didn't take it personally.

It never occurred to us they wouldn't want to come. It was just about being available. And they enabled us to wind down, to relax. It was really good for my children, and Quentin's if they happened to be staying for a few days with us at the time.

Quentin made a really tough decision to come and work in Sydney away from her own family. We were more than happy to have her. She was with us for six years. That is a lot of dinner parties—at least two a week. Between us we had a fantastic network of trusted friends, people you could rely on, when we wanted to discuss our work, as both our jobs were political. There were times after these dinner parties when we might sit for half an hour and talk. But somehow or other, in the company of friends and the breaking of bread, issues were simplified. The soup might have been complex, but the event was basic. It was about having friends over, sharing food and wine, and working out strategies and tactics, or talking about current affairs, but fundamentally about staying in touch.

Those years were rich in sharing ideas, and they built our confidence, as many of us were in workspaces we hadn't inhabited before, and we needed each other as back-up—always Chatham House rules, but fabulous experiences and spaces for women's friendships. No men.

In the first twenty years of this century, when I was in a one-bedroom apartment, I really missed those years. I would go out to dinner maybe three nights a week in Sydney, go to bed at seven o'clock the other night, and then head to the farm in between. I did have lots of friends coming to the farm, people loved to visit. They would come for the weekend, and I liked the cooking then. It was a different scale, of course—a roast chicken, a whole fish on the BBQ—simple and good food. And a lot of incidental entertainment was done there, but it wasn't done in the city anymore, where it became more about eating out, and it was much more expensive. And I don't think being in a restaurant creates the same sense of sharing ideas and strategies, and building trust in relationships, as it does when you are in your own dining room with people you really want to spend time with.

Maybe it's because I am older, but nowadays I think a lunch is a really good idea on the weekend, at home. During the week, if we are home working, we might decide to have a home lunch. But since time immemorial, people have eaten together, and when they eat, some things fall away, and we speak in a different way.

I would have loved to have had the culinary skills of the women I have modelled myself on: Elizabeth David, Claudia Roden, Irma Becker from Rombauer-Becker, Maggie Beer, Stephanie Alexander—they are the women who seriously understood how to set up a table where the overriding atmosphere was defined by friendship, curiosity and the pleasure of dining together.

Recently, my friend Bill Bowtell gave me a book by a woman who was Churchill's cook. I am longing to read it. I think she is going to claim in the book that without her Churchill wouldn't have been able to get through the war. And as Napoleon said, all armies march on their stomachs. Claudia Roden changed the food in British prisons. Regrettably, they didn't keep doing it—but for a while having decent food changed prison behaviour.

Food is to be worshipped. Even Gordon, as a beef breeder, felt thrilled when his meat was bought by David Jones, or good butchers who knew what he was trying to do without using a feed lot or loads of hormones.

I had become accustomed to being the solo person, the single woman in the group. And that was one of the reasons I so looked forward to having my and Gordon's next chapter in life, when we eventually sold the farm and Gordon came back to the city and we would be able to entertain in our lovely Potts Point apartment that I managed to find—yet another heritage place.

These things are not trivial.

Clothes

I have the same view about clothes in a way. Are we what we wear? Yes and no. But clothes define the impression we give when we arrive. Clothes are theatre. In all my management seminars, I would always have a session on how we walk into a room. It's not about cleavage or make-up, it's about how we make the first impression and the impression we want to convey. Do our clothes match who we are? And are these the right clothes for the time? It's about a skill, it's about respect for the people you are working with.

When I joined the Board of the ABC, I knew there would be a lot of cameras at our first meeting. My mother said to me—who was always beautifully dressed, even with nothing to her name she would look a million dollars—'Don't wear a black suit.' At that stage I never wore suits, only dresses. She said, 'Don't wear a black suit, go and buy yourself a suit of colour.' And I bought a beautiful red woollen Irish suit that became my go-to outfit for the ABC—my signature suit. The reason, my mother explained, 'was you will stand out from the men. You need to create your own look, and a black suit trying to look like the men won't do it.'

I've thought about this in the last couple of days because I recently came across Beyoncé's address to the graduate class of 2020, where she said, 'Build your own stage and make them see you.' And this has always been true. I dressed carefully earlier in my career. I wanted to have a particular look that defined me. I wasn't trying to be someone else. I was trying to be sure that I was comfortable in what I was wearing, that I knew when I would wear trousers and when I would wear skirts, or dresses. I never wanted my skin to be distracting. I wanted to look like the person I believe I am.

I love clothes. I love contriving that look. I was a great Carla Zampatti fan—I know she disapproved that I kept her clothes for so long, but they are some of my favourites and they adapt to many places. I love that her clothes were made in Australia. I try always to buy Australian designers. I was heartbroken when George Gross and Harry Watt closed their shops, and I still have some of their clothes fifteen or sixteen years later.

Clothes are fun. You get a reaction to what you wear. And you can do a lot without much money if you can put pieces together.

My greatest clothing challenge was when I presented a degree to the King of Thailand. I was told I couldn't turn my back on him, I had to have a full-length day dress, I couldn't 'look like a Thai woman', and under no circumstances was I to shake his hand. I spent hours agonising about what to wear and finally had a dress made that would also work with my university robes at the time.

I was in a room of such exquisite beauty. The men were dressed in white silk, the sofas were covered in pink silk, beautiful natural light, and pink and white orchids everywhere. My pale purple silk dress was not quite suited to the surroundings, I thought, and of course I hadn't known in advance about the decor. As I have mentioned before, the King insisted on shaking my hand, the courtiers got off their knees at that, but I did not turn my back on His Majesty.

Planning what to wear is endlessly engaging and doesn't require a lot of money, but it does require some thought, so it is best to enjoy it. I can sit with my friends and talk for hours about what we are going to wear, what impression we are trying to make.

When my mother died, my sisters Deborah and Sarah and I were deciding what she should wear to take her into the crematorium. We agonised over her Chanel shoes, which regrettably did not fit any of us. Really it was a no-brainer—she would wear the Chanel shoes. And she did. It seemed so right.

Travel

The 1960s left me with an enduring love of travel. Gordon's enthusiasm for travel was contagious. Travelling to London on a boat, exploring Europe every weekend and destination holidays for two years, and then on to America where we drove east to west on Highway 66 was a good base.

Growing up, my family rarely travelled. We could not afford it. A trip to Sydney, which I think happened three times before I finished school, was a big event. We went to Collaroy twice for a beach holiday, and twice I went to stay with my Aunty Ette at Huntleys Point, where she lived with my great-grandmother, Elizabeth McKenzie. Aunty Ette was flamboyant, exciting, had a married man as a lover, sang in a Pitt Street theatre in the evenings, and we could listen to her sing occasionally on 2GB.

Curiously, I did have the trip of a lifetime when I was eight. I was sent by myself to Perth to stay with the Rudwicks, who were family friends from Orange. Gail was my first school friend. I learnt to swim in Perth.

When I left Australia, I had not seen very much of my own country. The life of an expat is rethinking and reconsidering what it means to be an Australian. Understanding what you cherish and devising answers to the criticisms that others make. I knew, most of all, it was always the Australian light and bush for me. I understood people who longed for the landscapes of their countries.

A holiday to Greece during our time in Europe gave Gordon and me a wondrous moment to see the light of the Mediterranean. We were there in the wine grape season for the crushing of the grapes. The light was like what I knew on the central western plains of New South Wales, and I had a moment of intense homesickness that even being asked to join the virgins in the wine vats to crush the grapes did not alleviate.

One of the best moments of three years of travel was coming home. Returning to Sydney was a glorious moment. I marvel over the scene every time I fly over the harbour bathed in the Australian light. That's when I know I've come home.

Travel introduced me to different educational systems and to different lifestyles. One of the disadvantages of living on an island continent is that most European Australians are monolingual. Meeting Europeans who could speak three and four languages reminded Gordon and me of what we missed without another spoken language. My schoolgirl French can help me read a book in French, with a dictionary, but my capacity to speak it was entirely limited and it was a frustrating exercise.

Travel is never to be underrated. I had opportunities to observe the way women lived in different cultures. This was such a long way from my upbringing. And it was such a rich experience. Teaching in a convent and being encouraged to travel to Washington, where I otherwise might not have gone as it was not on the tourist list in those days, created new insights and understandings about what a faith-based school can provide. And the connections they created with colleges ensured their students had a continuity of faith during tertiary studies. This was so far away from my life experience.

I'm fond of saying to young people, 'Your first goal as part of your education must include travel. Not just vomiting in Earls Court or going to Bali and slapping oil on. But standing back and seeing new things, wondering why people behave differently in different cultures.'

Travel brings people together. We can all share our awe at the base of the pyramids in Egypt, or by looking at the Taj Mahal. We can wonder at the poorest people in Ireland trying to make a few shillings to contribute to a new cathedral.

Gordon and I wandered around the world, soaking up these experiences, meeting people in camping sites, tasting new food, learning to cook, observing poverty and wealth in the same country. Gordon was obsessed with how things worked. I was obsessed with how people lived. Travelling in a campervan meant we could talk to people about these things. It gave us a rich connection and it remained a reservoir of imagination and experience throughout our lives.

There were few years in my fifty-three years with Gordon McCarthy when we missed the opportunity to travel overseas. When other people started taking their children travelling, they took them to Europe. We took ours to Asia, on the grounds that it was the future, and it was their region. So, it might have been the Asia–Pacific, like the Solomon Islands, or Fiji, Malaysia, Vanuatu. These were the experiences we wanted our children to have, to give them a taste for travel and the curiosity about people. We wanted them to understand the world is not monochrome and there are many ways to be successful.

Travel creates new longings, and by the time Gordon and I were on the way home from living overseas, there had been a longing about having children. It seemed right to come back to Australia to start a family.

Returning for an expatriate is never easy. Over the years, I have mentored people—wonderful people, successful in other cultures—who have come back to Australia, which they dearly love, only to find, in effect, that no one could give a toss about what they had been doing. This is what we found on our return. Few of our friends or family had travelled and after a few obligatory questions people wanted us to be as we were three years ago. My mother would accuse me of having changed. And I had. My life was richer from my experience and new ways of living and thinking I had been exposed to. It was to be celebrated.

We left on a boat and returned on a plane, it was so unusual to fly in those days and all our relatives from Yass and Sydney met us at the airport to welcome us home. Travelling with Gordon was always an adventure. We always had to do new things. I'm probably the only person I know who went to the Volkswagen car factory on her honeymoon, because Gordon wanted to see how they were so successful. He was obsessed with Scandinavia and the fact that a country, with fewer people than us, could be such a leading nation in terms of manufacturing, design and lifestyle. And that stayed with him. And, indeed, with me, too. I have visited Scandinavian countries many times and still have a deep affection for them.

Being a director of Plan International meant extensive travel from Australia and that was a challenge. It was a

Eurocentric organisation, despite one of the founders having been Australian. At my farewell at Plan, I spoke of the places I had visited in the pursuit of improving the life of the child within a human rights framework. It was an arduous trip from Australia to other parts of the world. And there were times when I wondered why I did it. But there was always the hope that you really would make a difference, and I didn't want to be the person who sat in the armchair and talked about it, I wanted to talk to the people on the ground.

My job as Chair of the Australian Heritage Commission took me from one end of Australia to the other. It left me with a strong wish at this stage of my life to keep travelling around my country, ideally with a grandchild or two in tow.

CHAPTER 22

Creating a mentoring practice

> The delicate balance of mentoring someone is not creating them in your own image but giving them the opportunity to create themselves.
>
> Steven Spielberg

In 1996, I received a call from Tom McEwan, CEO of Citibank, asking me if I would come and meet him. I wasn't aware he wanted to discuss an article I had written for the *Bulletin* magazine. It had posed the question: Where are the women in corporate Australia? How sad it is that we are still asking the same questions in the early 2020s. He explained that as the recently arrived CEO from Taiwan, he was astonished to find that most of his colleagues were uniformly white men. He was equally astonished to find that they didn't see anything unusual about it. I looked at him and said, 'It doesn't surprise me.'

'I would like to find out why it is that we have such a monochrome culture,' he said. 'I want to place a couple of smart young women in the senior executive group. It is time to change, and the leadership of Citibank in New York is initiating a new program called Respect at Work. I would like to lead it with your assistance.'

The CEO also said, 'But, first of all, I need a status report. Does your firm do that?'

Well, my firm was me, so I said, 'Yes, I can do that. I can do a cultural survey and I can look at the opportunities for change, and I can look at what the current thinking is in the organisation. You just have to give me your blessing and I will do it.'

Over three months I interviewed people on a proforma, working closely with the HR Director, Elspeth Renshaw. I was doing qualitative interviews and another company was hired to simultaneously run a quantitative survey. I thought it was a good idea to keep the quantitative work independent, as it would give us a much greater insight into the thinking and behaviours of the organisation.

My report was disturbing. People said extraordinary things, which took me back to the days of the WEL survey. One-third of respondents said they didn't believe that women should come back to work after having a child. When pressed on that, some brave people volunteered that they didn't think their brains were working in quite the same way, and that they would always have their children on their minds and wouldn't therefore be able to do a proper job.

Of course, I restrained myself from the question that begged: *Why don't you boys think about your children?* There was a surprising hostility to women, especially on the trading floor, which was seen as the men's domain.

The compilation of the survey resulted in the CEO deciding that there would be some major work done. It would dovetail into the Respect at Work program. The Australian office was pleased to be ahead of the pack in developing this program for the rest of the organisation.

The first step for making change was to promote two women into the senior executive team, and both were extremely competent. The CEO said to me, 'I should probably get them a couple of people to act as mentors/coaches in case they need some extra support.' Although unfamiliar with the concept of coaches, I supported that idea.

A month later, he called me and said, 'This is not working.' He asked me to talk to the female senior executives to gauge their thoughts. The first woman said, 'I am just looking for someone whose shoes I can walk in. I want to know how women in front of me did it. I don't want to listen to men, like my father, telling old war stories. I want people to listen to me and help me find my voice.' The second woman echoed her comments.

After my report, the CEO asked that I meet them again and find a mentor for each. It sounded like the challenge I was seeking. I needed to create a professional development program that was ethical, sustainable, scalable and good value for money. There was not much available, and I could find no established programs in Australia. Coaching may have been flavour of the month, but mine would be mentoring.

I began following the work of David Clutterbuck at Oxford after finding his book, *Everyone Needs a Mentor*. It was a lightbulb moment. I thought of people who had encouraged and supported me in an organic way. OMG—they are mentors, I realised, but I didn't pay for them. I regularly sought their counsel, when we spoke, and I found my voice.

Here was a business opportunity that could work for women to be supported as they navigated their way through management layers in business. I would set up a mentoring practice as part of my portfolio and see how it went. Politically, the times were good. Individualism was the new black.

Citibank was the perfect first client. I was confident of my educational and learning foundation, and I had a large network of good businesspeople who could be excellent mentors. I developed a particular methodology. I was always looking for the perfect match. The chemistry was important, and people knew pretty quickly if they could work together for two hours a month for a year. I was fond of saying, 'In the best mentoring relationships there is mutual learning, integrity, respect and trust.' And there had to be.

By 1999, I had a mentoring practice firmly established in Citibank. When David Maister published *The Trusted Advisor* in 2000, it reinforced my belief that everyone does need a mentor.

The feedback was powerful and pleasing, and other companies were soon calling to explore opportunities. I was on a roll.

Some years into the program, I wrote two books. One, a mentee guide; the other, a mentor guide, which became a two-part series, *One2One*. They had a set of cards as part of the learning pack, and with them people selected choices about issues to discuss with their mentor, and to help the mentee focus on what they really wanted out of the relationship. At that level, it was a very efficient and powerful way to use the twelve sessions of two hours together. Demand for it grew and the pack still sells.

There is a magic about mentoring. It is beautiful work. You see people grow in front of you. And you understand the power of voice and the power of a trusted relationship that is mentee driven. There is no unaskable question.

It was during this time, that I became a mini entrepreneur and created Women's Business, Corporate Good Works, and the mentoring practice, the latter renamed as McCarthy Mentoring. They were all successful. But I was never especially interested in scaling up. It was enough to do the start-up and, in the case of McCarthy Mentoring, Sophie joined the business and decided it offered opportunities for her.

It made me appreciate the people in my life who had mentored me, although we didn't call it that then. People who listened, offered advice when asked, opened bigger worlds for me, and, just like the senior executive at Citibank said, allowed me to walk in their shoes.

Growing up, nobody spoke about mentors. You had people who helped you. I didn't come across the word mentor until the 1990s. Now it is a well-recognised professional development tool. In a perfect world, we would live and work in a mentoring space, where people are kind to each other, listen to what you have to say, and offer extra help and encouragement.

Growing up, I had teachers, a couple of school principals and a couple of aunts, who helped me realise that I could do things that I would never have dreamt were possible. That is the magic of mentoring. It broadened my world and helped me find my voice.

At Tamworth High School, one of my teachers suggested that I go to university. That was so far away from anything I had imagined. I was gobsmacked. I was planning a nursing career, and even that was outside my family experience. We are all within a family's knowledge of opportunity and background, and my family had ensured I could stay at school and encouraged me to be there. They didn't think much past school because they hadn't had that experience for themselves. Nursing sounded good, and they were shocked when they discovered I was too young to start training.

There were older women in the staffroom who took it upon themselves to help me, a very young teacher at a girls' school, find my way around. People whose wisdom I wanted to listen to, who were always there for support and advice.

I learnt to value the older women and men in my life who shared their wisdom with me.

It gave me confidence to challenge the status quo, take risks and achieve career opportunities beyond my wildest dreams.

But for me, the most beneficial outcome of mentoring is to hear and learn to trust your own voice. To hear your own voice, to be able to talk to someone and to be just prodded into speaking about yourself. It is a courageous thing to do.

When I was moving into a more business-oriented world, there were some good men who were my mentors. They gave me opportunities, and encouraged me to look for opportunities beyond my experience. I learnt about measuring risk from them.

There are two women, in particular, who supported me over an extended period of time. One was Dame Beryl Beaurepaire, who I met in 1978. We worked together on the National Women's Advisory Council for three years. We stayed in touch regularly after that, and she would always say, 'Don't give up, try something new, take a risk, what is the worst that can happen? And given the opportunities you have had to gain access to politicians and be rewarded with government roles, there is a reciprocity, Wendy, about giving back.'

The second was Joan Bielski, an educator and a librarian. We once worked at the same school although at different times. She was a woman, with completely different politics to Beryl, who would always encourage me and say, 'It is bigger than you, you have got to take the risk.'

Everyone needs a mentor. Thank you to all the people who have mentored me along the way, put their trust in me, and given me a bit of a nudge when I needed it. I am truly grateful.

My mentoring business became of particular interest to various government agencies, too. The Australia Council, for example, was interested in finding mentors for managers of performing arts boards. Louise Walsh and I interviewed people all over Australia during one monumental journey. Although I was never the mentor while I was running the practice, I did set up the relationships, and that began the story of my long relationship with Circus Oz.

Joining the circus

In 2007, the Circus Oz Board asked me if I would meet them as one of their members was accepting a placement, paid for by the Australia Council, to be a mentee. They wanted to discuss the program being offered by McCarthy Mentoring. After the quite rugged interview—which I valued—I was called a few days later by the General Manager to ask if I would consider joining their board as Chair. I was very flattered and said I needed to think about it for a few days. But I was interested in chairing an arts company and could think of no better fit than Circus Oz. So, I agreed to become the Chair.

Sitting in a Zoom meeting two days ago, I was reminded of a strategic plan put to the Australia Council by Jillian Segal, who was then on the Australia Council Board, saying it was the first she had ever seen where a company promised to be 'shit hot'. And that tells you a lot about the boldness of the Circus.

Circus Oz exists to create contemporary Australian circus performances that entertain, inspire and challenge locally, nationally and internationally. It has always strived to be the 'best little circus on earth', collaborative, culturally distinctive and sustainable. One of the great appeals for me was that the Circus was inclusive and diverse in its practices and its thinking. People could come from enormously varied backgrounds and find their way into a team, a troupe, and find a circus career. You didn't have to come from a wealthy family where you had to have a piano, trumpet or whatever—you came with a particular skill, and you learnt on the job.

Circus Oz is a truly remarkable organisation. As Chair, I decided to take myself to Broadway when they were performing. I can't tell you how excited you feel when you are walking down Broadway and you see a huge ad for Circus Oz next to *Batman*. Watching the show at the New Victory Theatre, your heart fills with pride. On opening night, we had a special event celebrating our thirty-fifth birthday. Sarah Jessica Parker and a few other stars attended. It was a truly stunning night.

I started a philanthropy program for Circus Oz. Most of these things had been done before, but not in a systemic, organised way. I felt sure that through the growing social enterprise network and the development in the sector, Circus Oz could become much more than an arts company. It is a living, breathing, creative industry, and it has offered, for nearly forty years, an ability to support the ecosystem, because it understands in the most mature way that without the ecosystem the show doesn't go on.

I was able to help bring one of its dreams about premises to fruition. Of course, it was a big team effort. For me, it was really interesting to get to know a whole lot of Victorian politicians and work in Melbourne. With commitments to both Circus Oz and headspace for a decade (2008–2016), I was in Melbourne at least three days a fortnight.

I stayed for exactly ten years. We did amazing work together. I agreed to the challenge of finding a new home for them. And, of course, they knew exactly where they wanted to be, and no matter how many politicians offered them other alternatives, we eventually landed in the old Collingwood TAFE, where they had started. The new building was a triumph, architecturally and functionally, with their own rehearsal hall, and the board decided we should buy a spiegeltent. I fulfilled my promise and commitments to them.

I love the fact that a small group of people who started Circus Oz, many of whom were still engaged there during my tenure, always had a big vision. And I remember in one of the reports, in 2016, we wrote: 'A future where the combination of our philosophy, our art, our training practice, our social enterprise programs, and our global development programs will add up to more than the sum of the parts. Nothing less than changing the world one irreverent, inspirational and innovative Circus Oz show at a time.'

It was a privilege to be part of the show. My farewell party was spectacular in the Melbourne spiegeltent. I wore a silver snakeskin suit, and one of the main performers, Sarah Ward, did what could be considered as her own version of a vagina monologue, as well as some songs. We all danced, ate and drank.

Corporate governance, like most things, can be fun. Although serious business. You have to deliver results. But to work in an arts company with less money than most, and to support people with extraordinary skills, is such a rewarding role. In my first year at Circus Oz, I learnt that when the red buckets went around after the show the money collected went to the Asylum Seekers Program. And during the time I was there, Circus Oz shows raised over $300,000. It is a company with a conscience and big dreams. It makes people laugh.

When my granddaughter, Lara, was very little and watching Rockie performing on the trapeze, she said she thought she would like to be Rockie when she grows up. I reminded her that she would have to get a degree first because that is what Rockie did.

It is the power of the relationships. I can trace the approach of Circus Oz to me, back through the mentoring practice, which came out of Citibank, and the Reconciliation Leadership Program I developed with Citibank and IATSIS in 1999 and 2000, and on it goes.

Meanwhile, my mentoring programs became a must-have for many of the legal firms in Sydney, Melbourne and Brisbane. When Sophie joined me in business in 2006, she quickly became engaged. We worked together happily, sitting almost side by side for five years, from 2007 to 2012. We celebrated when Kevin Rudd was elected. A few days later, when he announced he was holding a 2020 Summit to encourage a national conversation designed to help shape a long-term strategy for the nation's future we looked at the people attending and could see how many had been touched by our mentoring or leadership program. It was a very gratifying moment.

With Sophie there, the practice expanded. And it also enabled me to keep the rather crazy international travel that I was doing at a manageable level. On the night of the federal election when Kevin Rudd won, we were dancing in the street at a friend's house. And thinking, finally, some of our old issues around gender would be back on the agenda.

Sophie is now the sole owner of McCarthy Mentoring and more than two decades later it is a successful standalone business operating around the world. The new look is mother and daughter, not father and son.

As business management author Tom Peters famously predicted at a seminar I attended in 2006, the future is China, India and female.

CHAPTER 23

headspace

> What mental health needs is more sunlight, more candour, and more unashamed conversation.
>
> Glenn Close

In 2007, Kevin Rudd became Prime Minister. It was a stunning victory. In 2008, I accepted the offer from Minister of Health and Ageing Nicola Roxon to chair headspace, the National Youth Mental Health Foundation. It was another one of those self-questioning times. It would be exciting to be part of the new government. But did I have the energy to do this? I wondered.

The Howard years had not been good for women and the public sector, and I had invested my energy in those first years of the new century in health policy in New South Wales. I had become a trusted community adviser and consultant to the state health system. I co-chaired the Sustainable Access Health Priority Taskforce and, prior to that, had been a member of the Health Care Advisory Council and the Health Participation Council. I had travelled throughout New South Wales, listening to community expectations for their health services of the future. Better mental health services were high on the agenda. Youth suicide was a serious issue, and appropriate services were difficult to access. I could use my experience and knowledge to govern and grow headspace. Here was a new opportunity.

I rang a couple of friends, as I always do, to arrange to meet up and talk about it. And one of them looked at me and said, 'Wendy, you know I have lost someone to suicide, of course you have to do it. How could you refuse?'

I decided to accept the role.

headspace sounded like a wonderful initiative and had cross-party political support and a budget line item. I was experienced enough by now to know that in this game you need a clear line in the budget so you can be held accountable.

I confess to some doubts about ageing. I was by now sixty-seven. Was that too old to take this on? A quick look around my male peers put that negative thought to rest. Women live longer, I reminded myself. Get on with it.

Most of my work in the health sector has been in health promotion and disease prevention, so in many ways headspace was a natural fit for me. It focused on an emerging adult, 12–25, with an emphasis on prevention. It proved safe, feasible and highly accessible to young people and their families.

headspace was created in 2006 to promote and support early intervention for young people with mental and substance-abuse disorders. It was the culmination of the work and lobbying by Professor Patrick McGorry and Professor Ian Hickie—psychiatrists who felt deeply about the fact that mental health services for the twelve- to twenty-five-year-old cohort did not receive the share of the budget or the inclusion in the health portfolio that young people deserved.

In the first instance, headspace had been given $54 million from the Australian government. The main aim was to establish an accessible multidiscipline model of care to target the health needs of young people and to ensure that the schism between mental health and drug and alcohol services could be overcome with a common co-location and clinical governance. It was assumed that the physical health needs of young people would not be the primary focus as they represented only a minor component of the burden of the disease, though the service model would be able to address these needs as required.

I thought it was a magnificent and compelling proposition. When I became Chair, there were thirty centres. I prepared to meet the new directors. A couple expressed their astonishment at my appointment. One asked me how come he had never heard of me and was quite surprised when I said I supported the Schizophrenia Foundation in a very light-touch way, and had also been an Ambassador for Black Dog Institute for some years. I wondered if he would have posed that question to a man. I sensed there was outrage that the new minister Nicola Roxon was reorganising headspace and putting her stamp on the board without consulting them. It was with both enthusiasm and trepidation that I went to my first meeting.

It was one of the toughest gigs I have ever done. The governance structure was clumsy and from my perspective old-fashioned, with a central board and a large advisory group. Like many organisations that I have been part of, there was a sense that the experts on the board could micromanage the organisation. It never works—a boardroom is not a surgery or a clinic.

I realised that one of my first tasks would be to restructure the company, persuade the directors to keep their nose in and their fingers out of the day-to-day business, and let the management team get on with the job. This was not met with great enthusiasm. However, I was supported by Nicola

Roxon, and later her successor Mark Butler, who became the Minister for Mental Health and Ageing, a new and dedicated portfolio.

The first couple of years were both stressful and exciting. headspace directors and staff were passionate about their work and wanted their centres to be trusted providers. It was the go-to place for young people. Never underestimate the stigma of mental illness. Acknowledging their needs and seeking help is the first step as those of us with mental illness in our families well know. To have young people trusting our centres was both humbling and reaffirming. Everyone wanted a headspace centre, and I for one thought they should have one.

It seemed that the more successful we became, the less likely it was that we could retain our independence. We were in high-growth mode, and by 2016 we had a hundred centres. We'd also had four prime ministers and five health ministers. They all supported headspace, as did the Commonwealth Department of Health. During my time at headspace, my worst fear was that we would come to a point where it would be incorporated into the primary health networks (PHNs). That is exactly what happened in 2016 when Susan Ley became Minister. There is a reluctance in government to let these standalone entities remain independent and have their own budget line.

That was time for me. I had given it my best and did not agree with policy. After the election the independent directors resigned. headspace established the need for public provision for youth mental health and was admired as a leading mental health initiative for young people throughout the world. headspace Australia helped establish headspace Denmark, headspace Canada and headspace Israel. Our suicide-prevention program in schools was widely admired and sought after and e-headspace was a world-first. I felt very proud of the Australian leadership.

I still recommend headspace to young people. The board issues were irritating and challenging, but the service remains strong. If there is any criticism in that space, it is that the young people requiring acute care do not get the attention they need. Mental health is one of the fastest growing non-communicable diseases in the world. I am grateful that I had a chance to be steering some of those services and promoting the need for young people to have a fair go in mental health.

CHAPTER 24
A full dance card

Better to stay in the boardroom than die of boredom.
Dame Beryl Beaurepaire, seconded by Joan Bielski

At the end of 2012, I decided it was time to relocate from my McGrath Real Estate office space in Edgecliff where I had been for over a decade. I had accepted the invitation of Simon Longstaff from the St James Ethics Centre to move into his office space at Castlereagh Street. It was a beautiful new building and I was thrilled to be back in the city. I had forgotten how much of its buzz I had missed. Walking to work through the Domain was a spectacular way to start the day.

Sophie had taken over McCarthy Mentoring by this time and planned to keep the space at McGrath's and I thought she was best free of her mother and program founder. The St James Ethics Centre was a place to encounter a stimulating conversation in the kitchen. I loved working there and hosted many events, including the launch of Michael Traill's book *Jumping Ship* in 2016.

It was time for me to leave the McGrath Board, too. I was way past my use-by date. The years in Edgecliff being housed with McGrath were fun and energising—so many shiny young people with big dreams and eager for knowledge and skills. I was the Foundation Chair of the company in 2000. It was one of my outlier roles—people didn't see me as a real estate person, but I loved the company and reminded people that purchasing a house was the most significant spending decision of young people, and for those who thought real estate was naff it was best not to attend a Sydney or Melbourne dinner party where it was frequently the main topic of conversation. I introduced Corporate Good Works and philanthropy to the firm, which went on to win the Prime Minister's Award for Best National Philanthropic Program for our work with Youth Off the Streets.

Keeping faith with Beryl Beaurepaire's advice to stay in the boardroom, I had a full board dance card, which included Circus Oz, headspace, Goodstart Early Learning, Pacific Friends of the Global Fund, Plan International, McGrath Estate Agents and IMF Bentham.

IMF Bentham

I joined the board of IMF Bentham (now Omni Bridgeway) in 2013. It seemed a most unlikely role for me. I had not visualised myself as a director of a company in the financial services sector, but class actions and financial justice I liked. I was approached by Chairman Rob Ferguson to consider a role as a non-executive director. After the usual self-doubt about my capacity, I went back to my advice to others: if someone thinks you can do it, you most probably can. I like to think that with the experience I had had as a company director by 2013, I should be able to get my head around this.

I didn't know Rob well but was interested in his ideas about Androgyny in the Boardroom, after he gave a fascinating speech about it at the Sydney Institute in 1996. He defined an androgynous person as someone who possesses the whole range of human qualities. Qualities such as courage, compassion, competitiveness, sharing enthusiasm, guts striving for excellence and leadership. Such a person is not limited by normal social conditioning to the traditionally narrow perspective of either sex. Such a person has accessed their whole potential.

Before Rob Ferguson approached me, I had been a guest speaker at two legal lunches where people from IMF had also been in attendance. They were describing how they urged the directors to get a woman on their board. This opportunity came about again from my wonderful, serendipitous but real role in the community as a woman leader, a mentor, a female company director and, among those, I would like to think a teacher who wants to learn, enable and inspire people by saying, *This is not a bridge too far, Wendy, you can do it.*

I was the first female non-executive director at the company. For the first couple of meetings, I was struggling to see how I could contribute. My colleagues were smart with a strong sense of social and financial justice. And they knew how to play a long game. Still, when I asked to join the selection committee to find a new CEO, I was confident that I could bring a broader perspective to the appointment, and show I had a stake in the company.

When I was appointed to the board, a senior partner at a leading legal firm called me, asking, 'Why would you do that? It's not your scene. It's not a respectable industry for a woman, they are just bottom feeders. But,' he continued, 'if I was going to bring a class action against anyone, they are the best in the Australia, and probably in the world. I still would advise you not to do it, but as you have accepted it, at least you are joining the world's best practice.'

I tell this story to remind myself how many men in my life feel the need to advise me on these moves. Whereas they will often take the same role when offered. Are some roles not suitable for a woman? I don't think so. I don't call them and query their choices but, in the spirit of friendship, I accept that they were trying to protect me. Thank you, gentlemen.

When I look at the collection of corporate roles I had from 2010 to 2020, there are ways of seeing the things they have in common. I have a recurrent interest in doing corporate governance differently and better.

Every board is a learning opportunity. Meeting new people, solving new problems, meeting and working in New York, Hong Kong, Vietnam, Albania, Melbourne, Perth, Sydney, Adelaide, Brisbane, Canberra, Washington and the Hunter Valley—all rich experiences, and all creating and building new relationships. I felt privileged to have such a diverse portfolio. It sounds like a big load, but it was doable unless something went wrong. And there are concentric circles of relationships of people who have a primary role in one matter, and other relationships and engagements in other matters. I am often the connecting person.

Goodstart Early Learning

This remains my dream board. It is the one that reminds me of Nelson Mandela's oh-so-true quote: 'There can be no keener revelation of a society's soul than the way in which it treats its children.'

In late November 2008, a chain of childcare centres was on the brink of financial collapse. ABC Learning founded in the early nineties had just been placed into voluntary administration and a receiver was appointed. Tens of thousands of children, along with 13,000 employees, faced an uncertain future.

A phone call between social entrepreneur Evan Thornley and the then head of Social Ventures Australia, Michael Traill, sowed the seed of an audacious idea: purchase the ABC Learning network and use it to drive improved educational and social outcomes for Australia's children. The need was compelling. In 2009, 23.6 per cent of children in Australia were developmentally vulnerable as they entered school.

The buyout was a massive gamble. ABC Learning had attracted much criticism within the early childhood education sector for being of poor quality and profit focused. I was one of many people to publicly argue that case with Eddy Groves, the founder of ABC Learning, regarding the standards of its childcare operational chain and the quality on offer. The market was proving not to be the solution to Australia's childcare needs, despite the regulatory National Accreditation scheme.

The not-for-profit community sector still offered the best opportunity for pre-school experience in Australia. Their teachers were often better qualified, they were engaged with the local community, and they had better infrastructure. But there were not enough teachers, and it had to be acknowledged that tens of thousands of children had been denied early learning before Eddy Groves filled the space. It would take considerable expertise to transform the failed entity and operate it with a different philosophy. One with an emphasis on high-quality, education-focused childcare, supported by appropriate business discipline.

History records that an innovative partnership was formed, bringing together four of Australia's most respected community sector organisations: the Benevolent Society,

Social Ventures Australia, Brotherhood of St Laurence and Mission Australia. Their shared ambitions would improve the lives and education of Australia's children.

These organisations committed their own resources to the project and enlisted the help of former Macquarie Group Director Robin Crawford to win additional funding support from the National Australia Bank, the Australian government, and a small group of social investors. Some $95 million in cash was secured to purchase 678 ABC Learning centres, along with $70 million to fund the ongoing operations of a new social enterprise.

I was watching and reading what was happening to ABC Learning as this consortium started to become public. I thought to be a director of what would effectively be a start-up in the interests of children, where children and their families became the bottom line, would be fantastic. However, I was already chairing headspace, Circus Oz, Pacific Friends of the Global Fund and McGrath Real Estate. I had a pretty full plate, but I just kept watching the story. I was fascinated by the possibilities. I knew Robin Crawford, but it didn't even occur to me to call and see if he would consider me as a director, although we had been on the Clean Up Australia Environment Foundation together.

When I got a phone call from Robin asking me if I would be interested in being part of the first board, I was delighted. Gordon was pretty cool about on the idea, however, and thought I should leave it to someone younger—that didn't go down well. My friend and mentor Joan Bielski, an educational adviser to many ministers, said, 'You must do this because they must have a feminist lens on the board. This is unfinished business from the early feminist WEL agenda—this is an opportunity to really make a difference.'

When Robin rang me to confirm his offer, I said yes. Privately, I thought, *This is the hottest role in Australia for the next decade*. And it proved to be so. It was an amazingly audacious idea.

The first weeks and months were hard for everyone—debt, a lack of trained educators, uncertainty and anxiety of the staff and many families, and underdeveloped management systems. Many of the centres were shabby and no longer fit for purpose. There seemed to be an endless list of to-do items. We had to work hard to persuade the management and staff of our commitment. Equally, they needed to appreciate we were not there to maintain the status quo. This was about change.

We agreed we didn't want a hierarchical set-up, with the board sitting above the management team. We had to be one team with a common goal. We didn't want board members to micromanage either, but we wanted to make sure that their expertise was available at no extra cost to our people and the organisation.

I was chairing Circus Oz at the same time, and it had survived forty years with a flat leadership team. (Leadership shared between three managers meant it was as non-hierarchical as anything can be, but it worked and served the institution very well.) I could see that Goodstart offered us an opportunity to do corporate governance differently. So often highly skilled people join boards as non-executive directors, and no one even asks them a question about whether they can do anything to help. It was very innovative to think of ourselves as external consultants and to be listened to. It also meant a major commitment of time—we spent a lot of time together, referring to each other and assigning tasks to make sure we got it all done.

Quarterly, two-day board meetings became the norm. We started with a half-day informal session with senior management on topics such as talent, advocacy and government relations, usually followed by a dinner and a formal board meeting. Supporting a culture of open and informal engagement made a difference. We could all be part of a learning organisation. That was very satisfying. We also operated a quite informal and collegiate board. That is not unusual on some of the not-for-profit boards I have come from. I remember our CEO, Julia Davison, commenting that we didn't feel we had to take a vote on motions. We would have the formal papers and there would be a free-flowing conversation around it and then we would reach agreement.

This was an ego-free board. Many of the people sitting around the table had held authoritative places in other organisations. They were sitting at this table with a view to doing something significant and different. Discourse was always respectful. Robin Crawford was our Chair until illness intervened; he was succeeded by Michael Traill, and I became Deputy.

I was simultaneously chairing headspace, and the difference between headspace and Goodstart was astonishing. Both had a high moral and social purpose, but the headspace board was not as cohesive. Attending a Goodstart or Circus Oz board meeting was a dream by contrast. Of course, Goodstart had its tensions, though most of us felt comfortable to face it openly. That was very clear in feedback when we had our first board review. These became a biannual feature of the board, and showed the depth and experience of trust the directors shared.

How did we change the organisation? The timeline runs like this.

In 2010, there was 644 centres to care for 71,000 children. Over that first decade, more than five hundred centres were upgraded, occupancy rates lifted to about 80 per cent. More than 90 per cent of centres met the National Quality Standard, compared with 45 per cent of those assessed when the standard was introduced in 2012.

On average, in 2019, the 15,000 Goodstart staff members were paid 5 per cent above the award and staff turnover has almost halved from 2 per cent previously at ABC Learning. The company has invested more than $100 million in professional development and research since 2014. Staff were encouraged to enrol for learning and development in Goodstart's own institute of early learning.

That is the how. What was the purpose?

It's the social impact—more than five hundred vulnerable children have received two days a week of fee-relief care via a scholarship program. Almost 25 per cent of the centres are in some of Australia's lower socio-economic areas. Research has shown that high-quality pre-school is beneficial for children, especially from low-income families. It helps them prepare academically for kindergarten, socially, behaviourally, and shrinks achievement gaps. For poor children, it results in increased earnings and better health later in life.

We applied the best of development opportunities for the people in the organisation too: professional development, better salaries, learning about educational pedagogy. And at the same time, for those who wanted to be the people who run the centres with good business skills, we offered business development programs. Families were encouraged to be part of the centre and part of the educational development of their children.

I wanted us to reach out to Aboriginal communities, and I contacted June Oscar from Fitzroy Crossing, where an early learning centre had been set up adjacent to the women's centre.

The centre was having difficulty maintaining its funding and reporting to four different government departments was a heavy burden. I asked if they would accept Goodstart's help and support if we could find a way to work consistently with the local families. To be respectful, our CEO, our finance director and I made the long trek to Fitzroy Crossing, 400 kilometres east of Broome. We stayed for a couple of days to build relationships and identify how we might lessen the red-tape burden they carried. It was a wonderful journey.

In 2016, we launched the Fitzroy Crossing Secondment Program, supporting eight educators to spend several months at the Baya Gawiy Buga Yani Jandu Yani U Centre in Western Australia. Today, Goodstart continues to support some of the centre's administrative functions. People accepted that our offer and relationship was authentic. Twenty-three people have been placed, our educators loved the idea, and it remains an enduring program. It is probably the best legacy I can think of.

From the beginning, Goodstart was keen to create an international thought leaders' group with international experts to support the development of our research and evaluation strategy. This was a stimulating group and influenced our performance. It increased our determination that Goodstart would be best in class.

When my term ended in 2018, I left Goodstart as a voice to be listened to in the early learning community, one which works effectively and progressively with government, community, families and children. It was an exhilarating experience to be part of such a professional board. When I left it, it was already a billion-dollar company. What a result to have after a decade of experience. I feel confident it is a successful social model that can be duplicated elsewhere.

Today, Goodstart is the largest provider of childcare and early learning in Australia, with 665 centres catering for 75,600 children. It has a revenue of $1.1 billion. The surpluses it earns are invested in raising the quality of early learning and supporting centres in disadvantaged areas.

Employee surveys show that it has become a place where staff do want to work. But there is still a way to go. What it does demonstrate is a business can achieve a deep balance of skills and attributes without having to pay exorbitant director salaries. I hope it is an imitative model. There is definitely a place for a similar model in aged care and mental health.

When I finished my time at Goodstart it had satisfied my sense of moral and social purpose. I felt sad to leave, but proud that it was strong and thriving—a leading provider. And a respected voice in all layers of government. Goodstart is the exemplar of what can be achieved when a group of determined people connect head and heart to provide a better service for our most precious young citizens.

CHAPTER 25
Governance, boards and directors

> I always did something I was a little not ready to do. I think that's how you grow.
>
> Marissa Mayer

Boards exist to provide strategic oversight for a company and to protect the financial interests of shareholders. It takes a strong combination of people, rules, processes and procedures to manage the business of a company.

Corporate governance in the business context refers to the systems of rules, practices and processes by which companies are governed. In this way the corporate governance model followed by a specific company is the distribution of rights and responsibilities by all participants in the organisation.

People want to become directors in order to be active players in the governance of the institutions of our nation, despite the fact that they face the continual challenge of aligning the interests of the board, management, shareholders and stakeholders. They must respond to their duties and responsibilities with full regard to transparency and accountability.

It is often said that corporate boards are responsible for providing oversight, insight and foresight. That's a tall order in today's marketplace, which is complex and volatile. Good governance principles are fundamental to the work that board directors do.

The role of the board of directors in corporate governance

Corporate boards have many duties and responsibilities. With every decision the board makes, they must consider how it will affect their employees, customers, suppliers, communities and shareholders.

Good corporate governance relies on distinct differences in the roles between board directors and managers. It was never intended for board directors to be directly involved in the daily operations of a corporation, and they certainly shouldn't engage in micromanaging the management. The main roles of board directors are oversight and strategy. Despite the differences, board directors may delegate certain powers to the CEO or CFO under certain circumstances.

When I asked an experienced board director for advice in my new role as Deputy Chair of the ABC, he said, 'Keep your nose in and your fingers out.' It was good advice. Don't try to manage the organisation—you are part of a team whose task is to govern.

Boards regularly delegate some of their duties to board committees. Corporate board committees act as a subset of the full board. Committees devote the necessary time and resources to issues for which the full board doesn't have time. Committees delve deep into issues, often calling in experts to assist them. Committees provide regular reports to the board on the matters they're charged with handling.

I always volunteer for committee work as it offers an opportunity to work with management and develop trust and new insights.

Board composition and independent directors

Best practices for corporate governance encourage boards to offer the majority of board seats to independent directors. A well-composed board brings a diverse range of expertise, perspectives and knowledge into the boardroom. Regulators, investors and others are also making a big push for boards to consider diversity in a multitude of realms, including age, gender, experience, ethnicity, race, religion, skills and experiences.

Strategic planning

The role of the board is to plan and strategise goals and objectives for the short- and long-term good of the company and to put mechanisms in place to monitor progress against the objectives. Board directors must constantly review, understand and discuss the company's goals. In particular, the board relies on independent directors to challenge the board's perspectives to ensure sound decision-making.

The board must be confident in how they plan to address uncertainties and how they can capitalise on opportunities for the future, while identifying and managing real and potential risks. To inspire trust from investors, it's necessary for board directors to be able to articulate their plans for the future so that investors have a clear picture of the long-term outlook.

Stewardship

In essence, board directors act as stewards of the company they govern in the present and provide guidance and direction for the future. In their role as overseers, board members must continually assess a variety of risks in the following categories: financial reporting, reputation, litigation, ethics, technology, health, safety, climate change/environment and, most recently, cybersecurity.

Contemporary board members require curious minds to stay abreast of contemporary issues. That for me is part of the thrill and challenge of being a company director. You are constantly learning and working with new people and ideas. It is why people want to be part of a board. There are big issues with plenty at stake.

The board's relationship with management

It is in a board's best interest to develop good working relationships with managers. Corporations run best when the board and senior management hold the same perspectives on strategy, priorities and risk management. That is the sweet spot for a board, especially when you are the Chair.

Communication is a vital component of good corporate governance. Boards must communicate clearly and in a timely manner to develop a sense of mutual confidence and trust with their managers. It is important for board directors to have regular conversations with managers about risk mitigation and prevention. Managers need to understand risk so that they can put processes in place to protect the company.

Boards matter. They are the pinnacle entities in business and in the not-for-profit, for-purpose community. Service on a volunteer board of directors is a traditional form of citizen participation in the public sectors; as such, boards contribute to an evolving democratic process.

If you are seeking a role as an independent director, there are many areas of governance to consider. People of faith often seek roles with faith-based boards, sports people look for sports-based boards, arts lovers for arts boards, conservationists and those who care about heritage go to The National Trust and local environmental groups. Some of the best learning opportunities come from being a director of a government board and/or statutory authority. My book-loving friends compete to be on the board of the State Library. These are prestigious roles that recognise the importance of having directors who are seen as trustees of community values. It is also good to learn governance in subject areas in which you feel confident. You can branch out later.

All of these require good governance. It is the common thread that enables organisations to judiciously manage their affairs. I started what has turned out to be a significant board career in small not-for-profits (NFPs) where I felt passionate about the purpose of the company and, generally, I have joined boards across a broad spectrum where I have a sense of alignment and a curiosity. You don't need to start with Qantas or BHP, although don't say no to them. There is plenty of help around for new directors.

Being a company director in today's world is very different from the time I started. But in the beginning the point was always about wanting to be part of the entities that run our society, namely government, business and religion; they offer plenty of scope for people aspiring to be company directors. Women wanted a seat at those tables, and we are a better governed society as a result of their lobbying and professional persistence.

In the mid-eighties, a board appointment was often seen as a reward/sinecure for a mature male on his way to retirement. The board was seen as the last club before the exit lounge from a business, a way of staying in touch with his peer group who were members of similar clubs involving tennis/sailing/horse racing, The Australian and Melbourne Clubs or the Union Club. Their years of experience and networks were valued on both corporate and not-for-profit boards. Mature women did not have the same opportunities as most of those clubs did not permit women members. Women wanted to be included.

The Hawke government in 1983 committed to appointing women to statutory boards as part of its women's policy. I was a beneficiary of that policy and never for a moment felt like a token. This policy resulted in many women being board-ready for wider roles including non-government boards.

The barriers for women were high. Most appointments came through male networks. Most directors argued when challenged about the gender uniformity of their boards and insisted there was little demand and no supply anyway. A government minister called me about a board appointment in the late nineties. The conversation went like this: 'Good morning, Wendy. I am looking for a woman for an environmental board and wondered if you could help.'

I asked about required skills and he seemed surprised but hurriedly suggested a background in engineering or financial or legal would be valued. Within two hours I delivered him the names of three women who fit the bill. He was surprised, thanked me and hung up. Two weeks later I read in the paper he had appointed a professor of English literature, someone of his political persuasion.

I would never let those who protested get away with the response that no qualified women were available! When I joined the Board of the ABC in 1983, I read everything I could find to help me be a better director. I was surprised how much I enjoyed the literature—and what a new area of interest it opened up.

There are many ways to be a director. Corporate versus NFPs is not a binary choice. Some of my best years were when I was serving in both areas. It kept a balance in my brain. Also the distinctions between the NFP board and the corporate board are not as clear as they once were. A good example is Goodstart Early Learning, a billion-dollar company that reinvests its profit in the company. By contrast, commercial childcare operators share their profits with shareholders and investors. Increasingly what were once the province of the NFP sector has been monetised by corporates as in the rise of private higher education providers and private health services. The lines of difference can blur.

The AICD *Company Director Magazine* announced in September 2021 that:

- the latest percentage of women on ASX 200 boards was 33.5 per cent (31 July 2021)
- the percentage of women on boards of ASX 200 companies and the proportion of women comprising new appointments increased significantly from a low base of 8.3 per cent in 2009
- there are still two boards in the ASX 200 that do not have any women directors.

Australia is now one of just three countries in the world to have exceeded 30 per cent without mandated quotas. New research says the next target needs to be 40–40–20. This progress would have been unthinkable even a decade ago. Though sadly and disgracefully we are still lagging behind most of the Western world on workplace gender equity, having slipped from fifteenth in the world in 2006 to fiftieth in 2021 as reported by the World Economic Forum's Global Gender Pay Gap Report.

Boards are no longer exclusive clubs and are beginning to look like the communities they serve. One of my favourite lines in the seventies was 'A Woman's Place Is in the Senate'. Susan Ryan used it very effectively in her campaign to win the Canberra Senate seat in 1975. In the nineties we asserted 'A Woman's Place Is in the Boardroom'.

My own version of this continues to be 'A Woman's Place Is Everywhere'.

CHAPTER 26
The last lunch

> A single person is missing for you, and the whole world is empty.
>
> Joan Didion, *The Year of Magical Thinking*

Early in August 2017, one of my Plan colleagues and friends, Srilatha Batliwala, a most wonderful intelligent, thoughtful, international woman, rang me unexpectedly to say she would be in Sydney for a job with an aid agency for four days, and did I have any time on Sunday to catch up? I hadn't seen her for about four years and I was very excited. At one stage she had had a chair at Harvard, and I knew my friend Anne Summers was going off to New York to live, so I thought it would be great to introduce them. So I asked Anne along to our lunch too.

Gordon, Anne, Srilatha and I had one of those special Sunday lunches. We talked, laughed, workshopped the world, and agreed that it was good to be in Sydney in a relatively safe world, while acknowledging that there was still much to be done. And, of course, bemoaning the status of America, where all of us had lived and worked at various times in our lives.

Our guests left about four o'clock. Gordon and I had an afternoon sleep, some tea and toast at about eight, and then back to bed. Gordon said he thought he would go down to our beach house at Narrawallee on the South Coast and build the bookshelf purchased from Ikea a week or so previously. I thought that was a particularly good idea as it was a bit chaotic at the end of the room where it was to go. I checked my diary and said, 'Stay a couple of days if you feel like it because I am busy Monday and Tuesday.' He left on Monday morning, said he thought he would come back on Tuesday evening.

We spoke on Monday. He said he had a bit of a scratchy throat. And then on Tuesday he said he didn't feel so good. He had done most of the work that he had gone to do, and he would come back in the morning. When we next spoke he sounded really terrible. He said he had a blocked nose, clearly an infection, and that his chest hurt. He really wanted to come home, but he would stay in bed on Wednesday and get up early on Thursday morning to drive back to Sydney. I said to him that I had a big day of appointments on the Thursday and wouldn't be back until about three o'clock, but that there was chicken soup in the fridge and he should just come in and go to bed.

I got home about 3.30 p.m. I could tell immediately that something was deeply wrong. I probably never mentioned that Gordon is one of the tidiest, most organised men you could ever live with. His bag was flung just inside the door. Max, our dog, was looking anxious. I went into the bedroom and found Gordon in the foetal position.

When I asked what was wrong, he just said, 'Oh, I've got a really bad cold.'

I said, 'I think you've got more than a cold, darling. I think you have pneumonia. How about I take you to hospital?' He was adamant he did not want to go.

'If you can get the doctor,' he said, 'that's okay, but I want to stay here tonight no matter what. I don't want to go out in that weather again and I don't want to leave home.' It's a three-hour drive from our beach house so I understood.

I took his temperature and it was very high—104°F. I knew it was bad. I was pouring water into him; he clearly hadn't had any fluid for some time, and he was dehydrating rapidly. I couldn't find a medical practice that could provide a doctor, and eventually got on to a nursing site and the nurse who answered triaged me to make sure everything I was doing was appropriate.

It was a hideous night. Winds blowing, rain falling, and our airport and major roads were closed. I knew what it would be like at the emergency at St Vincent's Hospital. People who sleep on the streets, often very ill, would be there looking for somewhere warm to be. I settled in for a long night, making sure he was comfortable, and kept giving him water as required. We agreed he would go to hospital first thing in the morning.

It was a long night in Potts Point.

I had been here before. I remembered arriving at the farm on a Saturday evening about six when I found him dehydrated. I took him to Bowral Hospital early next morning, despite his protests it was not necessary. We knew the doctor on duty and he told him he was close to organ breakdown while he attached the drip. I did use the opportunity as he recovered to persuade him it was time to sell the farm we had bought next door in 1999. We agisted our cattle there and its owner was retired, widowed and desperate to sell. It was always intended as a twenty-year investment to scale up the beef-breeding program. I wanted him to accept the management responsibility was wearing him out. Getting on a motorbike chasing cows at seven o'clock every morning of his life was growing tedious. He agreed and I wondered why I had not done this earlier. It was time for a plan for a post-rural life. A year later we had moved our lives to Sydney.

The next morning, he insisted on getting dressed. He didn't want an ambulance to come to our place. I booked an Uber with a reasonably high seat so he could get in. It took Gordon about three hours to get dressed and he was clearly very unwell. But I had got his temperature down at about two o'clock in the morning. I made sure he kept drinking. The Uber driver arrived and it was another shocking day weather wise. Gordon liked his new doctor, Dr Jonathan Bentley at Kerryn Phelps's clinic, and he wanted to go there first. He wanted to be sure that if he went to emergency, it would be at St Vincent's.

We arrived at the Surry Hills practice just after midday. Jonathan came down the stairs to meet us. The wind was so strong that Gordon had to hold onto the Uber vehicle for support. He was shaking in the breeze. It was a terrifying sight. He got into the surgery and immediately they rang the ambulance. Jonathan said, 'Gordon, it's only been two weeks since I saw you last, how did this happen?' Gordon said, 'I really don't know. Last Sunday Wen and I and some friends had a wonderful lunch, and now I just feel terrible.'

The ambulance arrived within fifteen minutes. Gordon lost consciousness. They got him back. They worked on him for an hour in the surgery, and then took him to St Vincent's. At the hospital, he was taken straight into emergency, and within an hour he was tubed and pumped. The attending doctor said to me, 'This man is very, very sick.' I said, 'I know.'

Sam and Sophie arrived and were clearly shocked. The man they had been joking and laughing with the previous Saturday was nowhere to be seen, other than in his eyes and soul. He looked frail, thin and anxious. He said that we should go home. I said, 'No, we won't go home, but Sam and Sophie might go home for a while to tend to their families but I'll stay.'

Meetings with the doctors made us realise how dangerously ill he was. I felt in my heart that he was unlikely to be leaving cured. This had been a long haul, and he had nothing to fight it with. He was so thin.

At nine o'clock on Thursday night, they sent him up to critical care, where Sophie and I stayed for quite a bit longer, leaving the hospital after midnight. We had had a medical conference, and I stressed that Gordon would not want to be intubated; that he would want to die rather than live an incapacitated life. The team was fantastic. When we left him, he was aware we were leaving. We kissed him goodbye, and said, 'We will see you a little bit later.' The hospital team really wanted us to go home and get a couple of hours of sleep, and promised they would ring us if anything worse happened.

They rang at six o'clock in the morning to say Gordon was on a respirator, so we should come in. At eleven o'clock, it was all over. He didn't regain consciousness. We were all with him until they took off the respirator and he just slipped away.

It was so shocking for us, but probably relatively painless for him. We were so unprepared. But, in a way, we weren't really. We had been rehearsing this scene, one way or another, since he got leukaemia in 1981.

Our nephew Michael had arrived by that time. Michael, Sophie, Hamish, Sam and I went down to have a cup of tea in the St Vincent's café and join the grandchildren. They wanted to see Gordon—their parents had decided that would be appropriate, and I was very relaxed about it. The team needed about an hour to prepare him. We sat down and told a few Gordon stories. I don't think I cried. I was in deep, deep shock. I couldn't feel anything.

We went back upstairs. The children looked devastated. The three older ones, the Greens, started sobbing. But the little ones were intrigued. It was Luca's birthday. And he said, 'I hope Grandpa will remember to come to my party.' And Sam said, 'No, darling, Grandpa won't be coming to the party.' Luca was shocked. He could not believe that this peaceful-looking man in front of him was dead.

It was an unforgettable and unimaginable day. I went home later that evening and sat in my house feeling numb. How random life all seemed. He was the man with whom I spent fifty-four years of my life and he was not coming home.

I had to ring the hospital because he had made an appointment to meet a new haematologist on the Monday and I thought I would do that while I was on autopilot. They had been notified by an internal email of Gordon's death and they said, 'We are so sorry, but we want you to know that he died as Australia's longest-living bone marrow recipient.'

About two days later I was hit by the most overwhelming wave of grief.

I couldn't stand up. It just kept coming. I kept thinking, I have to plan a funeral. And somehow we did.

I was determined to speak at the funeral. I knew he would want me to honour him in that way and I managed to stay composed. But at the reception afterwards I found myself once again overwhelmed and sobbing in Sophie's spare room. For months, I'd find myself walking down the street or talking to someone, and just start crying. I am thinking, *This isn't what I do*. But it was what I did.

I remembered I had Joan Didion's book *The Year of Magical Thinking*, which I had read a couple of times, and often given to friends. I went foraging in my bookshelf, thinking it might help. And I remembered why I wanted it—she is such a wonderful wordsmith, saying of the death of her husband, John, 'Life changes fast, life changes in an instant, you sit down to dinner [in my case, lunch], and life as you know it ends.' Such comforting words.

It was the last meal I had had with Gordon, that Sunday before, and I am happy we shared it with two special friends. So many of our friends were generous and kind during that time. Although I still have trouble sorting out some of the memories. Without Mary Vallentine, we wouldn't have had beautiful music at the funeral. She and Margaret Throsby just came straight to my aid and helped us sort out the music and the recording. Geraldine Doogue held us all together as she led us through the funeral service. And, of course, our families and friends stood close.

I wasn't going to write this bit, but I need to help myself understand that the advice to get under a doona for twelve months was actually good. And, really, what brought me out from under the doona was the campaign to get Kerryn Phelps elected to federal parliament. It had a sense of purpose and fairness, and I needed something to change my mind.

I went through the motions of going to board meetings and began to think about winding down my workload. I had already made the decision that when Gordon came back from the farm, I would stop doing most of what I was doing, and we would have a different life together. The apartment I bought for us was probably not the place I would have bought just for me. But now it holds dear and special memories, even though he only lived there three months—it is still his place, as is our beach house on the South Coast.

Gordon would have loved his funeral. People were happy. Our children were magnificent, as were our grandchildren. It was a beautiful exit for a life well lived.

The last words

On 26 August 2017, I stood up in the Eastern Suburbs Crematorium and delivered my eulogy to Gordon, whose unexpected death had left me in almost demented grief. I wanted to make a statement about my soulmate and acknowledge his role in my life:

> I met Gordon McCarthy on a blind date in 1963 when I was twenty-two and he was twenty-three. We were meeting at an art movie with our respective flatmates. He arrived late and climbed over the seats in the theatre to sit next to me. I was grudgingly impressed by his audacity although less than impressed by his lateness. When he called me the next day, I found myself agreeing to have dinner with him.
>
> There was something special about him. He was different to the other men in my life. Cheeky, challenging, opinionated and drop-dead gorgeous with strong views about right and wrong.
>
> We were both country kids in pursuit of new adventures. He had a sense of where he was going. He wanted to see the world and planned to be only a year in Sydney before he started travelling, which he explained would be on his own. And he loved dancing.
>
> Despite his lofty ambitions to defer coupledom, love got in the way. Within two weeks we had agreed to spend our lives together.
>
> I have loved him deeply for fifty-four years and am struggling to think of life without him.
>
> We gave each other room to move. He assumed I would always have a professional career. He supported

everything—well, most—of my professional and personal aspirations. I trusted his judgement.

When he told me that he thought that sharing everything included us both contributing to the family income, I was taken aback. I had not factored that into our new relationship. All the marriages I knew had other assumptions. It was a liberating gesture for it assumed he would have the space to take his share of domestic life and I would have the space to have a career.

Fifteen months after we met, we were married and on a boat with a one-way ticket to London and a guaranteed job for him at Cooper's. It was a wonderful way to start a marriage. London in the sixties was fun. We knew no one and had to make it work. There was nowhere to hide if things went wrong. We had to hang together and carve out our own definition of what our marriage could look like.

It was a marriage of equals. There were few women I knew who could say that.

From the beginning, we worked in different spaces. He worked in the big end of town and I taught in disadvantaged schools in Hackney, Hammersmith and Fulham. As we made friends in our workplaces, we would bridge the class divide and bring them together over dinners in our basement flat on Queensway. We travelled every other weekend to the English countryside in our little green minivan and parked it overnight to sleep in country lanes. And at least four nights a week we went to concerts, jazz clubs, theatre. We were like two sponges soaking up another world, joined at the hip.

Gordon was intrigued by Scandinavia and wanted to understand why these countries with small populations were world leaders in so many areas. It was thus deemed that we would visit car factories and breweries to see how they worked and try to understand why Australia was not in that space.

My new husband's fascination with how and why things work became contagious, especially when observing different societies. That restless inquiring brain required answers. It was sometimes annoying when he interrogated people he had met twenty minutes before.

In 1966, we were transferred from London to Pittsburgh for a year. His work for the first six months was boring as no one really believed Aussies could do much, but it meant he observed corporate America at close quarters, and until he was assigned to good work he spent his days reading in the Carnegie Library. It was the beginning of a love of military history.

After a year in the US, we were on our way home. It seemed like time to put roots down and have a baby . . . We took our time driving across the USA on Route 66, through Mexico, and flew out of Acapulco to Sydney, hoping we were pregnant. We were and within five years our family included Sophie, Hamish and Sam.

We were determined to do birth together and joined the Childbirth Education Association, which was lobbying to give fathers the right to be present at birth. Together we became activists for choices in childbirth and took on the hospital systems and the obstetricians who did not want fathers in the labour wards. We were successful, and he was there for the births of Sophie, Hamish and Sam. Sharing birthing with families is now an accepted practice.

Our first house in McMahons Point brought to the fore Gordon the builder. Brick walls were built, floors were sanded, old bits of wood came out of the bay and turned into the dining room table, which has been the central point in all our homes since 1974.

Last Sunday week, we had our last luncheon party on it.

McMahons Point was where we became active citizens. It produced Gordon the urban guerrilla, determined to beat the developers. He could be seen pasting 'Save McMahons Point' on telegraph poles. The campaign was successful. McMahons Point is now a desirable residential suburb.

Life seemed perfect until a regular scheduled health insurance medical disclosed he had chronic myeloid leukaemia. It was a profound moment. Within a week from diagnosis, he was advised he had six weeks to live and should be sure he had his affairs in order.

His courage and stoicism were extraordinary. He made a plan and assured me he was not intending to die. I wanted to believe him. After seven years of on and off chemotherapy, he decided to try his luck with a bone marrow transplant. His brother was a perfect match, and in 1988 he had a transplant.

Last week in hospital, the medical staff told me he was officially the longest living bone marrow recipient in Australia. How could I doubt it?

I woke this morning feeling so sad, and then thought to myself, no, Gordon doesn't want that sadness. He wants me to tell you some of his story and celebrate his life. He has too much of the old warrior in him to waste time on despair. And then I smiled when I thought that, even in death, he cheated the leukaemia. It reminded me what an extraordinary person he was, and as well as loving him how much I admired him.

When I think of what he packed into his life: accountancy, travel, publishing, writing, establishing and running a manufacturing business, then breeding cattle and farming, I am just filled with awe. He was always in pursuit of excellence. No wonder he cheated the leukaemia; he treated it as seriously as it needed to be treated, and then got on with more fulfilling things and interests, like reading and music.

Our family was his bedrock, and he took his role as provider seriously so that if the leukaemia won, we would be cared for. The years between diagnosis and transplant were spent building businesses that he could sell to ensure we would be safe. He encouraged me to take on more so that I would be set up for life and could take over our affairs.

He was interested and articulate on a wide range of topics, from animal husbandry and jazz to politics, and the early days of management consultants, in which he was a pioneer. His pursuit of detail was relentless. When I first became a company director, he would interrogate me to ensure I fully understood my responsibilities.

His voice stays with me. He was the most constant, loyal friend.

His life was a life of goodness, courage, integrity and individuality. He had a particular toughness which reassured people that the homework was always done and could be trusted.

Our marriage was not conventional in many senses, but it worked.

He was my man, my mate and mentor.

He always had my back.

Our story is the story of a happy marriage, for which I will forever be grateful.

I was always loved.

There can be no greater gift.

CHAPTER 27
Doctor's orders

> I think if women are to have the influence they wish to have and if Parliament is to represent the community which it serves, then many many more women should be in Parliament.
>
> Senator the Hon. Margaret Guilfoyle

On 20 October 2018, the residents of Wentworth went to the poll in the by-election caused by the resignation of Prime Minister Malcolm Turnbull. As the Campaign Chair for Dr Kerryn Phelps, I was out in the electorate at 8 a.m., feeling the excitement and energy of the day. It had been a tough but exciting campaign, and our team was optimistic and believed we had the best candidate and a good chance of winning.

We were working on a shoestring budget with volunteers who had little prior experience of an election campaign. They were people who had a driving passion for change and saw an opportunity to challenge the complacency of the status quo. They saw it as a chance to make history. It was magical grassroots community politics.

Wentworth had never been represented by a woman or an Independent Member. It was solid-blue Liberal and many mature men counselled me during the day that that was how they liked it. Most added that their wives voted the same way. I thought not, but refrained from responding.

It felt like time for change.

Kerryn positioned herself as 'socially progressive and economically/fiscally conservative' and placed 'in the sensible centre'. She ran a strong message on health and climate change. She was also committed to getting the asylum-seeker children off Manus Island and Nauru. She had a history with this issue: while president of the Australian Medical Association, she advocated strongly for children to be removed from immigration detention.

Although a substantial number of voters had already done pre-poll voting, the polling stations were buzzing and our purple army was very visible. It was an extraordinary day, and having visited all the polling stations during the day the word on the street was that people were going to vote for Independent Dr Kerryn Phelps.

Kerryn, her wife Jackie and I had decided, on the advice of our media strategist Darrin Barnett, that at the end of polling we would go home, do whatever we needed to do to revive ourselves, and reconvene at about 8 p.m., to give us plenty of time to get a clear result by about 9.30 p.m.

I was exhausted when I got home. Jackie predicted rain, and suddenly a thunderstorm started. I thought—she's right again. The psychic powers were speaking from the heavens, and it bucketed down. So I took my time. I knew that everyone would be perfectly happy to be at the Bondi Surf Club—a glorious spot, having a few drinks, with all the volunteers sharing their experiences. At seven o'clock, I got a phone call—I still had wet hair—saying it looked like the result was going to be called in a very short time and we needed to leave immediately.

I hopped into the taxi, zhooshing my hair as I went, dressed to the nines in my silver snakeskin suit with my silver boots, thinking I might as well go right over the top. If it's all on national television, there is no point in hiding ourselves.

We had been inside for about ten minutes when Antony Green on the ABC broadcast called the election and said Kerryn had won. The place went into mayhem. Screaming, shouting and doing the things that we love to do when we are excited—girls started dancing, a couple of the boys started dancing, then everyone was dancing and singing.

Television cameras were everywhere. We were in a state of shock, excitement, disbelief and happiness. We had made history with some firsts to celebrate: the first woman to win Wentworth, and the first woman of the Jewish faith to be elected to parliament. And I had my first glass of champagne of the day.

However, the atmosphere was changing. It seemed that the pre-poll counting was narrowing Kerryn Phelps's margins from 54.4 to 45.6, to 51.9 to 48.1. In particular, the Rose Bay pre-poll booth gave Dave Sharma, her Liberal opponent, almost 70 per cent after preferences, with over 6400 formal votes at that booth. The two hospital booths also damaged Phelps. However, she was still ahead.

I went home to sleep, feeling pretty sure that it was going to be okay. I had the sleep of the exhausted person. When I got up in the morning to turn on Barrie Cassidy's *Insiders*, the first thing he said was that it looked uncertain, and they would still be counting today.

I dragged myself into the shower, then into some clothes, and went straight out to the polling booths to scrutineer. There was a discrepancy in one of the booths where the Phelps ticket performed much worse on preferences than expected, given the primary votes at those booths. If this was correct, and the count was indeed in her favour, she would then have enough to offset the postal votes. I felt exceedingly anxious.

Next morning, I was in this great big shed at Alexandria, watching the count. The Liberal scrutineers were beside themselves and being extremely aggressive in their challenges to the count. I decided to try and take control of the situation. I went and introduced myself as the person in charge of the Phelps team. I said I would take responsibility if there were any issues with any of my team as some had not much experience (I hadn't been a scrutineer since university days). Either way, if there are any issues please come and talk to me about it.

It turned out we had a couple of excellent scrutineers in our pack. They watched every vote.

On the early counting, the media commentators talked about a record win against the Liberals. That wasn't quite right. What was clear, however, is that when it was finally all counted, and the election was declared for Kerryn the following Tuesday, there had been a nineteen per cent swing—which is very high. The victory was sweet.

In our first post-mortem, the day after, we just prayed that there would not be a general election too early. Because the idea of raising funds and repositioning ourselves in three or four months was quite confronting. But that night, and the next week, belonged to Kerryn. And the first few months in parliament belonged to her too.

She made alliances with the centrist Independents. She delivered the promises she made to her electorate, which is to get the children out of detention and off Manus. She is one of the most naturally skilful politicians that I have seen after a very long period of observing parliamentary life. She is authentic, she is extremely well prepared, she is kind, and she is politically savvy. She really is the dream candidate.

How did I come to be doing this just one year after Gordon's death?

Kerryn and I first got to know each other properly sometime in the eighties, although I had previously been aware of her in a couple of Family Planning meetings and conferences. I kept a bit of an eye on her, along with some of those other wonderful young female doctors working really hard to keep their place in the world. It was clear they were the future.

I was chairing the National Better Health program at the time. I was asked by Mick Reid, who was then Secretary of the Department of NSW Health, to meet Kerryn and have a chat to her about her career. He saw her as a person of promise with great capacity to give to her community. She was working on daytime television as a health reporter, as well as running her medical practice. She was a young mother of two and already knew she wanted a political life in the community.

I met with her and we talked about what her future might be in public life. I remember her as a smart and shiny young woman who was looking to make a difference. She was committed to exploring new pathways for herself without leaving her professional practice work. She is a passionate GP.

I suggested she start thinking about a portfolio career. There are many ways to have political influence, and it would be a good idea to explore those. As a medical practitioner with a good practice in Double Bay and a media role, she had a great base to work from. She subsequently became the first woman to be President of the federal AMA.

In 2003, I had peritonitis and realised I needed to leave my North Sydney–based practice and find a GP closer to home in the eastern suburbs. Crossing the Harbour Bridge for a medical appointment seemed mad. I became her patient and sometime later her neighbour in an apartment building where I got to know Jackie and Gabi, their daughter. We would occasionally have a meal together and talk about what she was doing, and at that stage she was very keen on going into local government.

The day after Malcolm Turnbull had resigned as Prime Minister and quit parliament, she told me a few people had suggested she stand as an Independent for Wentworth.

'What do you think?' she asked.

A lightbulb moment. 'A great idea,' I said. 'Why don't you?'

She asked if I would like to be involved. My response was in the positive, it just came tumbling out. I immediately offered to chair the campaign. It felt right.

She was such an obvious candidate. I joined the team she had started putting together under her registered political party, Kerryn Phelps Independents.

This catapulted me out from underneath the doona. I had been so grief-stricken and lethargic since Gordon died in August 2017. Nothing seemed worth doing. Suddenly, I could see a bigger cause in my life than myself and my grief. Only political tragics would understand how a campaign would give me a new spring in my step, and it did.

A short campaign with an outstanding independent candidate is what you dream about. As a non-party person, my heart is with independent politics. It's a position of leverage and only suits some people. Most candidates feel happier with the security, information, intelligence and IP of a party and a big machine. People like Kerryn would prefer to have the direct accountability.

I saw myself as the campaign chair, mentor and supporter, and I took on the primary role of fundraising. It was a really exciting time. People were ringing up, offering to help—people who had never done anything political in their lives. There were others who had left the Liberal Party because they were so devastated by what had happened to Malcolm Turnbull.

For those of you who don't live in Wentworth, you've got to remember that for 117 years this had been an all-male Liberal seat. I am reminded of the day I got into a lift in the Renzo Piano building in the city. A man followed me, but then I stepped out of the lift because I needed to check the floor I was headed to. I went to look and when I went back to the lift he was still there. I felt apprehensive. He said, 'I know who you are, and we will be coming to get you. Don't think you are going to win that seat again. We know you are a stooge of the Labor Party.' It was a 44-floor ride. I was absolutely gobsmacked. And a bit scared. He said, 'You know you won't win it again, don't you?'

And I said, 'Oh, we will see.'

He said, 'It won't be long until you have to do it again. In Wentworth, we produce male prime ministers, and that is how we would like it to stay.'

I presumed immediately that he had come from Rose Bay, Vaucluse or Bellevue Hill. Which, in a sense, were other planets. Because when we looked at the vote distribution, you could see exactly how people had voted for their own view of what Wentworth should be. And it is an extremely well-off place.

Our purple army of volunteers with contagious enthusiasm, and rapidly focused and developed skills, had been well-behaved and courteous. We'd had help from all over New South Wales. My friend Anne-Marie Nicholson, for example, came from Manly, where she had run as an independent, to help. People we knew wanted to be part of a new voice in Wentworth. Scott Morrison begged voters in Wentworth not to push his government into minority as part of venting their anger about the conservative-led coup against Malcolm Turnbull. They turned their backs on him. It was a historic result.

Wentworth had elected a woman

It was a repudiation of the Liberals, their current policy direction, and the unhinged coup culture in Canberra. In *Guardian Australia*, Katherine Murphy wrote:

> It is a devastating night for the Liberals and there are messages here beyond the frustration of a single electorate in a single city.
>
> Australians, with this result, are telling the political class in Canberra that they want a different style of politics, a politics that comes from the community and serves the community. What we are watching tonight is nothing short of a revolution.

When it was settled and Kerryn went to Canberra to be sworn in, I invited my nephew, who is a senior legal figure in Canberra, to come with me to the ceremony, just to be part of the experience. It was a shocking moment in political history. Prime Minister Scott Morrison had pretty well ignored Kerryn, except for a momentary briefing before she walked into the parliament. Later, when she got up to make her maiden speech, the Liberal Party MPs walked out. It was one of the rudest things I have ever seen.

But Kerryn was not deterred. She gave a speech directed to young people and aspiring Independents:

> I would like to say to any young people, any woman, any aspiring Independents out there, if you are thinking of running for parliament or running for public office, yes it can be tough, yes the road can be hard, but it is so worthwhile,

> that we have the right people stepping up to represent Australia. I am so heartened by all the young people who volunteered in this campaign, people who shared the vision, people as young as thirteen and fourteen who have been learning about the political system at school, and about democracy, and want to play a part in it. Not to learn from a textbook from a distance, but to roll their sleeves up, come into the polling station with their parents, talk to people, hand out flyers, and really understand what the Australian democratic process is all about.

She continued:

> A few weeks ago, I was told this was an impossible task. And if we managed to win the seat of Wentworth, it would be a miracle. It was said if we won the seat of Wentworth it would make history, and my friends, we have made history.

After the thrill and high that came with winning, the next part was not so easy. As the member for Wentworth, Kerryn was given occupancy of the building that Malcolm Turnbull had been in, next to Edgecliff Station. It was a very prominent space, and she was advised that she would be there until the next election. It was hard to get your head around the idea that no sooner had you finished settling in that we were out having to begin a campaign again.

Though we had a couple of larger donors, the majority of the money we spent in the by-election came from small donations. There were no big events; there simply wasn't time to get our act together. That was a disadvantage. But the excitement on the streets, and the prominence of the people on our team, kept the dream alive to win.

Now that Kerryn was an MP, we were in new territory. And I pulled back from that. I continued to be the chair of the group, but I spent less time engaged with the team until the next election date was announced as May 2019. Really, she had three months on the job. She had wonderful support in parliament and delivered on her promises. Too soon we were gearing up for the next election. We knew this was going to be tougher.

Most people who win by-elections do not win in the next general election. That's the usual story which people never tired of repeating to us. We were better with our fundraising this time, and of course you get some government support as a sitting member. When Kerryn conceded defeat in the May election, she acknowledged the privilege of representing the electorate, and acknowledged that voters in Wentworth wanted a return of the Liberal/National government.

The removal of children from Nauru, and medical transfers from offshore detention, were two of Kerryn's proudest achievements. She made the point that one voice can make a difference. She said, 'I knew when I entered the house of reps it could be seven months or maybe many years.'

She still supported the idea of the sensible centre, and believed it would be more important than ever in Australian politics. There is still a crying need for socially progressive politics.

The second campaign had some very ugly moments. Shocking social media references of racist and homophobic stories circulating around the electorate, including one claiming Kerryn had died from AIDS during the campaign. Oh dear. And a lot of badly behaved people out in the streets. I am hardly an ingénue, but I was shocked by the behaviour of some working in the Liberal Party, maybe on the payroll, maybe volunteers—the dismantling of the candidate corflute posters every other night, the rudeness towards people, the aggressive mansplaining in some of the pre-polls.

I was out on the street every day. And I saw things that didn't make me proud of the behaviour of Australians in Wentworth. Not the candidates so much, just the supporters. However, I think we kept our cool. We did well. I was disappointed with the outcome, and I hope we see Dr Kerryn Phelps back in a leading political role sometime soon.

Postscript

We were talking with our PR people, and media people and others at the beginning of the campaign, and we discussed how we should refer to Kerryn. There were about eight of us there. Some people said, since she is Independent, and she is a woman—maybe we should just call her Kerryn Phelps? And others, 'Well, she is a professor and a doctor . . .' Anyway, we were all rabbiting on about this, trying to be democratic, and not look like we were taking ourselves too seriously. Then suddenly a voice said, 'Does anyone know that being a doctor gives you an extra five per cent?'

The matter was settled immediately. *Dr* Kerryn Phelps became the candidate for Wentworth, twice.

Finally, I just wanted to add here some words from a letter one of the volunteers wrote to me:

> Dear Wendy,
> What a ride this has been. I want to send you commiserations as I know these past weeks have been incredibly personally challenging for you. The result has been a huge blow. I was

> never particularly confident about returning to Wentworth in the face of a predicted Labor win. But the fact that we missed this seat, and a chance to reset the moral compass of the nation, has deeply affected me, as I am sure it has you.
>
> Thanks for the opportunity, Wendy, to work with you. I am glad I was able to have the experience. I have learnt and evolved so much in the past seven months. It is an experience I will always be proud of. I am a better person because of it.
>
> And that, in the cold light of day, is what I hope we will all take from it. The team has provided extraordinary service to Kerryn. It has been a pleasure to work with them. I think I am a better person. And I know now, I want to help to make our society, nation, and world, just a bit better.

I was so touched to receive this letter.

Building relationships throughout the community with wonderful people who had never done this sort of work before, and learning with them, is rewarding and exhilarating. The loss of the seat was shattering. But the journey was wonderful. I felt motivated and energised. Just what the doctor ordered.

I know Gordon would have been thrilled.

CHAPTER 28

Trust the Women campaign

> Arguably, the pill has had more impact on the 20th Century than jet aircrafts, space flight, computers, or even the atomic bomb. Perhaps television is its only rival.
>
> Sue Javes

In 1986, Sue Javes also wrote in the *Sun-Herald*:

> To be in the frontline of Australian women who first experimented with the contraceptive pill twenty-five years ago, almost to the day, was to be present at the dawning of a revolution without equal.
>
> It was a revolution that ignored the standard impediments of national boundaries, language, culture and creed . . .
>
> The release of the pill for general consumption in Australia 1961 was a social time bomb that virtually launched the women's movement, established morality was challenged, social mores were threatened by the single ability of a woman to live normally without the constant fear of pregnancy.
>
> Today, many of the women who've made it to the upper echelons of most professions give thanks to the pill as a fundamental factor in having got where they were.

How prescient. I am one of those women.

It was a major step in the long journey to an effective, safe and efficient contraceptive. I swallowed my first oral contraceptive pill, thoughtfully provided by a friend, in March 1964. I was twenty-two-years-old, in love, engaged to be married in December of that year, and had already survived one unplanned pregnancy and an illegal backyard abortion.

Few doctors would prescribe the pill for an unmarried young woman when it first became available, although the gynaecologist I was referred to (yes, a gynaecologist for a premarital check-up) gave me a lecture about saving myself for my husband before writing a script for Anovlar that would be effective on my wedding day. He assumed I was a virgin, and I did not disclose to him my abortion for fear of the consequences—up to ten years' jail for the doctor and the woman—and not wishing to admit that I had been sexually active!

I had been reading about the contraceptive pill and it sounded amazing. The idea that I could be in charge of my own fertility and having total protection against pregnancy and so not interfere with the sexual moment itself was breathtaking. When my friend asked her doctor to replace her 'lost' script, she offered the six-month supply to me.

It got me to the church on time.

Better still, the pill was medically endorsed and therefore assumed to be safe. After all, it was the sixties, and no one questioned doctors. Our trust in the medical profession was absolute and the risks seemed minimal.

The risk of an unplanned pregnancy was far greater for most young women back then. Access to abortion was secretive and limited, and the procedure was often dangerous. Women died from backyard abortions. Becoming a single mother or having to give a child up for adoption meant private anguish and public loss of reputation. Abortion had been on the Criminal Code since 1900. That has finally changed.

In 2019, the NSW Abortion Law Reform Act commenced. This Act was to amend the Crimes Act 1900, to repeal the provisions of that earlier Act relating to termination of pregnancy and to abolish the common law offences relating to termination of pregnancy. The 119-year-old law was overturned and a historic bill decriminalising abortion was passed. The new Act establishes:

> a health-centred approach for termination of pregnancy;
> supports a woman's right to health, including reproductive health and autonomy; and
> provides clarity and safety for registered health practitioners providing terminations of pregnancy.

The Trust the Women campaign was a community campaign that worked with a cross-partisan group of NSW MPs and many others to drive the changes and ensure the community support for these changes was enabled. There are many people who can claim victory. It does not belong to any one of us but all of us. This is my experience as the leader of the Pro-Choice Alliance.

The first public announcement of the proposed changes was an Australian Associated Press release published on Monday, 29 July 2019, announcing that NSW Premier Gladys Berejiklian would support a bill to decriminalise abortion. This came as a surprise to many. The Bill was to be introduced by Independent Sydney MP Alex Greenwich and a report by the Australian Associated Press (as picked up by *The Guardian Australia*) read:

More than a dozen MPs, including the health minister, Brad Hazzard, will co-sponsor a bill to decriminalise abortion in New South Wales . . .

In an unprecedented show of support, the reproductive health care reform bill 2019 will feature the names of 15 MPs from five different parties when it is tabled in the state parliament by the independent MP Alex Greenwich this week.

The historic bill would remove abortion from the state's criminal code and create a standalone health care act to regulate the procedure . . .

'If the legislation contains what I think it does I'll be supporting it,' Berejiklian said on Monday.

Coalition MPs will be given a conscience vote, but a number of key members of Cabinet support the bill, including Hazzard, Andrew Constance, Bronwyn Taylor, Gareth Ward, Shelley Hancock and Sarah Mitchell.

Another Liberal Party MP, Felicity Wilson, is one of the bill's 15 co-sponsors.

'NSW is the last state to decriminalise abortion and all members of the Liberals and Nationals will be given a conscience vote on this issue,' Berejiklian told reporters on Monday . . .

'The private member's bill is based on laws in Queensland and Victoria and has the backing of the NSW branch of the Australian Medical Association NSW and Pro-Choice Alliance.

Under the proposed legislation, a woman would not commit an offence if she procures a termination within the bill's framework. It would also repeal provisions of the Crimes Act relating to abortions and common law offences . . .

> The bill was developed by a cross-party working group including the Nationals MP Trevor Khan and Labor's Penny Sharpe and Jo Haylen. There was oversight from the health minister, Brad Hazzard.
>
> In a joint statement, the members of working group said the bill would 'ensure women in NSW can get access to safe and legal abortions, and that doctors have the legal certainty they have long asked for'.
>
> 'To mark the significance of the Reproductive Health Care Reform Bill 2019, this bill will be the first co-sponsored legislation ever introduced into the NSW Legislative Assembly, and has more co-sponsors than any other piece of legislation in the history of the NSW parliament,' the working group members said.
>
> Hazzard said the issue of abortion should be between a woman, her partner and her doctor, and not involve 'possible criminal proceedings against them—it's a medical issue'.
>
> 'We feel confident there will be a respectful debate,' he told reporters, adding he was 'hopeful' the bill would pass.
>
> The bill would ensure women in NSW have the same rights as those elsewhere in Australia,' Hazzard said. 'To my mind, in the 21st century, it's inappropriate for a woman who lives in Tweed not to have exactly the same right as a woman in Coolangatta or the Gold Coast.'

Behind this announcement is the story of the Pro-Choice Alliance group, made up of more than seventy organisations by the end of the campaign. It came out of the Roundtable established in 2017, as a result of discussions between Family Planning NSW, Women's Electoral Lobby NSW and Women's Health NSW. Each organisation believed that the time was right to get abortion off the Criminal Code.

We read the tea leaves in the United States after the election of Donald Trump, and the clawback of the assumptions that Family Planning was a Human Right, the withdrawal of US funds to International Planned Parenthood, the threats to women, the grotesque verballing directed at Justice Ruth Bader Ginsburg, who held the balance of power on the issue in the Supreme Court, and the oft-expressed hope that she would pass away soon.

The new receptiveness of elements in Australian conservative political parties to Trump's confected and reactionary views on women also really gave us the frights—and still does. Could it happen here we asked ourselves. Is this another expression of hostility to women around the world?

We were contending with a mix of same-old religious conservatives as the bill's likely. and overwhelmingly traditional opponents but also something disturbingly new, nasty, duplicitous and well-funded from the US's gender- and woman-phobic mainstream. We first saw it here in 2013 and 2014, when Fred Nile attempted to introduce 'foetal personhood' laws. In contrast, by 2018–19, there was an unprecedented opportunity presented to us by a both liberal and discretely feminist NSW Premier, and Labor leaders strongly influenced by feminists in their caucus. This combination heightened the odds for a win—as we read them—and made us press 'go'.

We observed the positive changes in Victoria since the law was reformed and we watched the campaign in Queensland. We believed we had a community responsibility to remove abortion from the Criminal Code in New South Wales. Despite people saying leave it alone, we were aware of a decline in access to safe terminations with women increasingly travelling across the borders.

I want young women to know this story because it stands as a reminder that we must always be vigilant about our right to inhabit the planet on our own terms. We are 51 per cent of the population, we must have 51 per cent of the decision-making and the responsibility. We must have autonomy over our body. It is ours, our agency, our way of being able to contribute to holding up the sky. Without reproductive autonomy, women's lives are so much harder.

We wished that we didn't have to fight for it constantly. We wanted leadership from the MPs. I wanted to be able to say to the MPs that you don't have to be hung out to dry, we are going to make sure that the community comes in behind you. We are planning a strategic, dignified campaign—research and relationship based.

Never be fooled by the apparent concern of those who oppose women's personal autonomy and authority in these matters. Once the opponents driven by religious conservatism lost their position, and the bill was passed, they disappeared. It's strange, but it has always been my experience. They tell us our lives are valueless if we don't agree to proceed with a pregnancy we didn't plan, but we know we can't manage, and we know is not the right time for us. There is no primacy for us in that position. And there is no equality.

But when the cameras are gone, they disappear too. They don't stay to look after the babies they talked about caring for, the children who might need adoption. The institutions they belong to that may have abused children relentlessly through the ages by removing them from their mothers, often using them as cheap labour, changing their names and denying their existence when families came in search of them.

The incense, chanting and speechmaking disappeared from Macquarie Street overnight. It is such a deeply deceptive, double-edged position. And it demonstrably downgrades the rights of women. The promises to protect the rights of the child seem hollow and already forgotten.

A few of us sat in the parliament for almost all the speeches as the bill was debated. It was a revealing experience. None of us could be described as political ingénues. But I wonder how some MPs would be prepared to claim the right to read into Hansard records outdated, incorrect and deeply distressing documents of dubious provenance. There was no compassion or understanding of what an enormous decision it is for most women to seek a termination.

I am writing this in the pandemic, when borders are closed and movement is restricted. And even under the new regime, I am worried about what happens next. Time is of the essence in an unwanted pregnancy—the earlier the better. In fact, until the legislation passed, twenty-nine women in New South Wales were crossing the border at Albury every fortnight for a termination in Wodonga.

We were aware that a recent case in New South Wales had been reported to the Magistrates Court, resulting in a woman being charged for procuring a miscarriage: Blacktown Local Court case 'Director of Public Prosecutions (NSW) v Lasuladu' on 5 July 2017. The first conviction of a woman under Section 82 of the Crimes Act 'self-administer drug with intent to administer own miscarriage'. We cited this case when we were told to leave it alone as a counter example to the frequent claims that the Crimes Act no longer mattered and abortion was essentially legal under common law. In fact, we said the case demonstrated the law could be activated against women and doctors at any time.

Reproductive rights have long been a part of my life. It had been fifty years since I attended my first abortion rights meeting. When we decided to run the decriminalisation campaign, I was sitting in my office space in the St James Ethics Centre, a non-executive director of six boards and busy, thinking, *How can I do this?*

To which my response had to be, *How can I not?*

I agreed to chair the group. Indeed, I was flattered to be asked. I immediately felt that sense of excitement that comes with campaign mode, where the odds were tight but winning was possible. I was anxiously following what was happening in the individual states in Australia—Victoria, Queensland and South Australia—and I was shocked to discover that abortion access had declined in New South Wales. My antennae went up immediately, and in the next couple of weeks I heard of women travelling from Bourke to Tamworth (nearly 600 kilometres) to ensure a termination. More stigma, secrets and lies when access to public hospitals was limited. Add to that the increase in the power of the conscientious objector who is rarely a friend to women in these matters, and it felt as though we could be going backwards.

We went to work. Setting up our contacts, bringing women together. Talking about the need, we discovered a significant enemy of change and advocacy was ignorance and many people were not aware that abortion remained on the Crimes Act. The passage of the bill in Queensland confirmed that New South Wales was the outlier, and we had to get a strong strategy together for a community campaign. Our plan was not to go into campaign mode publicly until after the state election. We had been watching the Coalition and the Upper House in New South Wales work and win the 2018 Safe Access Zones debate, and we talked to people in all parties who had worked on that and supported it.

Throughout two years we worked on bringing many groups together to demonstrate the large base in favour of changing the laws. This included the abortion providers, the educators, the women and community advocates. They made up Pro-Choice Alliance of seventy-plus organisations, not trumpeting loudly, speaking quietly and authoritatively, giving us the confidence to keep proceeding. The human rights lawyers who worked with us, along with the doctors and nurses' groups, were all vulnerable politically, but they still stepped up and offered support and resources.

This is the moment to acknowledge the contribution of women journalists who held truth to power. It may be what took it across the line. The decision that it would be a cross-party bill led to an agreement between fifteen MPs—the largest grouping in the history of the NSW parliament to sponsor a cross-party bill.

A critical difference between the United States and Australia is that abortion is still not a partisan issue here. One of the most pompous and rhetorically grotesque parliamentary opponents was a Labor MP. Yet we still won under a Liberal–National government, with the Nationals being critical to the passage of the bill.

We had a secure strategy. We wrote to political party leaders before the election, saying we wanted this matter addressed after the election. We were not trying to make it an election issue. When the Liberal Party won the election, I visited the Minister for Health Brad Hazzard and asked for the Liberals' support and leadership of the matter. He said, 'Trust me.' And I did.

As I trusted Alex Greenwich, the Independent member who led the bill, and Penny Sharpe and Trevor Khan from the Upper House whose leadership were crucial. They thought the numbers in the Lower House were solid. What we could offer was broad-based community support.

The bill sponsors accepted their responsibility and stayed on message for six weeks to lead one of the longest debates in the NSW parliament. I was impressed by their capacity to stay calm. I sat in the gallery feeling flustered and enraged.

We had hired Sinead Canning as our campaign manager. She had worked on the Queensland campaign. She was trusted by the MPs, and during the debates she was in parliament providing professional advice. Queries and fact-checking matters raised in the House that needed immediate research were dealt with quickly and accurately.

A significant issue was the ignorance of the community. There was little or no public awareness that there was really a problem. There was a credibility gap as everyone seemed to know someone who had an abortion without a problem. Given our limited sex education programs in schools, when many of these issues can be safely discussed, it was understandable.

Many people who thought abortion was readily available were surprised we needed a campaign. I could understand that as, technically, for most of their lives access had been lawful, as a result of the 1971 Levine ruling. Judge Levine established a legal precedent on the definition of 'lawful' in his ruling on the case of *R v Wald* in 1971. He ruled that an abortion should be considered lawful if the doctor honestly believed on reasonable grounds that 'the operation was necessary to preserve the woman involved from serious danger to her life or physical or mental health'. Levine also specified that two doctors' opinions were not necessary, and that an abortion did not have to take place in a public hospital. The problem with the ruling was that the women's view on why she needed termination could be rejected.

Many people said, 'Young women don't care about this anymore, so why are you bothering?' My reply was to say, 'I am bothering because women need this protection to lead full lives, and we are vulnerable to a challenge under the Criminal Code. We need to remove abortion from that code. I understand that this may not be a major issue for younger women, but for my generation it was the right to control our bodies. And we need to tidy this up.'

On the hustings, some young women turned up to see their grans demonstrating. One of the nicest things said to me on Macquarie Street one morning after I had a bit of a rant was from a young woman: 'You are just like my gran,' she said. 'She says all of that stuff. She can't be here today, but she told me to come—I don't know much about it, but I am learning very fast.'

This was the work and unfinished business of an earlier generation of feminists. It was our job to tidy up the legislation. It was clear during the campaign that our memories of the bad times were still vivid. We could see the decline in the acceptance by public hospitals of the responsibilities for women's health matters. Many public hospitals would only accept a woman for a termination of pregnancy in the emergency room—how utterly appalling is that?

This battle is a continuing one. We now have the best laws we can have to protect women's reproductive health. It is essential that we remain vigilant and protect our new legislation.

I have many memories to celebrate the courage of those who told their stories. 'Arrest Us', led by Emily Mayo, who along with fifty other women spoke about their terminations—just like we did in the seventies. These are some of the women's stories from the frontline.

There was a moment in the early morning gatherings on

the footpath of Macquarie Street outside Parliament House. A young woman, a paramedic, came up and talked about the shock and anger and sadness and pain she felt when she found a woman—I am talking *now*, not fifty years ago—who had tried to perform an abortion on herself in a bath. For this young woman, a call saying there is a woman bleeding in a bath will always be a subtext with the accompanying anxiety.

At our rally in Hyde Park, we sang of hope, for change and shared our memories. We kept a positive, friendly feel to the rally by focusing on our aspirations for safety, fairness and access to better health.

Then there was the extraordinarily moving march through the streets of Sydney to represent the women who'd had to travel to get a termination. Based on the demonstration in London by the women from Ireland who had to travel to England for a termination, fifty women walked from Hyde Park through the streets, each with a luggage trolley, to Parliament House in Macquarie Street to remind people these were not academic stories.

The MPs and the community advocates had some tough gullies to cross.

Penny Sharpe captured some of these when presenting the Bruce Childs Lecture in December 2019.

Most of our team would recognise this moment so vividly described by Penny Sharpe:

> **Wake in fright**
>
> I want to take you back to August this year.
>
> I'm in the spare room in my house, it's dark. I have come in very late from Parliament and slept here so I do not wake up my partner, Jo, and our daughter Pip, who has snuck into our room.

It is 4.23 a.m.

I'm bolt-upright. I am covered in sweat and my heart feels like it is going to pound out of my chest.

I wonder briefly if I'm having a heart attack. As my heart starts to slow, I accept I am not, in fact, dying. It dawns on me that I've just had my first anxiety attack.

As the attack passes, I realise that perhaps the NSW Reproductive Health Care Reform Bill is having a more difficult time going through the NSW Parliament than first anticipated.

We are a few hours into the amendments in the Legislative Council with many, many hours to go.

My anxiety is that the bill before the Parliament could be passed with amendments that would make the situation for women, and other pregnant people in NSW wanting to access a termination, harder than it already is.

This has never been the plan.

In the early hours of that morning, and after months of work with my Parliamentary colleagues and women's legal and medical organisations, I contemplated whether I would be forced to pull my support for the bill.

Just how bad would it have to get before I could no longer endorse it? What would it mean to withdraw support for a bill I had helped draft and spent my entire political life trying to get done?

These were the questions I asked myself every morning as the debate continued.

Then I got up and went back into Parliament.

It's a scenario we had all dreamt about. What if the outcome was worse? And we ended up with poor legislation that made access more difficult We all had to believe in and trust the MPs who had supported the bill. I would sit there and wonder how I could help more. I decided that just being there, constantly, was the best I could do.

I always thought this was our moment and we would get the bill through, but there was high anxiety for all as we closed in.

I had to appear in front of the Ministerial Enquiry at Parliament House, as part of the oversight process during the bill. For the record, as they are in Hansard, my own words:

> My name is Wendy McCarthy and I am proud to chair the NSW Pro-Choice Alliance, which collectively covers an extraordinary number of organisations and people who are frontline providers in all aspects of reproductive health.
>
> Most of these organisations have been campaigning on these matters since the seventies when incremental gains were made in access to abortion under common law. These groups are made up of the people who educate, advocate and care for the sexual and reproductive health and education of women and girls in our community. They hold the trust and confidence of thousands of women and girls.
>
> We feel confident of majority-community support for our assertion it is time to remove abortion from the NSW Crimes Act and regulate it as a health procedure.
>
> Access under common law ruling does not remove the criminal risk. The NSW abortion laws have been in place for 119 years, and while they may have been intended to protect women from backyard abortion providers, they also were designed to punish women who dared to stray outside the 19th-century boundaries of female sexuality when women were supposed to engage in sex only within marriage.

These laws have not matured with the times. They have contributed to the shame, stigma and secrecy surrounding abortion in NSW, and to the deaths of hundreds of women as well as to the chronic ill health and infertility of many others.

Many women of my age will remember visiting an underground abortion clinic: making furtive phone calls from public telephones to arrange the visit, driving to distant suburbs, passing through double doors after pre-paying cash for the operation. It was humiliating, shameful and degrading—an experience to bury in the deep recesses of consciousness.

I speak of a time before the Levine ruling, a time when contraception was still hard to access despite the availability of the pill since 1961. However, many doctors would prescribe to married women only.

The contemporary equivalent of this situation is the lack of timely access for women in remote and rural areas often forced to cross the state borders to obtain the health service they require.

I have this lived experience. Creating public debate about abortion, contraception and childbirth choices has been a major part of my professional life for over 50 years. This is not a new discussion.

Since the Royal Commission into Human Relationships was established in 1974–76, the Australian community has been debating these matters. All other states have come to an understanding that abortion is a health issue, not a criminal matter.

Our gift to our daughters and granddaughters must be the reproductive choices we did not have, and safety and protection from criminal prosecution.

As the 1908 suffrage banner mantra states: 'Trust the women Mother as I have done.'

It is time for change.

I commend our submission to Members.

Some of the words I used come from other women's war stories: a sentence here, an adjective somewhere, a new breakthrough, and maybe a new insight into your opportunities for leadership.

I was in London when the bill was assented to in the NSW parliament. I had Gordon business to attend to in London: I needed to go back and see the places in which we had lived. It all felt right. And I believed as I got on the plane that the bill would go through.

The matters were settled. I was settling my life by having a trip down memory lane to those first two years of our marriage. I stayed with my friend Caroline whose husband Patrick had worked with Gordon. We have been friends for more than fifty years. I looked at the tiny terraces we lived in and visited the school where I learnt so much about teaching.

My life has settled.

It was time to take my first sabbatical, write this book, and get a dog.

I have come full circle.

Postscript

A friend sent me this short email:

Subject: Done

Abortion Law Reform Act 2019

The Abortion Law Reform Act 2019 (Act) commenced on 2 October 2019. The Act amends the Crimes Act 1900 to repeal the provisions of that Act relating to termination of pregnancy and to abolish the common law offences relating to termination of pregnancy. The Act:

establishes a health centred approach for termination of pregnancy;

supports a woman's right to health, including reproductive health and autonomy;

provides clarity and safety for registered health practitioners providing terminations of pregnancy.

Enjoy your trip.

In case you missed it, this was my favourite article in 2019, published on 30 November. Who could believe that after fifty years this would be mainstream news and a cause for celebration?

THE SYDNEY MORNING HERALD: WHO MATTERED IN 2019
These people are defining Australia right now
HEALTH
Wendy McCarthy

You might think this 78-year-old feminist had done her most important work decades ago. But after helping Kerryn Phelps win Malcolm Turnbull's former seat of Wentworth last year, as her campaign chair—even if Phelps lost it back to the Liberals in the May federal election—Wendy McCarthy, teacher, writer, executive, activist, became the face of the movement to drag NSW's archaic abortion laws into the 21st century.

And who better to do so? McCarthy, who chairs the NSW Pro-Choice Alliance, was famously one of 80 women who included their names in a full-page newspaper advertisement in the early 1970s, acknowledging that they had illegally terminated pregnancies. (McCarthy's own covert abortion came in 1963 and cost 63 guineas.) She could not have imagined the issue would still require warriors more than half a century later.

'In September this year, NSW finally overturned its 119-year-old abortion laws, but the foundation for this historic moment was cemented in the early 1970s,' says the editor of *The Sydney Morning Herald*, Lisa Davies. 'McCarthy led the campaign effort for this bill, working tirelessly to convince MPs of its merits. Her persuasive lobbying was instrumental in achieving this historic moment.'

In fact, on the eve of the NSW bill's presentation to parliament, 60 Sydney women launched a social media movement daring police to arrest them for having had illegal abortions. 'The 2019 #ArrestUs Facebook page was a hat-tip to the 80 women led by McCarthy all those years ago,' says Davies. 'Imitation really is the sincerest form of flattery.'

With the support of a younger brigade of advocates, the legislation McCarthy had been hoping for all those years ago finally got through. 'McCarthy's advocacy and passion for women's rights has spurred a new generation,' says Davies. 'We wouldn't be where we are without her'.

The Nation Review, October 1972—Signatures of women who had had abortions

WE HAVE HAD ABORTIONS AND ARE WILLING TO ADMIT IT IN THE INTERESTS OF LEGISLATIVE CHANGE.

CHAPTER 29

The coming of Daisy May

Dogs do speak, but only to those who know how to listen.

Orhan Pamuk

There is a new being in my life, Ms Daisy May.

Ms Daisy May, a black miniature schnauzer, joined me on 18 December 2019, my wedding anniversary. She can't quite replace Gordon, but she is working hard at the task.

I needed another beating heart in my household. It had taken me quite a while to come to terms with this. The emptiness, sadness and grief after the death of Gordon had been somewhat assuaged by the presence of Max, our schnauzer.

Max developed severe anxiety and grief, something I've never seen in a dog before and may even have been dismissive of it. But each day when I left the house, Max would cry. He would, however, patiently go to other people's places and sit quietly. One young woman who was using her computer during the day told me when I collected him, 'Do you know he likes men better than women?' It had never occurred to me. As happy as he was with her, the minute her partner came in, he bounded over to the bloke and wanted to sit on his lap.

After three months, Max's grief, his weight loss, his teeth removal, his overwhelming sadness when I took him back to the farm, had our vet very tenderly saying, 'Max, mate, it's over, it's time for you to go back to your bloke.' And so Max had the needle and suddenly there was no beating heart in my household, just ashes in the cupboard, belonging to Gordon and Max.

I thought this is not a time in my life to get another pet. But I had forgotten that pets have been central to life in our family.

The very first thing Gordon and I did when we came back to Australia, after our three years living overseas, was to get a cat, the only pet allowed in our apartment in Kirribilli. Lucy, our half Burmese, joined us in late 1967. She lived for thirteen years. She was joined over the years by Hussy and Hannah, the cocker spaniels; Bridie the red setter; and Alice the springer spaniel.

Mostly the dogs had cats as friends. We had Toffee Apple, Sam's cat, Polly the Siamese, Lucca the farm cat. We also had tortoises, fish, rats, Bertie and Chloe the Bantams. There was always an animal who was part of our family. At the farm, there were disobedient donkeys, friendly ponies, and more dogs. I had grown up with pets; Gordon required some encouragement and subsequently became a dog lover.

Our first cattle were almost pets. We bought them from our neighbours, the Llewellyns, and they all had musical names because Ernest Llewellyn was the concert master of the Sydney Symphony Orchestra. We could walk around and talk to them, calling them by their name. Diva was a grand dame and lived to seventeen. Piccolo the bull was always naughty but would come for food at the fence.

There is something special about people who understand and are kind to animals, which distinguishes them from people who don't care. It's that extra capacity of being, thinking and loving.

I remember when Alice, our springer spaniel, who was part of our lives for sixteen years, had to be put down. The vet had called me from our house. I left the Bicentennial Authority desk and went up to Longueville, stayed with Alice while she was euthanised, came back to work, and when someone said I didn't look well, I burst into tears. The person quizzed my assistant and asked, 'What is wrong with Wendy?'

She replied, a bit weepy herself, 'Oh, her dog had to be put down.'

He said, 'She'd cry over a dog?'

It reminded me why I disliked him. Not much love for anyone except himself, that man, I thought.

Yet I could see the love, support and empathy that an animal brings to a family. After Alice died, I said, 'I think that might be it for pets.' But Sam said that he had never had a pet of his own, so it was his turn. And along came Ruby, our first schnauzer, then there was Otto and Max, and now there's Daisy May.

Why did it take me so long to understand I needed a companion?

I collected Ms Daisy May the puppy from Jervis Bay on my wedding anniversary. A date that keeps recurring in my life for good things to happen. Sam and his family decided to buy her brother, who was named Zeus, and we set about establishing a new family, with grandchildren Freya and Luca and the sibling mini schnauzers.

Mr Zeus and Ms Daisy May have become our new extended family. And in an unbelievable coincidence, her other brother Ziggy lives around the corner and they play together most days.

Since Ms Daisy May has joined my household, she has brought light and shade, comfort, company and joy. Teaching her to do things, seeing her joy in accomplishment—whether it's sitting, shaking hands, or just watching her run round and round our upstairs carpark with unfettered joy—is heart lifting.

As she becomes less shy, I think the world for Daisy May is increasingly a happy place, and she has found her special human friend, Orla, who lives upstairs in our apartment building. Orla is eleven and came to puppy training with us. They are in love.

In our first week together, we collected Daisy May from a bushfire-affected area, Jervis Bay. A week later, we were fleeing the South Coast, where the sky was red-brown, and the sea was grey and ashy with curled up gum leaves on the sand. There was lightning, thunder, all terrifying things for an eight-week-old puppy, but somehow she survived.

When she got to Potts Point, and we'd walk up Wylde Street, motorbikes and big trucks would frighten her. Wylde Street is pretty crazy to a puppy, but slowly she has found her space—at my place.

I am looking forward to many more summers with Ms Daisy May. She has been great company during the pandemic. Isolation is her favourite thing with me. I am the caricature of an older woman and a dog.

I could not be happier.

CHAPTER 30

Missing friends and family

The comfort of having a friend may be taken away but not that of having lost one.

Seneca

Kerry's story—Bye-bye, *Miss American Pie*

In October 1994, my brother Kerry died. His death made me stop and re-evaluate my life. The decision to leave the law practice, Price Brent, seemed a lot clearer. Why would I do a job that did not engage my head and my heart? Life was too short.

Kerry was four years younger than me, and for many years the only surviving mature Ryan male—a responsibility he took seriously. He was the sibling with whom I had the closest relationship, as my sister Deborah was eight years younger and only three when I went away to high school. So, apart from the years we shared at Garema, our lives connected only in school holidays. Separations of this kind are not unusual for country children who have to leave home to go to school. But families learn to adapt.

Kerry was a gentle boy, and our father preferred Deborah's company when they were young. She was a tomboy and fearless. Kerry was much more easily intimidated and bullied, and he would be very distressed when our parents argued. Like me, he was fearful for our mother, and throughout his life felt protective and responsible for her.

He was fourteen and boarding at Farrer Agricultural High School when our father died. It all happened so quickly. I don't think Kerry had even known that he was in hospital in Sydney. When my mother rang the school, the headmaster advised her it would be best if she didn't speak to her son. He would tell Kerry about his father's death and then help him get on with his life. He strongly recommended that my brother not attend the funeral either. This was not unusual advice and practice at the time, but Kerry always felt angry that he had been excluded from such a significant family event.

When he asked me much later in life about it, I lied and avoided telling him how deeply awful my father's funeral had been. I suspect the death of our father had been somewhat liberating for him because their relationship was unsatisfactory and unresolved.

Kerry grew up fast after finishing school, and like our father he went to work in a stock and station agency. He always wanted a country life, and he was a natural auctioneer with great people skills. He was called up in the first conscription ballot in 1966 and consequently spent a year in Vietnam—an experience he would rarely speak about. I recall only three conversations.

The first was the night before he was married. He was staying at my place, and he told me that he occasionally had nightmares and hoped they would not frighten Suzie, whom he adored. The second was to register his rage and disgust that Gordon and I had attended an anti–Vietnam War march. Years later, when I was on the board of the ABC, he asked if

I would arrange for him to view the archival film material on Vietnam, which is now at the War Memorial. I did, and that was a breakthrough. He saw himself in it and that helped him to decide to take part in the reconciliation march in Brisbane to honour the Vietnam veterans. Like many of his mates, he found it cathartic, as though he had finally come home. And was recognised for his service to his country.

He was a party boy, quick-witted with a great singing voice, a good rugby player, and had many girlfriends. He liked a drink, and people would say, 'He's a chip off the old block.' However, people who said that didn't really understand how important it was for him to gain respect as a serious and responsible person. When he met Sue Weaver, the love of his life, he became a successful and focused family man. No doubt determined to become a better father than the one he had known.

Our political beliefs were light-years apart. He supported the National Party, and saw my support of issues, rather than a party, as weak. He was outspoken and negative about feminism, the Labor Party, and Aboriginal people ('blacks', he called them). And claimed, at least in the case of Aboriginal Australians, that his home at Walgett entitled him to be an expert. We shared some very robust family moments, and occasionally our mother got caught in the middle. If she supported my views, he saw it as an urban plot and proved that city life had ruined her judgement.

Despite these differences, which we just had to manage, we remained friends as well as family, interested in and proud of each other's achievements, and our children. In 1993, with my sisters Deb and Sarah, Kerry and I, with all the children and our spouses, had one of the great family holidays at Blueys Beach on the mid-north coast of New South Wales. We rented four beach houses at Christmas, one for each family, and we also had a couple of friends join us. We met at the beach every day, ate lunch, played golf and tennis, and reminded ourselves that we still cheat to win at Scrabble. Our families moved into a new mode, more relaxed and tolerant, acknowledging the connections and differences in an affectionate and accepting way. How different it was from the Christmas we spent at Walgett when all my children got nits.

Eight months later, we were dancing and singing at Kerry's oldest son Nicholas's twenty-first birthday, held at the favourite motel in Walgett. Six weeks later, we returned to that motel for Kerry's wake. He was only forty-nine. Kerry was in the ranks of Ryan men who didn't make fifty. In his case, he died from a massive stroke. It happened quickly. He was out in the paddocks checking stock at five o'clock in the morning and was struck by a headache, then started feeling dizzy and tingling. By afternoon, he had been airlifted to Dubbo Base Hospital unconscious and paralysed.

Sarah and my mother, Bette, flew up from Sydney, and Deb drove from Tamworth. And by late afternoon, the diagnosed brain stem haemorrhage was determined as impossible to overcome. The bedside vigils continued. He was never alone. His Walgett friends filled up the waiting rooms and annexes—all regular Aussie blokes, off the land. I was so overwhelmed by their ability to show their love and affection for Kerry. When they weren't with him, they were telling stories about Kerry in the courtyard. It made my heart sing.

I thought of my father's last hours alone at RPA and his funeral in a no-name chapel in Chatswood, and the anxiety about who was paying the funeral bill. I thought about my Nana Ryan's pain. And the brother-in-law who refused to speak to my mother, as though it was her fault my father had died.

Kerry Rex struggled for three days while we talked and encouraged him to hang on until Nicholas came home from his rugby tour in Ireland. We will never know whether he recognised Nick, but we all wanted to think so. As we all wanted to believe that he knew we were with him, in one combination or another, until he died on the Saturday morning.

My brother's wake was a major Walgett event. The arrangements say so much about him. The funeral service was held in the local Catholic church, a new church with a design he liked, and there were two ministers officiating, Catholic and Protestant. He liked both those blokes. Almost a thousand people attended, and both family and friends spoke. As the service concluded, his coffin draped with the flag of his regiment was carried out to 'American Pie', the Vietnam War theme song.

As the cortege moved along the streets of Walgett, where businesses were closed and employees stood outside to pay their respects, we drove past his favourite places: Wickman and Ryan, his stock and station agency; the TAB; the RSL club, where his photograph remains today. Many of his regiment were present, and at the cemetery he was accorded a military burial. He would have been pleased with his funeral; it had a style and flare he would have appreciated.

Over the next couple of weeks, obituaries appeared in the rural press. On 20 October, the editorial obituary in *The Land* described Kerry as 'one of the great characters in agency work, who always looked on the bright side of life, and one of the best all-rounders in the game'. It talked of his love of racing and his sense of fairness. Mike Wilson wrote in *The Land* on 10 November: 'there must really be a big stock sale coming up in the sale yard in heaven, last month, god called home one of the best stock and station agents I have ever known to help him organise it. Kerry Ryan from Walgett was a great agent, a great bloke, and a good friend. He will be sadly missed.'

He was, and he is. I had been connected to Kerry for nearly fifty years. At that stage, longer than any man in my life. Gordon passed that figure. Kerry has a special place in my memories. He was so often the counterpoint, and I valued the tension as much as it enraged me when he'd say, 'Wake up to yourself, woman.'

When I returned to work, my decision to leave Price Brent was made. I advised them I would leave at the end of the year. We parted amicably. They no longer needed a change agent. That task was done.

On the way home from Kerry's funeral, in the car, Hamish wrote a few verses for Kerry:

> And the word did get around town that the legendary Kerry was now underground. So a large mustering took place to find all his peers and children, and put them in one space. To toast K. Rex Ryan was to toast the lifeblood of the bush. People endured, enjoyed and lived with a man whose heart was always in his gate. And the memories that everyone shared were in the traditional K. Rex style, with his friends milling around, sitting, smiling, and laughing at his jokes, while his spirit sailed safely away under town. It seemed a good ending to his life.

The records of the Royal Australian Regiment record that Kerry Ryan, ex 4 Platoon, B Coy:

> died suddenly on the 15/10/94. Kerry was a first intake National Servicemen who served in 4 Pl B Coy on the first tour. He will always be remembered not only as a fine soldier

but also for numerous tasks he did in running the company canteen. An example of his achievements was on one occasion he exchanged six cartons of Aussie beer with the Americans for a large refrigerator and a pallet of Budweiser beer. Kerry was a phenomenal negotiator as well as an entertainer with his characteristic auctioneering techniques.

In his home town of Walgett he was very popular, he had been President of the RSL, the Jockey Club, the Sporting Club, as well as a councillor on the local shire. He was in business in the livestock industry as well as farming.

A very large crowd of mourners attended his funeral including many of his National Service comrades.

Deepest sympathy from the 6 RAR Association is extended to his wife Sue and his young family.

Bette

In the years that followed my mother was still unsettled, and there had been another breakdown in our relationship. She remained unhappy and angry about my book, *Don't Fence Me In*, and probably displeased that most of the family had supported me. Fortunately, my sister Deborah stuck with my mother, whereas Sarah had tried to stay neutral despite her relationship with her having fractured, too.

One Sunday night, Bette rang me and asked if I would go to her place and do some shopping as she was not feeling well. I said, 'Of course.'

I thought and hoped this may be a rapprochement. When I walked into her room, I knew she was really sick. She looked so lost and frail, and when she described her symptoms, I said, 'I think you might have pneumonia.' She rejected the idea but was in no position to argue. I said, 'We are off to the emergency all-night clinic for advice.'

It was pneumonia, and after a couple of days she was in hospital.

Her life spiralled down from that point. For the next three months, she was hospitalised. The diagnosis was never clear, and there were various emergencies that took her from St Luke's in Potts Point to the larger hospitals.

As a post-seventy woman now, I realise there are a lot of things that happen in this age bracket to be put in the magical box called 'DOB'. When she got sick, my mother was seventy-nine, my age when I started writing this book. She had already had a fall, an ankle break and now pneumonia, known fondly as 'the old person's best friend'. I think she was a little tired of life.

When she was admitted to hospital, Sarah, Deborah and I ensured that one of us was always there with her. A lot of stuff gets decided by medical professionals in those times. I look back and think how grateful I am that, being in St Luke's, meant I could walk to her every day, which I did, unless of course I was on the road, in London, Africa, Indonesia, or any of the other places to which I was still travelling. In my heart, I knew she was never really coming home.

Lara Green was born in September 2002 and Bette met her first great-granddaughter. She died two days later, after three months in hospital. Her death was peaceful. She exited well. She had refused to eat for the last month and was wasting away. But relationships were repaired, every grandchild visited, people came and went. She rewrote her will to be inclusive. Everyone has a little memento from her.

She found it difficult to express her feelings, but we know she cared when the grandchildren visited. Everyone called her Bette, she never allowed anyone to call her Nana or, God forbid, Grandma. She didn't want that definition, and she made that very clear. She didn't have especially close relationships with her grandchildren, but as many lived in the country that was not surprising. It was not a role she craved.

At some stage, after her death, I moved out of my rented accommodation and into her apartment. I wondered if I could live there. I couldn't—Double Bay is not my place. I put the property on the market knowing that this was the end of the Bette era.

We farewelled Bette at a beautiful service at St Peter's at Watsons Bay, where Sarah and David Nichols had been married. We spoke of the things we loved about her. We three sisters acknowledged that she produced great daughters, and a gorgeous son, Kerry, whose death had shattered her. She never recovered.

She left the church with Frank Sinatra singing 'My Way' and a pair of Chanel shoes in the coffin. We retired to Sarah's house and shared Bette stories.

There was a symmetry about my mother's death. She had turned eighty a week before she died. We were all speaking to each other. There was no conflict in the family—we had worked hard to achieve it, and it had been done. We looked after Bette for the three months of her time in hospital. We made sure she was never alone.

My mother always wanted to be an independent woman. In the last decade of her life, with her alimony finally sorted, she had an income and a pension. Gordon and I had bought an apartment for her in Double Bay. She found a new life there. She learnt to play bridge and turned out to be good at it. She proved to herself what she didn't need to prove to us: she had a very smart brain.

Like so many women of her era with limited education, she was always reliant on other people for survival. It certainly produced in me a fierce independence, a sense that I would always be responsible for myself.

For at least twenty-five years of my life, I lived with my mother's edgy disapproval. The sense that somehow I betrayed her by living a public life she had not approved of. Our safest ground was books and films. We did do quite a lot of films, and some concerts, together. And we swapped books. She loved reading. And I thank her from my heart for the books in our house when I was growing up. And for the appearances before Canteen's Trust Fund to secure a secondary scholarship for me. Giving me the responsibilities of the eldest child in the family helped me grow up and be resilient. I remember *her* when I was growing up: it couldn't have been easy to have an eighteen-year-old daughter when you are only thirty-six.

In our relationship, there were few moments of truth. She really never understood the life of a family with two working parents. She saw no reason to babysit my children. If I wanted to work, I could pay for it. I understood that: I didn't want to be a permanent babysitter for my grandchildren either. I never imagined or longed for another mother. Sometimes she travelled with me. She came to Perth for the Bicentennial Celebration, and met the Queen and Prince Philip, and enjoyed those events.

When Bette died, I realised I was an orphan, and that more than ever I was now the matriarch of the family. That sounds better than being the oldest, although that too is a badge of honour. It offered a second chance to build strong networks in the expanding Ryan family.

I was a grandmother, a mother, a wife, a company director, an entrepreneurial business owner—and Women's Business was bubbling along. I could pull out a whole range of titles. And maybe this is who I really was. Maybe I liked to have that combination of things. It wasn't like the feeling of the young mother when you've got ten balls up in the air and if they didn't come down in the right sequence you were finished. This was different.

My sister Sarah had three children. And her father died not long before our mother, meaning she too was suddenly an orphan. We wrapped our arms, as a family, around her. But as the family started to grow, it was Sarah who suggested we should try to recreate some of the magic of the Blueys Beach family weekend. We instigated a new plan to keep everyone together. We would take a house on the South Coast, then the North Coast, every second year, and spend a week together over Christmas. It has turned out to be the most spectacularly successful strategy for keeping our family of more than forty people together.

I'm sure Facebook helps. But so does spending time together, talking, getting to know each other again, meeting the newest babies in the family. It's not just the fortieth birthdays that creep up on us now. It's that sense of engagement that we know who our tribe is on the Ryan side of the ledger. And people make their own decisions about the intervening year. When we missed a catch-up and got out of sync, I think every single one of us felt that we had lost something.

Family-building was part of Gordon's DNA too, and our farm became the touchpoint between Sydney and Canberra for McCarthy family days. The cousins know each other. Family-building with the Ryans is fun. They are noisy, they sing, they love a party, they love children, they are loyal to each other. They are raising good families. And they know where they come from. I love them.

I could never have said that as a child. I had my little nuclear family and my two grandmothers; everyone else—the aunties, uncles, and cousins—were denied to us, on the grounds my mother didn't like them. They appeared when my first book was published, all over the place. I'm your cousin, they would say, and we would explore the relationships. It has been an enriching process for our families as we go through life's ups and downs. We stick together. And we know who we are.

I take my role seriously. I want to be the wise, trusted woman in the centre. And I have never thought it was a disadvantage to be seen to be growing older, and therefore becoming a matriarch. I know that when I include my family in things that they may not have otherwise accessed, the shared experience is the better one. I also know that I transfer a lot of the things I learn in my family into my workplace. Negotiating difficult family relationships requires the same skills as negotiating difficult work relationships.

People ask me, 'Why did you keep working after sixty? Didn't you think that you'd had enough?' I can't imagine my life without a sense of purpose. And the sense of purpose I had around various issues hasn't changed in forty years of professional life.

My family is always with me. They balance everything I do. I see no reason to choose between having a family and having a professional life. I love being the matriarch, the aunty, the mother, the grandmother, and the sister. I don't want to sit on the sidelines of my country and my community without my rich extended family network. I want to be engaged until the day I die. I am having my first sabbatical this year to write this book.

There will always be another campaign.

Hazel Hawke AO

People often ask me how Hazel Hawke and I became friends and what she meant in my life. Hazel and I met sometime in the 1970s and we would have been introduced in a more formal way by Jan Marsh, who had been working at the ACTU and led the ACTU case for equal pay for women in 1976. Writing this now, I understand even more how important and wise she was.

Hazel was vigorous, opinionated, firmly spoken and fun, but had a wistfulness about her that I was beginning to recognise often indicated a woman who was ambivalent about feminism and perhaps concluding that it wasn't for her. She was not an active part of it, yet remained excited by the ideas, and the promises that engagement and action would produce a better life for all women.

We struck a bond from the first time we met. It was a comfortable and engaging relationship, but Bob was never part of it. My place was her time-out with women, away from the hustle and bustle of the Hawke government.

For many of my friends in the 1970s, appearing to be a feminist was a bridge too far. It was anticipated, rightly or wrongly, that their husbands would not approve, that it would damage their relationship and their marriage, and in some instances the purse strings might be tightened as a consequence. The authority of men was not to be questioned. Yet those women sniffing the times were longing to be engaged, and during that decade there were many who took the plunge and became part of an exhilarating movement. It had an edginess and a risk about it for those of us who were married and seemed to be challenging the very institution we had embraced.

I'm not sure Hazel was quite in that category when I met her, but she was just beginning to think about the opportunities of an education for herself. She volunteered at things while keeping hearth and home together for the Hawke household, which included three children and a mostly absent husband. She worked with the Brotherhood of St Laurence, and when an opportunity opened to get some formal training she grabbed it. In the early 1970s, the Whitlam government announced that women who wished to attend university could take their prior lives into account, and that universities would open up their degree courses without the requisite end-of-school-matriculation requirements.

I was so proud to be a part of this and was hoping my mother would apply. I was disappointed when she said she didn't need a university degree. I desperately encouraged her, no doubt I overdid it, to go to TAFE and do her Higher School Certificate. She was intelligent, well read, well spoken, but not formally educated. This inhibited her throughout her life.

Second-chance education offered women an opportunity to satisfy their longing for a formal education. I was working with various lobby groups to open up the classrooms, and could not understand why, having fought so hard for her children to have an education, that my mother could never take that step herself. If I mentioned any of her peers deciding on this pathway, she felt I was diminishing her.

When I taught in TAFE, I would tell stories of the admiration I had for people I was teaching who undertook this education journey. I knew it was scary, especially having to hand in the first assignment. I would turn myself inside out to help them. I kept in touch with some and felt proud of their achievements.

As I've previously mentioned, in 1988, the Sydney Symphony Orchestra was invited to perform in the US to celebrate Australia's Bicentenary and Hazel and I joined them. It was a wonderful trip and we became the closest of friends after attending fourteen gigs with the best band in Australia.

But it's our story in the last two decades that matters most. Hazel and Bob's marriage was in trouble. Despite a seemingly happy time in the Lodge, building a new house in Northbridge after his time in office didn't quite keep it together. Hazel was not well, and Bob had declared his love for Blanche d'Alpuget. This was a bitter blow for her, because while she was quite aware of his affair with Blanche, she had seriously believed that was in the past and they would have a happy future together. She even wrote a book expressing her hopes and dreams for this. But like the trooper she was, she faced up to facts, and set about organising the best divorce settlement she could and resetting her own life.

In a very orderly way, she became formally involved with issues she cared about: heritage, bush regeneration, drug programs and stillborn births. All personal political issues for her. She began writing, although remaining unsure about her skill as a writer. Her books sold in the thousands. She was offered various roles and began to earn her own income. She would say to me, 'I never thought I'd be back earning money, but here I am, Wen, and it feels good.' Her daughter, Sue, was a huge support to her through these years and managed her commitments. It was a satisfying, confidence-building period in her life.

In September 2009, I wrote a note to her friends and family advising them that the Guardianship Tribunal, together with the Office of the Protective Commissioner, had ruled that I would be the manager of Hazel's legal and financial affairs.

This was a hands-on role. It meant Sue relinquishing the responsibilities she had carried for so many years, and those that she and I had shared for the previous six months. I had been the executor of Hazel's estate since October 1999. I took my responsibilities very seriously and she had been very clear about her wishes regarding the estate.

After the Tribunal hearing, I went home thinking, 'How could it be that this woman, who has been so generous, so admired and been through so much, suddenly requires the care of a guardian, and that has to be resolved in a public process?' Sometimes these things happen. It's not a role I sought, but the thought that she would not be cared for was something I could not ignore.

Hazel was a trusted and dear friend. She was a bit older than me, though it was never a daughter–mother relationship; it was a genuine peer-to-peer friendship. The two hearings of the guardian tribunal were surreal. Unfortunately, Hazel's children were not in a position to accept responsibility, and Bob was not willing or appropriate as he had now established his relationship and life with Blanche.

What would Hazel do, I pondered that night, if she were in my position. That was the main question, and I was sure she would look after me. At the second hearing, it was agreed I would become responsible for her for the rest of her life.

I found selling up her house and distributing the contents to the family as gruelling a task as they did, but in the end it was my decision that went with being the executor and the guardian, though I sometimes felt very lonely doing that. She had two pianos; we gave one to the Institute of Music for students, a typically generous Hazel thing to do, and one she took with her to Hammondville, the care place that Sue had carefully chosen, and Ros and Steve supported.

It was a difficult place to access for the children. Steve lived in Perth and Ros didn't drive. Hammondville was 35 kilometres out of Sydney and wasn't an easy place to get to on public transport. But I managed to drive past there on my way down to the farm every Friday afternoon, so that became my drop-off point and my regular moment with her.

In the early days, when I would leave, Hazel would walk with me to the door and say, 'Wen, I think I'll come with you, I don't really belong here, I need to be somewhere else.' I'd have those moments that probably every mother has had of someone taking you with an iron grip, knowing that you are about to abandon them. Sometimes I would just get in the car and cry, wondering how it could come to this. But it does, and it's not a death or the end of a life to wish on anyone. Dementia is the cruellest disease.

After four years in care, Hazel died in 2013 at Hammondville. A last-minute visit from Bob, organised by Ros, made the end so much better. Her last moments were peaceful.

She would have loved her funeral in her favourite Concert Hall with her favourite band, the Sydney Symphony Orchestra, playing. The place packed with VIPs and many more everyday Aussies.

These are my farewell words to Hazel:

> Good afternoon, Hazel's family and distinguished guests.
>
> Thank you for coming to celebrate Hazel's life and her contribution to our community and our country.
>
> I am honoured to speak about our much-loved friend and why she meant so much to us and I thank her family for offering me this opportunity. How bemused and delighted she would be to see us gathered together in the Sydney

Opera house, her favourite place, with her favourite band the Sydney Symphony playing in her honour. She would wonder modestly whether she deserved it.

Equally, she would be astonished and humbled by the outpouring of love, affection and admiration expressed by the Australian community in the last month.

Let me share some of the words people have sent to me in the last few weeks:

'We have lost a National Treasure.'

'I can't think of a woman, or Australian citizen who is more respected and loved by the Australian people than Hazel Hawke: nor one who has shown greater leadership, warmth, courage and humanity.'

'Like many other women, I was inspired and encouraged in my journey by Hazel's values, strength and commitment to equity; all given in down-to-earth advice and a certain impatience with any suggestion of pomposity or inaction if you had the power to effect change.'

'I have never heard anyone say anything negative about Hazel. She must be the only Australian we universally loved.'

'I was so sad to hear of Hazel's passing today. She has been a very important part of my view of women in politics and leadership for many years. Her bravery and honesty around her life with Bob, and then her suffering with Alzheimer's, was inspirational.'

Hazel had a special relationship with people throughout Australia. People felt they knew her; that somehow, she would understand their stories and concerns, that she was one of them, and they shared a common narrative about the things that mattered in their lives—love, marriage, children, community, social justice and fairness and always hoping to leave the world a better place for the next generation

It was a constant feature of her life—the way she could establish a sense of intimacy and trust with people so quickly. When her book, *My Own Life*, was published, she spoke of the thousands of letters she received from people she had never met but who trusted her with their stories and empathised with her life experience.

She was a woman of her time; she took her marriage vows seriously and built her life around her family, but equally she took her life in the community seriously.

She said in an interview in 1991, 'Most women do all sorts of things that they never imagined they'd do, particularly in my generation, because our expectations were in the traditional role model without much in the way of expectations. We may have had hopes but we didn't have expectations.'

She lived through a shifting landscape of being female in Australia in a time when women of my age, a decade younger, were insisting that we should and could have expectations rather than hopes. It was in those years that I met Hazel, who was quietly intrigued by feminism and wondering what it might mean for her.

Like so many women of her age, she had a deep longing for a formal education, and the opening up of higher education for mature-age people offered her the opportunity to enrol in a welfare course. Her work with The Brotherhood of St Laurence as both volunteer and later paid worker gave her confidence, recognition and a broader perspective about her own life.

It was a great preparation for her role as the prime minister's wife.

At Julia Gillard's book launch in Sydney, September 2014.

Visiting Fitzroy Crossing with June Oscar for Goodstart, 2015.

Brisbane launch of the Early Learning campaign with Governor-General (and my good friend) Quentin Bryce, 2016.

With my granddaughter Lara at Uluru on our trip together, 2017.

Our Berrima farm, Mundi Mundi, as we were saying goodbye to it for the last time, 2017.

In conversation with Governor-General Quentin Bryce (left) at a Roads and Transport Breakfast, 2017.

With daughter Sophie (centre) and my younger sister Sarah (right) on the campaign trail for Kerryn Phelps, 2018.

Breakfast with June Oscar at NSW Parliament House, with my nieces Azura and Savannah, 2018.

With Kerryn Phelps (second from left), her partner Jackie and advertising guru Dee Madigan (second from right), during Kerryn's re-election campaign, 2019.

Having lunch with my dear friends. From left: Quentin Bryce, Susan Ryan and Elsa Atkin, Australia Day, 2019.

With my grandchildren, Elias, Lara, Aidan, Luca and Freya, 2019. Photo by Verve Portraits.

Women protesters march with suitcases as part of a campaign to highlight how often women had to travel interstate to get an abortion, Macquarie Street, Sydney, 2019.

At the book club with Jane Jose (centre) and Dinah Dysart (right) at S.H. Ervin Gallery in Sydney, 2021.

Women's Budget Statement Group. From left: Jennifer Westacott, Michelle O'Neil, me, Natalie Walker, Georgie Dent and Sam Mostyn, April 2021. Photo by Dan Nascimento.

Women's March, Canberra, with Aminata Conteh-Biger (centre) and Kerryn Phelps (right), March 2021.

In memory of my dearest friend Hazel Hawke, outside at The Lodge.

My loving miniature schnauzer, Ms Daisy May. Photo by Laura Reid.

Women's friendships are powerful bulwarks in our lives. They nourish and sustain us, and to the surprise of many of the men in our lives we do not talk about them. Hazel had a great capacity for friendship as many in the audience would know. Our 40-year friendship was one to celebrate.

We had a lot of fun together, and this is surely the place to tell of our travelling together in the USA with the SSO on its Bicentennial tour. We thought of ourselves as mature-aged groupies on a roadshow, in love with the music and bursting with pride for the orchestra.

Such ambassadorial opportunities do not come often, and when Hazel and the orchestra opened the day's trading on the New York Stock Exchange, I watched with pride her skill and composure, even when they played 'Yankee Doodle Dandy'.

It was during this trip that she developed a close friendship with Stuart Challender, and despite her misgivings about whether she was good enough she accepted his invitation to play with the orchestra at the Opera House. And being the woman she was, she set to work with her music teacher and her performance was a triumph.

I doubt that Hazel has ever lost a friend. They just kept accumulating. I loved:

- her curiosity;
- her loyalty once she was your friend;
- her engaging loud laugh;
- the no-nonsense cut-through when people were being pompous;
- the way she celebrated the achievements of her friends and was there to console us when things went wrong; and
- her passionate commitment to social justice

She brought out the best in us.

Hazel found her voice in her role as wife of the prime minister. She saw her role as a way of contributing to the wider community, and many of her friends supported her work.

When her marriage ended, her friends mattered a great deal, but with our many shared interests around women's issues, heritage and the natural environment, reconciliation and the Republic, it was possible to work together. It was a creative and a happy time for her as she found a new life rhythm and an unexpected career as a successful writer, community campaigner and admired leader in matters close to her heart.

Her voice was valued and listened to.

Alzheimer's was a doubly cruel blow and many times she wept with rage at the way it curtailed her new autonomy. She so hated having it, but decided if it was in the public interest and might do some good, she would speak out. As indeed she always did.

One woman wrote to me last week on Facebook, 'I loved how she inspired and supported other women . . . One of my heroes.'

As she was mine.

I was privileged to be her friend.

Thank you.

Susan Ryan AO

It is difficult to exaggerate the significance of the life of Susan Ryan. She was a woman of her time determined to make the world a different and better place. She had a fierce intelligence and the courage to take on changing the system when she saw the need to improve the lives of Australians.

Her sudden death on 27 September 2020 came as an unbearable shock to those as close to her as I was. We had been friends for nearly fifty years, brought together by the feminist politics of the early seventies. We were co-founders of the Women's Electoral Lobby (WEL); she in Canberra, me in Sydney.

She was a significant player in WEL politics, but what was so inspiring was that she pushed the ideals into realpolitik by putting theory into practice when she successfully ran for an Australian Capital Territory Senate seat for the ALP in 1975. Her campaign slogan was 'A Woman's Place Is in the Senate', an abbreviation of the WEL slogan 'A Women's Place Is in the House and in the Senate'. It was clever.

She had a remarkable group of WEL and other supporters who shared her triumph when she was elected in 1975, International Women's Year. Over the years those supporters have remained loyal and constant to the values they were endorsing.

Equally the feminist friendships that were forged in the seventies remained strong and idealistic. We all felt, in the words of Nina Simone, there's a new world coming, and our new friendships were helping that happen. We felt we were creating our histories.

And we were.

We never doubted Susan's integrity and capacity to represent us, even if we did not belong to the ALP. We felt she was there for all of us, and groups like Women into Politics grew their ambitions and encouraged others to follow her pathway. She was unfailingly kind and helpful and encouraging to would-be candidates.

She wrote in her 1999 memoir, *Catching the Waves*, that she was driven by the view that women should be able to pursue opportunities unencumbered by stifling stereotypes. There should be no unfair obstacles put in the way of them achieving independence. Women and men should be judged on their merits, not on how far they reinforce some socially useful or commercially contrived norm. Not everyone agreed, and it was a joy to watch her growing strength when she entered the Senate, disappointed by the dismissal of the Whitlam government and often feeling very alone.

Her leadership in delivering the Sex Discrimination Act was outstanding, and during the longest debate in parliament we had time to observe her intellect, her debating skills and her tenacity, despite the opposition of some residual misogynists in her own party. She just kept going—a mantra she encouraged in a recent interview about ageing and wisdom.

How perfect it was when she was appointed Age Discrimination Commissioner in 2011. She worked so hard, and when her term finished she transferred that experience to older women.

No matter what—she lived her mantra: Just Keep Going.

The Sex Discrimination Act is surely her finest achievement and most significant legacy. The bill outlawed discrimination on the basis of sex, marital status and pregnancy. Sexual harassment legislation was a world-first. She often reflected that 'it was probably one of the most useful things I have done in my life'. Many have tried to reinterpret or remove it, but it remains the instrument of the law available to all of us. Its application has changed the lives of many Australians, and forced organisations to change discriminatory employment practices. Now they ignore sexual harassment at their peril.

She turned her energy and intellect to the Republican cause, feminism and social justice, human rights, education, homelessness (especially for older women) and superannuation.

She was the first female Labor minister and the first female Minister for Women.

She was a loyal and wonderful friend, always the first to send a note of praise after a public event, even if you didn't do it well.

She was loved by her children, Justine and Ben, her partner Rory, and her large extended family. She loved everything Irish. I benefited by being born a Ryan and marrying a man born on St Patrick's Day.

She was the feminist we all aspired to be.

Glen Tomasetti

Glen Tomasetti was born in Melbourne, Australia. An academically and musically gifted woman, she was well-known throughout the Australian folk music circuit, working on commercial television and cutting eleven albums in the 1960s. A left-leaning environmentalist and feminist, Glen was vehemently opposed to the Vietnam War and was a member of the Save Our Sons Movement in Victoria. In 1967 she made headlines when she was subpoenaed to court for withholding one-sixth of her income tax on the grounds that this was the exact proportion used by the Holt government to finance the war in Vietnam.

She became a heroine of the feminist movement in 1969 when she adapted the words to an old shearing gang ballad, 'All Among the Wool, Boys', to be sung as 'Don't Be too Polite, Girls'. Glen's version of 'Don't Be too Polite, Girls'

> was written to support the 1969 case for equal pay that was being heard by the High Court.
>
> Glen Tomasetti had three children and believed that motherhood was the emotional core of her life. She has been described as 'a woman of singular passion that found focus in motherhood, friendship, art, the environment and justice for the oppressed. Her creativity was multifaceted. She was a historian, poet, novelist and actor. She was formidably intelligent, and her god had bestowed on her extraordinary physical beauty'.
>
> Australian Women's Register,
> www.womenaustralia.info/biogs/AWE0600b.htm

I wish I had met her.

When I chose the title for my book serendipity kicked in. Firstly, I discovered Glen Tomasetti had signed the abortion statement inviting the police to charge us for committing a crime. Her signature is one column from mine. Goosebumps.

Reading *Radicals: Remembering the Sixties* recently, I discovered she was friends with and a great career supporter of folksinger Margret RoadKnight, whose song, 'Girls of Our Town', remains one of my favourites. Oh, that I had been to a concert where they sang together. Then, I remind myself that three children under five meant I was not at song festivals often in those years. But the songs remain as powerful as ever.

I reflect that, when we add Helen Reddy's 'I Am Woman', we have three feminist Australian anthems. Quite an achievement.

Here is the first verse and chorus of 'Don't Be too Polite, Girls', written in 1969.

We're really on the way, girls, really on the way
Hooray for equal pay, girls, hooray for equal pay

They're going to give it to most of us, in spite of all their fears
But did they really need to make us wait for all those years?
Chorus:
Don't be too polite, girls, don't be too polite,
Show a little fight, girls, show a little fight.
Don't be fearful of offending in case you get the sack
Just recognise your value and we won't look back.

For those who wish to sing along go to YouTube.

Epilogue

> When the whole world is silent, even one voice becomes powerful.
>
> Malala Yousafzai

I still think of myself as a teacher, I just work in different classrooms. I can't think of any role I have taken on in my career where my professional training as a teacher has not been of great value to me. To the way I learn, to the way that I encourage and enable people to be curious, to the way that I refuse to accept the status quo, to the way I want to engage a team. No one learns in isolation. It works for governance, too. People say to me, 'How come you've been on the boards of Circus Oz, IMF Bentham and McGrath Real Estate . . . when you are just a teacher?'

Well, never call me just a teacher.

I have been to so many communities around the world where the teacher is a revered person. In Ghana, a teacher came to meet me on a Plan project—a young man, obviously nervous about meeting an older white woman whose organisation had invested in the community. He came out from this little cement-and-brick place that Plan had built. Inside it was incredibly hot, and totally inappropriate for a contemporary classroom, though at least there were windows for ventilation.

He was so proud of this space. And proud of the responsibility of hosting the donors. He confided to me that the brown woollen suit he was wearing was his best outfit. He was twenty-four and trembling with excitement at being a teacher. He couldn't wait to show his pupils how he could conduct himself, and demonstrate that his pupils were, as was required in that community, obedient and enthusiastically engaged in learning. It was such a touching moment and I will always remember the sign on the classroom wall: 'Reading makes a perfect man.'

A couple of years ago, I went to hear Malala Yousafzai speak. I was so overwhelmed by the power of that young woman and her words about teachers. As I came away, I thought to myself, *Why didn't I persevere and stay as a teacher?* The simplicity of her quote—'One child, one teacher, one pen and one book can change the world'—is just so true.

Teaching as a profession today doesn't respond to contemporary ways of evaluation and impact, producing answers in short timeframes. It can take a very long time to do these tasks. We see green shoots, we see weary classrooms and weary children, we see social dislocation. And then we see inspired people in our classrooms, and students are enabled to find the answers that they need to run their lives. So why do we go on a relentless pursuit of metrics? I wonder. Perhaps it's because we want immediate satisfaction—we are the donors, the benefactors, the voters. We want to know that our children can do certain things, at certain ages.

There is now enough evidence around the world to know in a congenial classroom with a good teacher, most of these things will happen. But we have to remind ourselves that not everyone is ready to learn at the same time. Classrooms based on age, where children move ahead for the convenience of the system, are not right for some. But most places around the world do it because it suits the majority of children.

There was one really humbling moment when I was a Chancellor. It began with the question: How can someone who hasn't even got a master's degree be a Chancellor? I mumbled, 'Well, I am a good team leader, I love learning, and someone asked me to do it, and I assumed that they must think I would be okay, so I accepted.' But what I learnt in that moment echoed what I had learnt when I was teaching at TAFE: when the circumstances required for learning are available, it doesn't matter if you haven't fitted into the system. As long as the society keeps it open, and believes passionately in learning, people will learn.

I think of the pregnant schoolgirls in my TAFE classes—my heart ached for them as the pregnancy developed and they pretended it wasn't happening. I felt so anxious about them, but I respected their boundaries. I was so proud of them when they all got through their Higher School Certificates, and hopefully went on to better lives.

It was a similar experience for the blokes coming out of the defence forces, or from very poor backgrounds, or on parole. How important it was for them to be able to sit as an equal human being in a group and learn, even if there was terror in their guts that they would not be able to do the first assignment. Good teachers recognise those signs.

I always think of what Einstein had to say, which seems so counterintuitive to the way we try to measure children's learning. He said, 'It is the supreme art of the teacher to awaken joy and creative expression and knowledge.' I carry that with me.

Teaching is so much a task of the heart and the head. The heart and the head need to be connected. Your classroom needs to know it is being cared for and loved. And it is building trust. In all my years of teaching, I have carried many secrets. They are the dreams and aspirations of young women, and some young men. Things they didn't want to disclose but were willing to share in a trusted environment. The best teachers are those who show you where to look, but don't tell you what to see.

As a high school student, I had some teachers who just dictated notes in History that you were expected to regurgitate. Yes, it mostly got you through the exams, but it didn't bring the subject to life. If you love History and the classroom, you love it for the rest of your life. If you love Geography, the same applies. The best company directors are those who know and share where to look inside the company to get the realities. They don't tell you what to see, but tell you what to look for.

Frank McCourt, author of *Angela's Ashes*, wrote a wonderful memoir called *Teacher Man* in 2005. He turns his attention to the subject he most often talks about in his lectures: teaching, why it is important, why it is so undervalued. I identified with his own coming-of-age as a teacher, a storyteller, and ultimately a writer—which is what I am trying to become. I recognised the humility, and the mischievous and rebellious storyteller that he was. When I read his book more than ten years ago, I felt that a lot of my aspirations as a teacher were worthy after all. McCourt says it took him fifteen years to find his voice in the classroom. I think I got there earlier than that. But, like McCourt, I am a storyteller. I like people to get inside the story.

I am a storyteller in the boardroom as well, sometimes to the irritation of my colleagues. But I am always looking for the narrative that fits the scenario. And there is almost always a narrative. It might be five pages of numbers, but there is a story *behind* the numbers, just as there is a story behind the words. And when you tell a story, the others who are listening because they trust your voice will start to share their stories too. And then the exchange is sublime.

Back in schools, I was always assigned the naughty classes. Not that I had naughty stories to tell them. But I could persuade them to tell their stories, to find their stories in their hearts, and to learn from what they told me. My first classroom was full of the naughtiest girls in the school at Cremorne. I had the naughty girls at Gilliatt School in London. And before I even graduated, I was the college tutor of the perceived 'naughtiest' group. But naughty only really meant not in line with other people's expectations.

When I worked in the Ravenscourt Park adventure playground in London, I wondered how the local immigrant children, many of whose parents were in Wormwood Scrubs Prison, could not feel like outliers. There were no places for them to play, and during the long school holidays they were often unsupervised and bored. The adventure playground movement was dedicated to finding adventurous spaces for play in highly manicured parks. I wanted to bring these kids into those safe spaces. If it meant I went against the rules and invited in the babies and the strollers, so be it, and I dared anyone to challenge me.

They never did.

Over my lifetime, so many talented people left teaching. I think of the waste of fabulous women who loved their profession, and who were not allowed to stay if they got married. While celebrating the number of women school principals we have now, I mourn the loss of those who had the odds stacked against them. They lost status, and in their early years spent their careers in a system where advancement was based on seniority. Motherhood and broken work forced many out of schools, and on their return, frequently as casuals, they were not considered leadership material.

This didn't happen to men.

It was no accident that many of the women who founded WEL were teachers who had also been forced out of the profession and lost the opportunity to be leaders in their community. They were generous volunteers and were crucial in changing the system for the betterment of others.

I do feel sad that teaching as a profession does not have the high regard it deserves. If there is one positive thing that comes out of the current pandemic, it may well be that parents finally understand the professional skill of a teacher. Society has indulged many parents into believing it is appropriate to bully teachers at school and tell them how to do their jobs. It is confronting as a teacher to have to spend your time defending your professional stance. Most of my generation of teachers left the education of their children in the classroom to their teachers.

As a teacher, I met the parents of my pupils at school events, hockey matches, debating competitions, parents' nights, and occasionally on school excursions. As a parent, I was not running up accusing the system of not favouring my children.

In most parts of the world, teaching is an admired profession. It is not a commodity; it is a profound human relationship—and, at its best, creates wonderful citizens. But teachers need to breathe. They need to be trusted. They need to be paid properly.

I was particularly sad and inspired when I read Gabbie Stroud's book *Teacher*. Her story about her struggle to 'keep the heart in teaching' needs to be shouted from the rooftop. She very eloquently shows us why and how education needs to change.

One day in the 1980s, during my first visit to China, I met parents who worked in a factory. They invited me to their home to meet their family. One couple had two little boys, ten and twelve. They were doing their homework, and they told me they were going to be teachers in physics. They were studying with the help of a modest 25W lightbulb. I have never forgotten the parents' pride in their expectations that their children would be teachers.

Life for children starts with trusted teachers in the community, and in the classroom. And it ends there as well.

Teachers have been central to my life. They rescued me, inspired me, advised me of futures I had never dreamt of. When I became one, I learnt about collegiality and mentoring. I am the beneficiary of great public-school education, for which I am truly grateful.

Teaching has been the platform of my professional life.

Friendship

> Abandon the cultural myth that all female friendships must be bitchy, toxic, or competitive. This myth is like heels and purses—pretty but designed to SLOW women down.
>
> Roxane Gay

> There is nothing I would not do for those who are really my friends. I have no notion of loving people by halves, it is not my nature.
>
> Jane Austen, *Northanger Abbey*

I could not imagine my life without my women friends. Some friendships span over fifty years, and we share precious memories and particular interests. In most, partners have not been integral to the friendship. Unlike my mother's generation, whose social lives were often dictated by their husbands, my generation has friends with whom we share political interests, commitment to women's issues, support feminist activities, go on holiday, attend concerts, sporting events and exchange stories about our health. All this enables rich, textured relationships. There are boundaries we recognise in equal friendships. I have never felt the need or inclination to discuss my sex life with anyone other than my husband, for example. And growing up in a co-ed boarding hostel and educated in co-ed schools, I have always had men friends as part of my life.

Recently I rediscovered the *Oxford Book of Friendship*, Quentin Bryce's Christmas gift to our family in 1992. Among many gems was the reference to *Testament of Friendship* by Vera Brittain, who was interested in the ideas and attitudes about women's friendships. Her book was published in 1940 in honour of her friend Winifred Holtby. I love this snippet:

> From the days of Homer, the friendships of men have enjoyed glory and acclamation, but the friendships of women in spite of Ruth and Naomi have usually been not merely unsung but mocked and belittled and falsely interpreted.
>
> I hope that Winifred's story may do something to destroy these tarnished interpretations and show its readers that loyalty between women is a noble relationship which far from impoverishing, actually enhances the love of a girl for her lover, of a wife for her husband, of a mother for her children.
>
> Some feminine individualists believe they flatter men by fostering the fiction of a woman's jealous inability to

love and respect one another. Other sceptics are roused by any record of affection between women to suspicions habitual to the over sophisticated. Although we did not grow up together, we grew mature together and that is the next best thing.

Women of the seventies might say the same.

The grandmothers are coming

As I learned from growing up, you don't mess with your grandmother.

Prince William

I wanted the last words to be about grandmothers. I recalled a speech I gave in 2015 about ageing and how I had found an article in *The Atlantic* comparing menopause in mammals. It was a great story and stayed with me. I went to the *Current Biology* journal looking for updates. I feel suddenly anxious that the story might have changed. Turns out, it is better than I thought.

Killer whales are one of the few animal species in which the females live long after they stop reproducing. Research scientist Darren Croft and his team published their report in 2015 and followed up in 2017. They discovered that the postmenopausal killer whales are key leaders, directing the group to the best feeding grounds.

It seems like a new reason to respect grandmothers.

The 'wisdom of elders may be one reason female killer whales continue to live long after they have stopped reproducing,' one of the researchers wrote.

The simplest theory is the grandmother hypothesis. It speculates that prehistoric humanity benefited from having built-in babysitters, or caregiving grandmothers, to provide an extra hand to help with the grandchildren, therefore improving survival rates and allowing the human race to flourish.

Imagine my delight to read a recent article by Joe Pinkstone in London *Telegraph* that giraffes are just as sociable as elephants as elderly females stay with their tower (or herd) long after they have stopped being fertile. This postmenopausal period accounts for almost a third of their lives, researchers at the University of Bristol found, and the fact they stay with their familial group until death indicates giraffes have more complex social groups than previously thought.

The so-called 'grandmother hypothesis' is a well-established theory that states that highly intelligent animals—such as whales, elephants and humans—have complex social lives and older family members help raise infants when they are no longer fertile themselves.

It is an anomaly in the animal kingdom, where an individual's worth is based solely on their ability to reproduce and pass on their genes. Elephants are the best-known example, with matriarchal groups headed by a sage female which is long past the point of being able to breed. Almost a quarter of a female elephant's lifespan is spent in a post-reproductive state and for killer whales this rises to thirty-five per cent. For humans it is about forty per cent, assuming a woman goes through menopause at fifty and lives until she is eighty. However, scientists have never before studied giraffes to see if they also fit into this exclusive group, with experts assuming they had a simplistic hierarchy and therefore were unlikely to have a prolonged post-reproductive lifespan.

Fresh analysis, published in the journal *Mammal Review*, proves this is not the case and that thirty per cent of a giraffe's life occurs after the menopause. Study author Dr Zoe Muller said:

> I hope that this study draws a line in the sand, from which point forwards, giraffes will be regarded as intelligent, group-living mammals which have evolved highly successful and complex societies, which have facilitated their survival in tough, predator-filled ecosystems.
>
> If we view giraffes as a highly socially complex species, this also raises their 'status' towards being a more complex and intelligent mammal that is increasingly worthy of protection.

What a great group of mammals to be part of.

Darren Croft noted mounting evidence that menopause in humans is adaptive, and that older women in prehistoric times may have similarly functioned as repositories of wisdom and knowledge. I like this interpretation, and if this is the case then the world is ready to offer new opportunities to older women whose careers may have been derailed when they became grandmothers.

Someone else will have to mind the grandchildren.

It may be time for women to run the world. We are living longer and more importantly living well. The world is now providing many, many examples of mature leadership. If we are looking for the wisdom of elders, it is hard to go past the experience of women who are now arguably better educated than they have ever been before.

Can you be a leader at an advanced stage?

Yes.

Janet Yellen became the first female Chair of the Federal Reserve Board of Governors when she was sixty-seven. Now in her seventies, she is the first woman Secretary of the Treasury in the United States. Christine Lagarde was Head of the International Monetary Fund and then President of the European Central Bank in her sixties. Angela Merkel, the German Chancellor, was during her tenure arguably the most important leader in the world during her sixties, and Dame Quentin Bryce became Australia's first female Governor-General post-sixty years of age.

As a society, we trust older women. They have raised generations.

I think of that scene in *Downton Abbey* when Dame Maggie Smith, the grandmother, speaks to her son, who is asking that she stop interfering in family matters. With a withering glance, she pulls herself to her full-seated height and says, 'It is the job of grandmothers to interfere.'

I like the idea.

There was no better example of a working grandmother than Ruth Bader Ginsburg, who didn't join the US Supreme Court until she was sixty, whereas her male colleagues had on average been seven years younger on their swearing-in. She was the second woman to serve on the Supreme Court, and a pioneering advocate for women's rights, and in her ninth decade became a much younger generation's unlikely cultural icon

She died in 2020 at age eighty-seven while still serving on the Supreme Court. Let me close on some of my favourite RBG quotes:

> My mother told me to be a lady. And for her, that meant be your own person, be independent.

> Women will have achieved true equality when men share with them the responsibility of bringing up the next generation.

> The state controlling a woman would mean denying her full autonomy and full equality.

> I'm sometimes asked when will there be enough [women on the Supreme Court] and I say, 'When there are nine.'

* * *

I want to end with the beautiful and generous words of the Uluru Statement from the Heart, which ask for the establishment of a First Nations voice to be enshrined in the Constitution.

I want them to be everywhere so that they become familiar and accepted. They are gentle, powerful and healing, and should be heeded.

ULURU STATEMENT FROM THE HEART

We, gathered at the 2017 National Constitutional Convention, coming from all points of the southern sky, make this statement from the heart:

Our Aboriginal and Torres Strait Islander tribes were the first sovereign Nations of the Australian continent and its adjacent islands, and possessed it under our own laws and customs. This our ancestors did, according to the reckoning of our culture, from the Creation, according to the common law from 'time immemorial', and according to science more than 60,000 years ago.

This sovereignty is a spiritual notion: the ancestral tie between the land, or 'mother nature', and the Aboriginal and Torres Strait Islander peoples who were born therefrom, remain attached thereto, and must one day return thither to be united with our ancestors. This link is the basis of the ownership of the soil, or better, of sovereignty. It has never been ceded or extinguished, and co-exists with the sovereignty of the Crown.

How could it be otherwise? That peoples possessed a land for sixty millennia and this sacred link disappears from world history in merely the last two hundred years?

With substantive constitutional change and structural reform, we believe this ancient sovereignty can shine through as a fuller expression of Australia's nationhood.

Proportionally, we are the most incarcerated people on the planet. We are not an innately criminal people. Our children are aliened from their families at unprecedented rates. This cannot be because we have no love for them. And our youth languish in detention in obscene numbers. They should be our hope for the future.

These dimensions of our crisis tell plainly the structural nature of our problem. *This is the torment of our powerlessness.*

We seek constitutional reforms to empower our people and take a rightful place in our own country. When we have power over our destiny our children will flourish. They will walk in two worlds and their culture will be a gift to their country.

We call for the establishment of a First Nations Voice enshrined in the Constitution.

Makarrata is the culmination of our agenda: *the coming together after a struggle*. It captures our aspirations for a fair and truthful relationship with the people of Australia and a better future for our children based on justice and self-determination.

We seek a Makarrata Commission to supervise a process of agreement-making between governments and First Nations and truth-telling about our history.

In 1967 we were counted, in 2017 we seek to be heard. We leave base camp and start our trek across this vast country. We invite you to walk with us in a movement of the Australian people for a better future.

Acknowledgements

My life has been rich with the friendships and trust of many women and some men. They are people who have been kind and generous to me over my eight decades. People who gave me a chance to do something I knew nothing or little about, who invited me to be part of a group I would never have entered otherwise, like government ministers who challenged my initial response of 'I know nothing about the issue' when asked to accept a public/statutory responsibility, reassuring me I could learn on the job, and I did.

I think of our neighbours in the bush, who kept an eye on my mother and her three children when my father was absent. My mother's mother, who took us all into her tiny house in Tamworth, where we enrolled in schools while the storm blew over before we went back home—providing us a time to breathe and heal.

The man I married—Gordon McCarthy—my life would have been unthinkable without him. He remains a guiding thought and presence.

My children, who stand as testimony that two working parents can build a family and raise wonderful children despite the naysayers. Children who understood they were deeply loved and that giving them wings to fly at the end of school was not pushing them out of the house but believing they would be capable of flight and would always know how to find their way home.

My grandchildren—grandsons, aged twenty-one, sixteen and eleven, and granddaughters, eighteen and eight—who have repurposed my life and given me a reason to stay a bit longer if I can. How I love looking at the patterns of their lives and their new discoveries and listening to the way they think and speak. How proud I am of them.

And always, the continuing thread of my life, the company of women. So many brave women who helped me be brave; smart women who encouraged me to be smarter, to take on risk and opportunity, reminding me that to fail is essential and mistakes are but battle scars; older women who thought I was worth mentoring and held me to account, reminding me that what I felt personally was political.

Women who would discuss preposterous ideas about a public issue, such as allowing fathers to be present at the birth of their child and being able to choose if you let the state be in charge of your fertility or if it's something you share only with your doctor.

Women who wanted to work out what politicians thought about women in society, women with seemingly crazy ideas that in so many cases turned into gold and are now part of the social fabric of our community

And the joy of discovering it was not just me who cared.

Thank you for enabling me to have a life of activism, purpose, friendship and trust with you.

Timeline

Bachelor of Arts, University of New England, 1960
Diploma of Education, University of New England, 1961
Teacher, Cremorne Girls High School, Sydney, 1962–64
Teacher, Gilliatt School for Girls, London, 1965–66
Co-founder, Ravenscourt Park adventure playground, London, 1966
Teacher, Fontbonne Academy, Pittsburgh, 1966–67
Secretary, Childbirth Education Association (NSW), 1968–70
Co-founder, Women's Electoral Lobby (NSW), 1972
Non-Executive Director, Family Planning NSW, 1973–74
Teacher, TAFE, Sydney, 1973–75
Media Information and Education Officer, Family Planning NSW, 1975–79
Founding member, National Women's Advisory Council, 1978–81
Advice columnist, *Cleo* magazine, 1978–84
CEO, Australian Federation of Family Planning Associations, 1979–84
Attendee, World Conference of the United Nations Decade for Women, Copenhagen, 1980
Member, NSW Higher Education Board, 1980–83
Executive Director, McCarthy Management Pty Ltd, 1980–2019
Commissioner, NSW Education Commission, 1981–83
Member, NSW Women's Advisory Council, 1981–83

Deputy Chair, Australian Broadcasting Corporation, 1983–91
Founding member, Chief Executive Women, 1985
General Manager, Australian Bicentennial Authority, 1985–89
Director, Young Endeavour Youth Scheme, 1988–90
Officer of the Order of Australia for service to the community, particularly women's affairs and to the Australian Bicentennial celebrations, 1989
Chair, National Better Health Program, 1989–92
CEO, National Trust of Australia (NSW), 1990–93
Member, Independent Panel on Intractable Waste, 1991–92
Member, University of Canberra Council, 1992–95
Member, CIRCIT Review, 1993
Chair, Visions for the Future, 1994
CEO, Price Brent, Sydney, 1994
Member, Macquarie Graduate School of Management Advisory Board, Sydney, 1994
Chair, Faculty Review, School of Social Sciences, University of Technology Sydney, 1994
Deputy Chancellor, University of Canberra, 1995
Executive in Residence, International Graduate School of Management, University of South Australia, 1995
Director, RACP Research and Education Foundation, 1995
President, Chief Executive Women, 1995–96
Founder and Executive Manager, Women's Business, 1995
Honorary Doctorate, University of South Australia, 1995
Member, EPAC Child Care Task Force, 1995–97
Chair, Australian Heritage Commission, 1995–98
Chair, Royal Hospital for Women Foundation, 1995–99
Director, Star City Pty Ltd, 1995–99
Chair, Clean Up Australia Environment Foundation, 1996–98
Member, Australian Advertising Standards Board, 1996–98
Trustee, Adelaide Festival Centre Trust, 1996–2000

Chancellor, University of Canberra, 1996–2005
Director, Plan International Australia, 1996–2009
Advisory role, Sydney Symphony Orchestra Honorary Council, 1996–current
Director, Australian Multicultural Foundation, 1997–2000
Member, Olympic Urban Design Review Panel and Olympic Public Art Committee, 1997–2000
Chair, Accreditation Advisory Board, Advertising Federation of Australia, 1998
Chair, Plan International Australia, 1998–2009
Founder and Executive Manager, McCarthy Mentoring, 1998–2012
Chair, The Look of the City Committee, City of Sydney, 1999–2000
Member, Australian State of the Environment Advisory Committee, 1999–2001
Chair, Advisory Committee, WHO Kobe Centre, Japan, 1999–2002
Founder and Executive Manager, Corporate Good Works, 2000
Chair, McGrath Estate Agents, 2000–15
Distinguished Alumni Award, University of New England, 1998
Chair, Symphony Australia, 2001–03
Centenary Medal for service to Australian society in business leadership, 2001
The Grand Stirrer Award, The EDNAs, 2002
Director, Jacobsen Entertainment Group, 2003–04
Chair, NSW Health Participation Council, 2003–04
Member, NSW Health Care Advisory Council, 2005–07
Featured, Australia's Top 100 Public Intellectuals list, *Sydney Morning Herald*, 2005
Co-chair, NSW Sustainable Access Health Priority Taskforce, 2006–09

Chair, Sydney Community Foundation, 2006–09
Vice Chair, Plan International, International Board, 2007–09
Director, Plan Hong Kong, 2007–09
Chair, Circus Oz, 2007–17
Founder and Patron, Sydney Women's Fund, 2007–current
Chair, Pacific Friends of the Global Fund, 2008–14
Chair, headspace National Youth Mental Health Foundation, 2008–16
Lecturer and course developer, Arts Board Induction, Master of Arts Management, Australian Institute of Music, 2009–10
Ambassador, 1 Million Women, 2009–current
Independent advisor, Cabinet Committee on NSW State Plan Performance, 2010–11
Deputy Chair, Goodstart Early Learning, 2010–18
Featured, *The Power of 100: One Hundred Women Who Have Shaped Australia*, International Women's Day publication, 2011
Mentor, McCarthy Mentoring, 2012–current
Inaugural inductee, Women's Agenda Hall of Fame, 2013
Non-Executive Director, IMF Bentham, 2013–18
Advisor, Grace Papers, 2015–current
Life Fellow, Australian Institute of Company Directors, 2017
Advisor, The Front Project, 2018–current
Patron, Regional Opportunities Australia, 2019–21
Chair, NSW Pro-Choice Alliance, 2019–current
Featured, 'Good Weekend's Who Mattered 2019: Health', *Sydney Morning Herald*, 2019
Honorary Doctorate, University of New England, 2019
Patron, The Parenthood, 2020

Index